GOVERNMENT RESEARCH ON THE PROBLEMS OF CHILDREN AND YOUTH

GOVERNMENT RESEARCH ON THE PROBLEMS OF CHILDREN AND YOUTH

BACKGROUND PAPERS PREPARED FOR 1970–71
WHITE HOUSE CONFERENCE ON
CHILDREN AND YOUTH

SUBMITTED BY THE

SUBCOMMITTEE ON EXECUTIVE REORGANIZATION
AND GOVERNMENT RESEARCH

ARNO PRESS
A New York Times Company
New York ★ 1973

Reprint Edition 1973 by Arno Press Inc.

Manufactured in the United States of America

———◆———

Library of Congress Cataloging in Publication Data

Government research on the problems of children and
youth.

Reprint of the 1971 ed.
Includes bibliographies.
1. Children in the United States. 2. Youth--
United States. 3. Child welfare--United States.
I. White House Conference on Children, Washington, D.C.,
1970. II. White House Conference on Youth, Estes Park,
Colo., 1971. III. United States. Congress. Senate.
Committee on Government Operations. Subcommittee on
Executive Reorganization and Government Research.
[HQ796.G684 1972]   362.7'0973   72-1301
ISBN 0-405-03148-3

92d Congress 1st Session	COMMITTEE PRINT

GOVERNMENT RESEARCH ON THE PROBLEMS OF CHILDREN AND YOUTH

BACKGROUND PAPERS PREPARED FOR 1970–71 WHITE HOUSE CONFERENCE ON CHILDREN AND YOUTH

SUBMITTED BY THE

SUBCOMMITTEE ON EXECUTIVE REORGANIZATION AND GOVERNMENT RESEARCH

(Pursuant to S. Res. 31, Sec. 7, 92d Congress)

TO THE

COMMITTEE ON GOVERNMENT OPERATIONS
UNITED STATES SENATE

SEPTEMBER 1971

Printed for the use of the Committee on Government Operations

U.S. GOVERNMENT PRINTING OFFICE
WASHINGTON : 1971

66-385

INTRODUCTORY STATEMENT

By Senator Abraham Ribicoff, Chairman, Subcommittee on Executive
Reorganization and Government Research

It has become a tradition over the last 60 years that a national
White House Conference on Children and Youth should be held at
the beginning of every new decade. The most recent Conference was
held in two stages. The problems of children were discussed in December 1970 at Washington, D.C., while the future of America's youth
was discussed in April 1971 at Estes Park, Colo.

In order to assist the delegates to the Conference, a series of background papers were prepared by experts within the Federal Government and by consultants retained by interested Federal agencies. The
papers survey our present knowledge and understanding of several
important problems affecting young Americans—population planning,
nutrition, health, day care, juvenile delinquency, and employment.
The special situations of handicapped and minority group children
are also studied.

Because the papers were circulated only to persons connected with
the White House Conference, the Subcommittee on Executive Reorganization and Government Research concluded that publication of these
products of Federal research would serve the public interest by making this material available to the Congress and the public.

Each of the eight papers in this volume deals with a major problem
affecting American children today. The papers reach many interesting and surprising conclusions on the present condition of children
and on the record of the Federal Government in providing for their
needs.

The paper on day care and preschool services lists 15 major Federal
programs administered by five different departments or agencies. In
1969 these programs aided over 600,000 children. However, even with
Federal aid all public and private child-care arrangements in 1969
served only 8.7 percent of our 3-year-old children and 23.1 percent
of our 4-year-olds. Moreover, the study indicates that children in poor
families did not receive a pro rata share of such services.

Proper human growth and development require adequate nutrition,
particularly during the time from 3 months before birth to age 3. The
paper on food and nutrition analyzes the data on the nutritional deficiencies which affect the 10 million children living in poverty and
surveys existing Federal programs for dealing with this problem.

The study on health cites a long list of quantitative estimates indicating serious health and dental deficiencies among children, including statistics that in 1967 4.4 million (18.7 percent) of children 0–5
years of age and 17 million (39.2 percent) of children 6–16 years of
age never saw a physician during the year.

The imbalance of Federal priorities and the failure of the Federal Government to help prevent the huge deficit in health services for children is indicated by the report that Federal health care outlays for children and youth under age 19 in fiscal year 1969 totaled $1.3 billion as against $11.5 billion for the rest of the population. Thus children and youth under 19, who represented about 36 percent of the entire population, received only about 10 percent of the Federal health care dollars.

The study on population change in the United States and the development of family planning services analyzes the growth of population and the relation of family size to the poverty status of families. Its description of Federal family planning services reveals that in fiscal year 1971 only 2 million of the 5 million women in need of subsidized family planning services were budgeted to receive such aid. A fourfold increase in funds was projected over the next 4 years.

Three of the papers in the compendium center on the large groups of children and youth with special problems. Because the country has not devoted the effort and resources necessary to prevent and solve the problems of these special groups, a vast reserve of human potential is wasted.

The poverty and deprivation of millions of black, Chicano, Indian, and other minority group children are discussed in the paper on minority children and youth. This study points out that in all the major areas of social and economic concern, such as home life, income and poverty, health, education, employment, and social unrest, children of minority group families are dramatically worse off than whites. The paper reveals that while there have been significant improvements in the last decade in the reduction of poverty (although not in the last year, according to the most recent census data), as well as increased education, and employment opportunity, there are signs of a worsening situation in terms of family stability and social unrest.

The conclusion of the 1970–71 White House Conference on Children—that the Federal Government neglects children in its budgetary priorities—is exemplified in the paper on special programs for handicapped children and youth. The study on this subject estimates that there are at least 8 million handicapped children in the ages 0–19 and that about one-third of all young males fail military entrance tests because of mental and physical disabilities. Mental retardation alone is estimated to cost the Nation economic losses of $8 billion annually. This dwarfs the total Federal expenditure for all special services to the handicapped.

The data in the report on handicapped children illustrate the underlying causes of the high prevalence of handicaps and failure among children of the disadvantaged:

1. Three-fourths of the Nation's mentally retarded are to be found in the isolated and impoverished urban and rural slums.

2. Conservative estimates of the prevalence of mental retardation in inner city neighborhoods begin at 7 percent.

3. A child in a low-income rural or urban family is 15 times more likely to be diagnosed as mentally retarded than is a child from a higher income family.

4. About three times as many low-income children as higher income children fail in school. A child whose father is an urban laborer has one chance in 3.5

million of being named a national merit scholar, compared with one chance in 12.6 thousand for children of professional or technical parents.

5. Students in the public schools of inner city low-income areas have been found to be from 6 months to 3 years behind the national norm of achievement for their age and grade. An appalling number of these children fall further behind with the passing of each school year.

One of the increasingly serious problems of our urbanized, youth-oriented society is documented in the paper on juvenile delinquency. The report makes clear that crime is primarily a problem of youth offenses. In 1969, for example, 64 percent of all serious crimes were committed by youths under age 21. However, our society has failed either to eliminate the basic conditions of poverty, racism, and deprivation which are often at the root of delinquent and criminal behavior; or to develop effective correctional and rehabilitation institutions or techniques. For example, one major study cited in the paper concluded that 70 percent of the boys in corrections programs became recidivists.

The monograph on Jobs for Youth documents the social and economic costs of the growing teenage unemployment problem. The paper analyzes the connection between poor preparation of youth for holding meaningful jobs and the high rates of unemployment among uneducated and untrained white and black youths and the problem of delinquency. Special attention is given to the problems of dropouts and veterans. The probable characteristics of the job market, by industry and occupation, during the 1970's are discussed. A large section considers the various programs to promote employment—from the traditional ones, such as vocational education and apprenticeship, to the experimental programs of the 1960's such as the Job Corps and JOBS.

America's children are the place to begin to rejuvenate a society in which 25.5 million Americans—1 in 8—do not even have an income which reaches the poverty level; in which millions of Americans go without health care because our medical system assumes that good health is a privilege to be paid for rather than absolute right; in which a high school education is often so inferior that graduates in effect have diplomas certifying functional illiteracy; and in which juvenile delinquency abounds because of a lack of jobs, substandard environment, and anyone to take a personal interest in the special and unique needs of each youngster.

These eight papers document this situation and should be read by all those concerned with the fate of our children.

PREFACE

This compendium assembles a series of background papers prepared for the 1970 White House Conference on Children and Youth. These papers were generally designed to assemble data on past trends, present status, current needs, and some potential alternatives for the future in selected program areas. They were written at the request of the national chairman of the 1970 White House Conference by experts mainly in Federal Departments or by consultants retained by the Departments. The purpose of these papers was to supplement the working papers of the various forums, which focused largely on policies and recommendations.

This compendium includes six background papers distributed to various forums of the Conference on Children, held in Washington December 13–18, 1970, as follows:

Day Care and Preschool Services: Trends in the Nineteen-Sixties and Issues for the Nineteen-Seventies by Ronald K. Parker, Ph. D. and Jane Knitzer, Ph. D.

Background Paper on Health by Richard W. Dodds, M.D., F.A.A.P.

Population Change in the United States and the Development of Family Planning Services by Carl S. Shultz, M.D., et al.

Background Paper on Minority Children and Youth by Pamela Haddy Kacser, Ph. D.

The Background Paper on Food and Nutrition by Ruth M. Leverton, Ph. D.

Background Paper on Special Programs for Handicapped Children and Youth by James W. Moss, Ph. D.

Two additional papers related more directly to the White House Conference on Youth which was held at Estes Park, Colorado, on April 18–22, 1971. These were the:

Background Paper on Juvenile Delinquency by Kenneth Polk, Ph. D., and John M. Martin, Ph. D.

Jobs For Youth by Herbert C. Morton.

The entire series was planned and monitored by Michael S. March, Ph. D., who served as Senior Research Consultant to the National Chairman of the White House Conference on Children and Youth. Pamela Haddy Kacser assisted in seeing the final papers through the publications stage. Appreciations is due the several authors for their efforts, which in many cases were carried out under great pressure of time and at substantial personal inconvenience.

CONTENTS

BACKGROUND PAPER ON MINORITY CHILDREN AND YOUTH FOR THE 1970 WHITE HOUSE CONFERENCE ON CHILDREN AND YOUTH

(By Pamela Haddy Kacser, Advisor on Socio-Economic Research, Office of Economic and Social Research, Bureau of Labor Statistics, U.S. Department of Labor)

INTRODUCTION

This paper seeks to review each of the problem areas discussed in the other papers as they collectively affect minority children and youth to measure the distance the Nation has come and the distance still to go toward racial equality. If one were to draw up a set of accounts of social and economic well-being from the decennial census data on the positive side, we would show improvements in three important areas, namely reductions in the incidence of poverty, increases in educational attainment, and in employment opportunity. On the other hand, there are some signs of a worsening situation in terms of family stability and social unrest. Many indicators which would accurately document the degree of progress will not be available until complete 1970 census data have been processed. Many indicators of welfare for non-Negro minority groups are nonexistent. Many of the improvements for the Negro are taking place too rapidly to be reflected fully in available statistics.

This report has seven main sections, each discussing a certain area of relevance to minority groups. The general subject areas covered are:

1. The demographic background
2. Home life
3. Income and poverty
4. Health
5. Education
6. Employment and job training
7. Social tranquility

In some of the sections, there is also a brief look at major government programs relevant to the economic and social welfare of minority children and youth pertaining to the topic on hand. These are mainly programs directed toward the general population or the general children and youth population, but which would be expected to aid minority children and youth more than children and youth in the general population.

Recent statistical information for minority groups are compared with indicators for earlier years and with the white majority. The comparisons, where feasible, are both in absolute and relative terms, in order to determine whether the situation of a minority group has improved, as well as whether any gaps are widening or narrowing.

Because of the limitations of the data, it is not always possible to present consistent comparisons. However, wherever possible, data are presented in the age categories: For children less than 1, 1–5, and 6–13; for youth 14–17 and 18–24. Comparison may be possible only for whites versus nonwhites, or whites versus Negroes (who constitute 91 percent of nonwhite children and youth). Very little separate data are available for other nonwhite minorities (native American Indians, Chinese Americans, Japanese Americans) and for predominately white minorities (Mexican Americans, Puerto Ricans).

For all groups concerned, the indicators are limited to those indices which have been traditionally used, are easily obtained, and which are objective and cardinally ordered.

1. THE DEMOGRAPHIC BACKGROUND

Since World War II, children and youth have gradually become a larger part of the American population, rising from 41 percent of the total in 1946 to 47 percent in 1969. However, this is far short of their share in 1900 and 1870 when those under 25 constituted 54 and 57 percent of the population, respectively. About 48 percent of the Nation's males and 45 percent of the females are now under 25, compared with 46 and 44 percent respectively in 1960. (See tables 1, 2, and 3, appendix.)

In minority groups, the young make up an even larger segment of the population. In 1969, Negro children and youth were 56 percent of the total Negro population. In part, this reflects higher Negro birth rates and earlier deaths, as well as the widening with age of the differences between the white and Negro death rates. For all minority races, the under-25 population was 56 percent of their total population.

Projections of the population indicate reversal of the trend of the past 25 years. By the end of this century, a smaller proportion of both the white and the Negro and other populations is expected to be under 25—the result of declining birth rates in the 1970's and 1980's. Actually, the population under 5 years old was already declining in the 1960's. Thus, despite increases in the total population, the proportion in elementary school ages is expected to grow very little, and of preschoolers to decline. (See table 4.)

Minority races account for a greater proportion of the young population than of other age groups. Today about 1 in 7 of those under 25 is a member of a minority race as compared to 1 in 10 of those over 25. By 1990, about 1 in 6 of those under 25 will be of a minority race. This represents a continuing increase since 1930, when one 1 in 9 of those under 25 was a member of a minority race. (See chart A.)

The most recent nationwide data for non-Negro minority groups, including Spanish-surnamed whites (who are included in statistics for all whites) are contained in the 1960 census. The more recent current population reports generally contain data only for whites, and Negroes and other races, often with separate data for Negroes.

Of the eight minority groups listed, all had lower median ages and larger proportions of people aged less than 25 in their populations than whites, and the American Indians, Oriental-Americans, Mexican-Americans, and Puerto Ricans had lower median ages and larger proportions of under 25 year olds than Negroes as well. (See table 5.)

Chart A

Negro and other minority races are accounting for larger proportions of the children and youth population.

Minority Races Under 25 Percentage of Total Under 25 Population

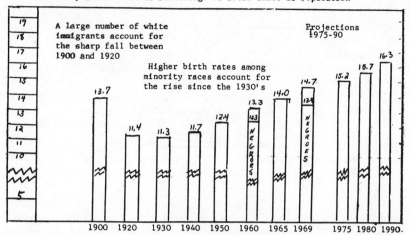

Source: U.S. Bureau of the Census, Current Population Reports, Series P-25, Nos. 311, 381, and 441, "Estimates of the Population of the U.S. by Single Years of Age, Color, and Sex 1900 to 1959," "Projections of the Population of the U.S. by Age, Sex, and Color to 1990," "Estimates of the Population of the U.S. by Age, Race, and Sex: July 1, 1967, to July 1, 1969."

Chart B

Minority Group Children and Youth Are Primarily
Negroes and Mexican-Americans

Percent of total minority group children and youth
in each minority group - 1960 distribution

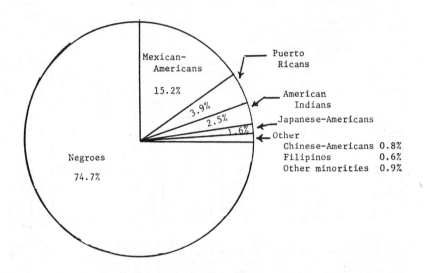

Source: U.S. Bureau of the Census, <u>1960 Census of Population</u>,
          Subject Reports, PC(2)1-B, 1-C, and 1-D. See Table 5.

In 1969, 52 percent of the Negro population lived in the South, 19
percent in the Northeast, 21 percent in the North Central States and 7
percent in the West. The most recent data on geographic dispersion for
other minorities are from the 1960 census. The 1960 data revealed that
Negroes were more dispersed throughout the United States than other
minority groups. Puerto Ricans were most concentrated with 69 percent of those in the United States in New York City, and 25 percent on
Manhattan Island alone. Puerto Ricans are most likely to live in urban
areas (96 percent) with Negroes second (75 percent). Half of all
Indians live in the West (50 percent) and 70 percent are in rural areas.
The majority of Japanese-Chinese and Filipino-Americans are concentrated in cities along the Pacific coast and on the Hawaiian Islands,
while most Mexican Americans live in the Southwest. (See table 6.)
    While the geographic dispersion of Negroes is greater than that of
the other minority groups, Negroes are more segregated within our
cities. One study of residential segregation analyzed population on a

city block basis for 207 cities in 1960, and revealed that, on average, 87.8 percent of the Negroes in these cities would have to move from their block to other areas of the city in order to have every block integrated according to the city's percentage of Negro population. Even in the most integrated of these large cities, San Jose, Calif., 60.4 percent of the Negro population would be required to disperse for full integration. The study also revealed considerable, although less, segregation of various minority groups from each other.[1]

Table A. Segregation of Minority Groups in Large Cities, 1960 [2]

In New York City:
    73.0 percent of Puerto Ricans; and
    79.8 percent of Negroes would have to move in order to fully integrate with the Anglo-white population.
In San Antonio:
    63.6 percent of the Mexican-Americans; and
    84.5 percent of the Negroes would need to move for full integration.
In Los Angeles:
    57.4 percent of the Mexican-Americans;
    60.5 percent of Oriental-Americans; while
    87.8 percent of the Negroes would have to move.
In San Francisco:
    37.3 percent of the Mexican-Americans;
    51.4 percent of the Oriental-Americans; while
    65.4 percent of the Negroes would have to move in order to fully integrate with the Anglo-white population.

2. HOME LIFE

The physical and other conditions of the homelife of many minority children and youth are indeed not as pleasant as for the white majority, aside from the average lower family income, discussed in part 3. Indicators such as children living with both parents, and marriage-divorce comparisons show a worsening situation as viewed by conventional standards of home life quality, despite a lessening of the incidence of poverty.

Most children (about 85 percent) who are under 18 years of age live with both parents, and the younger the child, the more likely he is to be in a two-parent family. Among white children, the proportion of children not living with both parents increased from 8 percent in 1957 to 11 percent in 1969. In nonwhite families, children undergo a greater disadvantage since a very large proportion of them do not live with both parents. In 1960, a quarter of unmarried nonwhites under 18 did not live with both parents, and the proportion has increased to 29 percent in 1965, and to 31 percent in 1969. (See chart C.)

---

[1] Karl F. and Alma E. Taeuber, "Negroes in Cities," ch. 3, passim.
[2] Latest available data.

Source: Karl E. and Alma F. Taeuber. "Negroes in Cities," ch. 3.

Chart C
Children and youth are more likely to be living with
both parents when they are very young and when parents have higher income.
Percent of unmarried persons under 18 living with both parents.

Percent living
with both parents

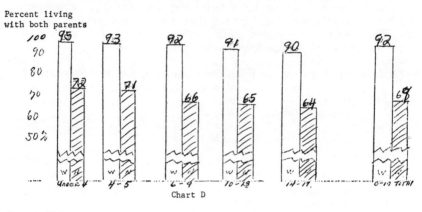

Chart D

Percent living
with both parents

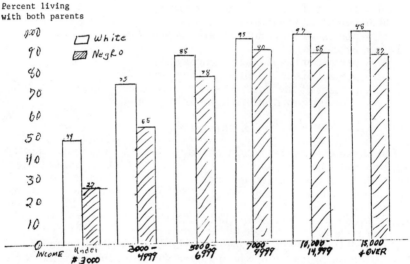

Source: U.S. Bureau of Labor Statistics, The Social and Economic Status of
          Negroes in the United States, 1969, (BLS Report No. 375), and U.S.
          Bureau of the Census, Current Population Reports, Series P-20, No. 198,
          "Marital Status and Family Status, March 1969."

As might be expected, for both white and nonwhite children, proportions not living with both parents are higher in urban than in
rural areas, reflecting, in part, the rural tradition of family
cohesiveness.

About four times the proportion of nonwhite children lived with their mother only, as compared with whites, and about five times the proportion lived with neither parent, compared with whites.

Marital discord for whites and nonwhites appears to be on the rise if figures on separations and divorces alone indicate discord.

The nonwhite figures are more than twice the white. A major source of discord is financial problems, which may explain some of the white-nonwhite differences. However, increasing urbanization and increased employment opportunities for women may also contribute to the financial independence of women. Female-headed families have been increasing for both whites and nonwhites, the trend being clearer and more pronounced, in the case of nonwhites. (See tables 7–9.)

Minority group children are more likely to have a working mother than others since they have a higher incidence of female-headed families. However, there were nearly five white children with working mothers for every one nonwhite. There were 2.2 million children of minority races under 14 years of age with working mothers as compared with 10.1 million whites. (See table 10.)

About 10 percent of the children of working white mothers were in families whose income was under $3,000 in 1964, while 40 percent of the children of Negro and other races were in that situation. About the same proportions of all races (32 percent) are in families with incomes between $3,000 and $6,000, while nearly twice the proportion of white children are in working-mother families with incomes of 6,000 to 9,000, and almost three times the proportion in working-mother families of $10,000 and over.

Although there were some differences by race, arrangements for the care of these children were quite similar. White children were somewhat more likely to be cared for by the father (14 percent compared to 11 percent) but less likely to be cared for in someone else's home, either by a relative or nonrelative (19 percent versus 24). Of the children of part-time working mothers, differences of care arrangements by color were more pronounced. Arrangements involving the mother were more frequent for white children, with 29 percent cared for by the mother while working as compared with 9 percent for Negro and other children. Twenty-five percent of whites had a mother who worked only during school hours as compared with only 16 percent of Negro and other children. Care in the child's own home by a relative other than the father, on the other hand, was far less common among white children. Care in someone else's home, particularly in homes of relatives was also more frequent among Negro and other races than among whites. (See tables 11 and 12.)

A particular disadvantage to which many nonwhites under 18 are subjected is the low educational attainment of the family head, even in the case of the child living with both parents. Whereas, for whites under 18 living in husband-wife families, only 15 percent of their fathers had not graduated from elementary school, half the comparable nonwhite heads were in this educational category.

Consumption patterns also point up the relative disadvantage of the minority child or youth. They are more likely to be living in a housing unit not meeting specified criteria of structural soundness and plumbing facilities. Recent (1968) estimates indicated that while 6 percent of the housing units occupied by whites failed to meet the criteria, 24 percent of the units occupied by Negro and other races failed. The 1960 census placed respective figures at 13 and 44 percent. As table 13 indicates, Negro housing in the central city is better than in the suburbs or in nonmetropolitan areas with respect to these criteria.

Along with their higher incidence of poor and old housing, minority group children and youth are more likely than whites to be exposed to its perils. These include the presence of rats and vermin, as well as a higher frequency of home accidents. Transcripts of hearings held by the Commission on Civil Rights and congressional committees cite many examples of those hazards. One subject of current interest concerns lead poisoning, a disease of slum areas, where dilapidated pre-World War II housing units contain peeling lead-based paint that young children chew and eat. Surveys in Washington, D.C., and other cities show a large proportion of children living in slum housing have excessive amounts of lead in their bloodstreams. The cost of treating one case of lead poisoning ranges from $1,000 to $220,000, and the cost in terms of poor health and physical defects is even greater.

Reflecting the lower average income, minority children and youth are less likely to be living in a home owned by the family, even less likely to be living in a new, family-owned home. According to Census Bureau figures, one in 83 households in America bought a new house in 1969, while only one in 250 Negro households did so. Negro households, however, are about as likely as white households, to purchase a previously occupied home. Negroes account for only 2 percent of new homes and 3 percent of used home purchases exceeding $20,000. (See table 14.)

As with housing, so with cars, during the 1967–69 period the Negro household was less than half as likely as white to have bought a new or used automobile. About 1 in 8 of the white, compared with only 1 in 19 of the Negro households, bought a new car per year, and 1 in 5 white and 1 in 6 Negro households bought a used car per year. On an average, the Negro household also spent less on household durables (furnishings and appliances) from 1967–69—about three-fourths as much—mainly, of course, because their income was lower. (See chart E.)

Chart   E

Negro Households are Less Likely to Purchase a New Car, or a
Higher Priced Home

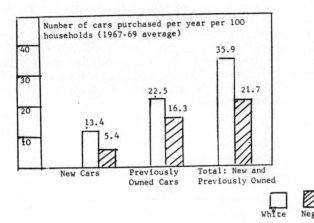

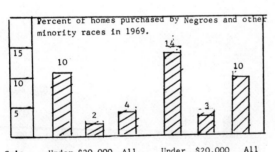

Source: U.S. Bureau of the Census; Current Population Reports, Series P-65, No. 31,
"Recent Purchases of Cars, Houses, and Other Durables and Expectations to Buy During
the Months Ahead: Survey Data Through April 1970."

Another aspect of homelife is the source of family income. The source is particularly important at a time when expressions such as black capitalism on one hand, and generation-to-generation welfare on the other hand, are commonplace. The 1968 income data reveal the fact that Negroes derive more of their total family income from wages and salaries than whites do. The figures are 85 percent for Negroes and 79 percent for whites. Self-employment, and income from dividends, interest, and rentals provided 4 percent of total Negro family income, but 14 percent of total white family income. Contrary to the idea held by a substantial number of people concerning widespread handouts to Negroes, welfare and public assistance accounted for only 4 percent of total income for the average Negro family. (See table 15 and chart F.)

Chart F

Percent of Total Family Income from Specified Sources in 1968, by Race

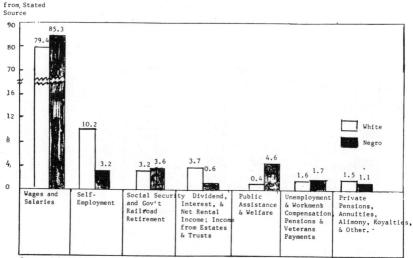

Source: Calculated from U.S. Bureau of the Census, Current Population Reports, Series P-60, No. 66, "Income in 1968 of Families and Persons in the United States."

Income of other races can only be deduced from 1968 data. They indicate that about 20 percent of family income was from sources other than wages or salaries among Japanese and Chinese who have been subjected to less discrimination than Negroes. Much of this was apparently entrepreneurial. American Indians, on the other hand, are known to be worse off in terms of income level and probably worse off in terms of income source than any other minority group.

The impact of lower average family income and higher unemployment affects the young, as indicated in this report, by a lower physical standard of living. In addition to this is the complex matrix of motivation and other psychological factors. How the family receives its income may be as important as how much income it gets in shaping today's youth and tomorrow's adults, although the process is uncertain.

3. INCOME AND POVERTY: PROGRESS IN THE BATTLE AGAINST POVERTY

While much attention has been placed on Negro poverty, a situation facing about 30 percent of all black families and about 40 percent of blacks under 18, it must be kept in mind that about 20 percent of all black families received more than $10,000 income in 1968. However, over 40 percent of white families receive more than $10,000. The 1968 median family income was $8,936 for whites and $5,359 for blacks, a difference of $3,577. This gap indicates the need for more progress in providing equal opportunity. To look at poverty alone, without presenting the whole income distribution would reveal a biased picture since almost 60 percent of blacks under 18 live above the poverty line.

Chart 1 (appendix) demonstrates the white-Negro income gap. For any specified amount of family income, a larger percentage of Negro families receive less than the amount than white families. Since larger family size is associated with lower income relatively more often among Negroes than whites, the gap is even greater in a distribution of family incomes of children under 18. (See table 16.)

Progress in the battle against poverty

Between 1959 and 1969, the number of family members of all races under 18 living in poverty had fallen from 17.2 million to 9.8 million, a drop of 7.4 million or 43 percent. For whites, family members under 18 in poverty fell from 11.4 million to 5.8 million, a drop of 49 percent, but for Negro and other races, the drop was only 30.5 percent from 5.8 million to 4 million.

In 1959, 21 percent of white children and 67 percent of the children of minority races were in poverty. By 1969, the poverty incidence had been cut by more than half to 10 percent, and 38 percent respectively.

Looking at children (under 18) of minority races alone, on and off the farm, we find that those on the farm are more than twice as likely to be in poverty than the children of nonfarm families. Furthermore, the improvement from 1959 to 1968 has been greater for those living off the farms than for those on farms.

Children in families with a female at the head are more likely to be poor than children of male-headed families whether they are whites or a minority race. In female-headed families, minority children are 2½ times as likely to be in poverty as in families headed by a man, and almost 5 times as likely to be in poverty as those in the average American family.

In 1968, 11 percent of white family members under 18 were in poverty. The incidence for Negro and other races was 42 percent. The white under 18 is only one-fourth as likely to be in poverty. (See tables 17–20 and chart G.)

Chart   G

Incidence of Poverty--Unmarried Family Members Under 18

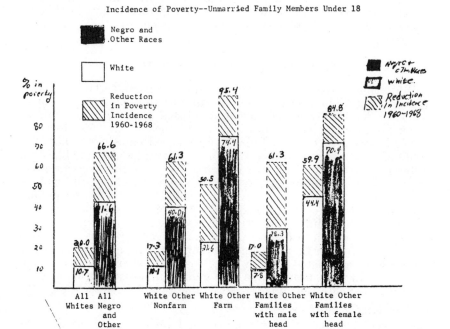

Source: U.S. Census Bureau, <u>Current Population Reports</u>, Series P-60,
No. 68, "Poverty in the U.S. 1959 to 1968."

Minority groups are accounting for a larger percent of the poor in both the total and the young population. In part, this is explained by the increases of minority children and youth as a proportion of total American population, and by the increases of minority children and youth in female-headed families as a proportion of total population.

The available data do not permit us to assess the reduction in poverty among individual minority groups. Based on 1960 income data, the incidence of poverty for different groups, albeit overlapping, probably lies in the following order:

Least poverty

    1. Anglo whites.
    2. Orientals.
    3. Spanish-surnamed whites.
    4. Negroes.
    5. American Indians, Aleuts, and Eskimos.

A number of Federal Government programs or joint Federal-State programs alleviate or reduce poverty among the young, including along with aid for dependent children, emergency welfare assistance, Cuban refugee program, social security to dependent and disabled youth, the Department of Agriculture food stamp program and the commodity distribution program, school breakfast and school lunch programs and the special food service for children in preschools of the Department of Agriculture. Many other Federal programs have direct or indirect effects upon the poor, including the manpower programs of the Department of Labor. All of these programs have a disproportionate effect upon minority youth—either for good or ill—since minorities are more likely to be poor and young.

The American public, in referring to Federal programs to alleviate poverty, however, is usually concerned with the aid for dependent children (AFDC), which has come to mean "welfare" in the United States.

During 1969, 1.6 million families in the United States containing 4.7 million children received AFDC benefits. Of these families, 783,000 were white (including Puerto Rican, Cuban, and Mexican-American), 736,000 Negro and 21,000 American Indian. Fifty-six percent resided within a central city of a metropolitan area, 16 percent lived elsewhere in metropolitan areas, and 28 percent in small cities, towns, or rural areas. Two percent lived on farms. Most AFDC children were 4 to 12 years old; relatively few were infants or over 16. The median age was just under 9 years.

Of 1.6 million AFDC families, the father was in the home in only about 300,000 cases, and of these 190,000 or more than half, were incapacitated. In most cases, the mother was in the home (1.5 million cases). Of these 330,000—roughly a fifth—were employed full or part time, in a work or training program, or awaiting enrollment after referral to the work incentive program. Of the 1.2 million remaining mothers, about 220,000 were incapacitated for employment, 110,000 had no marketable skills, or suitable employment was not available, and 580,000 were needed in the home full time in household duties. About one-third of the remainder were actively seeking work.[3]

4. HEALTH

The minority group child born in America is 3½ times as likely to have his mother die giving birth as a white child. The maternal death rate for minority races is 7 in 10,000. The minority races/white ratio is about the same as in 1960 when the odds against minority race mothers was 10 in 10,000.

The death rates, reflect in part, the fact that the minority race child is less likely to be born in a hospital or attended by a physician at birth; however, there have been great improvements in this situation, too, in recent years.

Minorities (in 1967) weighed less at birth than whites—3,130 grams, 5.4 percent or 180 grams less than whites. In all States, the white child was about half as likely to be born immature (weighing under 2,500 grams). Nationwide, 7 percent of white births and 13.6 percent of other births are immature.

The minority infant is about 1.8 times as likely to die during the first year, 1.6 times as likely to die between ages 1 and 4. One and a half

[3] U.S. Department of Health, Education, and Welfare, *Preliminary Report of Findings—1969 A.F.D.C. Study*, N.C.S.S. Report AFDC-1 (69), March 1970.

14

times as likely between 5 and 14, and 1.7 times as likely between 15 and
24. (See table 23.) Between 1 and 4, he is 1.8 times as likely to be
killed by an accident, 3.3 times as likely to die from influenza and
pneumonia, 2 times as likely to die from meningitis, but only 60 percent as likely to die from cancer. The death rate from tuberculosis
under age 15 is 21 times as high for Indians as for the entire U.S.
population.

Nonwhite infants are about 60 percent more likely to die during
their first 28 days after birth than whites, and more than 2½ times
more likely to die in the period from 28 days to 1 year after birth.
Oriental-Americans have lower infant mortality than whites, and
blacks have a higher rate than other minority races. (See table 21.)

The average infant mortality rate in the United States is higher
than for 16 other countries, including many European nations, Australia, New Zealand, and Japan. It compares favorably with the rate
in most countries of the world. However, the rate for black Americans
continues to lie halfway between the rates observed for white Americans and some of the underdeveloped nations. (See table 22.)

A continuing national health survey reports on the incidence of
various health problems by age and race. Whites are more likely to
have reported one or more chronic conditions. Two of the chief factors
contributing to the higher reported prevalence of such conditions
among whites are: [4]

"First, the better medical care of white persons which leads to
more frequent diagnosis of chronic conditions and, second, the
higher socioeconomic level of white persons which is associated
with better reporting. Conversely, less frequent medical attention
of nonwhite persons results in fewer diagnosed chronic conditions
among the nonwhite but in higher levels of activity limitation and
disability."

Members of minority groups experienced 8 percent more bed-disabil-
ity days per person during the 1965–67 period than whites but in the
case of persons under 17 years of age whites had about 18 percent more
such days.

More white persons (26.2 per 100 population) than others (19.1 per
100 population) were reported injured in accidents. White persons had
a higher rate of persons injured in each age group except 45 to 64, but
substantial differences between color occurred only at the youngest
and oldest ages.

Whites in all age groups experienced more hospital episodes than
others; however, once hospitalized, relatively more of the minorities
reported larger numbers of hospital days than did whites of the same
age and sex. More than twice the proportion of hospitalized nonwhites
under 17 reported 15 or more days in the hospital than whites.

Many of these white-nonwhite differences may be explained by differences in diagnosis which results from differences in number of
physician visits. Whites saw a physician about 50 percent more often
than others. In the case of children under 6, whites saw a physician
80 percent more often, and for those 6 to 16 it was 140 percent more

[4] Department of Health, Education, and Welfare, National Center for Health Statistics, Vital and Health Statistics: *Data from the National Health Survey,* Series 10, No. 56, page 1. This publication is hereafter cited as *NCHS,* Series 10, No. 56.

often. A greater proportion of the minorities visited doctors in hospital clinics or emergency rooms. (See table 24.)

Mental health

Psychological studies have shown that often the black child may become convinced that he is inferior, perceiving himself as a social reject and as unworthy of help and affection. Children who are discriminated against or otherwise deprived in a number of ways are likely to respond in ways showing various asocial or antisocial patterns. According to Charles S. Johnson [5] the frustrations accompanying this discrimination felt by black children may express themselves in direct aggression, antisocial behavior, neurotic repressions, withdrawing from reality, and other ailments. Dr. Fritz Redl has stated "a lot of youthful 'defiant' behavior is not the outcropping of a corrupt or morbid personality, but the defense of a healthy one against the kind of treatment that shouldn't happen to a dog, but often does happen to children." [6] The young victim of discrimination may seek security in a gang—such behavior has been seen by various groups in our history. Lewis Yablonsky has written: "In the modern disorganized slum, the gang has been for many Negro youths their only source of identity, status, and emotional satisfaction. They set goals that are achievable; they build an empire, partly real and partly fantasy, that helps them live through the confusion of adolescence." [7]

During hearings held before the Commission on Civil Rights in Cleveland, Ohio, Dr. Robert Coles, a child psychiatrist from Harvard University, who has made clinical studies of black children in Boston and Cleveland, as well as in the South, testified about black children in the North. A technique used by Dr. Coles in working with the children is to have them draw pictures of familiar things. He described a picture one child drew of his home: [8]

"This house is a shambles. It is a confused disorderly house for a child that can do better and has done better. He has much better drawing ability. The house is deliberately ramshackled. There is a black sky and what might pass for a black sun or in any event a cloud of black. The ground is brown and not green, and there are no flowers. It is a dismal place. There is a cross on the door. The child told me that the property was condemned."

The Federal Government has many programs relevant to the health for the young, particularly for children and youth in poverty. In the light of their heavy incidence of poverty, the benefits are disproportionately directed toward minority groups. The Department of Health, Education, and Welfare provides grants for health services for migratory workers. In many areas most migrant workers and their families are Spanish-Americans and Negroes.

[5] "Race Relations, Problems and Theory," Chapel Hill, University of North Carolina Press, 1961.
[6] "Our Troubles with Defiant Youth," Children, Jan. 2, 1955, DHEW.
[7] Cited in Young Children, May 1967, by J. H. Douglass—Mental Health Aspects of the Effects of Discrimination upon Children."
[8] U.S. Commission on Civil Rights, "A Time to Listen, A Time to Act," pp. 9–10, statement contained in USCCR, Cleveland Hearings, p. 283.

HEW's Indian health service provides health services for more than 400,000 Indians, Eskimos, and Aleuts through a system of 51 hospitals, 65 health centers, and about 300 health stations. Contract medical care is also available for these citizens through non-Federal facilities.

The Social and Rehabilitation Service of HEW provides grants-in-aid to States under the Maternal and Child Health Services improvement program, the maternity and infant care support program, and the medicaid program.

The most widely known program is medicaid program (title XIX of the Social Security Act). This program provides grants to States to administer medical assistance programs which benefit all public assistance recipients in the federally aided categories, those who would qualify for public assistance, all children under 21 whose parents cannot afford medical care, as well as (at the State's option) those with enough income for daily needs but not for medical expenses.

In addition, title V of the Social Security Act provides for Federal grants to State and local agencies and institutions to provide for health care and services to children of school and preschool age, particularly in areas containing concentrations of low-income families.

5. EDUCATION

Members of minority groups, on average, have received less education than whites, although progress is being made in narrowing the gap. The lower educational attainment of parents explain, in part, some of the present disadvantages experienced by today's minority group children and youth. Research indicates that the educational achievement of today's young is often dependent on the parents' education. Other functions, cited elsewhere in this paper also affect the young, as reported by the Office of Education.

Millions of deprived children suffer social handicaps that reach far beyond the classroom. Among these are the lack of prenatal care, basic medical attention, and a decent home environment. Children who are hungry cannot learn and if they are without proper clothing, they may not even reach the school door. Poor children are burdened with the despair that is handed down by generations of neglect and hoplessness. In the cities, the children of poverty are likely to be segregated in fixed racial ghettos which lock in despair and shut out opportunity.[9]

This same report cites evidence that the early years in a child's life can result in a difference of 20 to 40 IQ points as an adult. "Psycholo-

---

[9] Office of Education. *Title I, Year II, The Second Annual Report of Title I of the Elementary and Secondary Education Act of 1965*, p. 16.

gists know that the growth of a child's mind can be severely hampered by a repressing and restricted environment. It is important that planned educational experiences be introduced well before a child arrives at school. The cradle is not too early. Headstart programs may be too late." [10] In testimony on the Headstart Child Development Act (S. 2060) in August of 1969, the results of a scientific study of the development quotients (DQ) of 344 Negro infants in Mississippi were described. The average DQ at 3 months was 115, well above average. By the end of 36 months, the average DQ had fallen to a below average 85. A study in Washington, D.C., showed that there was a decrease in the average intelligence quotient from 108 to 89 between the ages of 3 months and 3 years for a group receiving no services to compensate for an environment of physical, educational, and psychological deprivation. A similar group receiving these services had an IQ of 105 at 3 months and 106 at 36 months.[11]

While improvements have been made in bringing the education level of minority group members up to that of whites, there continues to be a gap. In the 16–17 age group, a Negro was almost one and a half times as likely to have dropped out of school as his white counterpart in October 1969. For 18–21-year-olds, the ratio was approximately 2 to 1. (See table 25.)

Enrollments for Negroes and whites are highest in the suburban areas of metropolitan areas, and lower in descending order in the central cities of metropolitan areas, in nonmetropolitan areas, and in the poverty areas of the larger metropolitan areas. Negroes in metropolitan poverty areas fare only slightly worse in terms of enrollment than whites living there, perhaps because whites in some of these areas are often members of minority groups themselves (Puerto Ricans and Mexican-Americans).

School enrollment for children and youth between 7 and 15 is almost universal, with litttle difference between whites and Negroes. The nonenrollment rate for Negroes 5 and 6 years old is 1.5 times that of whites, while for children of 3 and 4, the ratio is reversed. Enrollment of 3 and 4 year olds has been rising despite a drop in the 3–4 population since 1960, and increased from 10 percent in 1964 to 16 percent in 1969. Fifteen percent of white children and 21 percent of Negro children, 3–4 are enrolled, the increase largely the result of Headstart programs at the nursery and kindergarten level. Enrollment rates have risen for all races since 1960, particularly Negroes and whites aged 5–6, and Negroes 16–17. (See table 26 and chart II.)

---

[10] Ibid., p. 59.
[11] Hearings, S. 2060, pp. 48–49.

18

Chart H

Except for Three- and Four-Year-Olds, Negroes Are Less Likely to be Enrolled in School.

Percent of persons by age and race no. enrolled in school and not having graduated
from high school, Ocrober 1969.

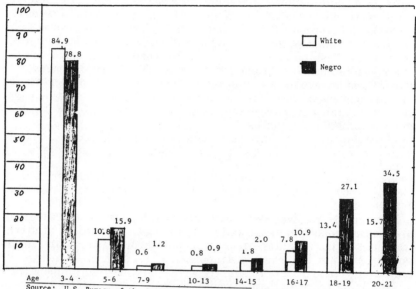

Source: U.S. Bureau of the Census, Current Population Reports, Series P-20, No. 206,
"School Enrollment: October 1969."

Enrollment rates alone can be misleading, for they do not indicate age-grade comparability. Ninety-eight percent enrollment at age 15 means little in itself as an indicator if one group's modal grade is the second year of high school while another group's mode is the eighth grade. Most children enrolled at age 6 attend first grade, advancing one grade each year until a plurality of 17-year-olds are in their final year of high school. The 1960 census contains data on enrollment by age, grade, and race. Of those enrolled, a greater percentage of Negroes and Indians were enrolled below the modal grade for all races, while Japanese and Chinese Americans outperform whites in this respect. (See table 28.)

Another comparative indicator of education is the educational attainment at a specific age, or the proportion of a group's population at a given age completing high school or college. In 1969, 77 percent of all whites and 58 percent of all Negro and other races 25–29 years of age had completed high school, a large improvement over the 64 and 39 respective figures in 1960. Of the 25–29 white population, 17 percent had completed 4 years of college in 1969, nearly double the 9 percent of Negro and other races. This compares with 12 and 5 percent respectively in 1960. At ages 20 and 21, 8 in every 10 whites, and 6 in every 10 Negro and other races had completed high school. About 1 in every 4 whites versus 1 in 8 Negro and other races had completed at least 1 year of college in 1969. The average white 20-year-old had completed 12.8 years of school compared with 12.3 years for Negro and

19

other minority races; while for those over 25, the respective medians were 12.2 and 9.8 years in 1969. It is clear that the gap in median years of schooling is closing for the young. (See chart I, and tables 29 and 30 appendix.)

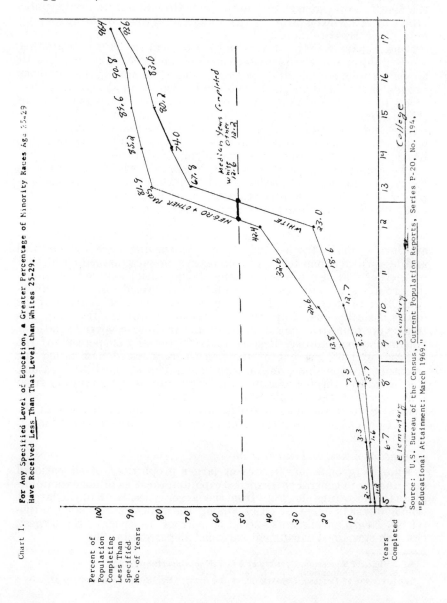

Chart I. **For Any Specified Level of Education, a Greater Percentage of Minority Races Age 25-29 Have Received Less Than That Level than Whites 25-29.**

Percent of Population Completing Less Than Specified No. of Years

Years Completed

Source: U.S. Bureau of the Census, Current Population Reports, Series P-20, No. 194, "Educational Attainment: March 1969."

However, studies of the quality of education shows an increase in the gap in performance between whites and others as they progress through school. Using the average scores for whites in metropolitan areas of the northeast portion of the country as a standard for verbal ability, reading achievement and mathematics achievement, Negroes were about two grades levels behind the standard at the sixth grades, while at the 12th grade level the gap was about 4 years. Whites in other parts of the Nation did not come up to standard, especially in the South; however, even Southern nonmetropolitan 12th grade whites (the whites with the largest gap) were behind the standard group by only 1.3 years. (See table 31.)

School characteristics studies in the Coleman report [12] indicate that white children tended to attend elementary and secondary schools with a smaller number of pupils per classroom than any of the minority groups, except Indians in high school. Negroes tended to have less access to science and language laboratories, fewer books per pupil in school libraries, and text books less often in sufficient supply. On the other hand, minority group students were more likely to have a cafeteria, a free lunch program, and free textbooks. Many characteristics, however, were about the same for students of all races.

The report reveals most teachers, Negro and white, prefer not to teach in schools that are predominately nonwhite; most future teachers prefer to teach high ability students in academic schools; white students training for a teaching career are better prepared academically than Negroes; and there are substantial differences between Negro and white teachers in verbal competence. Disadvantaged Negro children are thus taught by teachers who, generally speaking, are less qualified and less willing than teachers who teach more advantaged children.[13]

Another indicator of the educational deprivation suffered by minority groups is a comparison of results of the Armed Forces Qualifications Test for Negroes and non-Negroes. The "mental" portion of the test is basically one of aptitude at absorbing military training. The test covers four areas: vocabulary, simple arithmetic, spatial relations, and mechanical ability. Results for 1968 reveal 35.9 percent of the Negroes and 6.7 percent of the non-Negroes tested had failed for "mental" reasons alone, or for both "mental" and "medical" reasons. Results by geographic area indicate Negro failure rates ranging from 18.2 percent in the Pacific States to 47.4 percent in the East South Central States; and non-Negro failure rates from 2.5 percent in the West North Central States to 13.1 in the East South Central States.[14] (See table 32.)

Education, cities, and integration

Minority groups now represent larger proportions of educational enrollments in central cities of metropolitan areas as minorities immigrate to and whites emigrate from the larger cities. In 15 of the largest school districts (central cities among the Nation's 100 largest districts), Negro enrollments exceed 50 percent. In seven of the largest, Spanish-surnamed enrollment exceeded 20 percent in 1969.

---

[12] U.S. Office of Education, *Equality of Educational Opportunity,* 1966.
[13] U.S. Office of Education, "Title I," op. cit., p. 43.
[14] Department of Defense, Department of the Army, "Health of the Army," p. 51.

Large metropolitan school districts with Negro enrollment 50 percent or more
(October 1968)

Ranked by percent Negro:
  1. Washington, D.C_____ 93. 5
  2. Newark, N.J_____ 72. 5
  3. Richmond, Va_____ 68. 3
  4. Orleans Parish, La_____ 67. 1
  5. Baltimore, Md_____ 65. 1
  6. St. Louis, Mo_____ 63. 5
  7. Atlanta, Ga_____ 61. 7
  8. Gary, Ind_____ 61. 6
  9. Detroit, Mich_____ 59. 2
  10. Philadelphia, Pa_____ 58. 8
  11. Cleveland, Ohio_____ 55. 9
  12. Oakland, Calif_____ 55. 2
  13. Memphis, Tenn_____ 53. 6
  14. Chicago, Ill_____ 52. 9
  15. Birmingham, Ala_____ 51. 4

Source : HEW News, Jan. 4, 1970.

Metropolitan districts with Spanish surnamed enrollment 20 percent or more
(October 1968)

1. San Antonio, Tex_____ 58. 2
2. El Paso, Tex_____ 54. 2
3. Corpus Christi, Tex_____ 46. 6
4. Albuquerque, N. Mex_____ 35. 3
5. Tucson, Ariz_____ 25. 7
6. New York, N.Y_____ 23. 0
7. Los Angeles, Calif_____ 20. 0

October 1968 figures for Negroes and the Spanish-surnamed alone
indicate that their enrollments are the majority in 19 of the 100 largest
school districts.

Over 50 percent_____ 19
Over 60 percent_____ 11
Over 70 percent_____ 3
Over 80 percent_____ 2
Over 90 percent_____ 1

Desegregation

In a 1963 Commission on Civil Rights report, only 8 percent of total
Negro public school pupils in 17 Southern and border States and the
District of Columbia attended schools with white children. Alabama,
Mississippi, and South Carolina had no Negroes in desegregated public
schools. Desegregation in the 11 Southen States alone was less than 0.5
percent, while in border areas the figure was 51.8 percent. By fall 1968,
the 11 Southern States had 32 percent of their Negro students attending schools with whites and 18.4 percent in predominantly white
schools. While segregation in the South remains the established pattern as late as the fall of 1969, 36 percent of blacks in voluntary plan
districts and 20 percent in court-ordered districts attended white-
majority schools, according to HEW preliminary figures. Segregation

is not an exclusively Southern institution. Detailed enrollment figures for the fall, 1968 show segregation existing in other areas as well, but to a lesser degree. Likewise, segregation exists, but to a lesser extent, in public school systems for other minority groups. (See table 33.)

The largest Federal program for preschool, elementary, and secondary education, spending $1.5 billion this fiscal year, is the educationally deprived children program, often referred to as the title I program (title I of the Elementary and Secondary Education Act of 1965) which provides grants to States for allocation to local education agencies operating schools with concentration of children from low-income families, schools for the handicapped, and institutions for neglected or delinquent children. Also, in the title I program are schools for Indian children and special grants to States with concentrations of children from agricultural migrant families.[15] The ultimate goal of the program "is to overcome the educational deprivation associated with poverty and race." [16]

Project Headstart has more than proportionately aided minority group children in both its year-round and summer programs. Negroes represent about one-half, Mexican-Americans about one-tenth, and Puerto Ricans, one-twentieth of total enrollment, which are all larger proportions than their proportions in the age 3 to 6 population. Estimated fiscal 1971 enrollment will be 260,000.

The Follow Through program is designed to extend and supplement the gains made in Headstart or similar preschool training. As estimated 70,000 children will be served by Follow Through this fiscal year.

Other education programs include the dropout prevention program, bilingual education program, civil rights education, Indian education, neighborhood Youth Corps-in school, and enforcement of desegregation laws.

An important, though not the only, prerequisite for a high income level during the adult years is a college degree. In October of 1969, 6.1 million youths between 16 and 24 were enrolled in college. College enrollments accounted for 21 percent of the 16 to 24 population and 36 percent of the 18 to 21 population. Only 14 percent of the 16 to 24 population and 24 percent of the 18 to 21 population of minority races were enrolled. Minority-race youth constituted 13 percent of the total 16 to 24 population, but only 8 percent of the 16 to 24 college enrollments, despite rapid increases in Negro college enrollments since 1964—still only a little more than half the white proportion. (See tables 34 and 35.)

Enrollment rates for Negroes are highest for those living in the suburbs of the central cities, and lowest for those living in nonmetropolitan areas and in poverty areas of the large metropolitan areas. This is the same pattern as observed for white youth, but in each group at a lower level.

Like white students, seven out of eight minority-race college students attended classes full time, but proportionately fewer of them were men, 42 percent, compared with 60 percent among whites. Relatively fewer were working in the fall of 1968. The labor force participation

---

[15] Office of Economic Opportunity, *Catalog of Domestic Assistance Programs* * * * p. 122.
[16] *Title I Evaluation 1966–67* * * * p. 16.

rate among white college students was 42 percent, while among students of Negro and other races it was 33 percent. The fact that half of all minority group students attend schools in the South and Southwest, where job opportunities may not be as plentiful as in other regions of the country may partially account for this difference.[17]

A fall 1968 survey of State universities and land-grant colleges indicate that the 6.6 percent of the college population which is black is not distributed evenly. In the 80 predominantly white State universities and land-grant colleges covered in a nationwide survey conducted by the Southern Education Reporting Service, Negroes constituted under 2 percent of all the full-time undergraduate students. On the other hand, at 17 originally all-Negro schools in 16 Southern and border States, the full-time undergraduate population was almost 96 percent Negro.[18]

A large proportion of black students—between 40 and 50 percent—are enrolled in predominantly black institutions, largely in the Southern and border States, many of which are below average in financial support, in institutional excellence, and in student body quality. The better students are more likely to enroll in the predominantly white colleges, having higher credentialed faculties, better facilities, and more student financial aid available.

According to the results of a survey of entering college freshmen in 1968 conducted by the American Council on Education, Negroes attending predominantly Negro colleges are more likely to have lived on a farm while growing up than both Negroes and whites attending predominantly white colleges. Blacks at predominantly white colleges are more likely to have lived in a large city (over 40 percent) than Negroes at Negro colleges (under 20 percent). The student entering the predominantly Negro college had lower parental income and had a father with a lower educational attainment than the Negro entering a predominantly white college.[19] (See table 36.)

In response to concerns about the relatively low proportion of Negroes in higher education, there are programs including financial assistance to the student and the school, institutions reviewing administrative and admissions policies on the composition of their entering freshman classes, as well as the active recruiting of students who are members of minority groups.

Federal programs directly involving college students of minority groups are of three forms: (1) equal opportunity requirements; (2) forms of student financial aid having a weighing in favor of the low-income student; and (3) recruitment and supplemental education programs such as Talent Search and Upward Bound. The Office of Education administers student-aid programs which mainly assist undergraduates. Three of these programs have been initiated to help increase the number of capable but economically disadvantaged students entering college.

---

[17] U.S. Bureau of Labor Statistics, "Employment Status of School Age Youth," Monthly Labor Review, August 1969.
[18] All 100 member institutions of the National Association of State Universities and Land Grant Colleges in 1968 except University of Hawaii, University of Puerto Rico (prohibited by law from collecting statistics by race), and Washington, D.C., Federal City College.
[19] Fall 1969 issue of Educational Record, American Council on Education, Washington, D.C., Alan E. Bayer and Robert F. Boruch.

Educational opportunity grants provide assistance for students of exceptional financial need. Work-study grants assist students earning a portion of their educational expenses through employment opportunities. Direct (NDEA) loans provide low-interest long-term repayment loans to needy students. The guaranteed loan program is available to students of all income levels.

The social security program provides benefits to students age 18–21 who are children of retired, disabled, and deceased workers. Negro and other races accounted for 13 percent of students receiving benefits and 9 percent of dollar outlays as of December 1968.

Upward Bound, a program to supplement the education of financially and academically disadvantaged high school students, includes summer study and school year tutorial services. In 1969, almost three-quarters of Upward Bound students completing the program went on to college. About half of these go on to graduate. Minority youth comprise about 75 percent of those enrolled. Another program is Talent Search, which is expected to increase the number of minority youth attending college.

The 2-year colleges enroll more than one-third of all Negro students. They can facilitate opportunity in three ways. They are academically accessible; tuition fees are low and in some cases nonexistent; and admission policies are relatively open. For example, in California, admission to the 92 2-year institutions is granted ot anyone who can benefit from the institution.[20] On the other hand, the 2-year colleges, particularly those located in low-income areas, may create a de facto segregation at the freshman and sophomore levels with Negroes and Mexican Americans primarily attending the 2-year schools, while most whites would be attending the 4-year colleges, which generally have higher admission standards.

Much attention (and statistics) has been given to the educational problems of Negroes, while American Indians, Eskimos, and Mexican Americans, however, have as much, if not more, deprivation in this area than Negroes.

AMERICAN INDIANS

In 1969, there were about 200,000 Indian children and youth between 5 and 18; 90 percent were known to be enrolled in school. Of these, two-thirds attended public schools, one-fourth attended Federal schools operated by the Bureau of Indian Affairs, and the small number remaining attended mission and other schools.[21] The proportion of Indian high school graduates has increased somewhat in the past 2 years but this proportion remains much lower than that of the general population, reflecting a continued very high dropout rate,[22] as high as 90 percent in some areas. Many children are 3 years behind grade in performance on standardized tests. In the Albuquerque area, 30–40 percent of Indian children are behind in grade, and in a sample of 74 children beginning first grade in three districts of Idaho, only 15 eventually graduated from high school.[23]

[20] "Manpower Report of the President, 1970," p. 180.
[21] Department of the Interior, Bureau of Indian Affairs, "Education of Indian Children in 1969."
[22] "Manpower Report of the President, 1970." p. 6.
[23] "The Education of American Indians Field Investigation and Research Reports," prepared for the (Senate) Subcommittee on Indian Education, hereafter cited as Indian Subcommittee Reports, p. 51.

The Senate Subcommittee on Indian Education field report on California lists nine reasons for much of the educational failure, including home, culture, and health problems and poor or irrelevant school programs.[24]

As in the case of Negro children there is a culture clash. Indian children, many from homes where English is not spoken at all, or not spoken well, find themselves suddenly placed in the midst of another culture, one presented to them as superior.[25]

Values, beliefs, ideas, and ideals clash, with little, if any, understanding on the part of teachers, of the problem suddenly thrust upon the child * * *. For 12 years, if he is not a dropout, he will be taught the "white man's way" while the Federal Government—in teaching Indian schoolteachers—provides a 2-week (at most) orientation for teachers to learn the "Indian way."

The frustration and powerlessness of the Indian resulting from social disorganization in their communities have become manifest in two notable ways—alcoholism and suicide. During 1968, on one pueblo in New Mexico there were five suicides involving Indian men under 25.[26]

On the brighter side of the picture is the increase in Indian youth entering college, usually with Federal or tribal scholarships; the substantial amount of aid under the Elementary and Secondary Education Act; and other legislation providing special assistance to needy school districts serving Indian children. In 1969, the first college with an all-Indian board of regents—the Navajo Community College at Many Farms, Ariz.—was established on a reservation.[27]

ESKIMOS

The educational situation of the Eskimo is harsh also. College graduates form less than 1 percent of the population, and only 2 percent of the population have completed high school. More than half have not gone beyond sixth grade, while the current elementary school dropout rate is in excess of 64 percent and the high school dropout rate is 54 percent. One study revealed only 40 percent of those in school are average in relation to normal age/grade placement.[28]

SPANISH AMERICANS

Mexican Americans and Puerto Ricans have many of the educational problems faced by Negroes and other minority races. Although more than 99 percent of Spanish-surnamed Americans are classified as white, they are subject to discrimination. In December 1969, the U.S. Commission on Civil Rights held hearings which for the first time focused entirely on problems facing the Mexican American in the Southwest. The Mexican American has had less years of education, and higher school dropout rates, than the Negro, but fares better than Indians and Eskimos. One reason for low educational attainment is the langauge barrier. In many homes, English is not spoken

---

[24] Ibid., pp. 178–179.
[25] Ibid., p. 33.
[26] "Indian Education : A National Tragedy—A National Challenge, 1969" Report of Special (Senate) Subcommittee on Indian Education, p. 17.
[27] "Manpower Report of the President, 1970," p. 6.
[28] "Indian Subcommittee reports," op. cit., p. 30.

at all; in others, not very well. In Texas, Spanish-surnamed individuals 17 and older have completed, on average, only 4.7 years of school. In California, the average is only 8.6 years.[29] Added to the language barrier is the fact of the migratory occupations followed by many Mexican-American parents, resulting in unstable school attendance. In 1968, more than 95 percent of the 150,000 migratory farmworkers coming from Texas were Mexican Americans.[30]

When the child enters school, "about the first thing he encounters at school is an IQ test—in English. Usually he makes a bad showing because of his limited knowledge of English. This means that at best he will be considered a 'slow learner' and treated accordingly; at worst, he will be placed in classes for the mentally retarded." [31]

Some programs have been undertaken to correct the language problem. Many schools in the past had prohibited the use of Spanish, punishing children for violations. Testimony before the U.S. Commission on Civil Rights indicates this may still be the practice at some schools. However, there are bilingual education programs, which are reaching 36,000 students, many of which involve teaching English as a second language, an approach also being used at some Indian schools. Also, a high-intensity language training program has been used to prepare Teacher Corps members to help Spanish-speaking students. These efforts are helping to develop students who will function well in two languages rather than well in one and poorly in the other, or poorly in both languages.

6. EMPLOYMENT AND JOB TRAINING

In 1969, the total U.S. civilian labor force was 80.7 million, a 16-perecnt increase over 1960. Of these, 9 million or 11.1 percent were nonwhite. Youths aged 16 to 24 comprise 20.6 percent of the white labor force; 23 percent of the Negro and other races labor force.

It is interesting that for a variety of reasons, the labor force participation rates (the percent of the population working or looking for work) is higher for white teenagers than for the minority races, but lower for whites, 20 to 24. Some possible explanations are the greater availability of part-time and part-year jobs to white teenagers (as suburban yardboys, newsboys, babysitters, camp counselors, and so forth) contrasted with their wider tendency to attend college, while Negroes over high school age are overwhelmingly likely to enter the full-time labor force. (See tables 37 and 38.)

For all races aged 16 to 24 years, the male labor force participation rate has been falling and the female rate has been rising since 1960, as more men entered college, while new opportunities opened for women.

The occupational distribution of young workers differs by race and school status. About half the white and one-third of the black young men 16 to 21 are enrolled in school. A large proportion of employed white youths hold white-collar and blue-collar jobs (rather than service jobs) than minorities. The pattern for young women is different. Only 40 percent of the whites and one-third of the blacks are en-

---

[29] Rubén Salazar. "Stranger in One's Land," U.S. Commission on Civil Rights, Clearinghouse Publication No. 19, p. 23.
[30] "Manpower Report of the President, 1970," p. 101.
[31] "Stranger in One's Land," op. cit., p. 24.

rolled in school, and a larger proportion of young whites than minority women who are employed are in service jobs. Of the large group not enrolled in school, although most are blue-collar workers, a greater proportion of employed whites of both sexes hold white-collar jobs, and a larger proportion of employed Negroes and other minorities of both sexes hold blue-collar jobs. The proportion holding service jobs is greater for minority workers except in the case of females enrolled in school. (See table 39.)

Unemployment

The average unemployment rate for Negroes and other races of all ages has remained at about double the white rate in 1969 and 1970, about the same proportion as in most earlier years since 1955.

However, there has been a worsening ratio in the past decade for minority teenagers, especially the younger males.

While youths 14 to 15 are not included in the national unemployment rate, the Bureau of Labor Statistics collects information on their labor force participation and employment. In 1969, the unemployment rates for 14- and 15-year-old whites were 8.5 percent for males, and 6.4 percent for females, versus 22.1 percent for males of Negro and other races and 23.1 percent for females. For the 16 to 19 age group, the unemployment rate in 1969 was 10.7 percent for whites and 24.0 percent for Negro and other races. By October 1970, the rates had risen to 15.3 and 32.9 percent, respectively.

Once out of their teens, unemployment rates for youth of all races are much lower, and the nonwhite-white unemployment rate ratio is also lower.

Youth unemployment rates are high and rising compared to the national rate; but it must be kept in mind that often the young job-seeker (particularly one enrolled in school) is looking for work during certain hours, days, or months only, and that such schedules may not match a prospective employer's manpower requirements.

The same trend is very clear in the case of the minority races in spite of lower labor force participation rates for males since 1960. (See tables 40–42.)

Teenage unemployment is often merely an inconvenience in relatively affluent families. In middle-income families, the consequences may be felt in the necessity to attend a less expensive college as a result of less savings accumulated during those years, or the inability to maintain an automobile. For youth in poverty families, unemployment may mean no college education or the need to borrow for college. Worse yet, it may mean fewer vital necessities for maintaining a family, since youth earnings may be supplementing parental income.

In urban poverty areas, unemployment rates for 16- to 19-year-old youths are very high for all races, particularly Negroes and minority group whites.

Most Anglo whites in poverty do not live in poverty areas. However, Negroes, in particular, are often found to live in poverty areas whether or not they are in poverty.[32]

Poverty areas suffer from high unemployment for all groups, particularly youth, with Negro youth being in the worst situation in

[32] U.S. Bureau of the Census, "Current Population Reports," series P–23, No. 19, "Characteristics of Families Residing in Poverty Areas," March 1966.

five of the six cities studied. Tables 43 and 44 present a summary of results from urban employment surveys conducted in the major poverty areas of six large cities.

Manpower training

There are many Federal manpower programs to provide training and job opportunities for the young, particularly in poverty areas, where many minority youth reside. The programs are not confined to urban ghetto or barrio areas alone; they reach out to those areas which contribute to sending the poor into the cities. These programs include job opportunities in the business sector (JOBS), Manpower Development and Training, Neighborhood Youth Corps, Job Corps, Special Impact, and work incentive programs, in addition to Operation Mainstream for Adults, veterans training and rehabilitation, and programs for Government employment.

While the Department of Labor administers most of these programs and would probably receive more than one-half of the total budget of $3.2 billion for manpower programs in fiscal 1971, the Office of Economic Opportunity, the Department of Health, Education, and Welfare, the Veterans' Administration, and other agencies also share in manpower programs. The JOBS program is intended to stimulate private industry's interest in hiring and training the hard-core unemployed and to encourage the hiring of unskilled, disadvantaged, workers for first jobs. Of the workers hired in the federally financed projects, about four-fifths were Negro, one-tenth white, and one-tenth other races. About one-half of the enrollees were under 22 years of age.[33] As part of the administration's effort to consolidate categorical programs, funding for the Manpower Development and Training Act's (MDTA) on-the-job (OJT) program will be merged with the JOBS program. During fiscal 1969 nearly 85,000 persons were given on-the-job training on nearly 500 MDTA projects. About two-fifths of those receiving on-the-job and institutional training under the MDTA program were Negro, and about the same proportion were under 22 years of age.[34]

Two programs with virtually 100 percent of its enrollment under 22 years of age are the Neighborhood Youth Corps and the Job Corps. The Neighborhood Youth Corps has an in-school program which provides part-time work and on-the-job training for students of high school age from low-income families; a summer program that provides these students with job opportunities during the summer months; and an out-of-school program to provide economically deprived school dropouts with practical work experience and on-the-job training to encourage them to return to school, or if this is not feasible, to help them acquire work habits and attitudes that will improve their employability.

In fiscal 1971 the Neighborhood Youth Corps in-school and summer programs are expected to have 427,000 new enrollees, while the out-of-school program should have 59,000. About one-half of Neighborhood Youth Corps enrollees were Negro and about one-tenth members of other nonwhite minority groups.

---

[33] Manpower Report of the President, 1970, p. 60. See table 45 appendix.
[34] Executive Office of the President, Bureau of the Budget, "Special Analyses, Budget of the United States, Fiscal year 1971," pp. 143–44. (Hereafter cited as Budget Analyses).

The Job Corps, established in 1965, had the purpose of removing disadvantaged youth from an environment so deprived or disruptive as to prevent their rehabilitation. The emphasis was on locating ghetto youth in rural centers or urban centers some miles from the city.

During fiscal 1969 about three-fifths of the enrollees were Negro, and one-tenth members of other nonwhite races. In fiscal 1971 the Job Corps is expected to have 49,000 new enrollees. Extremely high drop-out rates and the isolation of training sites from prospective employment, as well as the cost of self-sufficient residential centers, have led to a reshaping of the entire program. New, relatively small (some nonresidential) centers have been planned and opened. The new emphasis in the Job Corps will be on the coupling of its residential services with other manpower programs as well as the use of volunteers from such programs as VISTA.

The concentrated employment program (CEP), with approximately a 40-percent youth enrollment and a 65-percent Negro enrollment, is a system of packaging and delivering manpower services within a poverty neighborhood. It works through a single contract with a single sponsor (usually a Community Action Agency), to provide such services as outreach and recruitment, orientation, counseling; basic education, day care, work experience or vocational training under a variety of individual manpower programs, job development and placement, and followup.

Other manpower programs include veterans on-the-job training, vocational rehabilitation, veterans rehabilitation, project 100,000, public service careers, and Operation Mainstream. The Federal Government also provides Government jobs through the youth summer employment and the stay-in-school campaign for low-income youth. These are in addition to funds for the Federal-State employment services with 2,100 local offices and funding for manpower research, evaluation program direction and support services.

Of particular relevance to minority groups is the Equal Employment Opportunity Commission which receives, investigates, and conciliates complaints of discrimination in employment based on race, color, religion, sex, or national origin.

The newest large manpower program is the work incentive program (WIN) which is directed toward recipients of the AFDC program. Its intention is to remove men, women, and out-of-school youth 16 or older from the welfare rolls and into productive employment. It includes: (1) placement or on-the-job training and follow-through supportive services for the job ready; (2) work orientation, basic education, skill training, work experience, and follow-through supportive services to improve employability for individuals who lack job readiness; and (3) placement in special work projects arranged with public or private nonprofit organizations for individuals not ready for employability development. These manpower services are supplemented by supportive social services offered by State welfare agencies, such as day car for children, medical, legal, and homemaking aid; aid with family problems; and consumer education.

In 1969 the WIN program had an enrollment of 81,000. The expected number of new enrollees in 1971 will be 180,000. The WIN program in 1969 had about 40 percent Negro enrollees. The relation of WIN with AFDC recipients and its similarity to the manpower training and related services in the proposed family assistance program, make it extremely important to minority children and youth despite the fact that it had only a 16 percent youth enrollment in 1969.

The Labor Department administers safety and labor standards, and minimum wage and hours standards, in addition to other services. These standards help to protect youth from hazardous occupations, extremely low wages, and working schedules detrimental to health and education. Certificates authorizing special minimum wage rates are issued for learners, full-time students, student workers, apprentices, and handicapped workers to the extent necessary to prevent the curtailment of opportunities for employment. However, most agricultural occupations are exempt. An example of the effect of this exemption is the situation of migrant farmworkers and their families where poor housing, poor nutrition, and poor health; combined with working hours detrimental to health and education are observed. Many children miss school to supplement family income. Mexican-Americans comprise a large part of the migrant farm labor force, particularly in the Southwest.

7. SOCIAL TRANQUILLITY

A discussion of crime and race must tread carefully to make it clear that in the Nation's largest cities, where crime statistics are best, minority groups are more numerous and visible; however, crime statistics and arrest rates are presented in raw numbers and not adjusted for differences in the social and economic conditions which may breed crime, or which may affect the likelihood of being arrested and convicted even if crime rates among the races are equal FBI arrest statistics indicate that the arrest rate of young Negroes (ages 10 to 17) for criminal homicide is 12 times the rate of young whites. For forcible rape, robbery, and aggravated assault, the arrest rates of young Negroes are 12 times, 20 times, and 8 times, respectively, the rates of young whites.

Except for aggravated assault the 10- to 17-Negro rate has been rising faster than for whites in the same ages, and for all four crimes, faster than for Negroes 18 and over. Most of these crimes are intraracial except robbery, consistent with higher Negro victimization rates.

Of total arrests for FBI index crimes in 1969 (murder and nonnegligent manslaughter, aggravated assault, forcible rape, robbery, burglary, larceny over $50, and auto theft) 50 percent of the whites arrested were under 18, while 45 percent of the Negroes arrested were under 18. Sixty-three percent of youth under 18 arrested in 1969 were white, 35 percent were Negro, and the remainder were of other races or race unknown. The FBI figures do not show rates for convictions.[35]

This disproportionately large percentage of arrests as well as the greater likelihood that Negroes will be victims of crime (especially

---

[35] FBI. "Uniform Crime Reports, 1969," and, National Commission on the Causes and Prevention of Violence, Staff Report: "Crimes of Violence," ch. 3, passim.

violent crime) raises many problems, both for Negroes and all Americans. Crime statistics, by race, however, have more validity when they are considered in light of other statistics presented in this report.

One study of a Michigan industrial community (based on arrest data) compared whites and Negroes with respect to such socioeconomic variables as employment status, occupation, and migration for the 1942–65 period. It found that with these variables controlled, arrest rates were about equal; for some crimes Negro arrest rates were higher, for others white arrest rates were higher. For example, at each occupational level, migrant whites incur higher arrest rates than native born (Michigan) Negroes although raw arrest statistics reveal a greater preponderance of Negro as compared to white arrests than for any other major crime category.[36]

A major deterrent to crime is respect for the law and this depends on many factors. To a large number of people, the most visible symbol of the law is the policemen on the streets. Many minority youth complain they are treated less fairly than white youth by police.

Abrasive relations with the police are not only a racial problem but also one of youth. The young are much more likely to complain of police than the older population regardless of race or ethnic group, especially of actions involving bodily contact. This age trend, however, is about equally pronounced in the whole population.[37]

A study done for the Kerner Commission revealed that among those blacks interviewed, the young have a higher propensity to advocate or participate in violence. Young men were about twice as inclined as women, but for each sex the under-20-age group was about twice as inclined as the 30- to 50-age group. The interviewers asked questions concerning (1) readiness to use violence as a way to gain Negro rights; (2) readiness to join a riot if it occurred; (3) use of violence against a discriminatory storekeeper if other methods failed; (4) having actually participated in a riot.[38]

In recapitulation there has been substantial improvement in the position of minority children and youth in the areas of income, education, and occupational status. At the same time, there has been some deterioration in the area of family stability, and social unrest. As has been indicated, there are many programs directed at the first three above areas, in which improvement has occurred. It is more difficult to improve the last two areas by means of Federal Government programs, although some currently proposed legislation does attempt to do just this.

---

[36] Edward Green, "Race, Social Status, and Criminal Arrest," American Sociological Review, XXXV: 3 (June 1970), pp. 476–490.
[37] U.S. Commission on Civil Rights, "Mexican-Americans and the Administration of Justice in the Southwest," 1970.
[38] National Advisory Commission on Civil Disorders, "Supplemental Studies," July 1968, p. 43.

Chart 1   Family Income Distribution: 1968

At any specified level of income a greater percentage of Negro families receive
less than that level than white families.

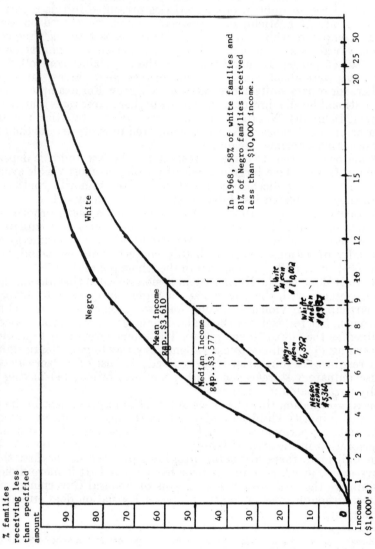

% families
receiving less
than specified
amount

Income
($1,000's)

In 1968, 58% of white families and
81% of Negro families received
less than $10,000 income.

Source: Calculated from data contained in U.S. Bureau of the Census, Current Population Reports,
Series P-60, No. 66, "Income in 1968 of Families and Persons in the United States."

Table 1. Children and Youth, 1969 and 1960, by Race and Sex

Race/Sex	1969 (Population, thousands)										1960									Percent increase 1960-1969			
	USA total population of race/sex	Children under 14		Youth 14-24		Children and youth					USA total	Children		Youth		Children and youth			USA total population of race/sex	Total population	Children	Youth	Children and youth
		No.	% of USA total	No.	% of total	No.	%					No.	% total	No.	% total	No.	%						
All races																							
Both sexes	203,216	55,291	27.2	39,068	19.2	94,359	46.4				180,007	53,047	29.5	27,136	15.1	80,183	44.5			12.9	4.2	44.0	17.7
Male	99,771	28,170	28.2	19,778	19.8	47,948	48.1				89,011	26,969	30.3	13,670	15.4	40,639	45.7			12.1	4.5	44.7	18.0
Female	103,445	27,120	26.2	19,290	18.7	46,410	44.9				90,996	26,077	28.7	13,466	14.8	39,543	43.5			13.7	4.0	43.2	17.4
White																							
Both sexes	178,225	46,580	26.1	33,904	19.0	80,484	45.2				159,467	45,700	28.7	23,817	14.9	69,517	43.6			11.8	1.9	42.4	15.8
Male	87,654	23,795	27.2	17,209	19.6	41,004	46.8				78,998	23,295	29.5	12,047	15.3	35,342	44.7			11.0	2.1	42.8	16.0
Female	90,571	22,784	25.2	16,694	18.4	39,478	43.6				80,469	22,403	27.8	11,771	14.6	34,174	42.5			12.6	1.7	41.8	15.5
Negro and other races																							
Both sexes	24,991	8,712	35.0	5,164	20.7	13,876	55.5				20,540	7,347	35.8	3,320	16.2	10,667	51.9			21.7	18.6	55.5	30.1
Negro																							
Both sexes	22,727	7,943	35.0	4,747	20.9	12,690	55.8				18,916	6,780	35.8	3,058	16.2	9,838	52.0			20.1	17.2	55.2	29.0
Male	10,973	3,984	36.3	2,360	21.5	6,344	57.8				9,158	3,386	37.0	1,489	16.3	4,875	53.2			19.8	17.7	58.5	30.1
Female	11,754	3,959	33.7	2,387	20.3	6,346	54.0				9,759	3,395	34.8	1,568	16.1	4,963	50.9			20.4	16.6	52.2	27.9
Other minority races*																							
Both sexes	2,264	769	34.0	417	18.4	1,186	52.4				1,624	567	34.9	262	16.2	829	51.9			39.4	35.6	59.2	43.1

*Obtained by subtracting Negro from Negro and other races.

SOURCE: U.S. Bureau of the Census, Current Population Reports, Series P-25 #441. Estimates of the Population of the U.S., by Age, Race, and Sex.

Table   2.   Median Age by Race and Sex, 1969 and 1960

Race/Sex	1969 median	1960 median	Decrease, # years	Decrease as % of 1960 median
All races	27.7	29.5	1.8	6.1
Male	26.5	28.6	2.1	7.3
Female	29.0	30.3	1.3	4.3
White	28.7	30.3	1.6	5.3
Male	27.4	29.3	1.9	6.5
Female	29.9	31.1	1.2	3.9
Negro and other races	21.6	23.5	1.9	8.1
Negro	21.5	23.5	2.0	8.5
Male	20.4	22.5	2.1	9.3
Female	22.5	24.4	1.9	7.8

SOURCE: U.S. Bureau of the Census, <u>Current Population Reports</u>, Series P-25, #441, 3/19/70.

Table   3.   Minority Races as a Percent of Total Population by Age Groups

	1969			1960		
	Negro and other races % total population	Negro as % population	Other as % population	Negro and other %	Negro %	Other %
All ages	12.3	11.2	1.1	11.4	10.5	0.9
Under 1	17.8	16.2	1.6	14.9	13.7	1.2
1-5	16.8	15.3	1.5	14.5	13.3	1.1
6-13	15.0	13.6	1.4	13.3	12.3	1.0
14-17	13.9	12.8	1.1	12.3	11.4	0.9
18-21	13.3	12.2	1.1	12.2	11.3	0.9
22-24	12.0	11.0	1.0	12.2	11.1	1.0
0-24	14.7	13.4	1.3	13.3	12.3	1.0
25 and over	10.2	9.2	1.0	9.9	9.1	0.8

Minority Races as Percent of Children and Youth for Selected Years

Year	Percent	Year	Percent
1969	14.7	1940	11.7
1965	14.0	1930	11.3
1960	13.3	1920	11.4
1950	12.4	1900	13.7

SOURCE: U.S. Bureau of the Census, <u>Current Population Reports</u>, Series P-25, Nos. 441 and 311.

Table 4. Population Projections 1975-1990 by Age and Race
(Numbers in thousands)

Age	1975 Total	1975 White	1975 Negro and other races	1980 Total	1980 White	1980 Negro and other races	1990 Total	1990 White	1990 Negro and other races
1	3,821	3,192	629	4,360	3,633	727	4,746	3,936	810
1-4	14,502	12,149	2,353	16,375	13,688	2,687	19,020	15,815	3,205
5-13	34,209	28,719	5,490	32,695	27,437	5,258	40,224	33,617	6,607
Total children	52,532	44,060	8,472	53,430	44,758	8,672	63,990	53,368	10,622
14-17	16,896	14,414	2,482	16,005	13,444	2,560	15,469	12,994	2,475
18-24	27,535	23,735	3,800	29,612	25,309	4,303	25,621	21,581	4,040
Total youth	44,431	38,149	6,282	45,617	38,753	6,863	41,090	34,575	6,515
Total children and youth	96,963	82,209	14,754	99,047	83,511	15,535	105,080	87,943	17,137
Total population	215,367	188,211	27,156	227,665	198,117	29,548	255,967	220,805	35,162
Children as percent of total population	24.4	23.4	31.2	23.5	22.6	29.4	25.0	24.2	30.2
Youth as percent of total population	20.6	20.3	23.1	20.0	19.6	23.2	16.1	15.7	18.6
Children and youth as percent of total population	45.0	43.7	54.3	43.5	42.2	52.6	41.1	39.8	48.7
White children and youth as percent of total population	84.8			84.3			83.7		
Negro and other as percent of total population	15.2			15.7			16.3		

Source: U.S. Bureau of the Census, Current Population Reports, Series P-25, No. 381, "Projections of the Population of the U.S., by Age, Sex, and Color to 1990, with Extensions of Population by Age and Sex to 2015," Series "D" Projections. Published December 1967. Total population figures differ less than 0.4% below Series "D" projections made in 1970 (not published by race).

Table 5 . The 1960 Census Presents Detailed Figures with Regard
to Children and Youth of All Minority Groups

Group	Total 1960 population	Age * 0-14	Age 15-24	% under 14	% 15-24	% 0-24	Median age
American Indian	546,228	230,733	89,564	42.24	16.40	58.64	19.2
Japanese	473,170	148,167	58,798	31.31	12.43	43.74	28.4
Chinese	236,084	77,894	27,397	32.99	11.60	44.60	28.3
Filipino	181,614	60,732	22,747	33.44	12.52	45.97	27.9
Negro**	18,723,297	7,075,727	2,697,361	37.79	14.41	52.20	23.3
Other non-white minorities	202,281	83,200	37,184	41.13	18.38	59.51	19.7
Spanish surname in Arizona, California, Colorado, New Mexico, Texas 1/ (Mexican Americans)	3,464,999 1/	1,449,629	557,258	41.84	16.08	57.92	19.6
Puerto Rican 2/	892,513 2/	344,996	164,242	38.65	18.40	57.06	21.4
Total minority groups 3/	24,648,659	9,457,718	3,648,509	38.31	14.05	53.09	--
Minority group as % total population	13.77	16.95	15.14	--	--	--	--

1/ Of whom 36,443 are Puerto Ricans and also counted below.
2/ Of whom 35,084 are Negroes and also included above.
3/ Total minority group population figures exclude double counting of
Puerto Ricans in the Southwest and Negro Puerto Ricans. See Notes 1 and 2.

*Data not presented so as to allow 0-13 and 14-24 categories used elsewhere.
**1960 data published in Current Population Reports, p-25, No. 441 (3/19/70) differs
by 0.7 percent due to revisions of 1960 data.
SOURCE: 1960 Census - Non-white Population by Race PC (2) 1-C; Persons of Spanish
Surname PC(2) 1-B; Puerto Ricans in the U.S. PC (2) 1-D.

Table 6 . Dispersion of Minority Groups Among States, 1960

(Percent of total population of listed minority group residing in State)

Rank	Negroes State	Percent	Rank	Japanese-Americans State	Percent	Rank	Chinese-Americans State	Percent
1	New York	7.5	1	Hawaii	43.8	1	California	40.2
2	Georgia	6.0	2	California	33.7	2	Hawaii	16.6
3	North Carolina	5.9	3	Washington	3.6	3	New York	16.0
4	Louisiana	5.5	4	Illinois	2.9	4	Illinois	2.8
5	Illinois	5.5	5	New York	2.0	5	Massachusetts	2.7

Rank	Filipino State	Percent	Rank	American Indians State	Percent	Rank	Mexican-Americans Five S.W. States State	Percent
1	Hawaii	38.6	1	Arizona	15.2	1	California	41.2
2	California	37.0	2	Oklahoma	11.5	2	Texas	40.9
3	Washington	3.7	3	New Mexico	10.3	3	New Mexico	7.8
4	New York	3.1	4	California	7.5	4	Arizona	5.6
5	Illinois	2.1	5	North Carolina	7.1	5	Colorado	4.5

	Puerto Ricans	
1	New York	72.0
2	New Jersey	6.2
3	Illinois	4.0
4	California	3.2
5	Pennsylvania	2.4

Source: U.S. Bureau of the Census, 1960 Census of Population, cited for table 5.

Table 6 Continued

Dispersion Among Metropolitan Areas

(Percent of total population of listed minority groups)

	Negroes			Japanese-Americans			Chinese-Americans	
Rank	SMSA	Percent	Rank	SMSA	Percent	Rank	SMSA	Percent
1	New York	6.5	1	Honolulu	31.8	1	San Francisco-Oakland	22.6
2	Chicago	4.7	2	Los Angeles-Long Beach	17.4	2	Honolulu	15.6
3	Philadelphia	3.6	3	San Francisco-Oakland	5.2	3	New York	15.5
4	Detroit	3.0	4	Chicago	2.7	4	Los Angeles-Long Beach	8.2
5	Washington	2.6	5	Seattle	2.3	5	Sacramento	2.7

	Filipinos			American Indians			Mexican-Americans	
Rank	SMSA	Percent	Rank	SMSA	Percent	Rank	SMSA	Percent
1	Honolulu	25.0	1	Los Angeles-Long Beach	1.7	1	Los Angeles-Long Beach	18.2
2	San Francisco-Oakland	12.3	2	Phoenix	1.6	2	San Antonio	7.4
3	Los Angeles-Long Beach	7.2	3	New York	1.5	3	San Francisco-Oakland	5.1
4	San Diego	2.8	4	Tulsa	1.4	4	El Paso	4.0
5	New York	2.7	5	Tucson	1.3	5	Brownsville-Harlingen-San Benito	2.8

	Puerto Ricans	
Rank	SMSA	Percent
1	*New York City	68.6
2	Chicago	3.6
3	Philadelphia	1.6
4	Newark	1.1
5	Jersey City	0.8

* Puerto Rican data for Central Cities only.

Source: U.S. Bureau of the Census, 1960 Census of Population, cited for table 5.

Table 7. Percent of Children (unmarried, under 18) Living with
Both Parents by Income, 1969

Annual income	White	Negro	Negro % Ratio White %
Less than $ 3,000	49	27	.55
$ 3,000- $ 4,999	75	55	.73
5,000- 6,999	88	78	.89
7,000- 9,999	95	90	.95
10,000- 14,999	97	88	.91
15,000 and over	98	87	.89
All incomes	92	69	.75

SOURCE: The Social and Economic Status of Negroes in the United
States, 1969, page 75.

Table 8. Percent of Ever-married Women Not Living with Their
Husbands Because of Marital Discord

Year	White	Nonwhite
1950	5	14
1960	5	16
1965	6	17
1969	7	18

SOURCE: The Social and Economic Status of Negroes in the United
States, 1969, page 72.

Table 9. Percent of Families with Female Head

Year	White	Nonwhite
1950	8.5	17.6
1960	8.7	22.4
1966	8.9	23.7
1969	8.9	27.3

SOURCE: The Social and Economic Status of Negroes in the
United States, 1969, page 70.

Table 10. Children of Working Mothers by Color, Age, and Family Income
(Numbers in thousands)

Color	Age	All families	Less than $3,000	$3,000-5,999	$6,000-9,999	$10,000 and over
White	Total	10,056	970	3,185	3,980	1,922
	Under 6	3,066	318	1,038	1,206	496
	6-13	6,990	652	2,147	2,774	1,426
Nonwhite	Total	2,231	879	706	485	162
	Under 6	729	289	249	143	57
	6-13	1,502	590	457	342	105

U.S. Department of Health, Education and Welfare, Children's Bureau and
U.S. Department of Labor, Women's Bureau, Child Care Arrangements of Working
Mothers in the United States, p. 65.

Table 11.   Children of Working Mothers, by Color, Age of Child
and Employment Status of Mother
(Numbers in thousands), 1965

Age	Total		Children of full-time working mothers		Children of part-time working mothers	
	White	Non-white	White	Non-white	White	Non-white
Total under 14	10,056	2,231	6,773	1,580	3,283	651
Under 6	3,066	729	2,067	506	998	224
0-2	1,207	288	832	196	374	92
3-5	1,859	441	1,235	310	624	132
6-13	6,991	1,501	4,705	1,075	2,285	427
6-8	2,261	555	1,503	410	758	146
9-11	2,693	581	1,801	411	892	171
12-13	2,037	365	1,401	254	635	110

Source: U.S. Department of Health, Education, and Welfare, Childrens Bureau, and
U.S. Department of Labor, Womens Bureau, Child Care Arrangements of
Working Mothers in the United States.

Table 12. Child Care Arrangements--Percent Distribution
Of Children by Type of Arrangement, Color, Age, and Employment Status of Mother. 1965

	Children of full-time working mothers		Children of part-time working mothers	
	White	Nonwhite	White	Nonwhite
Total (Numbers in thousands)	6,773	1,580	3,283	651
Care in own home by:	50.8	41.8	35.3	47.7
Father	14.5	10.8	18.9	8.2
Other relative	23.6	25.3	10.7	35.6
Under 16	4.8	4.6	2.9	11.5
16 and over	18.8	20.8	7.8	24.2
Non-relative	12.7	5.6	5.6	3.9
Who only looked after children	5.3	4.7	3.9	3.9
Who usually did additional chores	7.4	1.0	1.7	--
Care in someone else's home by:	18.9	24.0	5.6	17.1
Relative	9.2	12.0	2.5	11.2
Non-relative	9.7	12.0	3.1	6.0
Other arrangements:	30.3	34.2	59.1	35.2
Care in group child center	2.9	2.7	0.5	0.9
Child looked after self	9.3	11.3	4.3	8.3
Mother	17.8	19.0	54.0	25.6
Looked after child while working	7.0	7.0	28.9	9.3
Worked only during school hours	10.8	12.0	25.1	16.3
Other	0.5	1.3	0.3	0.3

Source: U.S. Department of Health, Education, and Welfare, Childrens Bureau, and
U.S. Department of Labor, Women's Bureau, Child Care Arrangements of
Working Mothers in the United States.

Table 13. Housing Units Not Meeting Specified Criteria*

| | Occupied by white | | Occupied by Negro and other races | |
	1960 Percent of Total units	1968 Percent of Total units	1960 Percent of Total units	1968 Percent of Total units
U.S. total	13	6	44	24
Central cities	8	3	25	9
Suburban areas	7	3	43	16
Outside metropolitan areas	23	11	77	55

* If the unit is either diliapidated (defects are so critical or widespread that the building is unsafe or otherwise evaluated as inadequate for human shelter; that razing, rebuilding, or textensive repairs are required or the building eas inadequately constructal originally) or lacks one or more basic plumbing facilities (hot running water inside the structure, flush toilet and bath tub or shower for private use by members of a household.)

Source: U.S. Bureau of the Census and Bureau of Labor Statistics, The Social and Economic Status of the Negro in the United States, 1969, pp. 56-57.

Table 14.   Purchase of Automobiles, 1967-1969 and Houses, 1969

Number of Automobiles Purchased Per 100 Households

New automobiles	1967	1968	1969	3-year average
All households	12.3	13.2	13.0	12.8
White	12.7	13.8	13.6	13.4
Negro	4.1	6.5	5.7	5.4
Previously owned automobiles				
All households	22.7	22.2	20.8	21.9
White	23.2	22.4	21.8	22.5
Negro	15.6	17.5	15.8	16.3
Total: New and previously owned				
All households	35.0	35.4	33.8	34.7
White	35.9	36.2	35.4	35.9
Negro	19.7	24.0	21.5	21.7

Number of Houses on One-Unit Properties Purchased, 1969
(Thousands)

Race	Total	New homes Sale price				Total	Previously owned homes Sale price			
		Under $20,000	$20,000-24,999	$25,000-34,999	$35,000 & over		Under $20,000	20,000-24,999	25,000-34,999	35,000 & over
All races	724	194	109	219	202	1,979	1,214	239	340	186 '
White	688	174	102	216	196	1,765	1,032	231	324	178
Negro	28	20	8	-	-	192	172	4	12	4
Other	8	-	-	3	6	22	9	4	4	4
White as % of total	95	90	94	99	97	89	85	97	95	96

Individual cells do not necessarily add to totals due to rounding.

Source: U.S. Bureau of the Census, Current Population Reports, Series p-65, No. 31,
"Recent Purchases of Cars, Houses, and Other Durables and Expectations to
Buy During the Months Ahead: Survey Data Through April 1970."

Table 15. Source of Income in 1968--Families, by Race

Income source	Race	Number families receiving this type of income (X 1,000)	Median amount received (dollars)	Mean amount received (dollars)	Total amount received ($millions)	Percent of total amount by race	Percent total family income of race from listed source	Percent of families receiving this type income
Wage and salary income	All races	43,638	8,362	8,918	389,164	100.0	79.7	86.4
	White	39,197	8,646	9,202	360,691	92.7	79.4	86.3
	Negro and Other	4,441	5,641	6,413	28,480	7.3	83.8	87.5
	Negro	4,079	5,453	6,208	25,322	6.5	85.3	87.8
Non-farm Self-employment	All races	6,180	3,958	6,581	40,671	100.0	8.3	12.2
	White	5,834	4,098	6,735	39,292	96.6	8.6	12.8
	Negro and Other	346	2,310	3,967	1,373	3.4	4.0	6.8
	Negro	275	1,974	3,111	856	2.1	2.9	5.9
Farm Self-employment	All races	3,014	1,296	2,460	7,414	100.0	1.5	6.0
	White	2,852	1,393	2,523	7,196	97.1	1.6	6.3
	Negro and Other	162	674	1,356	220	3.0	0.6	3.2
	Negro	133	603	685	91	1.2	0.3	2.9
Social Security and government railroad retirement	All races	9,778	1,457	1,615	15,791	100.0	3.2	19.4
	White	8,918	1,488	1,643	14,652	92.8	3.2	19.6
	Negro and Other	860	1,160	1,328	1,142	7.2	3.4	16.9
	Negro	814	1,162	1,328	1,081	6.8	3.6	17.5
Dividend interest, Net rental, income from estates or trusts	All races	19,913	618	858	17,085	100.0	3.5	39.4
	White	19,195	620	871	16,719	97.9	3.7	42.2
	Negro and Other	719	571	506	364	2.1	1.1	14.2
	Negro	520	548	344	179	1.0	0.6	11.2
Public assistance and welfare	All races	2,471	1,082	1,402	3,464	100.0	0.7	4.9
	White	1,536	1,004	1,330	2,043	59.0	0.4	3.4
	Negro and Other	935	1,205	1,519	1,420	41.0	4.2	18.4
	Negro	903	1,194	1,506	1,360	39.3	4.6	19.4
Unemployment and Workmen's compensation, Government employees pensions, and veterans payments	All races	6,445	794	1,192	7,682	100.0	1.6	12.8
	White	5,916	795	1,209	7,152	93.1	1.6	13.0
	Negro and Other	530	789	1,001	531	6.9	1.6	10.4
	Negro	490	782	1,000	490	6.4	1.7	10.5
Private pensions, annuities, alimony, royalties, etc.	All races	4,548	1,014	1,570	7,140	100.0	1.5	9.0
	White	4,185	1,044	1,608	6,729	94.2	1.5	9.2
	Negro and Other	363	833	1,132	411	5.8	1.2	7.2
	Negro	315	798	998	314	4.4	1.1	6.8
Total income*	All races	50,510	8,632	9,670	488,431	100.0	100.0	100.0
	White	45,437	8,937	10,002	454,461	93.0	100.0	100.0
	Negro and Other	5,074	5,590	6,695	33,970	7.0	100.0	100.0
	Negro	4,646	5,360	6,392	29,697	6.1	100.0	100.0

*Sum of individual items exceed 100 percent as a result of multiple income sources.

Source: U.S. Bureau of the Census, Current Population Reports, Series P-60, No. 66, "Income in 1968 of Families and Persons in the United States."

Table 16. Family Income Distribution, by Race 1950-1968, Current Dollars
Percent of Families with Income in Specified Range

Income	1950 White	1950 Negro and other races	1955 White	1955 Negro and other races	1960 White	1960 Negro and other races	1968 White	1968 Negro and other races
Under $1,000	10.0	28.1	6.6	19.0	4.1	13.4	1.5	3.9
$1,000-$1,499	5.7	12.4	4.2	11.8	3.1	10.2	1.3	4.0
1,500-1,999	6.5	12.9	4.5	8.9	3.8	8.1	1.6	5.1
2,000-2,499	8.6	13.1	5.1	9.5	4.2	8.1	2.3	5.6
2,500-2,999	8.7	10.4	5.3	8.1	3.9	6.7	2.2	5.4
3,000-3,499	11.9	9.0	7.1	10.2	4.6	7.5	2.8	6.7
3,500-3,999	9.4	4.5	7.2	7.0	4.8	6.5	2.6	5.6
4,000-4,499	8.3	2.9	8.4	6.4	5.2	5.3	5.6	10.6
4,500-4,999	6.1	1.4	7.6	4.7	5.3	5.1		
5,000-5,999	9.6	1.9	13.4	5.8	13.3	8.7	6.7	8.8
6,000-6,999	5.5	1.5	9.9	4.8	11.2	6.7	7.6	7.6
7,000-7,999					9.2	4.5	8.3	7.2
8,000-8,999	6.1	1.7	13.9	3.1	12.1	4.2	8.1	6.0
9,000-9,999							7.6	4.4
10,000-11,999	3.5	0.3	5.3	0.6	11.2	4.3	13.0	7.8
12,000-14,999							13.2	6.2
15,000-24,999			1.0	-	3.1	0.6	12.9	4.7
25,000-49,999							2.5	0.4
50,000 or more			0.5	-	1.0	-	0.3	-

Source: U.S. Bureau of the Census, *Current Population Reports*, "Consumer Income," Series P-60, Nos. 9, 24, 37, and 66.

Table 17. Family Members Under 18 in Poverty
(Other than head or wife)
By Sex of Family Head
(Numbers in thousands)

	Male Head						Female Head					
	All races		White		Negro and Other races		All races		White		Negro and Other races	
	Incidence		Incidence		Incidence		Incidence		Incidence		Incidence	
Year	Number	Percent	Number	Percent	Number	Percent	Number	Percent	Number	Percent	Number	Percent
1959	13,063	22.4	8,966	17.4	4,097	60.8	4,145	72.2	2,420	64.6	1,725	86.5
1960	13,193	22.3	8,872	17.0	4,321	61.3	4,095	68.4	2,357	59.9*	1,738	84.8
1965	9,826	15.7	6,274	11.4	3,552	48.0	4,562	64.2	2,321	52.9	2,241	82.2
1968	6,330	10.2	4,298	7.8	2,032	28.3	4,409	55.2	2,075	44.4	2,334	70.4
1969	5,444	8.8	--	--	1,640*	25.3	4,377	54.4	--	--	2,239	68.1
1959-68 reduction	51.5%	54.5	52.1	55.2	50.4	53.5	-6.4	23.5	14.3	31.3	-35.3	18.6

* Negro only.
Source: U.S. Bureau of the Census, Current Population Reports, Series, P-60, No. 68, "Poverty in the United States 1959 to 1968," and Series P-60, No. 71.

Table 18. Family Members Under 18 in Poverty, Farm and Nonfarm
(Other than head or wife)

| | All races | | White | | Negro & other races | |
Year	Number (x 1,000)	Incidence (Percent)	Number (x 1,000)	Incidence (Percent)	Number (x 1,000)	Incidence (Percent)
			NONFARM			
1959	13,533	23.5	9,069	18.0	4,464	61.3
1960	13,629	23.0	8,920	17.3	4,709	61.3
1965	12,497	19.2	7,457	13.4	5,040	54.5
1968	9,700	14.6	5,697	10.1	4,003	40.0
Percent reduction	28.3	37.9	37.2	43.9	10.3	34.7
			FARM			
1959	3,675	57.8	2,317	47.2	1,358	93.7
1960	3,659	61.1	2,309	50.5	1,350	95.4
1965	1,891	41.4	1,138	30.7	753	87.4
1968	1,039	28.8	676	21.6	363	74.4
Percent reduction	71.7	50.2	70.8	54.2	73.3	20.6

Source: U.S. Bureau of the Census, Current Population Reports, Series P-60, No. 68, "Poverty in the United States 1959 to 1968."

TABLE 19. Family Members Under 18 in Poverty
(Other than head or wife)

Year	All races Number (x 1,000)	Incidence (percent)	White Number (x 1,000)	Incidence (percent)	Negro & other races Number (x 1,000)	Incidence (percent)
1959	17,208	26.9	11,386	20.6	5,822	66.7
1960	17,288	26.5	11,229	20.0	6,059	66.6
1965	14,388	20.7	8,595	14.4	5,793	57.3
1968	10,739	15.3	6,373	10.7	4,366	41.6
1969	9,821	14.1	5,777	9.8	4,044	38.0
1959-68* reduction	37.6%	43.1%	44.0%	48.1%	25.0%	37.6%

Source: U.S. Bureau of the Census, Current Population Reports, Series
P-60 No. 68, "Poverty in the United States 1959 to 1968, and
Series P-60 No. 71, "Poverty Continues to Decline in 1969,"
(advance report).

Table 20 Percent of Total U.S.A. Poor Persons Who Are Family
Members Under 18
(Other than head or wife)

Year	Male and female head All races	White	Non-white	Male head All races	White	Non-white	Female head All races	White	Non-white
1959	43.6	28.8	14.7	33.1	22.7	10.4	10.5	6.1	4.4
1960	43.4	28.2	15.2	33.1	22.3	10.8	10.3	5.9	4.4
1965	43.4	25.9	17.5	29.6	18.9	10.7	13.7	7.0	6.8
1968	42.3	25.1	17.2	24.9	16.9	8.0	17.4	8.2	9.2

Source: U.S. Bureau of the Census, Current Population Reports, Series P-60, No. 68.

Table 21. Maternal Mortality, Infant
Mortality, and Related Indicators

Maternal Mortality per 10,000 Live Births

Year	White	Minority races
1941	26.6	67.8
1951	5.5	20.1
1961	2.5	10.1
1967	2.0	7.0

Percent of Births in Hospitals

Year	White	Negro and other races	Indians	Alaska natives
1950	92.8	57.9	--	--
1960	98.8	85.0	95.1	70.9
1965	98.9	89.8	96.7	84.0
1967	99.4	92.9	97.8	90.4

Percent Attended by Physicians

Year	White	Minority races
1950	98.7	72.2
1960	99.5	88.5
1965	99.5	91.8
1967	99.6	94.0

U.S.A. Infant Mortality
(Rate per 1,000 live births)
1966

Race	Male	Female
All races	26.6	20.6
White	23.5	17.7
Negro	44.0	36.2
American Indian	39.0	34.7
Chinese-American	10.5	9.3
Japanese-American	12.2	8.3
Alaska Native	-------55.6--------	

Source: HEW/NCHS, Vital Statistics of the United States, Vol. 17, No. 13,
and Department of Health, Education, and Welfare, Indian Health
Trends and Services, 1969 Edition, and 1970 White House Conference
on Children and Youth, Chartbook on Children.

Table 22. Infant Deaths per 1,000 Live Births
(Selected Nations)

Norway 1/	13.7
Japan 3/	15.3
Denmark 2/	15.8
Australia 1/	17.8
United Kingdom 1/	18.8
France 1/	20.4
United States 3/	20.8
Canada 1/	20.8
West Germany 1/	22.8
Israel 3/	23.0
U.S.S.R. 1/	26.4
Mexico 3/	65.7
Pakistan 4/	142 est.

1/ 1968
2/ 1967
3/ 1969
4/ 1965

Source: U.S. Bureau of the Census, Statistical Abstract of the United
States, 1970, page 809.

Table 23. Age Specific Death Rates, 1968
(per 1,000) By Races

Age	White	All minority races	Indian and Alaska native 1965-67 average
0-1	19.6	33.1	35.3
1-4	0.8	1.1	2.8
5-14	0.4	0.6	0.8
15-24	1.2	1.8	3.6
25-34	1.3	3.8	6.1
35-44	2.7	7.2	8.7
45-54	6.8	13.3	12.2
55-64	16.1	27.2	19.6
65-74	36.6	58.6	⎰
75-84	80.8	74.3	⎱ 58.0
85 and older	206.5	110.3	

Source: Public Health Service, Vital Statistics, Vol. 17, No. 13, and
Indian Health Trends and Services, 1969 Edition.

Table 24. Selected Health Indicators 1965-1967

Number of Bed Disability Days Per Person Per Year

Age	Male and female White	Male and female Negro and other races	Male White	Male Negro and other races	Female White	Female Negro and other races
All ages	5.9	6.4	5.1	5.3	6.6	7.4
Under 17	4.7	4.0	4.6	3.8	4.7	4.2

Percent of Persons Injured per 100 Persons Per Year

Age	Male and female White	Negro and other races
All ages	26.2	19.1
Under 17	30.9	15.6

Percent of Persons With Short-Stay Hospital Days in a Year

Age	Both sexes White	Both sexes Nonwhite	Male White	Male Nonwhite	Female White	Female Nonwhite
All ages	10.2	8.2	8.2	5.9	12.1	10.3
Under 6	7.5	6.4	8.2	6.8	6.7	6.1
6-16	4.8	2.9	5.1	2.8	4.4	3.0

Percent of Persons With Short-Stay Hospital Days in a Year Who Reported 15 or More Hospital Days

Age	Both sexes White	Both sexes Nonwhite	Male White	Male Nonwhite	Female White	Female Nonwhite
All ages	15.6	18.6	19.9	27.7	12.8	13.8
Under 17	7.9	18.9	7.9	19.7	7.9	18.0

Number of Physician Visits Per Person Per Year July 1966-June 1967

Age	Male and female White	Male and female Negro and other races	Male White	Male Negro and other races	Female White	Female Negro and other races
All ages	4.5	3.1	4.0	2.7	5.0	3.5
Under 6	5.8	3.2	6.0	3.6	5.6	2.7
6-16	2.9	1.2	3.0	1.2	2.8	1.3

Source: National Center for Health Statistics, Differentials in Health Characteristics by Color. (Series 10, No. 56 from the National Health Survey.)

Table 25

Non-enrollment in School By Age, Residence, and Race
October 1969

(Percent of population not enrolled in school and
not having graduated from high school)

Age	Race	U.S.A. total	Metro-politan areas	Central cities	Suburbs of central cities	Non-metro politan areas	Poverty areas of metropolitan areas over 250,000
3-4							
	White	84.9	82.2	82.8	81.8	89.4	89.4
	Negro	78.8	74.0	74.6	72.0	89.9	77.6
	N/W Ratio	0.9	0.9	0.9	0.9	1.0	0.9
5-6							
	White	10.8	8.8	9.9	8.2	14.4	17.1
	Negro	15.9	9.2	8.8	10.7	29.6	11.1
	N/W Ratio	1.5	1.0	0.9	1.3	2.1	0.6
7-9							
	White	0.6	0.6	1.0	0.4	0.7	0.3
	Negro	1.2	1.1	0.9	2.3	1.3	1.2
	N/W Ratio	2.0	1.8	0.9	5.8	1.9	4.0
10-13							
	White	0.8	0.8	0.9	0.8	0.9	0.7
	Negro	0.9	1.2	1.2	1.2	0.3	1.3
	N/W Ratio	1.1	1.5	1.3	1.5	0.3	1.9
14-15							
	White	1.8	1.6	1.8	1.5	2.1	3.8
	Negro	2.0	2.1	2.5	0.7	1.8	2.4
	N/W Ratio	1.1	1.3	1.4	0.5	0.9	0.6
16-17							
	White	7.8	6.5	9.9	4.6	9.9	16.5
	Negro	10.9	10.9	11.8	7.9	11.0	12.5
	N/W Ratio	1.4	1.7	1.2	1.7	1.1	0.8
18-19							
	White	13.4	13.0	14.2	12.3	14.0	31.0
	Negro	27.1	26.2	27.8	21.6	28.9	31.5
	N/W Ratio	2.0	2.0	2.0	1.8	2.1	1.0
20-21							
	White	15.7	13.6	15.3	12.2	19.8	32.1
	Negro	34.5	31.2	32.1	28.6	41.4	41.5
	N/W Ratio	2.2	2.3	2.1	2.3	2.1	1.3

Source: U.S. Bureau of the Census, Current Population Reports, Series P.20,
No. 206, "School Enrollment: October 1969."

Table 26. School Enrollment By Age and Race 1960, 1969

(percent of population enrolled in school)

Age	White 1960	White 1969	Negro 1960	Negro 1969	Increase in enrollment % points 1960-1969 White	Negro
5-6	64.4	89.2	59.7	84.3	24.8	24.6
7-9	97.8	99.4	95.9	98.8	1.6	2.9
10-13	97.7	99.2	95.9	99.1	1.5	3.2
14-15	94.6	98.2	90.0	97.9	3.6	7.9
16-17	82.0	90.2	73.1	86.4	8.2	13.3

Source: 1960 Data from Coleman Report, p. 450. 1969 Data from U.S. Bureau of the Census, Current Population Reports, Series P-20, No. 206, pp. 8-9.

Table 27. School Enrollment By Age and Ethnic-Group 1960

(Percent of population enrolled in school)

Age	All Whites	Native-Born Whites	Foreign Born Whites	All Non-Whites	Negro	American Indian	Japanese and Chinese	Other	Puerto Rican	Spanish Surname 5 S.W. States
5	45.2	45.1	52.7	42.7	41.8	32.3	68.9	65.6	66.4	55.6
6	84.1	84.0	85.6	79.1	78.6	72.3	94.4	91.5		
7-9	97.8	97.8	97.1	95.9	95.9	91.7	97.8	97.5	94.9	96.0
10-13	97.7	97.8	96.5	95.9	95.9	93.4	97.7	97.2		
14-15	94.6	94.6	93.3	90.2	90.0	88.7	97.3	95.2	86.7	88.0
16-17	82.0	82.1	77.5	73.8	73.1	69.9	93.7	81.4	61.2	66.9

Source: Department of Health, Education, and Welfare, Office of Education, Equality of Educational Opportunity, By James S. Coleman, et. al., p. 450. Hereafter cited as Coleman Report.

Table 28. Enrollees Attending Modal
Grade or Higher, By Age and Race, 1960

(Percent of total students enrolled, selected ages)

Age	Modal Grade	All Races	White	Negro	American Indian	Japanese and Chinese	Other Races
8	3rd	60.2	60.9	55.2	38.8	72.2	60.5
9	4th	57.0	58.2	49.2	34.2	70.3	58.8
11	6th	56.5	58.0	46.2	32.0	66.6	55.4
13	8th	54.1	55.6	41.2	29.9	72.5	53.9
14	H.S. 1	54.9	56.9	40.1	29.5	69.4	48.9
15	H.S. 2	53.3	55.3	37.6	26.5	69.4	47.5
17	H.S. 4	53.2	55.4	33.1	18.7	67.5	45.7
19	Coll. 2	42.8	45.8	17.1	6.8	45.6	30.9

Source: Calculated from U.S. Bureau of the Census, U.S. Census of Population: 1960, Subject Reports. School Enrollment. Final Report PC(2)-5A, pp. 1-3

Table 29

Level of School Completed By Persons 25-29, By Race

(Percent of 25-29 population, selected years)

Year	Completed at least 4 years of high school			Completed at least 4 years of college			White/Negro ratio	
	All races	White	Negro & other	All races	White	Negro & other	4-Yrs. high school	4 yrs college
1940	37.8	41.2	12.1	5.8	6.4	1.6	3.4	4.0
1950	51.7	55.2	23.4	7.7	8.1	2.8	2.4	2.9
1960	60.7	63.7	38.6	11.1	11.8	5.4	1.7	2.2
1964	69.2	72.1	48.0	12.8	13.6	7.0	1.5	1.9
1967	72.5	74.8	55.7	14.6	15.5	8.3	1.3	1.9
1968	73.2	75.3	57.6	14.7	15.6	7.9	1.3	2.0
1969	74.7	77.0	57.5	16.0	17.0	9.1	1.3	1.9

Source: U.S. Bureau of the Census, Current Population Reports, Series P-20, No. 194, "Educational Attainment March 1969," and Current Population Reports, Series P-23, No. 30 "Characteristics of American Youth."

Table 30. Educational Attainment, March 1969, by Age and Race

Race and age	Total percent	Elementary school				High school				College					Median years completed
		0-4	5	6-7	8	1	2	3	4	1	2	3	4	5+	
All races															
20 and 21	100.0	1.3	0.3	2.0	2.5	4.2	5.0	5.7	40.9	13.5	15.8	7.9	1.0	*	12.7
22-24	100.0	1.0	0.4	2.3	3.4	4.5	5.6	5.0	43.8	6.7	6.3	6.7	11.4	2.9	12.6
25-29	100.0	1.3	0.5	2.4	4.8	4.8	6.5	5.0	44.1	5.9	6.0	2.7	10.0	6.0	12.6
25 and older	100.0	5.6	2.0	7.5	13.7	5.7	6.9	4.6	33.5	3.5	4.6	1.7	6.5	4.2	12.1
White															
20 and 21	100.0	1.1	0.2	1.6	2.4	3.5	4.5	4.8	41.6	13.7	16.9	8.4	1.1	*	12.8
22-24	100.0	1.0	0.4	1.9	3.1	4.0	4.9	4.3	44.8	6.9	6.4	6.9	12.3	3.2	12.7
25-29	100.0	1.2	0.4	2.1	4.6	4.4	5.9	4.4	44.8	6.2	6.2	2.8	10.6	6.3	12.6
25 and older	100.0	4.5	1.7	6.9	14.0	5.5	6.7	4.5	34.8	3.7	4.8	1.8	6.8	4.4	12.2
Negro and other races															
20 and 21	100.0	3.1	0.6	4.3	3.1	8.9	8.5	11.4	35.9	11.7	7.9	4.4	*	*	12.3
22-24	100.0	1.5	0.8	5.6	5.3	8.7	10.6	10.1	36.5	5.5	5.6	5.1	4.2	0.7	12.2
25-29	100.0	2.5	0.8	4.2	6.3	7.8	11.0	9.8	39.5	3.3	4.4	1.2	5.6	3.4	12.2
25 and older	100.0	15.2	4.5	12.9	11.4	7.1	8.2	6.2	22.7	2.0	2.9	0.9	3.7	2.4	9.8

* Less than 0.05 percent.
Source: U.S. Bureau of the Census, Current Population Reports, Series P-20, Number 194, "Educational Attainment: March 1969."

Table 31

Number of Grade Levels Behind the Average White in Metropolitan Areas
of the Northeast: Average of Verbal Ability, Reading Achievement,
and Mathematics Achievement Gaps:

Group and Location	Grade levels behind at			No. levels Negroes behind whites in specified area		
	Grade 6	Grade 9	Grade 12	6	9	12
White						
Nonmetropolitan						
South	0.6	0.9	1.3			
Southwest	0.2	0.3	0.7			
North	0.2	0.3	0.7			
Metropolitan						
Northeast	0*	0*	0*			
Midwest	0.1	0.0	0.3			
South	0.4	0.5	0.8			
Southwest	0.5	0.7	0.6			
West	0.3	0.4	0.7			
Negro						
Non-Metropolitan						
South	2.6	3.7	5.4	2.0	2.8	4.1
Southwest	2.3	3.3	4.9	2.1	3.0	4.2
North	2.1	2.7	4.4	1.9	2.4	3.7
Metropolitan						
Northeast	1.8	2.6	3.8	1.8	2.6	3.8
Midwest	1.9	2.3	3.6	1.8	2.3	3.3
South	2.2	3.0	4.6	1.8	2.5	3.8
Southwest	2.1	3.0	4.7	1.6	2.3	4.1
West	2.1	2.9	4.3	1.8	2.5	3.6
Mexican-American	2.2	2.5	3.6			
Puerto Rican	2.9	3.2	4.0			
American Indian	1.9	2.3	3.5			
Oriental American	1.0	0.8	2.9			

* Metropolitan area performance in the Northeast used as norm.
Source: Coleman Report, pp. 274-275

Table 32

Armed Forces Qualification Test Failures
By Race and Region 1968

(Percent Failure for "Mental" Reasons and "Mental and)
Medical Reasons"

Region	All races	Non-Negro	Negro	Negro/Non-Negro
USA Total	10.5	6.7	35.9	5.4
Northeast	8.5	6.8	27.5	4.0
New England	6.7	6.2	21.8	3.5
Middle Atlantic	9.1	7.0	28.2	4.0
North Central	6.0	4.1	27.1	6.6
East North Central	7.2	4.7	27.5	5.9
West North Central	3.1	2.5	24.6	9.8
South	17.5	9.8	41.5	4.2
South Atlantic	18.4	9.6	41.5	4.3
East S. Central	21.0	13.1	47.4	3.6
West S. Central	12.0	7.4	36.1	4.9
West	6.1	5.4	19.9	3.7
Mountain	6.2	5.6	36.5	6.5
Pacific	6.1	5.4	18.2	3.4

Source: Department of Defense, Department of the Army, Health of
the Army, p. 51.

Table 33. Public School Integration, Fall 1968 by Minority Group and Region.

Minority, Group and Region	Total Number of students (X 1,000)	Number of minority group students (X 1,000)	Percent minority of total	Percent minority group students attending school With specified percent minority enrollment			
				Under 50 percent	95-100 percent	99-100 percent	100 percent
Negroes							
U.S.A.* total	43,354	6,282	14.5	23.4	61.0	53.0	39.7
32 Northern and Western States	28,580	2,703	9.5	27.6	44.3	30.9	12.3
6 Border States and D.C.	3,730	636	17.1	28.4	57.9	46.3	25.2
11 Southern States	11,043	2,943	26.6	18.4	77.0	74.8	68.0
5 Southern States	3,649	1,363	37.4	10.5	87.6	87.2	81.9
Spanish-Surname							
U.S.A.* total	43,354	2,003	4.6	45.3	16.6	--	1.9
Arizona, California, Colorado, New Mexico and Texas (Mexican-Americans)	8,144	1,398	17.2	45.9	15.4	--	2.2
Connecticut, Illinois, New Jersey, and New York (Puerto Ricans)	7,651	394	5.2	28.0	27.6	--	1.5
Florida (Puerto Ricans and Cubans)	1,341	53	3.9	49.9	6.2	--	0.5
39 Other States and D.C.	26,218	158	0.6	81.7	2.6	--	0.6
American Indians							
U.S.A. total**	43,354	177	0.4	61.7	16.7	--	6.3
Orientals							
U.S.A. total	43,354	194	0.4	72.2	8.7	--	0.1

*Excludes Hawaii. **Excludes students attending Federal Indian Schools.
Source: Department of Health, Education, and Welfare, News release, January 4, 1970.

Table 34

College Enrollments of Youth by Age and Race, Fall 1969

Age	All races Total population	Enrolled	Percent enrolled	White Total population	Enrolled	Percent enrolled	All minority races Total population	Enrolled	Percent enrolled	Negro Total population	Enrolled	Percent enrolled
16-17	7,481	242	3.2	6,465	222	3.4	1,016	20	2.0	924	19	2.0
18-19	6,677	2,601	39.0	5,762	2,377	41.3	915	224	24.4	837	193	23.1
20-21	5,958	1,945	32.6	5,168	1,762	34.1	790	183	23.2	725	149	20.5
22-24	8,727	1,294	14.8	7,676	1,208	15.7	1,051	86	8.2	980	65	6.6
18-21	12,635	4,546	36.0	10,930	4,139	37.9	1,705	407	23.9	1,562	342	21.9
18-24	28,843	6,082	21.1	25,071	5,569	22.2	3,772	513	13.6	3,466	426	12.3

Table 35

College Enrollment Rates of Youth by Age, Race and Residence
Percent Enrolled in College

Age	U.S.A. total White	Negro	Metropolitan areas White	Negro	Central cities White	Negro	Suburbs White	Negro	Poverty areas large SMSA White	Negro	Non SMSA White	Negro
16-17	3.4	2.0	3.9	2.1	4.2	1.5	3.8	4.1	2.6	2.0	2.6	1.9
18-19	41.3	23.1	43.2	25.0	39.7	24.2	45.5	27.4	15.3	23.3	38.0	18.7
20-21	34.1	20.5	36.8	21.8	34.9	21.9	38.2	21.5	21.2	16.2	28.7	17.8
22-24	15.7	6.6	17.8	6.1	18.9	5.4	16.8	9.0	12.2	1.8	11.7	8.4

Source: U.S. Bureau of the Census, Current Population Reports, Series P-20, No. 206, "School Enrollment: 10/69."

Table 36. Percent of Blacks in State Universities and Land Grant Colleges

Fall 1968

Region/School	Full-time undergraduate-enrollment	Percent Black	Graduate and professional students	Percent Black
17 originally all black State universities and land grant colleges in southern and border states	44,803	95.6	3,576	93.4
28 predominantly white State universities and land grant colleges in southern and border states	398,249	1.76	91,732	1.69
11 Southern universities and land grant colleges in 9 eastern states	169,070	1.84	32,835	1.69
15 in 7 midwestern states	348,978	2.98	110,981	2.85
26 in 16 western states	306,085	1.34	86,521	1.13
Total predominantly white: 80 schools	1,222,382	1.93	322,069	1.91

SOURCE: John Egerton, State Universities and Black Americans, Southern Education Foundation, 1969

Table 37. Civilian Labor Force 1955-1969 by Race and Sex

	White				Negro and other races			
	Civilian labor force		Labor force participation rate (Percent)		Civilian labor force		Labor force participation rate (Numbers in thousands)	
Year and Age	Male	Female	Male	Female	Male	Female	Male	Female
1955 14-15	487	224	23.5	11.2	79	34	27.1	11.4
16-17	934	576	48.0	29.9	135	65	48.2	22.7
18-19	1,121	966	71.7	52.0	178	117	75.7	43.2
20-24	2,802	2,137	85.6	45.8	419	307	89.7	46.7
Total youth	5,344	3,903	60.4	37.3	811	523	63.7	34.6
1960 14-15	555	300	22.2	12.5	83	47	23.3	13.2
16-17	1,140	731	46.0	30.0	150	74	45.6	22.1
18-19	1,293	1,112	69.0	51.9	203	139	71.2	44.3
20-24	3,559	2,228	87.8	45.7	564	352	90.4	48.8
Total youth	6,547	4,371	60.0	36.9	1,000	612	62.7	35.5
1965 14-15	669	382	21.7	12.9	90	39	18.9	8.1
16-17	1,359	862	44.6	28.7	172	92	39.3	20.5
18-19	1,639	1,405	65.8	50.6	226	154	66.7	40.0
20-24	4,279	2,910	85.3	49.2	614	454	89.8	55.2
Total youth	7,946	5,559	58.3	37.9	1,102	739	56.9	34.6
1969 14-15	788	534	23.0	16.1	86	39	15.8	7.1
16-17	1,583	1,115	48.8	35.2	187	125	37.7	24.4
18-19	1,830	1,640	66.3	54.6	271	219	63.2	45.4
20-24	4,615	3,999	82.6	56.4	667	598	84.4	58.6
Total youth	8,816	7,288	58.7	44.0	1,211	981	53.6	38.3

Source: Manpower Report of the President, 1970, pages 217-219.

Table 38

Growth in Civilian Labor Force by Age, Color, and Sex, 1960-1969

	White male		White Female		Negro and other races Male		Negro and other races Female	
	1969 (x1000)	% increase from 1960	1969 (x1000)	% increase from 1960	1969 (x1000)	% increase from 1960	1969 (x1000)	% increase from 1960
14-15	788	42.0	534	78.0	86	3.6	39	-17.0
16-17	1,583	38.9	1,115	52.5	187	24.7	125	68.9
18-19	1,830	41.5	1,640	47.5	271	33.5	219	57.6
20-24	4,615	29.7	3,999	79.5	667	18.3	598	69.9
14-24	8,816	34.7	7,288	66.7	1,211	21.1	981	60.3
16-19	3,413	40.3	2,755	49.5	458	29.7	344	61.5

Source: Manpower Report of the President, 1970, p. 217.

Table 39

Major Occupation Group of Employed Persons 16 to 21 Years Old, by Race, Sex, and School Enrollment Status, October, 1969.

(Percent distribution)

Major occupation and sex	Enrolled in school			Not enrolled in school		
	Total	White	Negro and other races	Total	White	Negro and other races
MEN						
Total: Number (thousands)	2,449	2,239	210	2,408	2,021	387
Percent	100.0	100.0	100.0	100.0	100.0	100.0
White-collar	29.4	29.9	23.8	18.6	20.0	11.6
Professional and technical	7.2	7.3	5.7	3.5	4.0	1.0
Managers and officials	1.5	1.6	.5	2.6	2.9	1.0
Clerical	10.8	10.4	14.8	8.9	9.1	8.0
Sales	9.9	10.6	2.9	3.6	4.0	1.5
Blue-collar	43.3	43.8	38.1	69.8	69.1	73.2
Craftsmen	5.2	5.4	3.3	15.6	16.3	11.9
Operatives	17.9	17.8	18.6	36.3	35.9	38.4
Nonfarm laborers	20.2	20.6	16.2	17.9	16.9	22.9
Service workers	20.3	19.5	28.1	6.5	5.8	9.8
Private household	.3	.4		.1	.1	
Other service	19.9	19.2	28.1	6.4	5.7	9.8
Farm workers	7.0	6.7	10.0	5.2	5.1	5.4
WOMEN						
Total: Number (thousands)	1,746	1,592	154	2,847	2,530	317
Percent	100.0	100.0	100.0	100.0	100.0	100.0
White-collar	58.4	58.1	62.5	64.0	66.3	45.5
Professional and technical	6.7	6.6	7.2	4.3	4.6	2.5
Managers and officials	.6	.6		.9	1.0	.....
Clerical	36.3	35.4	45.4	53.7	55.4	39.8
Sales	14.9	15.4	9.9	5.1	5.3	3.1
Blue-collar	5.0	4.9	6.6	16.0	14.9	24.8
Craftsmen	.2	.2		.9	.9	.9
Operatives	3.7	3.5	5.9	14.4	13.3	22.9
Nonfarm laborers	1.1	1.1	.7	.7	.7	.9
Service workers	35.1	35.8	27.6	19.6	18.4	28.8
Private household	14.3	14.8	8.6	3.4	3.0	6.3
Other service	20.8	21.0	19.1	16.2	15.4	22.6
Farm workers	1.4	1.3	3.3	.4	.3	.9

NOTE: Because of rounding, sums of individual items may not equal totals.

Source: Monthly Labor Review, September 1970.

Table 40

Youth Unemployment Rates By Age, Sex, and Race, 1955-1969

Year	National rate	White 14-15 M	White 14-15 F	White 16-17 M	White 16-17 F	White 18-19 M	White 18-19 F	White 20-24 M	White 20-24 F	Negro and other races 14-15 M	Negro 14-15 F	Negro 16-17 M	Negro 16-17 F	Negro 18-19 M	Negro 18-19 F	Negro 20-24 M	Negro 20-24 F
1955	4.4	5.1	7.1	12.2	11.6	10.4	7.7	7.0	5.1	12.7	5.9	14.8	15.4	12.9	21.4	12.4	13.0
1960	5.5	8.1	6.3	14.6	14.5	13.5	11.5	8.3	7.2	13.3	10.6	22.7	25.7	25.1	24.5	13.1	15.3
1965	4.5	7.1	15.0	14.7	13.4	11.4	6.3	5.9	4.4	20.3	17.9	27.1	37.8	20.2	27.8	9.3	13.7
1969	3.5	8.5	6.4	12.5	13.8	7.9	10.0	4.6	5.5	22.1	23.1	24.7	31.2	19.0	25.7	8.4	12.0
1970	4.8	--	--	15.1	14.9	11.4	11.5	7.4	6.9	--	--	26.4	37.5	22.9	31.8	11.9	15.1

Table 41

Ratio of Unemployment Rate: $\frac{\text{Non-white}}{\text{white}}$ By Age and Sex, 1955-1969

Year	14-15 M	14-15 F	16-17 M	16-17 F	18-19 M	18-19 F	20-24 M	20-24 F
1955	2.5	0.8	1.2	1.3	1.2	2.8	1.8	2.6
1960	1.6	1.7	1.6	1.8	1.9	2.1	1.6	2.1
1965	2.9	1.2	1.8	2.8	1.8	4.4	1.6	3.1
1969	2.6	3.6	2.0	2.3	2.4	2.6	1.8	2.2
1970	-	-	1.7	2.5	2.0	2.8	1.6	2.2

Table 42

Unemployment Rate as Percent of National Rate By Age, Sex, and Race, 1955-1969

Year	National rate	White 14-15 M	White 14-15 F	White 16-17 M	White 16-17 F	White 18-19 M	White 18-19 F	White 20-24 M	White 20-24 F	Negro and other races 14-15 M	Negro 14-15 F	Negro 16-17 M	Negro 16-17 F	Negro 18-19 M	Negro 18-19 F	Negro 20-24 M	Negro 20-24 F
1955	4.4	116	161	277	264	236	175	159	116	289	134	336	350	293	486	282	295
1960	5.5	147	115	265	264	245	209	151	131	242	193	413	467	456	445	238	278
1965	4.5	158	333	327	298	253	140	131	98	451	398	602	840	449	618	207	304
1969	3.5	243	183	357	394	226	286	131	157	631	660	706	891	543	734	240	343
1970	4.8	-	-	315	310	238	210	154	144	-	-	550	781	477	663	248	315

Source: Manpower Report of the President, 1970.

Figures for 1970 from BLS tabulations for Jan.-Sept. (Not seasonally adjusted).

65

Table 43

Teenage Unemployment Rates in Poverty Areas of Six Cities,
by Racial/Ethnic Group, July 1968-June 1969

City	Group	Unemployment rate ages 16-19 (% of civ. labor force)	Rate as a percent of national rate of 3.5%
Atlanta, Ga.			
	Total	28.6	820
	White	25.0	710
	Negro	29.4	840
Chicago, Ill.			
	Total (96% Negro)	31.1	890
Detroit, Mich.			
	Total	36.4	1040
	White	18.2	520
	Negro	40.0	1140
Houston, Texas			
	Total	30.2	860
	Mexican-American	20.0	570
	Other White	14.3	410
	Negro	37.5	1070
Los Angeles, Calif.	Total	31.8	910
	Mexican-American	15.8	450
	Other White	33.3	950
	Negro	45.5	1300
New York, N.Y.			
	Total	25.3	720
	Puerto Rican	30.4	870
	Other White	25.0	710
	Negro	23.1	660

Manpower Report of the President, 1970, p. 132.

Table 44

Poverty Areas of Six Large Cities by Age, Sex, and Racial-Ethnic Group, 1969

| Racial-ethnic Group | Unemployment Rates (weighted average) | | | | | |
| | Total 16-64 labor force | | 16-19 labor force | | 20-24 labor force | |
	Male	Female	Male	Female	Male	Female
All groups	7.1	9.7	28.3	31.1	8.1	16.2
Total white population	6.3	7.5	25.4	20.4	4.4	12.7
White Spanish-Americans	6.7	9.4	23.1	23.3	3.6	17.1
White Puerto Ricans	8.8	10.4	27.8	28.6	3.6	19.0
White Mexican-Americans	3.6	6.5	18.2	14.3	6.3	9.1
Other whites ("Anglos")	6.2	5.3	28.0	15.0	6.1	6.9
Total non-white population	7.5	10.4	29.3	35.0	9.2	17.8
Total Negro	7.5	10.5	29.7	34.8	9.3	17.6
Negro Spanish-Americans	9.8	12.0	*	*	*	*
American Negro	7.4	10.5	29.7	34.4	9.6	17.9

* Small population too small to indicate statistical significance.

Source: Department of Labor Urban Employment Survey Tabulations.

Table 45

Estimated Characteristic of Enrollees in Manpower Programs, by Approach in 1969

Approach	Percent poor	Percent Less than a high school education	Percent minority races	Percent under 22	Percent ale	Percent welfare recipients	Percent disabled	Estimated 1971 participant unit cost (dollars)
On the job training	51	53	45	47	79	9	3	1,350
Institutional training	81	67	57	43	55	34	7	1,800
Rehabilitation	70	56	22	24	56	11	100	1,500
Post-school work support	95	85	53	65	51	38	2	1,850
Total out of school	73	62	42	40	60	21	38	1,600
In-school work support	100	97	58	100	54	31	0	450
All approaches	83	75	48	63	58	25	24	1,200

Source: Executive Office of the President; Bureau of the Budget, Special Analyses, Budget of the United States, Fiscal Year 1971, pages 143-144.

White House Conference on Children and Youth
Minority Children and Youth

Selected Bibliography

United States Government Publications*

U.S. Senate, Committee on Labor and Public Welfare, Subcommittee on
Employment, Manpower, and Poverty, Hearings, S. 2060 Headstart
Child Development Act.

U.S. Senate, Committee on Labor and Public Welfare, Special Subcommittee on Indian Education, The Education of American
Indians--Field Investigation and Research Reports, October 1969.

Indian Education: A National Tragedy--A National Challenge, 1969.

Executive Office of the President, Education for the 1970's Renewal
and Reform, messages to the Congress by the President, March 1970.

Executive Office of the President, Office of Management and Budget,
Special Analyses, Budget of the United States, Fiscal Year 1971, 1970.

National Advisory Commission on Civil Disorders, Report of the National
Advisory Commission on Civil Disorders, March 1968.

Supplemental Studies for the National Advisory Commission on
Civil Disorders, July 1968.

National Commission on the Causes and Prevention of Violence, Staff
Report, Crimes of Violence, 1970.

The President's Commission on Campus Unrest, The Report of the President's
Commission on Campus Unrest, September 1970.

The President's Commission on Law Enforcement and Administration of
Justice, Criminal Victimization in the United States: A Report
of a National Survey, prepared by the National Opinion Research
Center, 1967.

* Published by the Government Printing Office, Washington, D.C.

U.S. Department of Commerce, Bureau of the Census, U.S. Census of
Population: 1960, Subject Reports, "Persons of Spanish Surname,"
Final Report PC(2)-1B, 1963.

U.S. Census of Population: 1960, Subject Reports, "Non-white
Population by Race," Final Report PC(2)-1C, 1963.

U.S. Census of Population: 1960, Subject Reports, "Puerto Ricans
in the United States," Final Report PC(2)-1D, 1963.

U.S. Census of Population: 1960, Subject Reports, "School
Enrollment," Final Report PC(2)-5A, 1964.

U.S. Census of Population: 1960, Supplementary Reports, Series
PC(S1)-55, "Population Characteristics of Selected Ethnic Groups
in the Five Southwestern States," 1968.

Current Population Reports, Series P-20, No. 182, "Educational
Attainment: March 1968," April 1969.

Current Population Reports, Series P-20, No. 190, "School
Enrollment: October 1968 and 1967" 1969.

Current Population Reports, Series P-20, No. 200, "Household and
Family Characteristics March 1969," May 1970.

Current Population Reports, Series P-20, No. 206, "School Enrollment:
October 1969," October 1970.

Current Population Reports, Series P-23, No. 30, "Characteristics of
American Youth," 1970.

Current Population Reports, Series P-25, No. 311, "Estimates of the
Population of the United States, by Single Years of Age, Color, and
Sex 1900 to 1959," July 1965.

Current Population Reports, Series P-25, No. 321, "Estimates of the
Population of the United States, by Age, Color, and Sex: July 1, 1960
to 1965," November 1965.

Current Population Reports, Series P-25, No. 381, "Projections of the
Population of the United States, by Age, Sex, and Color to 1990, with
Extensions of Population by Age and Sex to 2015," December 1967.

Current Population Reports, Series P-25, No. 441, "Estimates of the
Population of the United States by Age, Race, and Sex: July 1, 1967
to July 1, 1969," March 1970.

U.S. Department of Commerce, Bureau of the Census, Current Population Reports, Series P-60, No. 66, "Income in 1968 of Families and Persons in the United States," December 1969.

Current Population Reports, Series P-60, No. 67, "Socioeconomic Trends in Poverty Areas 1960 to 1968," December 1969.

Current Population Reports, Series P-60, No. 68, "Poverty in the United States 1959 to 1968," December 1969.

Current Population Reports, Series P-60, No. 71, "Poverty Continues to Decline in 1969, (Advance Data From the March 1970 Current Population Survey)," July 1970.

Current Population Reports, Series P-60, No. 72, "Household Income in 1969 and Selected Social and Economic Characteristics of Households," August 1970.

Current Population Reports, Series P-65, No. 31, "Recent Purchase of Cars, Houses, and Other Durables and Expectations to Buy During the Months Ahead: Survey Data Through April 1970 (Including Annual Purchase Data, 1967-1969)," June 1970.

U.S. Department of Defense, Department of the Army, Office of the Surgeon General, Supplement to Health of the Army, Results of the Examination of Youths for Military Service, 1968, June 1969.

U.S. Department of Health, Education, and Welfare, Office of Education, Title I/ Year II: The Second Annual Report of Title I of the Elementary and Secondary Education Act of 1965, School Year 1966-67, 1969.

Education of the Disadvantaged: An Evaluative Report on Title I, Elementary and Secondary Education Act of 1965--Fiscal Year 1968, 1970.

Equality of Educational Opportunity, 1966.

U.S. Department of Health, Education, and Welfare, Office of the Secretary, HEW News, January 4, 1970 edition.

Toward A Social Report, January 1969.

U.S. Department of Health, Education, and Welfare, Public Health Service "Mental Health Aspects of the Effects of Discrimination Upon Children," by Joseph H. Douglass (reprint by PHS from Young Children, Vol. XXII, No. 5, May 1967).

U.S. Department of Health, Education, and Welfare, Public Health Service, Vital Statistics of the U.S., 1960, Vol. II, Section 1, "Mortality Analysis and Summary."

U.S. Department of Health, Education, and Welfare, Public Health Service, Indian Health Service, Indian Health Trends and Services, 1969 edition.

U.S. Department of Health, Education, and Welfare, Public Health Service, National Center for Health Statistics, Data from the National Health Survey, Series 10, No. 56, "Differentials in Health Characteristics by Color, United States--July 1965-June 1967," October 1969.

Vital and Health Statistics, Data from the National Vital Statistics System, Series 21, No. 19, "Natality Statistics Analysis, United States, 1965-1967," May 1970.

U.S. Department of Health, Education, and Welfare, Social Security Administration, Social Security Bulletin, Statistical Supplement, 1968.

U.S. Department of Health, Education, and Welfare, Social and Rehabilitation Services, The Nation's Youth, 1968.

Preliminary Report of Findings--1969 A.F.D.C. Study, NCSS Report AFDC-1 (69), March 1970.

Project Headstart 1965-67 (report and evaluation).

U.S. Department of Health, Education, and Welfare and U.S. Department of Labor, Womens Bureau, Child Care Arrangements of Working Mothers in the United States, by Seth Low (HEW) and Pearl G. Spindler (DOL), 1968.

Inter-Agency Committee on Mexican-American Affairs, The Mexican-American, A New Focus on Opportunity, 1968.

U.S. Department of the Interior, Bureau of Indian Affairs, Fiscal Year 1969, Statistics Concerning Indian Education.

U.S. Department of Justice, Federal Bureau of Investigation, Crime in the United States--Uniform Crime Reports--1969, August 1970.

U.S. Department of Labor, Manpower Report of the President, 1970.

U.S. Department of Labor, Bureau of Labor Statistics, Monthly Labor Review, XCIII: 9, September 1970.

U.S. Department of Labor, Bureau of Labor Statistics, Poverty--The Broad Outline, Urban Employment Survey, Report No. 1, Detroit, 1970.

Poverty--The Broad Outline, Urban Employment Survey, Report No. 2, Chicago, 1970.

Poverty in Houston's Central City, Region 6, Regional Report Series No. 1.

Labor Force Experience of the Puerto Rican Worker, Mid-Atlantic Regional Report No. 9, June 1968.

Poverty Area Profiles, New York, Mid-Atlantic Regional Report No. 13, October 1969.

The Social and Economic Status of Negroes in the United States, 1969, BLS Report No. 375 and U.S. Bureau of the Census, Current Population Reports, series P-23, No. 29.

U.S. Commission on Civil Rights, Hearings Held in San Antonio, Texas, December 9-14, 1968, 1969.

Mexican-Americans and the Administration of Justice in the Southwest, March 1970.

Stranger in One's Land, Clearinghouse Publication No. 19, May 1970.

BACKGROUND PAPER ON SPECIAL PROGRAMS FOR HANDICAPPED CHILDREN AND YOUTH FOR THE 1970 WHITE HOUSE CONFERENCE ON CHILDREN AND YOUTH

(Prepared by Dr. James W. Moss, December 1970)

CHILDREN WHO ARE HANDICAPPED

INTRODUCTION

Over 10 percent of the children born every day in the United States are destined to be called handicapped. These children may be deaf, blind, physically or mentally disabled, or in some other way set apart from their more fortunate peers. Over 8 million children living today will not progress normally through the schools without special attention of a continuing nature. Four times that number will need some type of special services before completing high school. Unless society makes a special effort, the lives of many of these children will be set aside and their hopes for the future discarded.

Today's society is dedicated to the provision of equal opportunities for all citizens. There are no acceptable exceptions to such a principle.

The principle of equal opportunities is a recent development and one which is not fully accepted by all peoples even today. The handicapped have not always had the good fortune of being considered equally participating members of their society. The earliest history of Sparta (circa 700 B.C.) suggests that defective children were deliberately exposed to the elements or sacrificed to the river Eurota. Evidence, even justification, for this has been reportedly found in the ancient laws of Lycurgus whose system of education in early Greece subordinated the needs of the individual to the needs of the state. In such a society which emphasized the achievements of physical prowess, the supremacy of the state, and the invincibility of its warriors, there was no place for the intellectually or physically defective.

A handicapped person may have had no role to play in ancient Sparta but today's society offers many opportunities for significant contributions to be made by the disabled provided they are properly prepared.

SCOPE AND NATURE OF THE PROBLEM

Handicapped children defined

The concept of "handicapped children" evokes a variety of images. There is no universally accepted definition and there is no real need for one. What constitutes a handicap for one person might well be only an inconvenience for another. Practically speaking, a person may be considered handicapped if he is prevented from taking full advantage of the opportunities which society provides him and is consequently unable to achieve his expected place as a contributing member of society. Such a definition, however useful, is far too broad for the purposes of this paper. For this purpose, a child who is handicapped is one who is mentally retarded; has impaired vision, speech, or hearing; has a serious and specific learning disability, or is severely emotionally disturbed or physically disabled to the extent that he cannot lead a normal life at home, in the school, or on the playground. He is a child who needs special services in order to obtain an education and to take his place in the community as a successful adult.

The inclusion of the need for special services in the definition of "handicapped children" is important in order to establish a distinction between the concept of "handicap" and that of "impairment" or "disability." A person may have a physical impairment, such as a finger missing on one hand, which in no way restricts his opportunities in life and which in no way requires special attention. Since the focus of this paper is on the need for and provision of special services, the definition of "handicapped" relates as much to appropriate services as it does to the condition of the child. As will be noted in the next section, however, such a definition will create some problems with reference to statistics on prevalence.

The definition of "handicapped children" used in this paper focuses upon the problems which are generally inherent within the child rather than imposed by society or the conditions of life. This rather restrictive definition is used because it is consistent with the majority of State and Federal laws and because it relates to special rather than general services. The definition does not, therefore, include the large numbers of children who appear to be handicapped because of cultural discrimination, poor economic conditions, geographical isolation, inadequate parental involvement, or the wide variety of other factors which interfere with the development of relevant life goals and behaviors appropriate to reach such goals. Temptation to include these latter groups in the definition should be avoided. It is no asset to be identified as "handicapped." Services necessary to the disadvantaged and, in fact, to children now identified as handicapped should increasingly be provided by society without the requirement that the recipient be labeled as handicapped.

Magnitude of the problem

The data on prevalence are somewhat inconsistent and incomplete because of the need to relate the definition to services required. Since the definition is dependent upon the need for services, the prevalence figures will also be a function of the type of service required. This means that the numbers of children reported as handicapped by one profession or agency will differ somewhat from those presented by another profession or agency. For example, an organization concerned with visual acuity will report, quite accurately, that a large number of children have eye defects which require attention. In fact, approximately 23 percent of school age children have impaired vision to the extent that corrective action is necessary. In the large majority of cases, the children need corrective lenses. Once a child is fitted with appropriate corrective lenses, in the majority of cases, he does not present any special problems to the schools. The schools are concerned with the provision of special services only where children cannot learn through normal procedures after the best possible correction. Thus, the educational agencies will report only about one-tenth of 1 percent of school-aged children with visual problems so great as to require special attention by that agency. Thus it is possible to find one agency reporting as many as 23 percent school-aged children with visual defects while another agency reports only 0.1 percent.

The accuracy of prevalence figures is somewhat dependent upon the degree of precision in determining the condition in question. Some handicapping conditions are relatively easy to recognize with a high degree of agreement by various professionals. Deafness, for example, can be measured scientifically in terms of decibels of hearing loss, at least for legal purposes, although two persons with the same decibel loss may behave quite differently in the hearing world. There can also be some degree of disagreement relative to the extent of hearing loss necessary before special attention is necessary, but it is not particularly difficult to define deafness arbitrarily and therefore to determine its prevalence in the population. This is in contrast to a condition such as emotional disturbance and how to describe it. While some agencies or professions might count only those children who are autistic or otherwise severely impaired, others might count all children who have some degree of social-emotional problems which could profit from counseling or guidance. For this reason, the prevalence figures reported can range from 1 to 2 percent to as high as 8 or 9 percent or more.

Prevalence data may be obtained from most agencies concerned with children. Those reported here come from the U.S. Office of Education, the Social and Rehabilitation Services, the Public Health Service, and the National Institute of Mental Health. Some gross figures have been obtained from the Department of Defense but these do not appear to be useful for education or health planning. The U.S. Office of Education reports the data presented in table 1. These data show the speech impaired child as constituting the largest number of children of concern to the schools.

TABLE 1.—PREVALENCE OF HANDICAPPED CHILDREN ACCORDING TO THE U.S. OFFICE OF EDUCATION ESTIMATES
[Ages 5 to 19]

Type of handicap	Total number	Percent
Visually impaired	60,400	0.1
Emotionally disturbed	1,207,200	2.0
Speech impaired	2,112,600	3.5
Hearing impaired	347,100	0.6
Crippled and other health	301,800	0.5
Learning disabled	603,600	1.0
Multiple handicapped	35,800	0.06

The prevalence data from the Health Services and Mental Health Administration of the Public Health Service report the prevalence data in table 2. These figures show the relatively large figure for visual impairment due to the inclusion of children who require corrective lenses. The second largest prevalence according to these data is for those children considered emotionally disturbed. It may be noted that the Public Health Service also has a broader definition for emotionally disturbed than does the Office of Education.

TABLE 2.—ESTIMATED NUMBER OF CHILDREN WITH CHRONIC HANDICAPPING CONDITIONS

Condition	Estimated number of handicapped children		Percent
	1965	1970	
Eye conditions needing specialist care	11,404,000	12,500,000	23.5
Emot'onally disturbed	4,600,000	5,400,000	8.5
Speech disorders	2,829,000	3,270,000	5.9
Mentally retarded	2,400,000	2,720,000	3.0
Orthopedic	2,153,000	2,425,000	3.5
Hearing loss	725,000	900,000	.0
Cerebral palsy	406,000	465,000	.0
Epilepsy	400,000	450,000	.8

Data from the National Institute of Mental Health, reported in "Crisis in Child Mental Health: Challenge for the 1970's" [1] generally agree with the U.S. Office of Education figures with an estimate of 2 to 3 percent of all children or apprixomately 1.4 million, as seriously emotionally disturbed. About one-sixth of these children are considered seriously psychotic. The Joint Commission on the Mental Health of Children, however, suggests that the magnitude of the problem is far greater than the numbers of seriously impaired children might indicate. It was the finding of the Commission, reported in the above referenced source, that an additional 8 to 10 percent of all children are sufficiently afflicted by emotional problems to require some specialized services.

Available data from the Armed Forces, from preinduction examinations, do not provide the kind of subcategorizations which permit direct comparisons with data from other agencies. They do, however, contribute to an understanding of the magnitude of the problem. Data from the 1968 preinduction examinations show that only 58.3 percent of all potential inductees were acceptable for the Armed Forces. Thus, over 40 percent of all individuals examined exhibited some problem serious enough to keep them out of the service. These figures varied dramatically with reference to race. Of the non-Caucasians examined, 30.7 percent were rejected because of a failure to meet the mental requirements as compared with only 5.4 percent of Caucasians. The figures reverse themselves with reference to rejects for health reasons. Approximately 42.3 percent of Caucasians failed to come up to medical standards while only 16.8 percent of non-Caucasians were rejected for health reasons.

Unfortunately, data from preinduction examinations are not readily available with reference to the numbers of individuals rejected for the specific categories of deficit reported by the U.S. Office of Education or the Public Health Service. It would probably be fair to assume, however, that not all of the individuals rejected by the Army would have required special attention by the schools or other agencies.

In summary, a minimum of 10 percent of school-aged children require some continuing special attention by agencies concerned with children. A much larger number, 25 percent or more, require some special service at some time during their developing years. The prob-

[1] Joint Commission on Mental Health of Children, "Crisis in Child Mental Health; Challenge for the 1970's," Harper & Rowe, 1970.

lem is of sufficient magnitude that it cannot be ignored by any of the agencies concerned with children.

Parents and guardians have almost total responsibility for the care and treatment of their children. They are not interfered with in this role unless there is a clear threat to their children's lives and welfare. The significant exception is in the area of education. Parents may opt to raise their children without adequate health services, without proper nourishment, without proper infant care, and without an environment which promotes effective mental health and moral stability, but with few exceptions they must send their children to school.

A variety of services is available to parents to assist them in raising and caring for their children. The support of these may be the responsibility of Federal, State, or local government, but the responsibility for the actual delivery of services, whether educational or health related, generally rests at the State and local levels. Federal programs usually work to assist State and local agencies. As this paper is being written, there are seven Federal cabinet departments and five other Federal agencies containing well over 100 separate, identifiable programs which in some way relate to the health, education, and welfare of children. All of these can and do relate to handicapped children and a number of them have been established specifically for that purpose. The specific programs focusing on the problems of handicapped children and their areas of responsibility are as follows:

Bureau of Education for the Handicaped, U.S. Office of Education, DHEW.—The Bureau of Education for the Handicapped is responsible for supporting a wide range of activities relating to the education of handicapped children. Aside from the support of research, demonstration, development activities, and professional training activities, the Bureau provides funds to the States for the support of educational programs for handicapped children. The Bureau also provides support for model early education centers for the handicapped, regional centers for deaf-blind children, and various media development and dissemination activities to permit teachers to cope more effectively with their handicapped pupils.

Crippled Children's Service, Health Service and Mental Health Administration, DHEW.—Since 1935, the Crippled Children's Service has been making grants to States to help them extend and improve "(1) services for reducing infant mortality and otherwise promoting the health of mothers and children; and (2) services for locating, and for medical, surgical, corrective, and other services and care for facilities for diagnosis, hospitalization, and aftercare for, children who are crippled or who are suffering from conditions leading to crippling." Half of the funds granted to each State must be matched dollar for dollar by the States. The other half does not have to be matched by the States. Every State has a crippled children's agency. In most cases it is a part of the State department of health.

Maternal and Child Health Services, Health Services and Mental Health Administration, DHEW.—The maternal and child health services provided by State and local health departments include: maternity clinics where women are seen by doctors, nurses, nutritionists, and medical social workers; family planning; visits of public health nurses to homes before and after babies are born; well-child clinics for child health supervision where mothers can get competent medical and nursing care for their babies and preschool children; pediatric clinics; school health programs that spot the youngsters who need medical or dental treatment and help them get it; dental care for children and pregnant women; immunizations; and mental retardation clinics for diagnosis, evaluation, treatment, and followup care.

National Institute of Mental Health, DHEW.—The National Institute of Mental Health is concerned with the mental health of children and adults. The Institute supports a variety of research and manpower development programs, provides funds for the construction and staffing of community mental health centers, operates narcotic addiction rehabilitation programs, as well as a variety of other activities designed to reduce the mental health problems of children and adults.

Rehabilitation Services Administration, Social and Rehabilitation Services, DHEW.—Federal funds are administered by the Rehabilitation Services Administration in order to promote more effective rehabilitation of handicapped adults. These funds are matched at the State level by programs usually managed by an appropriate rehabilitation agency. Rehabilitation services include a broad range of activities designed to overcome handicapping conditions, including corrective medical treatment where possible, provision of orthodepic and prosthetic devices, skill development through training, and other activities designed to help the disabled individual to earn a living and participate in today's society.

State and local responsibility.—The responsibility for programs at the State level are scattered through a number of agencies with enough differences among the States to make generalizations impossible. In most States, there is a director of special education within the jurisdiction of the chief State school officer to handle educational matters. Other services are administered within departments of health, welfare, mental health, et cetera, and within special institutions. The provision of services at the local level are the responsibility of both governmental and voluntary agencies. By far the majority of educational services are provided through the public school system. Health services and mental health services are provided to a large degree by nongovernmental agencies although often with Government support.

State and local authorities, even with Federal assistance, are not presently able to provide all the services required. For example, a recent survey by the Bureau of Education for the Handicapped found that over 15,000 school districts across the country are offering appropriate special educational services to less than half of the handicapped children within their districts.

Committees and organizations.—A number of committees and organizations have either been given or have assumed some responsibility relative to services for handicapped children. Several committees have been established for the purpose of advising the Federal Government concerning the handicapped. The most relevant of these are (1) the National Advisory Committee on Handicapped Children, (2) the

National Advisory Committee on Education of the Deaf, (3) the President's Committee on Mental Retardation, (4) the Secretary's Committee (HEW) on Mental Retardation, and (5) the President's Committee on Employment of the Handicapped.

A large number of professional organizations exist for the purpose of disseminating professional information through journals and conferences to members working with the handicapped. Parents have organized associations for the purpose of promoting more and better service for their children.

Parents.—In the final analysis, it is always the parent who must be responsible to see that the children receive the necessary services to the extent that such services are available.

PREVENTION OF HANDICAPPING CONDITIONS

The problem of the handicapped must be faced along two fronts. It is important to prevent as many handicapping conditions as possible. It is equally important to do whatever is necessary to help those for whom prevention comes too late. Medical science has indeed made great strides in preventing some handicaps, not only through significant breakthroughs such as the polio and measles vaccines but through the general improvement of health practices and services. Changing attitudes about abortion and genetic counseling will serve to reduce even more the numbers of handicapped children. The restrictions on fireworks on the Fourth of July reduced substantially the numbers of such children. Further reduction in the numbers of handicapped youngsters could be achieved through better accident prevention programs for automobile drivers.

It is difficult to estimate the number of children who are not handicapped today because of preventive measures. Conditions such as polio hardly emerge anymore as new cases (although the numbers are likely in increase because of reduced national interest in the immunization program). There were 25,000 children seriously affected by the last rubella epidemic, many of whom would not have been damaged had there been an effective immunization program. The reduction in numbers of disabled children through improved prenatal and postnatal care is impossible to determine with any accuracy. There can be no doubt that improved living conditions and health services result in decreases in the numbers of handicapped children. Some of these gains are offset because improved medical care makes it possible for some children who are born damaged to survive whereas they might not have done so previously.

The concept of "prevention" requires special attention with respect to the mentally retarded who are found within large cities. There is no common agreement as to the role of economic deprivation as a cause of mental retardation. The possibility that "cultural deprivation" can result in mental retardation has raised questions about the definition of mental retardation. The issue has been brought into focus because more and more culturally different children are being placed in special classes for the retarded because they fail in school and score low on intelligence tests. This is quite likely to occur if the child speaks a language different from that used in the school or represented by the intelligence test. A few simple facts can be noted.

1. Three-fourths of the Nation's mentally retarded are to be found in the isolated and impoverished urban and rural slums.

2. Conservative estimates of the prevalence of mental retardation in inner city neighborhoods begin at 7 percent.

3. A child in a low-income rural or urban family is 15 times more likely to be diagnosed as mentally retarded than is a child from a higher income family.

4. About three times as many low-income children as higher income children fail in school. A child whose father is an urban laborer has one chance in 3.5 million of being named a National Merit Scholar compared with one chance in 12,600 for children of professional or technical parents.

5. Students in the public schools of inner city low-income areas have been found to be from 6 months to 3 years behind the national norm of achievement for their age and grade. An appalling number of these children fall further behind with the passing of each school year. The data from the Army preinduction examinations certainly verify this fact.[2]

The inappropriate placement of disadvantaged and otherwise culturally different children in classes for the mentally retarded is often perpetrated as a misguided effort to help the children. The justification is often given that classes for the mentally retarded have better pupil-teacher ratios (usually a maximum of 15 to 1) and that teachers of the mentally retarded are more trained to cope with individual differences. Since the children are often failing in regular class settings, many school administrators see the special class for the retarded as offering some hope where none exists otherwise. Such administrators fail to see the disadvantage of placing such children in classes for the retarded and lack the imagination or resources to develop educational programs appropriate for the children in their schools.

Children who are raised in culturally different situations too frequently lose out no matter what name they go by. To label them as mentally retarded is to add an additional burden. Once a child has been labeled "mentally retarded" he will be treated as if he were mentally retarded. This is indeed appropriate if the child is truly retarded because he will need a special program with more intensive drill, more repetition, more careful explanations, and a generally slowed down program. To provide such a program to a child who is not retared will inhibit his educational development. Furthermore, nonretarded culturally different children often require highly specialized programs quite different from those required by the mentally retarded. They often require extensive language development work, enrichment activities to form an experience base for learning, more attention to the development of learning skills, and a better orientation to the value of learning and the schools in today's society.

It is unfortunate that the educational system is not sufficiently flexible to provide appropriate services for the full range of children who attend school.

---

[2] *MR 68 : The Edge of Change,* President's Committee on Mental Retardation. Superintendent of Documents, U.S. Government Printing Office, Washington, D.C.

If it is possible to provide culturally different children with more favorable teacher-pupil ratios by labeling them mentally retarded, it should be possible to provide the same without a label. If it is possible to provide special and appropriate services for children who are deaf, speech impaired, or mentally retarded, it should be possible to provide language development programs for children who need them. It is unfortunate that school administrators feel required to force children into inappropriate categorial programs rather than develop programs appropriate for their children. These should not be "special" programs but rather a natural extension of existing programs. It should not be necessary to create separate educational systems for every type of child who deviates from the traditional norm.

SERVICES FOR HANDICAPPED CHILDREN

When one thinks of services related to handicapped children, one may think of three broad categories of professional services: Those which seek to prevent handicapping conditions from occurring, those which seek to eliminate or reduce the impact of a condition which handicaps, and those which seek to enable a child to function effectively in spite of an impairment.

Medical research and treatment has made great strides toward eliminating some handicapping conditions. The most dramatic breakthrough was the discovery of the Salk vaccine and its successors which virtually eliminated the problem of polio in children. The rubella vaccine shows great promise of eliminating some problems of a multihandicapping nature. Control of viruses and bacteria which attack the nervous system has brought about reductions in the numbers of children with handicaps. Aside from these specific examples, general advances in obstetrics, prenatal care and public health programs have prevented some children from having handicapping conditions.

Conditions which handicap children can often be treated in such a way as to eliminate them as problems or reduce the impact of the condition. This is most easily recognized with reference to corrective surgery and optometrics where corrections sometimes result in immediate or very quick changes in the condition. It is equally true with other services which sometimes take longer but which can eliminate a handicapping condition. Speech and language disorders can often be eliminated completely through effective treatment as can some types of emotional disorders. The effect of an impairment can often be reduced significantly through early treatment or training. A deaf child, for example, who learns language during the first few years of life will be markedly better off than one who waits until school age before being introduced to language. Many emotionally disturbed children are in the same position where early treatment can be far more effective than treatment postponed until later in life.

Finally, there are those children who, after all possible correction, must learn to live with their handicaps and to make the most of life in spite of them. These children require specialized services in order to get through school and often require special help in order to take their places in an economic society.

The focus of this paper is on services to children who are handicapped more so than upon services required to prevent handicapping conditions. These services fall into four major categories: health services, mental health services, educational services, and rehabilitation services.

Health of the handicapped child.—It is axiomatic that all children are entitled to good health just as they are entitled to clean air to breathe, clear water to bathe in, and sufficient nourishment to build healthy bodies. Handicapped children are no different from other children in this respect except that they often require more services just to achieve this goal at a marginal level.

A general discussion of health services for children and the organization of these services at State and local levels is presented in the briefing paper on health prepared for the White House Conference on Children. This paper will not attempt to duplicate that information but will focus on those services specific to the needs of handicapped children.

A discussion of health services for handicapped children should hopefully be able to differentiate those services which in some way relate directly to the handicapping condition from those of a more general nature. For example, health services which improve a deaf child's hearing are more relevant to such a discussion than services which remove an appendix or otherwise improve conditions generic to all children.

Unfortunately, it is impossible to provide data on general health services for handicapped children apart from those for non-handicapped children. It is possible, however, to sort out specific health programs which exist primarily to help children with specific handicapping conditions. An examination of these programs can give some idea of the range of special health services available to the handicapped child. It must be taken for granted that handicapped children receive all the general health services which all children receive or should receive through local pediatricians and community health services.

The health programs which are particularly relevant to handicapped children are those which have been supported traditionally through the Federal Children's Bureau with matching funds at State and local levels. Almost $200 million was invested by the Federal Government in fiscal year 1969 for health programs. Most of these health programs at the Federal level are administered by the Health Services and Mental Health Administration. Included within this agency are the Maternal and Child Care Services, the Crippled Children's Service, Maternity and Infant Care projects, and Projects for Health of School and Preschool Children. Public health nursing, diagnostic clinics for mentally retarded children, hearing and vision screening, immunizations, prenatal and post partum care in maternity clinics, and in-patient hospital care for premature infants are all included in the above services administered by the Health Services and Mental Health Administration.

Crippled Children's Services.—The Federal investment for Crippled Children's Services has increased substantially over the past two decades. The growth in support for this program at State and local and Federal levels is shown in table 3. Services through the crippled children's program reached almost a half-million children in 1968. Thirty percent of these children were under 5 years of age, reflecting an inter-

est in early diagnosis and treatment. The majority of the children
served averaged two to three visits each and are seen in clinics. Approximately 25 percent of the children served are seen by physicians
during office or home visits.

The crippled children's programs involved a total of $113.9 million
for fiscal year 1968 with State and local agencies contributing $63.1
million of that amount.

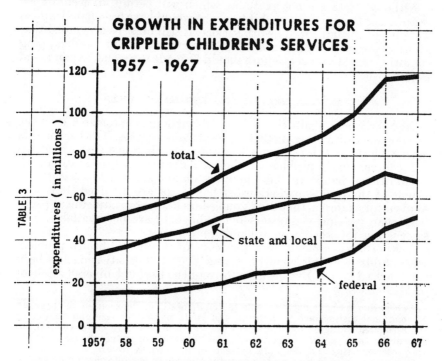

GROWTH IN EXPENDITURES FOR CRIPPLED CHILDREN'S SERVICES 1957 - 1967

TABLE 3

expenditures (in millions)

Maternal and Child Health Services.—The enactment of the Social
Security Act in 1935 was a major step forward in the development of
health services for mothers and children in this country. Maternal and
Child Health Services, administered by the Health Services and
Mental Health Administration of HEW, represents the most comprehensive medical approach to the prevention of handicapping conditions
through improved health care. During fiscal year 1970, the Maternal
and Child Health Services expended $50 million in grants to the States
to improve and expand medical services, another $38.7 million for
projects to develop comprehensive health services for preschool and
school-aged children, and another $36.6 million for special maternity
and infant care projects. During fiscal year 1969 over 300,000 women
received maternity nursing services. Millions of children were immunized against smallpox and diphtheria while almost 10 million
children were screened for vision. Mental retardation clinics served
40,000 children with more than 21,000 new applications for service.

The relationship between preventive medical care and handicapping
conditions can only be estimated. It is well documented that infant

mortality can be reduced through appropriate prenatal care, hospitalization, delivery and postpartum care. The special maternity and infant care projects have consistently demonstrated such a decrease in mortality wherever such services are established. Adequate health care not only reduces infant mortality, but also handicapping conditions which result from complications of pregnancy and delivery and poor post partum care.

Although data are not available which will permit an accurate assessment of the numbers of children who would have been handicapped were it not for improved health service, it still must be concluded that appropriate mother and infant health services prevent handicapping conditions and that every effort should be made to extend, expand, and improve such services.

MENTAL HEALTH AND THE HANDICAPPED

Over and over again the lack of adequate data interferes with the development of a clear picture of needs and services. Nowhere is this more true than with reference to mental health. Some data are available concerning the problem of emotional disturbances in children with no additional handicaps but there are almost no data to indicate the extent of the problem where other handicaps are involved. It is well known, for example, that deaf youngsters have more adjustment problems than hearing youngsters but valid data are not available. The same is true for other types of handicaps.

Neither the complexity nor the scope of the mental health problem with children in this country is well known. The situation has been summarized by Dr. Eveoleen Rexford of the Boston University School of Medicine: [3]

As a nation we have not been able to look honestly at the scope of the problem of emotional disturbance in children and youth nor at the size and quality of the resources available to cope with these children. We have not developed the systematic surveys, the categories of conditions, the conceptual models, nor the adequate reporting and analyzing systems to know where we are.

However concerned we may be about the lacunae in our information regarding emotional disturbed children identified by psychiatric facilities, the total situation may be far more serious. A large population of the children residing in correctional institutions, welfare homes, State schools, and foster homes undoubtedly suffer from emotional and behavioral disturbances. They may be labeled dependent, neglected, delinquent, or retarded and there is no way under present circumstances to include them in a comprehensive mental health survey.

Data from the National Institute of Mental Health suggests that 8.5 million of the 71 million children in the United States have mental health problems. Two million of these children are in need of psychiatric help while 6.5 million require help for emotional problems.

Appropriate mental health services for children require a complex network of coordinated elements including: diagnostic, consultative, and treatment services available in out-patient clinics, residential centers, halfway houses, and so forth. Special programs in regular schools and mental health consultation to parents and teachers are important components to the full provision of services.

[3] Rexford, E., "Children, Child Psychiatry, and Our Brave New World," "Archives of General Psychiatry," 20 (January 1969), 25–37; quoted from "Crisis in Child Mental Health," Harper and Rowe, N.Y., 1970, p. 257.

According to figures issued by the National Institute of Mental Health, 84 percent of children receiving psychiatric services receive them from out-patient clinics. The distribution of children receiving services from various types of facilities are presented in table 4. These data suggest that only about one-third of the children in serious trouble are receiving professional assistance. The data in table 4 also point out the emphasis our society has on adult care. Of the two and a half million patients receiving help, less than a half million are under the age of 18.

TABLE 4.—NUMBER OF PSYCHIATRIC FACILITIES AND ESTIMATED NUMBER OF CHILDREN UNDER CARE DURING THE YEAR IN EACH TYPE OF FACILITY. 1966

Type of facility	Facilities		Total Patients, all ages		Children under 18 years	
	Number	Percent	Estimated number	Percent	Estimated number	Percent
Outpatient psychiatric clinic	2, 122	56	1, 186, 000	46	399, 000	84
State and county mental hospitals	297	8	807, 000	31	27, 400	6
Private mental hospitals	175	5	105, 000	4	8, 400	2
General hospitals with psychiatric services	888	23	466, 000	18	28, 000	6
Psychiatric day-night units	173	5	15, 700	1	2, 500	1
Residential treatment centers (not in State mental hospital)	149	4			8, 000	2
Total	3, 804	100	2, 579, 600	100	473, 300	100

Source: "Crisis in Child Mental Health: Challenge for the 1970's," Harper & Rowe, New York, 1970, p. 268.

The data in table 4 do not include figures on the numbers of children helped by nonpsychiatric facilities. The latest figures from the U.S. Office of Education suggest that there are about 800,000 children in the schools who require special programs because of emotional disturbances and that approximately 100,000 received some sort of service during the 1968–69 school year.

If the cost of appropriate, comprehensive mental health services are difficult to determine, the cost to society for failing to provide such services is even more difficult. Some cost figures are available which can provide some basis for future planning.

The cost of treatment and prevention of mental illness in the United States is estimated at approximately $4.2 billion annually. State and local government pay $1.4 billion of this. The Federal Government's share is $1.1 billion. The cost to private insurance companies runs $0.8 billion. Finally, the patients themselves spend $0.9 billion annually for services. The National Institute of Mental Health estimates that the cost to the mentally ill and their families through lost productivity reaches $12.4 billion. The loss in tax revenues alone comes to $3.6 billion, a figure three times as great as the amount invested each year by the Federal Government in prevention and treatment activities.

Data from the American Association of Psychiatric Clinics for Children provide some cost estimates for the provision of mental health services to children. Table 5 shows the cost of operating psychiatric clinics for children and the source of funds. The same table also shows the difference in costs for the years 1955 and 1965. The data in this table, representing the costs for median sized clinics, shows a substantial increase in costs with the greatest increase in support from State and Federal tax dollars.

TABLE 5.—DOLLAR VALUE FOR SOURCES OF FINANCIAL SUPPORT FOR MEDIAN CLINICS, 1955 AND 1965

Source of funds	1955		1965	
	Percent	Proportionate amount	Percent	Proportionate amount
Fees	12	7, 200	13	21, 700
Community Chest, United Fund, etc	31	18, 600	14	23, 600
Federal and State	26	15, 600	44	74, 300
All others	31	18, 600	29	49, 000
Total	100	60, 000	100	168, 600

Source: American Association of Psychiatric Clinics for Children, "Children and Clinics," 1968, p. 13.

An important observation from table 5 is that support for psychiatric clinics for childern from the public sector has increased 4½ times between 1955 and 1965 while the private sector's contribution has increased little more than one-fourth times. Although the cost of providing services through community based mental health clinics has been rising, these services have been assuming the burden of caring for many patients who earlier would have been admitted to far more costly mental hospitals. Figures released by the National Institute of Mental Health show a decline of State and county mental hospital patients from 559,000 in 1955 to 401,000 in 1969 with a projected reduction to 252,000 by 1973.

Data from table 5 refer to the cost of psychiatric services only. Educational costs for emotionally disturbed children also run high. It costs approximately $2,000 per year to provide an education for an emotionally disturbed child in a public day school. This is two to three times the cost of educating nonhandicapped children. Services in residential schools run considerabley higher. The average cost for educating an emotionally disturbed child in a residential facility in 1967 was $3,226. Estimates for 1970 are that the costs will average as high as $4,825 per year per child. It is difficult to obtain figures on the total cost for providing adequate psychiatric, educational, and rehabilitative services to all of the children who require such services. Data from the public schools alone suggest that it would require $800 million over and above the normal costs of education to provide adequate psychoeducational services to all children needing such services.

The situation with reference to mental health for children cannot be described in positive terms. What data are available suggest that there are too many emotionally disturbed children and too little being done about it. The National Institute of Mental Health, in recognition of this problem, has joined forces with the Bureau of Education for the Handicapped within the U.S. Office of Education to develop a "child advocacy" system on a pilot basis.

Education and the handicapped.—There are approximately 8 million children today who can be considered sufficiently handicapped to require special education services at the preschool and school aged levels. Approximately 40 percent of the school aged children who require special educational services receive them at the present time. The most frequently mentioned type of public day school service is the "self-contained special class" where children with similar handicaps are grouped together for instructional purposes. Such special classes are most frequently organized for mentally retarded children although it is not unusual to find such special classes for the deaf, the blind, the orthopedically handicapped, and the emotionally disturbed. Children with speech impairments, children with learning disabilities, and some children who are blind receive services through an itinerate specialist. In some cases, children spend part of the day in a "resource room" for special instruction while spending the remainder of the day in their regular class.

Aside from these direct, more or less basic educational services to children, there are other special services which are required on an intermittent basis such as psychological testing, social worker contacts, hearing and vision screening, counseling and guidance, et cetera.

An estimated 200,000 handicapped children receive their education in State-supported residential schools. This is particularly true for the deaf and blind. Residential facilities for the mentally retarded are increasingly providing education and training for their patients. A relatively small proportion of handicapped children receive their education within private, residential settings.

The excess cost for educating handicapped children has generally been borne by the State and local governments. Local educational agencies are generally reimbursed by the State through some sort of an excess cost formula. The basis for reimbursement varies from State to State and not all States follow the same pattern. Most residential facilities for the handicapped are also State supported. The Federal Government plays only a minor role in the support of educational programs for handicapped children. At the present time, the Federal investment in education for the handicapped is approximately $170 million. These Federal funds are used to stimulate new program developments, new educational procedures, et cetera.

The distribution for costs of education has been undergoing a gradual shift over the years with the Federal Government taking more and more responsibility. Table 6A shows the gradual shift in Federal support for education from 0.3 percent in 1920 to 7.3 percent in 1969. The Federal involvement in education for the handicapped started as recently as the early 1960's with the major upswing occurring within the past 4 years.

TABLE 6.—CURRENT GROSS PER PUPIL COST FOR SPECIAL EDUCATION FROM SELECTED AREAS, 1968

Type of handicap	Selected areas				
	St. Louis	Cleveland	Cincinnati	Dayton	San Diego
Educable mentally retarded	$1,206	$802	$725	$1,000	$928
Trainable mentally retarded	1,363				1,539
Crippled	1,953	1,960	1,537	2,093	2,075
Visually handicapped	1,765	1,363	1,825	1,395	1,425
Deaf and hard of hearing	2,175	1,658	1,725	1,395	1,607
Average State per pupil expenditure	499	497	497	497	576

TABLE 6A.—PERCENT CONTRIBUTIONS TO PUBLIC SCHOOL FUNDING

School year	Federal	State	Local
1919–20	0.3	16.5	83.2
1929–30	0.4	16.9	82.7
1939–40	1.8	30.3	68.0
1949–50	2.0	39.8	57.3
1959–60	4.4	30.1	56.5
1968–69	7.3	40.7	52.0

While there has been a gradual increase in the amount of State and local funds for the support of educational programs for the handicapped, only about 40 percent of the children requiring help are currently receiving the special help they need. The most current figures from the U.S. Office of Education (1968–69 school year) indicate that of the 6 million school aged children identified as needing special services, only 2.1 million actually received such services.

The high cost of educating these children is the most frequently heard explanation for so few receiving services. The unwillingness of society to provide funds for such programs is a reflection of unfortunate attitudes toward the handicapped. Lack of familiarity with handicapped people plus a lack of information about the success of such programs lead to attitudes of hopelessness, pity, and charity. Such attitudes result in low priorities being assigned to educating handicapped children. With limited dollars for education and a desire to make dollars go as far as possible, most school officials appear to prefer investing in such a way as to affect the largest number of children.

Cost data on educating handicapped children have not been systematically collected until recent years. The data in table 6 have been collected from a selection of States to provide an indication of the per pupil cost for special education during 1968. These data show considerably variability but a comparison with the average State per pupil expenditure for education shows that the cost of educating handicapped children are from two to four times as high as for nonhandicapped pupils.

The cost benefits to society more than compensate for the increased cost of instruction. The cost to society to maintain one mentally retarded individual in a State institution can be as high as $250,000 over a lifetime. It can cost as little as $15,000 to provide the same individual with an education to make him independent and a contributor to society.

The data in table 6 show the per pupil cost of educating handicapped children in selected public day schools. The cost of educating such children in residential schools is markedly higher and increasing rapidly. Table 7 shows the actual cost computed by the Buerau of Education for the Handicapped (USOE) for the 1965–66 and 1966–67 school year with an estimate for the 1970–71 school year. The figures in these tables also give some indication of the differences in costs for different types of handicapped children.

TABLE 7.—AVERAGE ANNUAL COST PER PUPIL FOR HANDICAPPED CHILDREN IN RESIDENTIAL FACILITIES

[In dollars]

Type of handicapping condition	School year		
	1965–66	1966–67	[1] 1970–71
Visually handicapped	3,113	3,498	5,580
Deaf and hard of hearing	2,787	2,910	3,314
Emotionally disturbed	2,821	3,226	4,824
Mentally retarded	2,445	2,774	4,048

[1] 1970–71 data extrapolated from 1965–66, 1966–67 increases.

There has been a substantial increase in Federal programs for handicapped children over the past decade. The Federal investment for the

education of handicapped children has increased from approximately
$1 million in 1959 to approximately $170 million in 1970. The increase
in funding has been the result of a rapid increase in the number of
laws passed during that period providing support for a variety of
specific programs. A summary of the growth in legislation can be seen
in figure 1 which gives the titles of the different laws and the years in

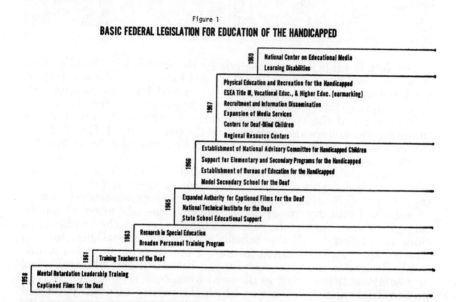

Figure 1

BASIC FEDERAL LEGISLATION FOR EDUCATION OF THE HANDICAPPED

which they were passed. In all, 20 major pieces of legislation were enacted into law during the period 1958 to 1969. The majority of these
laws provide funds which are administered by the Bureau of Education for the Handicapped of the U.S. Office of Education. A sizable
proportion, however, are administered by other components of the
U.S. Office of Education as a function of specification of funds not
originally authorized for the handicapped. The increase in Federal
support for the education of handicapped children since 1958 can be
seen in table 8. It should be noted that these funds are for a variety
of programs and are not all used directly for the support of local
educational programs for children. Until 1966, all of the moneys appropriated for the handicapped went into research, training of personnel, or media services for the adult deaf. It was not until 1966 that
any funds were made available for direct services to children. Even
today, little more than $100 million of the $170 million is committed to
programs which assist children. This would make the direct Federal
investment about $12 per child under the age of 18.

TABLE 8.—FEDERAL FUNDS AUTHORIZED AND APPROPRIATED SPECIFICALLY FOR THE EDUCATION OF HANDI-
CAPPED CHILDREN

[In thousands of dollars]

Fiscal year	Authorized	Appropriated	Fiscal year	Authorized	Appropriated
1959	$1,250	$1,000	1966	28,500	28,300
1960	1,250	1,050	1967	91,500	37,900
1961	1,250	1,150	1968	211,500	53,400
1962	2,825	2,782	1969	239,125	79,795
1963	4,000	3,040	1970	321,500	85,850
1964	16,500	15,384	1971	326,000	105,000
1965	19,500	17,884			

The data in table 8 do not include funds expended for handicapped children which were originally authorized for general educational purposes but which were subsequently earmarked for handicapped children. Approximately $85 million was appropriated for fiscal year 1970 as parts of the vocational education program, the program for supplemental centers and services, and the part of title 1, ESEA funds earmarked for State-operated and State-supported schools for the handicapped.

The financial data reported above relate to specific programs for which funds are appropriated directly or earmarked for the handicapped. The U.S. Office of Education invests an undetermined amount of general funds for programs to improve the education of handicapped children. As was the case with health services, the handicapped child is entitled to all the benefits of existing educational services whether specifically designed for him or not. This again makes it difficult to determine the exact cost for just those children whose physical or mental condition result in the need for special services. There is no way to determine the extent to which the variety of pupil personnel services, the cost for such services, are related to handicapped pupils. School nurses, attendance officers, psychologists, and social workers all spend part of their time working with the unique problems of the handicapped. Many federally supported educational programs benefit handicapped pupils because of the nature of the programs. Cost data for these programs are difficult to extract for just those who are handicapped.

Rehabilitation services.—In many ways the cost of not providing adequate health care and education for handicapped children is reflected in the costs of rehabilitation services at the adult or near adult level. This is not completely true since many rehabilitation clients are handicapped through accident or illness after reaching adulthood. Nevertheless, neglect at younger age levels leaves the entire burden of preparing individuals to assume a meaningful role in society to the rehabilitation agencies. The costs to provide vocational rehabilitation services for disabled persons to make them more employable, counting only those funds administered by the Department of HEW (not including the Veterans' Administration) are presented in table 9.

TABLE 9. FEDERAL-STATE BASIC SUPPORT PROGRAM UNDER SECTION 2 OF THE
VOCATIONAL REHABILITATION ACT

Fiscal years	Federal grants	Average cost per rehabilitation [1]	Fiscal years	Federal grants	Average cost per rehabilitation [1]
1960	$49,072,022	$892	1966	153,566,C26	1,385
1961	54,3C2,012	953	1967	235,926,260	1,750
1962	62,950,000	990	1968	286,861,083	1,816
1963	71,038,954	1,027	1969	340,485,879	1,888
1964	84,856,371	1,113	1970	435,000,000	[2]2,089
1965	96,949,721	1,143			

[1] Average cost per rehabilitation based on section expenditures (Federal, and State).
[2] Estimate.

The figures in table 9 represent rehabilitation services to both adolescents and adults. Over the years, youths under 20 have made up approximately 20 percent of the total of all persons served. The number of younger persons has been steadily increasing over the years. An important aspect of the rehabilitation service focuses on the special needs of the mentally retarded with the result that the number of persons served over the years has included more and more retardates. The percentages for the mentally retarded served and those under the age of 20 since 1960 is shown in table 10 for the purpose of illustrating the nature of the trends.

TABLE 10.—SELECTED DATA FOR REHABILITATION CLIENTS: 1960–69

Fiscal year	Percent of rehabilitants under age 20	Percent of mentally retarded	Fiscal year	Percent of rehabilitants under age 20	Percent of mentally retarded
1960	17.1	3.3	1965	21.3	7.6
1961	17.8	3.9	1966	22.9	9.3
1962	18.8	4.4	1967	22.7	10.2
1963	20.1	5.4	1968	22.5	10.7
1964	20.2	6.0	1969	23.3	11.4

The data in table 9 show a Federal investment of $435 million for fiscal year 1970 for rehabilitation services. This amount of money could be disturbing to many taxpayers if they saw it as a charity or some form of welfare plan for the disabled. More thoughtful people perhaps see it as an investment which, in general, brings a return to society. Very few have a full understanding of the specific value of this investment in terms of dollars in the taxpayer's pocket. It has been estimated that the yearly increase in Federal taxes due to rehabilitation rose from $9.4 million in 1961 to $29 million in 1967, while the yearly saving in public assistance payments due to rehabilitation rose from $9.6 million in 1961 to $16.4 million in 1967, giving a net benefit that ranged from $19 million in 1961 to $45 million in 1967. At that rate of return, it takes approximately 5 years for the taxpayers to recoup their share of the rehabilitation cost out of increased Federal taxes paid by rehabilitants and lowered welfare payments. The average number of years each rehabilitant will work is three to four times the number of years needed to repay the taxpayer. The return of tax dollars in excess of the cost of rehabilitation is clear profit to the taxpayer.

Although the rehabilitation services sponsored through the Department of Health, Education, and Welfare were originally designed to promote vocational independence for handicapped persons, the program is far more comprehensive than most people are aware. In many ways it is analogous to the Crippled Children's Service but serving an older population. Basic services include (1) comprehensive evaluation, including medical study and diagnosis; (2) medical, surgical, and hospital care, and related therapy to remove or reduce disability; (3) prosthetic and orthoptic services; (4) training services; (5) services in comprehensive or specialized rehabilitation facilities; (6) mantenance and transportation as appropriate during rehabilitation; (7) tools, equipment, and licenses for work on a job or in establishing a small business; (8) initial stock and supplies; (9) reader services for the blind and interpreters for the deaf; and many more.

Funds for rehabilitation services are allotted to appropriate State agencies to augment State appropriations for such services. In 1970 the Federal share was about 80 percent. Aside from the basic support program there are a number of special activities which are designed to focus on particular areas of need. It is not easy to break out cost data with reference to youth under 20, but all of the services available to adults through the Rehabilitation Services Administration are available to youngsters beginning about age 16.

One special service managed by the Rehabilitation Services Administration is a recently established center for deaf-blind youth and adults. This center is to demonstrate methods of providing intensive and specialized services for the deaf-blind and to offer an opportunity for the training of professional and allied personnel.

The Rehabilitation Services Administration shares many of the concerns of the Bureau of Education for the Handicapped of the Office of Education. The two agencies are concerned with promoting social and economic independence in handicapped persons. Both deal with the same population between the ages of 16 and 20. The fact that the two agencies have overlapping interests permits them to bring their special resources together to provide the most comprehensive of all possible services. An example of such cooperative efforts is the mutually supported postsecondary technical and vocational programs for deaf youngsters. Educational resources made available through the Bureau of Education for the Handicapped are combined with such rehabilitative services as interpreter services, counseling services, and the provision of special materials to enable deaf youngsters to participate in technical and vocational schools designed for hearing youngsters and adults.

AN OVERVIEW AND POSSIBLE OPTIONS FOR THE FUTURE

In our society the highest value is ascribed to the individual as a person. The data in table 1 indicate that there are some 6 million handicapped children from ages 5 to 19 who are mentally retarded and

emotionally disturbed or have speech, hearing, visual, and other imped-
iments which impair their ability to learn and to function effectively.
If infants and younger children are included at least 8 million children are handicapped. From table 2 it is evident that much larger numbers of children have lesser mental and physical conditions which are
chronically handicapping and which require care and attention.

The large number of handicapped children in our society presents a
serious and challenging national problem. First, the human and emotional cost of mental and physical disabilities is huge to the children
and to their families. Second, disability represents a large and unnec-
essary economic loss in productive human resources, for many of the
handicaps are preventable, remediable, or rehabilitatible. A disabled
person may lose $500,000 in lifetime earnings. Third, serious handi-
capping conditions among children represent a financial burden on
families and a large cost to the society. The cost of keeping a handicapped child in a dependent State can readily run to $100,000 or $200,-
000 in a lifetime. Fourth, the general standard of living in the
country and its national strength are diminished when handicapped
people cannot function productively and when the economy is burdened with the costs of their maintenance.

The costs of handicapping conditions are sizable indeed. For instance, selective service and military statistics indicate that about one-
third of all males fail military entrance tests because of mental and
physical disabilities. The President's Task Force on the Mentally
Handicapped, Action Against Mental Disability, September 1970, estimated that the cost of mental retardation alone comes to $8 billion a
year, including $2.5 billion for residential services and $5.5 billion for
loss of earnings. The estimated costs of mental illness are even higher
and the costs and losses attributable to physical handicaps are also
large. While precise data are not available, it is clear that a substantial part of these foregoing high costs are attributable to prenatal.
natal, and childhood handicaps—many of which could be prevented
through proper care of mothers and children if available knowledge
were applied. Research is further broadening possibilities for success.

Existing services

The costs of educational and other special services for handicapped
children often run several times those for normal children. These exceptional costs are typically borne by families or by local and State
governments. For extremely disabled children care is often provided
in private or public institutions.

Despite long concern over the problems of mentally retarded, emotionally disturbed, and physically handicapped children, the national
network of service systems and special programs for handicapped children is far short of meeting the needs. This is traceable to the high cost
of special services, the lack of trained manpower in many instances,
and a tendency on the part of society with many competing needs to
neglect the handicapped who are not readily visible. Handicapped
children bear the twin burden of neglect as children and as handicapped persons.

The Federal Government has expanded its resources for the handicapped in many directions in the last decade:

In the health area about $200 million was provided by the Federal Government in fiscal year 1969 for maternal and child health and crippled children's services programs originally authorized under the Children's Bureau. Among these programs were special maternity and infant care projects and comprehensive health services projects for preschool and school-age children which were developed in a special effort to prevent mental retardation and other defects.

Support for mental health services, particularly through comprehensive centers, has been augmented.

Special funds for the education of handicapped children have grown from over $1 million in fiscal year 1960 to nearly $86 million in 1970.

Funds for Federal grants under the Vocational Rehabilitation Act have likewise expanded from $49 million in 1960 to nearly $435 million in 1970, although most of these resources are used for individuals who were disabled as adults.

A substantial effort has been mounted to prevent mental retardation and to plan and finance services for the mentally retarded.

In addition, large but unestimated amounts which assist the handicapped are financed through the general social security, health, education, and other welfare programs of the Federal Government which provides payments to families, grants-in-aid to State or local governments, and, in some instances, finance direct Federal services.

Notwithstanding the progress that has been made, large unmet needs remain. In the health area there is a major problem of availability of health services in urban and rural poverty areas, where the incidence of prematurity and mentally defective children is the highest. It is likewise estimated that less than 40 percent of the handicapped children receive appropriate educational services. Moreover, the special educational services that are provided are largely in surburban metropolitan areas; the children living in the inner cities or in more isolated areas have less access to such services. Much the same may be said regarding mental health and rehabilitation services.

Moreover, while the needs are large, it is evident that the local and State governments in many instances face difficult financial problems and many more demands for resources confront the Federal Government than it can possibly finance. The society, it is clear, will have to set its priorities carefully to assure that handicapped children receive an adequate and just proportion of national resources for the expensive services which they require if they are to be helped to overcome their handicaps—and if the cohorts of newly handicapped in future years are to be reduced by effective preventive measures.

Possible alternative approaches for the future

What strategies and priorities offer the best hope of reducing the prevalence of mental and physical handicaps among children and youth and of securing for handicapped children their proper share of resources? What strategies and programs would be most effective against these humanly and socially costly conditions?

1. A prevention strategy.—From the standpoints of the individual child, the family, and the society, the best course is to prevent the physical or mental disability from arising. Prevention is likely to be less costly than remediation and for many types of mental and physical disability it is the only means of assuring that the child will not be handicapped throughout his lifetime.

Among ongoing programs prevention has not received as much emphasis as care. However, strong evidence has been marshaled in favor of prevention. For example, the President's Task Force on the Mentally Handicapped in its report pointed out that the lifetime care and earnings loss of a seriously retarded child may come to three-fourths of a million dollars. It also indicated that the more serious forms of mental retardation stem from internal infections, malnutrition during pregnancy, and birth injuries—which are preventable if adequate prenatal and obstetric care can be assured. To cite one instance, the 1964 rubella epidemic resulted in an estimated 20,000 children born with defects, including one-fourth to one-third of them mentally retarded.

Premature birth which is known to be associated with retardation and other disabilities has a link to low socioeconomic status. The President's Task Force on the Mentally Handicapped strongly urged that early attention be given to prevention of mental disability by use of measures in the social field, particularly programs directed toward improving conditions in the inner cities and impoverished rural areas. The President's Task Force on Physically Handicapped in its report "A National Efford for the Physically Handicapped," July 1970, likewise emphasized the importance of prevention through measures to reduce birth injury, safety programs, emergency care to accident victims, educational programs, early case finding, and initiation of services to minimize development of severe handicaps.

Programs for prevention for the physical and mental handicaps might be designed specifically for this purpose and targeted at high risk groups. Alternatively, prevention might flow from more general programs for proper health, nutritional, and early educational care of all children, particularly the young children. The President's Task Force on the Mentally Handicapped suggested that in considering priorities in the field of prevention, children from birth to age 5 should be given first priority, because this is the period when preventive intervention has its highest potential. Among such broader preventive measures might be education for family life, family planning, early screening, prenatal and perinatal services, maternal and infant nutrition, day care and preschool, and provision of other services and assistance.

2. An early care and rehabilitation strategy.—A prevention strategy alone is not sufficient because there will be some instances where preventive measures fail and a child is born handicapped or a handicap arises after birth. Thus, another significant line of attack is early intervention. Early intervention has weight because it is well known in health, education, and rehabilitation fields that treatment and rehabilitation are generally most successful and effective if provided as soon as possible after the injury or handicapping condition arises. Special health care and education to help children overcome their problems is a particularly fruitful type of rehabilitation because adjustment occurs most easily in the early years.

Effective treatment and rehabilitation require good diagnostic capacity, particularly for conditions such as mental retardation and mental illness, and also effective treatment services. The large relative neglect of health and education and day care programs for the early years plays a substantial part in negating the effectiveness of early intervention for children who are injured or mentally handicapped or live under deprived conditions where their physical and mental growth is stunted. While crippled children's health programs serve substantial numbers of children, they also fall short of full coverage. The gap in resources on the learning side is even more substantial. Children with mental retardation or emotional handicaps are particularly vulnerable in their early years. Blind and deaf children also cannot afford to lose their preschool years, when learning is most rapid.

Thus, early intervention is a significant contender for favorable national priorities with respect to the 8 million preschool and school-age children who face or are likely to face significant learning and health problems.

3. An extended care and maintenance strategy.—Even under the most enlightened prevention and early remediation approaches it is likely that some children are likely to be born severely impaired or subsequently to be injured to a degree that they cannot be restored to social effectiveness and ultimate self-sufficiency. The proportion of such children will, of course, be higher if the prevention or early intervention strategies are neglected.

In an advanced society with substantial material resources, it is clearly appropriate and feasible to care adequately for the individuals who are physically or mentally disabled to the degree that they cannot function effectively in our society. The national burden of such care is already substantial. For example, the President's Task Force on the Mentally Handicapped pointed out that 215,000 mentally retarded Americans were in institutions and an additional 367,000 mentally ill were in public hospitals. The objective of such care would be to provide maximum independence, security, and dignity.

The three foregoing strategies are not mutually exclusive. They are all needed in some appropriate mix—although it is far from clear that in the country at present this mix is such as to produce the most effective result, as is evident from the large number of handicapped children present in the society. Resources must be directed to geographical areas where the relative incidence of handicapping conditions is high, as is true in most poverty areas. Resources must also be balanced among different age groups of children, among different handicapping conditions, and among various functional program areas. These alternatives merit analysis in a broad context to determine the optimum mix.

The implementation of these strategies entails the consideration of many aspects, including many that come under the category of means. Fragmented programs must be coordinated and organized into effectively concerted service delivery systems dealing with the whole child and the whole family. A broader and more scientific base for action should be amassed through systematic research and experimentation. Trained manpower and adequate physical facilities for service delivery systems are necessary. An appropriate blend of State-local government, private, and Federal cooperation must be structured. New and improved financing mechanisms and fiscal arrangements will be involved.

Most important of all, however, is the question of the relative priority which the Nation is to accord to its children generally—and to those children who are most prone to fall victim to handicapping conditions. Can the Nation afford to allow large numbers of children to be born with or incur mental and physical handicapping conditions? And if they arise, what priorities does the country place on the remediation, rehabilitation, and care of the afflicted children?

BACKGROUND ON JUVENILE DELINQUENCY FOR THE 1970–71 WHITE HOUSE CONFERENCE ON CHILDREN AND YOUTH

(Prepared by Dr. Kenneth Polk, University of Oregon, and Dr. John M. Martin, Fordham University)

A. INTRODUCTION

1. THE SCOPE AND SIGNIFICANCE OF DELINQUENCY

For most young persons, growing up involves the normal ups and downs, even a routine of good times and bad. For others, and we are often surprised to find out how many others, growing up is more problematic. For these, "trouble" can become an important part of their lives. Law violation is one of the more dramatic forms such trouble can take.

Juvenile delinquency has become one of the words we associate with any discussion of youth and their problems, and well we might. As a problem it is perhaps even more prevalent than many think. The most recent Government estimates indicate that something like 2.9 percent of children between the ages of 10 to 17 will be referred each year to the juvenile courts of this country. According to this report prepared by the Youth Development and Delinquency Prevention Administration in Washington, in 1968 (the most recent year for which figures are available) a total of 1,455,000 delinquency cases were disposed of by the juvenile courts of the Nation. As large as these figures are, they probably in fact represent a gross underestimation of the actual number of young persons involved in criminal activity.

---

[1] "Juvenile Court Statistics 1968," Washington, D.C.: Office of Juvenile Delinquency and Youth Development, U.S. Department of Health, Education, and Welfare, No. SRS–JD–131, 1970.

CHART A

THE VOLUME OF DELINQUENCY[*]

THE DELINQUENCY PROCESS SIEVE

SCREENING, OF "PROBLEM" CHILDREN IN LOS ANGELES COUNTY
TO EFFECT SOCIAL CONTROL –1956

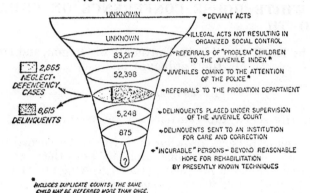

UNKNOWN   → DEVIANT ACTS

UNKNOWN   → ILLEGAL ACTS NOT RESULTING IN
ORGANIZED SOCIAL CONTROL

83,217   → REFERRALS OF "PROBLEM" CHILDREN
TO THE JUVENILE INDEX *

2,865
NEGLECT·
DEPENDENCY
CASES

52,398   → JUVENILES COMING TO THE ATTENTION
OF THE POLICE *

→ REFERRALS TO THE PROBATION DEPARTMENT

8,615
DELINQUENTS

5,248   → DELINQUENTS PLACED UNDER SUPERVISION
OF THE JUVENILE COURT

875   → DELINQUENTS SENT TO AN INSTITUTION
FOR CARE AND CORRECTION

?   → "INCURABLE" PERSONS – BEYOND REASONABLE
HOPE FOR REHABILITATION
BY PRESENTLY KNOWN TECHNIQUES

* INCLUDES DUPLICATE COUNTS; THE SAME
CHILD MAY BE REFERRED MORE THAN ONCE.

[*]Joseph W. Eaton and Kenneth Polk, Measuring Delinquency, Pittsburgh: University of Pittsburgh Press, 1961, p. 5.

There are two ways of demonstrating this underestimation phenomenon. First, there is operating a "funnel" or "sieve" process which weeds out many deviant acts so that official action (necessary for a person to enter the formal statistics as a "juvenile delinquent"—this being a legal term) is not taken. In a study in Los Angeles a few years ago (see chart A), it was shown that of 52,398 juvenile acts which come to the attention of the police, only 8,615 individuals were brought to the court, with a small number, 875, being sent to an instiution for care and correction.[2] While the 52,398 figure does, to be sure, represent an overestimate of the number of individuals involved (since a person might appear more than once in these police records), still the drastic reduction from the police to the court level is one indication of how official court referrals underestimate the actual number of offenses and offenders. The effect of the sieving process also can be seen in the self-report studies, which suggest that perhaps as many as 90 percent of all young persons have commited at least one act for which they could have been brought to juvenile court.[3]

Second, recent research in the Pacific Northwest reveals that while the yearly rate of official delinquency may vary between 2 or 3 percent, the chance of becoming a delinquent at some time before the 18th

[2] Joseph W. Eaton and Kenneth Polk, "Measuring Delinquency," Pittsburgh : University of Pittsburgh Press, 1961.

[3] Austin L. Porterfield, "Delinquency and Its Outcome in Court and College," American Journal of Sociology, 49 : 199–208, November 1943 ; idem, "The Complainant in the Juvenile Court," Sociology and Social Research, 28 : 171–181, January 1944 ; James F. Short, Jr., and F. Ivan Nye, "Reported Behavior as a Criterion of Deviant Behavior," Social Problems, 5 : 205–213, Winter 1957 ; John P. Clark and Eugene P. Wenninger, "Socio-Economic Class and Area as Correlates of Illegal Behavior Among Juveniles," American Sociological Review, 27 : 826–834, December 1962.

birthday, for males at least, is much higher and ranges somewhere between 20 and 25 percent.[4] That is, roughly one young male in every four or five will have some encounter with the juvenile court before he reaches the age which puts him under the jurisdiction of adult criminal law and courts. Comparable rates have been reported elsewhere.[5]

A first point to be made about delinquency, then, is that it is more common than many realize. A second point is that it is becoming increasingly difficult to separate the problem of crime generally from problems of youth. The Uniform Crime Reports which contain national crime and arrest information gathered by the Federal Bureau of Investigation show that in 1969, over half, 51.4 percent, of all the arrests were accounted for by persons under the age of 25,[6] 38.9 percent were under 21, 25.6 percent were under 18, and 9.7 percent were under the age of 15 (see table 1). Some individual offenses are virtually youth offenses: 87.7 percent of the arrests for motor vehicle theft, and 83.5 percent of the arrests for burglary involve persons under the age of 24. In fact, for property offenses (such as larceny, burglary, and car theft), over 50 percent (54.0, to be exact) of the arrests involve persons under the age of 18, while 70.1 percent involve persons under 21. Youth hold a virtual monopoly, then, on some forms of criminal behavior.

To give a balanced picture, we should add that in the case of offenses involving violence or bodily harm (willful homicide, rape, robbery, aggravated assault) only 22.3 percent of the arrests are accounted for by persons under the age of 18. While we may have some problems with crime among young people, if violence is our concern we should look elsewhere (76.1 percent of the arrests for murder, and 70.2 percent of the arrests for aggravated assault are accounted for by persons over the age of 21 in 1969). For serious "index" crimes as a whole, the subtotals in table 1 show that youths under 18 comprise 47.7 percent of those arrested and persons under age 25, 76.4 percent.

[4] Figures obtained from a sample of over 1,200 adolescent males being investigated by the Marion County Youth Study, a study in Marion County, Oreg. (1960 population 120,888) funded by the National Institute of Mental Health (Grant No. MH14806 "Maturational Reform and Rural Delinquency"). Virtually identical results were obtained in similar research undertaken by Kenneth Polk in Lane County, Oreg. (Population 1960, 180,000).
[5] The President's Commission on Law Enforcement and the Administration of Justice has estimates that, while still large, are a shade lower: one in six for males. See The Challenge of Crime in a Free Society, New York: Avon Books, 1968, p. 170.
[6] Uniform Crime Reports—1969, Washington, D.C.: Federal Bureau of Investigation, U.S. Department of Justice, August, 1970, p. 115.

TABLE 1.—TOTAL ARRESTS OF PERSONS UNDER 15, UNDER 18, UNDER 21, AND UNDER 25 YEARS OF AGE, 1969

[4,759 agencies; 1969 estimated population 143,815,000]

Offense charged	Grand total all ages	Percentage			
		Under 15	Under 18	Under 21	Under 25
Total	5,862,246	9.7	25.6	38.9	51.4
Criminal homicide:					
(a) Murder and nonnegligent manslaughter	11,509	1.4	9.4	23.9	42.1
(b) Manslaughter by negligence	3,197	.9	7.5	24.8	44.7
Forcible rape	14,428	3.7	20.1	42.1	65.1
Robbery	76,533	11.8	33.4	56.2	76.8
Aggravated assault	113,724	5.3	16.4	29.8	47.0
Burglary—breaking or entering	255,937	25.3	53.7	71.2	83.5
Larceny—theft	510,660	27.7	53.1	67.8	77.9
Auto theft	125,686	15.9	58.0	76.7	87.7

TABLE 1.—TOTAL ARRESTS OF PERSONS UNDER 15, UNDER 18, UNDER 21, AND UNDER 25 YEARS OF AGE, 1969—Continued

		Percentage			
Offense charged	Grand total all ages	Under 15	Under 18	Under 21	Under 25
Violent crime	216, 194	7. 3	22. 3	39. 7	58. 5
Property crime	892, 283	25. 3	54. 0	70. 1	80. 9
Subtotal for above offenses	1, 111, 674	21. 8	47. 7	64. 0	76. 4
Other assaults	259, 825	7. 0	17. 6	29. 9	46. 2
Arson	8, 691	43. 4	62. 1	71. 4	79. 1
Forgery and counterfeiting	36, 727	2. 3	11. 3	29. 2	52. 5
Fraud	63, 445	1. 5	4. 7	14. 7	34. 2
Embezzlement	6, 309	. 7	3. 9	13. 9	35. 1
Stolen property; buying, receiving, possessing	46, 176	10. 4	31. 6	51. 8	68. 5
Vandalism	106, 892	48. 1	73. 5	82. 4	88. 2
Weapons; carrying, possessing, etc	88, 973	4. 5	17. 1	32. 5	49. 9
Prostitution and commercialized vice	46, 410	. 2	2. 0	17. 7	58. 5
Sex offenses (except forcible rape and prostitution)	50, 143	8. 6	21. 8	34. 0	51. 0
Narcotic drug laws	232, 690	3. 5	24. 7	54. 8	77. 2
Gambling	78, 020	. 3	2. 2	6. 4	14. 7
Offenses against family and children	50, 312	. 3	1. 6	12. 5	30. 8
Driving under the influence	349, 326	(¹)	1. 1	7. 0	19. 7
Liquor laws	212, 660	2. 9	33. 5	74. 4	81. 7
Drunkenness	1, 420, 161	. 4	3. 0	8. 6	17. 2
Disorderly conduct	573, 502	7. 2	20. 4	36. 6	52. 4
Vagrancy	106, 269	1. 8	10. 4	27. 6	43. 8
All other offenses (except traffic)	664, 634	11. 9	30. 6	47. 3	62. 0
Suspicion	88, 265	6. 0	23. 6	47. 6	66. 5
Curfew and loitering law violations	101, 674	25. 7	100. 0	100. 0	100. 0
Runaways	159, 468	39. 6	100. 0	100. 0	100. 0

¹ Less than 1/10 of 1 percent.

Note: Violent crime is offenses of murder, forcible rape, robbery and aggravated assault. Property crime is offenses of burglary, larceny $50 and over and auto theft.

Source: Uniform Crime Reports—1969, Washington, D.C.: Federal Bureau of Investigation, U.S. Department of Justice, August 1970, p. 115.

There is a further factor to be considered as we examine the scope of the problem of juvenile delinquency: our inability to deal with it. This is reflected, on one hand, by the continued rise in rates of juvenile delinquency. On the other, at this time we appear to be unable to correct effectively the problem of law violation itself, or the cluster of maladaptive behaviors which accompany it. Not only do courts and (especially) institutions have high rates of recidivism (rehabilitation, in other words, does not occur), but post-correctional experience in such areas as education, employment, or the military suggests that the attempt to correct may in many instances actually aggravate the young person's problem.

One of our reasons for being concerned with delinquency is its continual rise both in raw numbers and in rates. In the period from 1958 to 1968, the actual number of delinquency cases disposed of by the juvenile courts doubled, going from 703,000 to 1,455,000 (including traffic cases—comparable figures obtained when traffic cases are excluded, as table 2 shows). During this same period, the rates of delinquency (per 1,000 child population) rose from 20.1 to 28.7. (See table 2 and chart A.) While there are well-known pitfalls in the interpretation of such figures (such as the fact that part of the increase is to be accounted for by changes in police and court practices), at a minimum the figures alert us to the fact that increasing large numbers of our youth are seen as troublesome enough to require formal attention.

TABLE 2.—NUMBER AND RATE OF DELINQUENCY CASES DISPOSED OF BY JUVENILE COURTS, UNITED STATES, 1958–68 [1]

| Year | Delinquency cases [2] | | Rate per 1,000 child population [3] |
	Including traffic	Excluding traffic	
1958	[4] 703,000	473,000	20.1
1959	[4] 773,000	483,000	19.6
1960	813,000	510,000	20.1
1961	801,000	503,000	19.3
1962	867,000	555,000	20.5
1963	967,000	601,000	21.4
1964	1,128,000	686,000	23.5
1965	1,157,000	697,000	23.6
1966	1,268,000	745,000	24.7
1967	1,360,300	811,000	26.4
1968	1,455,000	900,000	28.7

[1] Juvenile Court Statistics—1968, Office of Juvenile Delinquency and Youth Development, U.S. Department of Health, Education, and Welfare, No. SRS–JD–131, 1970, p. 11.
[2] Data for 1958–67 estimated from the national sample of juvenile courts. Inclusion of data for Alaska and Hawaii beginning in 1960 does not materially affect the trend.
[3] Based on U.S. child population 10–17 years of age.
[4] Much of the increase is accounted for in one State by administrative in the method of handling juvenile traffic cases.

8

CHART A

TREND IN JUVENILE COURT DELINQUENCY *
CASES AND CHILD POPULATION 10 - 17 YEARS
OF AGE, 1940 - 1968 'semi-logarithmic scale)

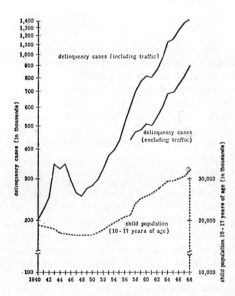

* Juvenile Court Statistics--1968, Office of Juvenile Delinquency and Youth Development, U.S. Department of Health, Education and Welfare, No. SRS-JD-131, 1970, p. 9.

Equally problematic is our current, and abominable, track record for rehabilitation. We have our choice of an abundant array of statistics here. For example, the "Careers in Crime Program," followup study of offenders conducted by the FBI shows that of offenders released from the Federal criminal justice system in 1963, for those under 20, virtually three of every four (74.3 percent, to be exact) had been arrested on new charges by 1969.[7] While this report, in a classic bit of understatement, suggested that such facts call "for greater rehabilitation efforts directed at the young offender," it is not quite clear what such efforts should include. Few treatment programs have been effective, and even such reasonable activities as education or vocational training have little impact. Glaser, in his analysis of the impact of the prison experience found, for example, that very few inmates actually used any vocational training they had received once they went outside the walls (although at the same time, unemployment is a persistent problem among ex-offenders).[8]

In this paper, we will review both the scope of the problem of juvenile delinquency and youth offenses, and review strategies for the prevention and control of such behavior. The paper's significance lies jointly in: (a) its contribution to the understanding of the specific problems faced by the large number of individual young people who come to be labeled "delinquent," and (b) its analysis of the range of strategies for institutional and community action (and change) to develop correctional strategies for more effective prevention and control of juvenile delinquency.

2. SOME FACTS ABOUT DELINQUENCY

Before we can do anything about a problem (except perhaps to ignore it—which might not be a bad suggestion for some so-called juvenile offenses), we need to know something about it. Here are some of the more central facts about juvenile delinquency:

First, juvenile delinquency is predominately a male phenomenon. Most recent records (1969) show that boys outnumber girls in arrest and court statistics roughly 4 to 1. Furthermore, they get into different kinds of trouble. The Crime Commission observed that—

* * * more than half of the girls referred to juvenile court in 1965 were referred for conduct that would not be criminal if committed by adults; only one-fifth of the boys were referred for such conduct. Boys were referred to court primarily for larceny, burglary, and motor vehicle theft, in order of frequency; girls for running away, ungovernable behavior, larceny, and sex offenses.[9]

Review of most recent FBI information corroborates these observations (see table 2), where it can be seen that in only one arrest category—prostitution and/or commercialized vice—did females outnumber males in arrests (594 to 270). A fact to ponder here is that while the

[7] Uniform Crime Reports—1969, op. cit., p. 39.
[8] Daniel Glaser, The Effectiveness of a Prison and Parole System. Indianapolis: Bobbs-Merrill, 1964.
[9] The Challenge of Crime in a Free Society, op. cit., p. 173.

problem of delinquency—both in numbers and in character (if we are concerned about serious offenses) is a male one, the rates of delinquency for girls are increasing at a more rapid rate than is true for males (as can be seen in table 2, for male arrests between 1960 and 1969 increased by 93.2 percent, while for the same time period arrests for girls increased by 175.8 percent), suggesting that we should begin to examine more closely the problem of female delinquency—since few existing authoritative studies deal with this problem.

TABLE 2.—TOTAL ARREST TRENDS BY SEX, 1960–69 [1]

[2,474 agencies; 1969 estimated population 94,853,000] [2]

Offense charged	Males (under 18)			Females (under 18)		
	1960	1969	Percent change	1960	1969	Percent change
Total	406, 473	785, 188	+93. 2	70, 789	195, 265	+175. 8
Criminal homicide:						
(a) Murder and nonnegligent manslaughter	340	838	+146. 5	24	76	+216. 7
(b) Manslaughter by negligence	132	135	+2. 3	7	17	+142. 9
Forcible rape	1, 191	2, 214	+85. 9			
Robbery	7, 471	20, 179	+170. 1	366	1, 534	+319. 1
Aggravated assault	5, 722	12, 341	+115. 7	661	1, 868	+182. 6
Burglary—breaking or entering	52, 752	89, 830	+70. 3	1, 640	3, 898	+137. 7
Larceny-theft	78, 483	140, 414	+78. 9	13, 361	43, 677	+226. 9
Auto theft	31, 521	50, 632	+60. 6	1, 260	2, 925	+132. 1
Violent crime	14, 724	35, 572	+141. 6	1, 051	3, 478	+230. 9
Property crime	162, 756	280, 876	+72. 6	16, 261	50, 500	+210. 6
Subtotal for above offenses	177, 612	316, 583	+78. 2	17, 319	53, 995	+211. 8
Other assaults	10, 701	25, 411	+137. 5	1, 857	6, 216	+234. 7
Forgery and counterfeiting	1, 161	2, 235	+92. 5	348	702	+101. 7
Embezzlement and fraud	642	2, 001	+211. 7	145	504	+247. 6
Stolen property; buying, receiving, possessing	2, 335	9, 638	+312. 8	168	705	+319. 6
Weapons; carrying, possessing, etc	6, 225	10, 460	+68. 0	188	509	+170. 7
Prostitution and commercialized vice	121	270	+115. 7	272	594	+120. 2
Sex offenses (except forcible rape and prostitution)	6, 659	5, 747	−13. 7	2, 638	1, 574	−40. 3
Narcotic drug laws	1, 421	33, 835	+2, 281. 1	241	8, 599	+3, 468. 0
Gambling	1, 390	1, 288	−7. 9	42	45	+7. 1
Offenses against family and children	328	351	+7. 0	160	114	−28. 8
Driving under the influence	1, 025	2, 401	+134. 2	55	102	+85. 5
Liquor laws	14, 195	33, 664	+137. 2	2, 369	6, 592	+178. 3
Drunkenness	11, 210	26, 267	+134. 3	1, 290	3, 954	+206. 5
Disorderly conduct	38, 374	65, 612	+71. 0	6, 132	12, 762	+108. 1
Vagrancy	5, 885	6, 636	+12. 8	655	1, 116	+70. 4
All other offenses (except traffic)	127, 180	242, 798	+90. 9	36, 910	97, 177	+163. 3
Suspicion (not included in totals)	16, 830	12, 500	−25. 7	2, 586	2, 025	−21. 7

[1] Uniform Crime Reports—1969, Washington, D.C.: Federal Bureau of Investigation, U.S. Department of Justice, August 1970, p. 117.

[2] Based on comparable reports from 1,832 cities representing 78,027,000 population and 642 counties representing 16,826,000 population.

Note: Violent crime is offenses of murder, forcible rape, robbery and aggravated assault. Property crime is offenses of burglary, larceny $50 and over and auto theft.

Second, for purposes of guiding programs, we need to know when the problem is most likely to occur in the age cycle. The uniform crime report data for 1969 arrests, consistent with other data sources, show that relatively few delinquency cases occur under the age of 11, that arrests begin to build in early adolescence (11–14), peaking at 16 and 17, tapering off gradually until 21 or 22, then dropping off more rapidly with the onset of early to middle adulthood. (See table 3.)

TABLE 3.—TOTAL ARRESTS BY AGE, 1969[1]

[4,759 agencies; 1969 estimated population 143,815,000]

Age	Total number	Percent distribution	Cumulative percent	Age	Total number	Percent distribution	Cumulative percent
10 and under	76,429	1.3	1.3	24	148,000	2.5	51.4
11 to 12	128,564	2.2	3.5	25 to 29	560,732	9.6	61.0
13 to 14	361,413	6.2	9.7	30 to 34	429,429	7.3	68.3
15	292,479	5.0	14.7	35 to 39	406,454	6.9	75.2
16	328,733	5.6	20.3	40 to 44	416,714	7.1	82.3
17	312,597	5.3	25.6	45 to 49	363,709	6.2	88.5
18	307,474	5.2	30.8	50 to 54	271,398	4.6	93.1
19	259,366	4.4	35.2	55 to 59	188,044	3.2	96.3
20	215,541	3.7	38.9	60 to 64	112,227	1.9	98.2
21	214,961	3.7	42.6	65 and over	98,032	1.7	99.9
22	203,057	3.5	46.1	Not known	884	(2)	
23	165,909	2.8	48.9				

[1] Uniform Crime Reports—1969, Washington, D.C.: Federal Bureau of Investigation, U.S. Department of Justice, August, 1970, pp. 113–114.

Third, we need to know where the problem is located regionally. Juvenile delinquency occurs disproportionately in the cities. The juvenile court statistics for 1968 show the rate (per 1,000 youth population) of referrals of juveniles was higher in urban areas, 48.5, compared with 19.3 for rural areas, that is, the chance of being referred to a juvenile court was two times higher in urban areas. Furthermore, 65 percent of the total number of cases disposed of by juvenile courts were in urban areas, in contrast with 29 percent in semiurban, and only 6 percent of all cases occurring in rural areas. Both in relative and absolute numbers, then, delinquency is fundamentally an urban problem (see table 4).

TABLE 4.—NUMBER OF DELINQUENCY CASES (EXCLUDING TRAFFIC) DISPOSED OF BY JUVENILE COURT, UNITED STATES, 1968*

Type of court	Total		Boys		Girls	
	Number	Percent	Number	Percent	Number	Percent
Total	899,800	100	708,200	100	191,600	100
Urban	588,200	65	453,200	64	135,000	70
Semiurban	256,400	29	209,000	30	47,400	25
Rural	55,200	6	46,000	6	9,200	5

*Juvenile Court Statistics—1968, Office of Juvenile Delinquency and Youth Development, U.S. Department of Health, Education and Welfare, No. SRS–JD–131, 1970, p. 10.

This does not mean that the problem can be ignored elsewhere. Simply in sheer numbers, the arrest data for 1969 shows that in that year there were 324,068 under 18 arrests in suburban, and 51,732 in rural jurisdictions. Furthermore, in these areas there are dramatic signs of change. For example, in 1963 a total of 281 individual arrests were recorded for narcotic offenses for persons under the age of 18 in the suburbs. Suburban arrests in this under 18 group for drug offenses rose to 12,044 in 1968, and 14,396 by 1969. This 7-year, 5,123-percent increase (compared with the 1960–69 10.5-percent increase of arrests for all offenses for the 18 and over group, and the 105.4-percent increase in arrests for all offenses for the under 18 category) suggests that however we may want to focus on urban delinquency, to give adequate coverage to the changing patterns of youthful trouble at least some effort must be expended elsewhere.

Fourth, we must consider the thorny questions of social class and race. These social categories pose the following kinds of analysis problems[10] (1) classification of persons into "upper class," "working class," black or whatever is arbitrary, often clumsy and inept; (2) arrest figures or other official statictics may be reported for areas or groups while the class or ethnic characteristics of the base population for the areas or groups cannot be determined, rendering it impossible to determine comparative rates of behavior, and (3) procedures in the administration of criminal justice are biased against economically and ethnically disadvantaged population—a fact which is commonly accepted yet which functions in an unknown and nonspecifiable way; thus we can expect the delinquency of lower-class blacks, for example, to be much more visible in official statistics than would be true of middle-class whites even if the actual rates of deviance were identical.[11]

With these qualifications, what can be said? With respect to social class, official statistics and investigations utilizing official definitions of delinquency indicate that rates of delinquency are higher among lower and working class population.[12] Chilton in his study set in Indianapolis, reports that the lowest income areas, which accounted for 37 percent of the juvenile-court-age children, contributed 65 percent of the juvenile court cases. He concluded:

Our findings suggest that delinquency still appears to be related to transiency, poor housing, and economic indices; this supports the assumption of almost all sociological theories of delinquency, that delinquency is predominately a lower class phenomenon.[13]

Similarly, Reiss and Rhodes argue that while no simple relationship exists between class background and delinquency, higher levels are found among lower stratum youth in terms of: (a) self-reports of serious delinquent deviation, and (b) career orientation to delinquency.[14] Support for similar conclusions can be found in a number of other investigations,[15] although as we shall see in a moment, the phrase "no simple relationship" is an important qualification in this conclusion.

Comparable findings occur in the case of race, where official statistics, again with important qualifications, show higher rates of criminality for blacks than for whites. The 1969 uniform crime reports arrest data, for example, indicate that Negroes, who constitute 11.2 percent of the Nation's population, contribute 25.8 percent of all arrests of persons under the age of 18. This evidence indicates that Negroes are particularly overrepresented in offenses such as murder (contributing 73.4 percent of all arrests) and robbery (74 percent of

[10] For a more extended discussion, see Edwin H. Sutherland and Donald R. Cressey, *Criminology*, New York: J. B. Lippincott, 8th edition, 1970, pp. 132–151.
[11] See William J. Chambliss, *Crime and the Legal Process*, New York: McGraw Hill, 1969, pp. 85–89.
[12] Sutherland and Cressey, op. cit., p. 220.
[13] Ronald J. Chilton, "Continuity in Delinquency Area Research: A Comparison of Studies for Baltimore, Detroit, and Indianapolis," *American Sociological Review*, 29 (February 1964), pp. 71–83, pp. 82–83.
[14] Albert J. Reiss, Jr. and Albert L. Rhodes, "The Distribution of Juvenile Delinquency in the Social Class Structure," *American Sociological Review*, 26 (October 1961), pp. 720–732.
[15] M. G. Caldwell, "The Economic Status of Families of Delinquent Boys in Wisconsin," *American Journal of Sociology*, 37: 231–239, September, 1931; W. C. Kvaraceus, "Juvenile Delinquency and Social Class," *Journal of Educational Sociology*, 18: 51–54, September, 1944; William Lloyd Warner and Paul S. Lunt, *The Social Life of a Modern Community* (New Haven: Yale University Press, 1941), pp. 373–377.

arrests) among young persons. While such figures are important in directing some of our strategies of prevention and control, even without qualification it should be noted that of the 1,427,632 arrests of persons under the age of 18, the overwhelming proportion, 1,030,239 (72.7 percent), were white (see table 5).

What must also be recognized as operating conditions influencing both class and racial differentials in official delinquency statistics are the phenomena of cultural differences, as well as the varying capacities of different groups to care for the needs of their children. While the cliche "the American way of life" is a common one, one need not be a trained anthropologist to recognize that there are actually many ways of life in the United States. Power and influence, however, are not randomly distributed across such life styles. The poor, and the minority poor especially, exert little influence on the law enforcement, judicial, and correctional bureaucracies. This creates a threefold problem for such deprived people. One, some of the behavior of their adolescents, although often seem as "hell-raising" to be sure, is defined by such people as relatively normal behavior not meriting the official police action which it often evokes. Two, in the middle-class oriented view shared by most officials, there is an idealized conception of a good youth, a proper family style, and a wholesome neighborhood, and patterns different from these views are likely to be judged as problematic by such officials. On such evaluations, the minority poor are very likely to receive the lowest of ratings. Three, once deprived youths are identified as delinquent, their life style differences affect the course followed by authorities in yet another way. The official disposition processes in delinquency cases taken into account the ability of the young person involved, his family, and his local community to correct or to otherwise deal with the problem presented in an unofficial way. Where such resources are inadequate, there is an increased likelihood of continued official intervention, such as formal arrest, court referral, probation, or commitment to a correctional institution. Since such resources are almost always inadequate among the deprived, official police intervention and subsequent court referral are much more likely to occur in cases of deviancy among their children and youth.

Another important qualifying factor is time. Times change, and with them, patterns of delinquency. The studies of the citywide distribution of delinquency conducted in the 1930's uniformly reported a heavy concentration of youthful misbehavior in low-income areas. More recent, studies suggest that although delinquency continues to disproportionately burden poverty and disadvantaged areas, this correlation may be weakening somewhat, indicating the spread of delinquency outward into higher income areas. Other evidence supports this conclusion. For example, the Uniform Crime Report data shows a more rapid rate of increase in arrests of persons under 18 in the suburbs than in cities.[16] These trends have been reflected in the growing concern with the problems of middle-class delinquency.[17]

[16] *Uniform Crime Reports, op. cit.,* pp. 121 and 130.
[17] See for example, Edmund W. Vaz, *Middle-Class Juvenile Delinquency,* New York: Harper & Row, 1967.

TABLE 5.—TOTAL ARRESTS BY RACE, UNDER 18—1969 [1]

Offense charged	Percent distribution					
	White	Negro	Indian	Chinese	Japanese	All others (includes race unknown)
Total	72.2	25.8	0.8		0.1	1.1
Criminal homicide:						
(a) Murder and nonnegligent manslaughter	23.5	73.4	.7		.3	2.1
(b) Manslaughter by negligence	75.1	20.7	.8			3.4
Forcible rape	38.1	60.2	.5		.1	1.1
Robbery	24.3	74.0	.4		.1	1.3
Aggravated assault	46.7	51.4	.5		.1	1.3
Burglary—breaking or entering	64.6	33.6	.6		.1	1.1
Larceny—theft	66.8	31.3	.6	0.1	.2	1.1
Auto theft	63.4	33.8	.7		.2	1.8
Violent crime	34.0	64.1	.5		.1	1.3
Property crime	65.6	32.3	.6		.2	1.2
Subtotal for above offenses	63.0	34.9	.6		.1	1.2
Other assaults	53.9	44.2	.5		.1	1.3
Arson	72.6	26.4	.3		.1	.5
Forgery and counterfeiting	73.5	25.4	.6		.1	.4
Fraud	61.4	37.7	.2			.7
Embezzlement	74.1	24.5	.9			.5
Stolen property; buying, receiving, possessing	60.6	37.9	.4			1.1
Vandalism	80.2	18.6	.4			.8
Weapons; carrying, possessing, etc	55.9	42.4	.4		.1	1.3
Prostitution and commercialized vice	37.5	63.9		.1		.3
Sex offenses (except forcible rape and prostitution)	67.3	30.6	.4			1.7
Narcotic drug laws	85.7	12.7	.3		.2	1.1
Gambling	22.6	71.5			.1	5.8
Offenses against family and children	84.6	14.1	.4		.1	.7
Driving under the influence	90.5	7.9	1.0			.6
Liquor laws	94.3	3.7	1.6			.4
Drunkenness	85.2	10.0	4.2			.6
Disorderly conduct	66.5	31.9	.5			1.0
Vagrancy	71.4	25.2	.4	.1	.4	2.5
All other offenses (except traffic)	76.7	21.4	.7		.1	1.0
Suspicion	69.7	29.5	.5			.3
Curfew and loitering law violations	7.0	20.6	1.0		.2	1.1
Runaways	83.1	14.5	1.0		.1	1.3

[1] Uniform Crime Reports—1969, Washington, D.C.: Federal Bureau of Investigation, U.S. Department of Justice, August 1970, p. 120.

Note: Violent crime is offenses of murder, forcible rape, robbery and aggravated assault. Property crime is offenses of burglary, larceny $50 and over and auto theft.

Closely related to these trends has been the emergence of the importance of the school experience in the generation and support of delinquent careers. Over the years, a number of investigations have pointed out that delinquency is higher among those who do poorly in school.[18] What more recent research suggests is that the effects of school experience may be "mixing" with effects of other variables, such as social class, in important ways. In one study it was reported that any potential effect of social class was "washed out" by school experience. Among young persons who did well in school, the levels of delinquency were low and virtually identical for boys from both white and blue collar homes. Among those who did poorly, delinquency rates were high, this being true for both white and blue collar boys.[19]

[18] See William C. Kvaraceus, "Juvenile Delinquency and the School," New York: World Book Co., 1945; Martin Gold, "Status Forces in Delinquent Behavior," Ann Arbor: University of Michigan, 1963; Jackson Toby and Marcia Toby, "Low School Status as a Predisposing Factor in Subcultural Delinquency," U.S. Office of Education, Cooperative Research Project, No. 526, 1961.

[19] Kenneth Polk and David Halferty, "Adolescence, Commitment and Delinquency, "Journal of Research on Crime and Delinquency," 4, 82—96. Comparable findings have been reported in other communities by Arthur L. Stinchcombe, "Rebellion in a High School," Chicago: Quadrangle, 1964, and Kenneth Polk, "Class, Strain and Rebellion Among Adolescents," "Social Problems" (fall 1969), 17: 214—224.

What these investigations suggest is that there may be occurring over time a shift in the role that class and ethnic variables play so that the relevance of economic status may be eroded to a significant degree by an emerging search for talent on the part of schools, and a consequent increase in emphasis on achievement and its consequences. Cicourel and Kitsuse have suggested the importance of a specific dimension regarding the changing function of the school; namely, the preparation of youth for college:

The differentiation of college-going and non-college-going students defines the standards of performance by which they are evaluated by the school personnel and by which students are urged to evaluate themselves. It is the college-going student more than his non-college-going peer who is continually reminded by his teachers, counselors, parents, and peers of the decisive importance of academic achievement to the realization of his ambitions and who becomes progressively committed to this singular standard of self-evaluation. He becomes the future-oriented student interested in a delimited occupational specialty, with little time to give thought to the present or to question the implications of his choice and the meaning of his strivings.[20]

It is within this framework that the functional relationship between class background and school behavior may be changing:

* * * we suggest that the influence of social class upon the way students are processed in the highschool today is reflected in new and more subtle family school relations than the direct and often blatant manipulation of family class pressure * * *. Insofar as the highschool is committed to the task of identifying talent and increasing the proportion of college-going students, counselors will tend to devote more of their time and activities to those students who plan and are most likely to go to college and whose parents actively support their plans and make frequent inquiries at the school about their progress; namely, the students from the middle and upper social classes.[21]

Such a view emphasizes the role of the school in the life of the individual, and focuses on the question of the consequences that accrue to those who are unable to achieve within that system. Vintner and Sarri have pointed out that the school has a multitude of punishments which it can mete out to the malperforming youngster.[22] In "Valley City," Call reports that delinquent youth not only were likely to do poor academic work, but were less likely to participate in school activities, and more likely to see themselves as outsiders in the school setting.[23] For such youth the future begins to take on a different meaning. It they lack an orientation to the future, and appear unwilling to defer immediate gratifications in order to achieve long-range goals, it may be that they see fairly clearly that there is little future for them. Pearl suggests that such youth:

* * * develop a basic pessimism because they have a fair fix on reality. They rely on fate because no rational transition by system is open to them. They react against schools because schools are characteristically hostile to them.[24]

The hostility engendered is not simple individual hostility; there seems to occur a "trouble-making" subculture which may have its roots in the "locking-out" process of the school. Such an interpretation

---

[20] Aaron V. Cicourel and John L. Kitsuse, "The Educational Decisionmakers," New York: Bobbs-Merrill, 1963, p. 146.
[21] Aaron V. Cicourel and John I. Kitsuse, op. cit., pp. 144-145.
[22] Robert D. Vintner and Rosemary C. Sarri, "Malperformance in the Public School: A Group Work Approach," Social Work (January 1965) 10, 3-13.
[23] Donald J. Call, "Delinquency, Frustration, and Noncommitment," Eugene, Oreg.: Unpublished Ph. D. dissertation, University of Oregon, 1965.
[24] Arthur Pearl, "Youth in Lower Class Settings," in M. Sherif and C. Sherif. "Problems of Youth," New York: Aldine Press, 1965.

is not inconsistent with the observations of Empey and Rabow in a small city in Utah:

Despite the fact that Utah County is not a high urbanized area when compared to large metropolitan centers, the concept of a "parent" delinquent subculture has real meaning for it. While there are no clear cut gangs, per se, it is surprising to observe the extent to which delinquent boys from the entire county, who have never met, know each other by reputation, go with the same girls, use the same language, or can seek each other out when they change high schools. About half of them are permanently out of school, do not participate in any regular institutional activities, are reliant almost entirely upon the delinquent system for social acceptance and participation.[25]

Call presents evidence which suggests that delinquent youth not only are more likely to spend their spare time with friends, but that their friends are much more likely to be outside the school system.[26] Polk's factor analysis study suggests that delinquency fits into a pattern of rejection of commitment to school success accompanied by an involvement in a pattern of peer rebellion against adults.[27] Pearl expresses the role such processes play in enabling youngsters to cope with the locking-out process:

A limited gratification exists in striving for the impossible and as a consequence poor youth create styles, coping mechanisms, and groups in relation to the systems which they can and cannot negotiate. Group values and identifications emerge in relation to the forces opposing them.[28]

The point of this discussion is that these youth are not passive receptors of the stigma that develops within the school setting. When locked out, they respond by seeking an interactional setting where they can function comfortably. The fact that the resulting subculture has built-in oppositional forces becomes an important aspect of the delinquency problem encountered in a community. We deal not with isolated alienated youth, but with the loosely organized participants of a subculture which provides important group supports for the deviancy observed. Individualized treatment aimed at such youth which does not take into account the importance and functioning of the group supports within this culture can have limited, if any, impact. What is needed is an approach that will counteract the social processes which generate this subcultural response.

Cutting across these trends, and qualifying any assumptions we might make about the class and ethnic concentrations of delinquency and crime, are the forms of law violation connected with rapidly emerging patterns of youth protest. There is scarcely anything new in the conflict between generations as an idea.

The rapid social change over the past century, and the close involvement of young persons in that change, inevitably has convinced at least some of the older generation that the young are hopelessly degenerate, and at least some of the younger generation that the old are hopelessly old-fashioned and out of touch. In some respects, there is little new in the nature of the differences that currently separate the old from the young—for many years youth have continuously evolved their own styles of dress, language, music, and fun, with some of this fun result-

[25] Lamar T. Empey and Jerome Rabow, "The Provo Experiment in Delinquency Rehabilitation," "American Sociological Review" (October 1961) 26 :674–695.
[26] Call, op. cit.
[27] Polk and Halferty, op. cit.
[28] Pearl, op. cit.

ing in potential contact with police (drinking and fighting being two of the more common examples).[29]

There is one theme, however, that runs through some of the current youth culture activity that gives this group of young persons a characteristic posture seen only rarely in earlier groups of youth—this being the protest theme. One central function performed by this protest theme is to legitimize engaging in behavior that violates some existing codes of behavior, including the legal codes. To be sure, in previous decades young people together would violate the law, and would draw support for such violation from some form of what sociologists call a subculture. Thus, a group of boys might go out for an evening to have a good time, and during the evening might drink because, after all, that's what the guys expect. We find nothing new, then, in the idea that adolescent groups occasionally pressure members to engage in behavior which violates the law.

Where the newness lies is in the posture taken toward the law and supporting legal and community structures themselves. Much of what went on in earlier youth cultures (and to some extent still goes on today) involved an elaborate "conspiracy of silence," which served to protect the individuals from the consequences of law violation by concealing the behavior. The "conspiracy of silence" does not openly raise questions about the legitimacy of laws—in fact it most often assumes that the law is legitimate but weaves a protective rationale around the given instance so that under the given circumstances engaging in the illegal act is permissible.

The open character of much of the current youth protest behavior contrasts sharply with the secrecy that is essential to the "conspiracy of silence" characteristic of more traditional forms of delinquency. This openness derives from the fact that often the issue is the law or the legal structure itself, which can only be challenged in a public, highly visible setting. Sit ins, political rallies, demonstrations, marches (all of which may or may not result in law violations and/or arrests) are dramatic because of the openness and visibility of their confrontation with "authority." Confrontation is basically what they are about, so that the secrecy of other styles of youthful behavior makes no sense.

In addition to the public character, a second distinctive feature that separates youth protest activity involving law violation from traditional delinquency seems to be the ideological base of much protest. There seems to be little in the way of theory, ideology, or any form of a framework of formal, political ideas that young people draw upon when they fight, steal, rob, or drink (or whatever) in more traditional delinquent or youth subcultures. In protest activity, however, the ideological components usually appear as central distinguishing features, as for example, in the conflict theories of social change articulated by some radical youth groups.

In terms of the present discussion of trends in crime and delinquency, the protest style as it expands will confound statements about the class or ethnic distributions of delinquency. Three main forms of protest can be identified for purposes of the present discussion: (a) "campus unrest" where the context is the high school and college setting and where in addition to campus issues, the targets are part of the wider political scene of today, such as war, the draft, poverty, or racism; (b) "ethnic identity protest," which centers around ethnically defined claims and grievances such as among blacks or chicanos; and (c) "youth culture withdrawal," which focuses on those aspects of youth life styles that cause conflict with the law, most notably because of drug use and addiction, but also occasionally in terms of codes dealing with sex or obscenity.

Campus unrest poses a particular problem for many because, far from deriving from those at the "bottom of the heap," it is found among those with the most advantages. It is concentrated among those who are, or have been, in colleges or universities. It is concentrated among those who have demonstrated high levels of academic performance. It is found among persons who come from homes that are both stable and economically advantaged.

Especially problematic in the matter of campus protest and in ethnic identity protest is that most of what constitutes the behavior is legitimate political activity, motivated out of social concern, and which is clearly protected constitutionally by the first amendment guarantees regarding freedom of speech and assembly. We thus must carefully distinguish such behavior from problems ordinarily dealt with by law enforcement agencies. Certainly it cannot be easily argued that a national goal is to create compliant youth who are either too timid or fearful to raise their voices to oppose what they sincerely believe to be injustices.

Terrorism is another matter. The Bill of Rights does not give protestors the right to bomb and to otherwise destroy property. When protest reaches such levels, it will not be tolerated. Yet, the bind in part remains. It is not easy to permit, even encourage, legitimate youthful protest, on the one hand, yet control violent protest on the other. This is, however, the challenge.

Ethnic protest also has altered some of our earlier notions about ethnicity and delinquency, partly because it, too, leads to a different form of behavior (protest) some of which may at times violate the law. Such protest has also resulted in a new social mixture for the groups involved—for example, in black action groups both middle-class and lower-class blacks are involved and also a few whites.

Youth cultural withdrawal can be seen posing three particular problems. First, it provides supports and rationale for engaging in behavior which violates the law, and, as in the case of "hard" drugs, at least, endangers the very lives of the young persons involved. Second, it results in a spreading of "troublesome" behavior throughout the class and ecological structure—being common among the poor, as well as among the more affluent. Third, the withdrawal itself means the loss of talent and resources which might be utilized in a variety of ways to increase the quality of the human condition in the Nation.

Each of these three forms of protest shares an attribute that is fundamental in guiding any societal response. Such protest is collective behavior—that is, it is not under the control of the dominant cultural norms or established social relations. In fact, in essential ways such protest activities represent widespread social movements against the norms and institutions of established society. For those aspects for which some corrective action is seen as necessary, action of necessity would seem best aimed at not only individual actors, but also at the variables which contribute to their collective response as well.

3. IMPLICATIONS

If all present trends are maintained, we can anticipate a continued rise in rates of delinquent and criminal behavior in the United States. But this rise, if our earlier facts are correct, is not going to be a simple increase of the present problems. Instead, we can expect that youthful deviance, since it is increasing more rapidly, will come to occupy an even more central position in the crime picture of the United States. A by-product of this, of course, will be that we can expect a more rapid increase in the rise of property crimes than crimes of violence, since the property offenses are predominantly juvenile, while violence offenses most often involve older persons (drug offenses also can be expected to rise, of course). Such predictions are consistent with the 1960–69 trend figures where the greatest increases (in terms of percent change) were observed in such offenses as drugs, stolen property, robbery, and larceny (see table 6).

The first programmatic implication that can be drawn, then, is that strategies for the prevention and control of law violating behavior should plan for an increasing emphasis on programs targeted at children and youth.

TABLE 6.—TOTAL ARREST TRENDS, 1960–69 [1]

[2,474 agencies; 1969 estimated population 94,853,000 [2]]

Offense charged	Number of persons arrested, total all ages		
	1960	1969	Percent change
Total	3,323,741	4,126,216	+24.1
Criminal homicide:			
(a) Murder and nonnegligent manslaughter	4,809	8,827	+83.6
(b) Manslaughter by negligence	1,931	2,016	+4.4
Forcible rape	6,862	10,747	+56.6
Robbery	32,538	63,534	+95.3
Aggravated assault	54,893	84,573	+54.1
Burglary—breaking or entering	117,359	178,334	+52.0
Larceny—theft	192,450	353,897	+83.9
Auto theft	54,369	94,329	+73.5
Violent crime	99,102	167,681	+69.2
Property crime	364,178	626,560	+72.0
Subtotals for above offenses	465.211	796,257	+71.2
Other assaults	121,179	187,381	+54.6
Forgery and counterfeiting	20,529	26,911	+31.1
Embezzlement and fraud	33,114	49,540	+49.6
Stolen property; buying, receiving, possessing	9,476	34,405	+263.1
Weapons; carrying, possessing, etc	30,736	66,750	+117.2
Prostitution and commercialized vice	25,633	41,265	+61.0
Sex offenses (except forcible rape and prostitution)	45,246	37,452	−17.2
Narcotic drug laws	30,904	182,909	+491.9
Gambling	118,299	67,590	−42.9
Offenses against family and children	37,010	35,690	−3.6
Driving under the influence	138,390	239,776	+73.3
Liquor laws	81,029	130,945	+61.6
Drunkenness	1,204,668	1,040,493	−13.6
Disorderly conduct	396,155	426,588	+7.7
Vagrancy	127,319	83,980	−34.0
All other offenses (except traffic)	438,843	678,284	+54.6
Suspicion (not included in totals)	89,449	72,391	−19.1

[1] Uniform Crime Reports—1969, Washington, D.C.: Federal Bureau of Investigation, U.S. Department of Justice, August, 1970, p. 110.

[2] Based on comparable reports from 1,832 cities representing 78,027,000 population and 642 counties representing 16,826,000 population.

Note: Violent crime is offenses of murder, forcible rape, robbery and aggravated assault. Property crime is offenses of burglary, larceny $50 and over and auto theft.

Viewed broadly, an effective national effort to prevent and to cure delinquency and youth crime would have three major salients: First, a broad-scale attack upon the fundamental social conditions of poverty and degradation, and social and economic discrimination, which do not give large groups of children a fair start in life and constitute the root causes of youth failure and resort to delinquency as an alternate way of life. This approach was stressed by both the President's Commission on Law Enforcement and Administration of Justice in 1967 [30] and the National Commission on the Causes and Prevention of Violence in 1969.[30a] The areas where high ratio of illegitimacy, broken families, and school drop-outs are prevalent are typically the very areas where delinquency rates are high. The seeds of delinquency may well be planted in the early years. Expenditures to provide better health, education, and social conditions for children, especially disadvantaged children, would seem to rank high in such a positive social effort to eradicate the breeding ground of much delinquency. But the costs will be high and major social realignments essential to such a social effort are, obviously, not to be easily nor rapidly achieved.

Second, an improved antidelinquency effort would be needed, targeted at the youths who, despite some gains in a basic, general preventive effort, still remain highly delinquency-prone or become enmeshed in delinquent behavior: Such a more targeted effort would involve strengthening of (a) the youth-oriented portions of the criminal justice system, namely the law enforcement, adjudicative, and rehabilitational areas, and (b) special community-centered services to keep the near-delinquent from sinking into delinquency by giving them better educational, training, job, and other opportunities and to serve likewise as a more efficient bridge between the criminal justice process and the regular community for those delinquents who are completing their rehabilitation.

But the development of plans to deal with delinquency must take into account the trends that are reshaping the composition of the population of delinquents as well. The rise in rates of "white collar" and of female delinquency suggest that: (a) we need to gather more information about these forms of deviance, and (b) new strategies for dealing with these populations will need to be developed.

The possibility that school experiences contribute fundamentally to the development of delinquency also suggests that mechanisms need to be created with link educational and correctional systems to provide new kinds of effective delinquency prevention and control programs. Even beyond this, it is probable that we should give support to the development of new kinds of educational procedures which alter the present "locking-out" process and which provide ways for "problem" children to become responsible participants in the school community.

Third, the emergence of illegal forms of youth protest suggest that for certain types of youth there is a need for entirely new strategies of intervention. The collective character of such protest means that

[30] President's Commission on Law Enforcement and Administration of Justice, "The Challenge of Crime in a Free Society," Washington, D.C.: Government Printing Office, 1967, pp. 59–60.
[30a] U.S. National Commission on the Causes and Prevention of Violence, "To Establish Justice, to Insure Domestic Tranquility: Final Report" Washington: U.S. Government Printing Office, 1969, pp. 27–28.

traditional individually oriented treatment processes are inappropriate. Instead, what would seem to be required is: (a) an understanding of the social and cultural forces which provide the supports for such collective phenomena, and (b) the development of strategies which intervene in appropriate, acceptable, and effective ways to develop similar collective supports for legitimate behavior.

B. THE RESPONSE: THE JUVENILE POLICE-COURT-CORRECTIONAL SYSTEM

As the problem of youthful law violation has become more visible in contemporary times, and as the yearly population of youthful offenders has surpassed the one million mark, a large scale police-court-correctional system has been developed in response (see chart D).

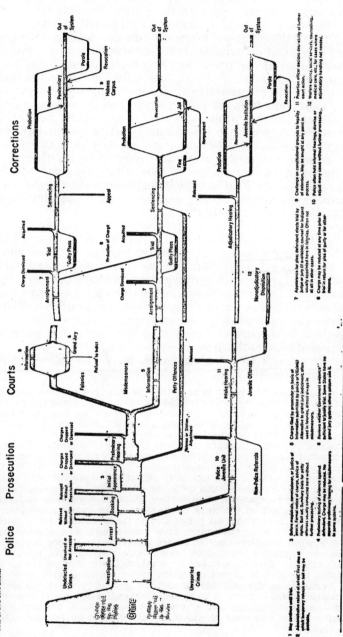

This chart seeks to present a simple yet comprehensive view of the movement of cases through the criminal justice system. Procedures in individual jurisdictions may vary from the pattern shown here. The differing weights of line indicate the relative volumes of cases disposed of at various points in the system, but this is only suggestive since no nationwide data of this sort exists.

CHART D

This chart is taken from pp. 8–9 of The President's Commission on Law Enforcement and Administration of Justice, The Challenge of Crime in a Free Society (Washington: U.S. Government Printing Office, 1967).

*The Challenge of Crime in a Free Society, New York: Avon Books, 1968, pp. 72–73.

Two points should be made about this system. First, this system as a legal system is separated by the law itself from other community institutions (schools, for example) both in procedure and logic—however important integration with these other elements may be. To put it another way, the legal mandates given to police, courts, and corrections give the principal responsibility for dealing with the problems of crime and delinquency to these three institutions, even though the root causes of the problems dealt with may lie outside of these institutions themselves. By implication, then, much of the leadership for improved intervention strategies for dealing with crime and delinquency must come from the police, courts, and corrections even though such intervention may often involve other community institutions. Yet the resources provided to the criminal justice system have been extremely meager and it is becoming increasingly clear that this system alone does not possess the necessary range of tools either to prevent delinquency in the first place or to rehabilitate the youth who becomes serious delinquents. Further, the links between the specialized system and broader community institutions, for example, the schools, are often weak and sometimes entirely absent.

Second, within the criminal justice system, planning for youth is complicated by the fact that two kinds of systems exist for this group. For those under a certain age (the age varying by State and within some stages, by offense), there is a juvenile justice system (the lower line of chart D), while for young persons above that age, the adult criminal justice system applies. Both systems must be considered since in virtually all States young persons above the age of 18 will be treated as adults (in some adult procedures apply to those over 16) and in many there is concurrent jurisdiction for certain age groups at the discretion of local authorities.

The President's Crime Commission made the following observations about these systems:

Any criminal justice system is an apparatus society uses to enforce the standards of conduct necessary to protect individuals and the community. It operates by apprehending, prosecuting, convicting, and sentencing those members of the community who violate the basic rules of group existence. The action taken against lawbreakers is designed to serve three purposes beyond the immediately punitive one. It removes dangerous people from the community; it deters others from criminal behavior; and it gives society an opportunity to attempt to transform lawbreakers into lawabiding citizens.

The criminal justice system has three separately organized parts—the police, the courts, and corrections—and each has distinct tasks. However, these parts are by no means independent of each other. What each one does and how it does it has a direct effect on the work of the others. The courts must deal, and can only deal, with those whom the police arrest; the business of corrections is with those delivered to it by the courts. How successfully corrections reforms convicts determines whether they will once again become police business and influences the sentences the judges pass; police activities are subject to court scrutiny and are often determined by court decisions. And so reforming or reorganizing any part of procedure of the system changes other parts or procedures. Furthermore, the criminal process, the method by which the system deals with individual cases, is not a hodgepodge of random actions. It is rather a continuum—an orderly progression of events—some of which, like arrest and trial, are highly visible and some of which, though of great importance, occur out of public view.[31]

---

[31] "The Challenge of Crime in a Free Society," op. cit., pp. 70–71.

The Crime Commission also compiled data on the number of individuals who receive institutional commitments, and the cost of such programs (see table 7). In 1965, the total average daily population of 62,773 juveniles were institutionalized, at a cost of $226,809,600, with an average yearly cost per offender of $3,613. Some idea of the comparative costs can be found in the fact that while many more individual juveniles, 285,431, were involved in the average day, both the operating costs ($93,613,400) and the average cost per offender per year ($328) were much smaller for community correctional programs.

What can we conclude about the effectiveness of these programs? Don C. Gibbons has the following to offer:

"The efficiency of training schools in arresting progress of deviant careers is largely conjectural, in that careful follow-up studies of these places are hard to find. However, one study has been carried out in California, a State which has a juvenile correctional system widely acknowledged to be the most advanced in this Nation. The results of that investigation are not encouraging and surely do not lead to much confidence in the operations of training schools in other States. In this research, 4000 delinquent wards discharged from the Youth Authority in 1953 and 1958 were examined. Less than 20 percent of the female wards acquired any sort of criminal record in the 5 year follow-up period after discharge, so the girls most commonly become "successes." Quite different paths are followed by boys. About 22 percent of the male wards had been discharged from Youth Authority custody as a result of being sent to prison. Another 22 percent were sentenced to prison within 5 years after discharge, while another 26 percent received one or more nonprison sentences (fines, jail, and/or probation). Thus only 30 percent of the boys managed to remain free from detected criminality."[32]

TABLE 7.—SOME NATIONAL CHARACTERISTICS OF CORRECTIONS, 1965 [1]

	Average daily population of offenders	Total operating costs	Average cost of offender per year	Number of employees in corrections	Number of employees treating offenders
Juvenile corrections:					
Institutions	62,773	$226,809,600	$3,613	31,687	5,621
Community	285,431	93,613,400	328	9,633	7,706
Adult felon corrections:					
Institutions	221,597	435,594,500	1,966	51,866	3,220
Community	369,897	73,251,900	198	6,352	5,081
Misdemeanant corrections:					
Institutions	141,303	147,794,200	1,045	19,195	501
Community	201,385	28,682,900	142	2,430	1,944
Total	1,282,386	1,005,746,500		121,163	24,073

[1] The Challenge of Crime in a Free Society, New York: Avon Books, 1968, p. 391.

Similar pessimistic figures can be found on adult corrections, where estimates of recidivism among parolees range from 20 to 30 percent (see table 8). Glaser in his study of Federal adult offenders reports that the common assumption of a two-thirds recidivism rate was not accurate (although it does seem to be true for juveniles as noted by Gibbons above), the actual rate being closer to 25 percent. He also identified, as associated with parole failure such factors as long periods of prior confinement, leaving home at an early age, records of property offenses, and age (younger offenders having higher violation rates).

[32] Don C. Gibbons, "Society, Crime, and Criminal Careers," Englewood Cliffs, N.J.; Prentice-Hall, 1968, p. 517.

TABLE 8.—CALIFORNIA PAROLE VIOLATORS RETURNED TO PRISON, 1954–65[1]

	New commitments	Technical returns	Total violations
1954	10.8	9.7	20.0
1955	7.6	8.7	16.7
1956	8.5	7.4	15.1
1957	9.4	8.7	18.2
1958	11.0	13.1	24.8
1959	10.0	11.2	21.1
1960	11.9	12.8	24.5
1961	10.9	16.9	27.3
1962	11.0	17.1	28.9
1963	10.4	21.6	32.0
1964	8.4	21.2	29.6
1965	8.9	22.4	31.3

[1] "State of California, Crime and Delinquency in California," 1965 (Sacramento: State of California, Bureau of Criminal Statistics, 1966), p. 136 in Don C. Gibbons, "Society, Crime and Criminal Careers," Englewood Cliffs, New Jersey: Prentice-Hall, 1968, p. 518.

If the results from more traditional correctional efforts have been less than successful what about more specialized treatment programs? The evidence would indicate that most institutionally based treatment or therapy programs have had limited success. Some of these programs include: (the description of programs are drawn from Gibbon's excellent summary in his "Society, Crime and Criminal Careers," pp. 515–529).

(1) *Wayne County Clinic for Child Study.*[33]—From 1924 to 1948 a heavy increase of psychiatric professionals was added to the clinic staff of the juvenile court in Detroit, and an analysis of the outcomes of this program should indicate the effects of psychiatric treatment within the court framework. But the follow-up study of boys who had been in court in 1930, 1935, 1940 and 1948 showed no such effectiveness. In 1930, 45 percent of the boys were later arrested by the police, as contrasted to 39 percent of those who had been in the clinic in 1948. The significant increase of costs in the clinic operations in other words, did not seem to be accompanied by decreased recidivism.

(2) *Intensive Treatment Project at San Quentin and Chino Prisons.*[33a]—A second study of psychotherapy occurred in these two California prisons in the form of an experimental program where treatment groups received intensive individual and group therapy, with control groups being processed through the regular institutional program. The results of the program showed no important differences in parole adjustment between the treated and untreated prisoners.

(3) *Pilot Intensive Counseling Organization Program.*[34]—A third case of psychotherapy is the PICO project which involved treatment and control groups of prisoners at Devel Vocational Institution in California. The treated subjects were given intensive, individual therapy, administered by trained therapists, along with some group counseling. The control group wards received regular institutional attention which consisted of much less counseling. All individuals in

[33] LaMay Adamson and H. Warren Dunham, "Clinical Treatment of Male Delinquents: A Case Study in Effort and Result," American Sociological Review, XXI, (June 1956), pp. 312–20.
[33a] California Department of Corrections, Second Annual Report, "Intensive Treatment Program" (Sacramento: State of California, Department of Corrections, 1958).
[34] Stuart Adams, "The PICO Project," in The Sociology of Punishment and Correction, ed. Norman Johnston, Leonard Savitz, and Marvin E. Wolfgang (New York: John Wiley and Sons, Inc., 1962), pp. 213–24.

the project were placed into categories of "amendable" and "non-amendable," depending on the level of anxiety which would make them likely to respond to therapy.

The criterion of failure for the program was "return to custody" or parole violation. The treated amendables showed the best post-release performance, followed by the control group amendable prisoners. The treated nonamendable inmates showed the poorest post-release record. They apparently became worse rather than better as a result of treatment. In this case, then, some positive effects of treatment were suggestive, but the negative impact also noted tempers any optimism about this form of treatment.

(4) *Highfields.*[35]—This experimental program at Highfields in New Jersey is an example of what has been termed "milieu management." (Milieu programs usually occur in institutions where efforts are made to coordinate all aspects of the operation into striving for the goal of rehabilitation.) The delinquent boys in this program were placed in a small institution and were subjected to a full "treatment diet" of "guided group interaction."

Two major efforts have been made to assess the effectiveness of this program. In both evaluations, the Highfields boys were compared to youths from the Annadale Reformatory (boys from both institutions were judged to be similar). In the first evaluation, recidivism comparisons showed that 18 percent of the Highfields boys violated parole in the first year after release, as contrasted to 33 percent of the Annadale boys. Highfields boys also performed better over extended periods of time. The second evaluation found that 63 percent of the Highfields youth completed treatment and remained in the community at least a year as contrasted with 47 percent of the Annadale youths. Early optimism concerning Highfields has been tempered both by more careful assessment of Highfields itself, and by the failure of similar programs (see below).

(5) *Paso Robles School.*[36]—An experimental group counseling program was established using various combinations of group counseling and community meetings in three dormitories. A fourth living unit served as a control in which the conventional institutional pattern was maintained.

The findings are much less impressive than those from Highfields. The major result was the improvement of the institutional atmosphere in those dormitories where the counseling and group meetings were held. But, the wards who had been in the experimental program did no better on parole than the control group.

(6) *The Fremont Experiment.*[37]—This California milieu venture involved the random assignment of 16- to 19-year-old males, eligible for a work therapy program, into either the Fremont program or a regular institutional program. The Fremont boys were subjected to a "treatment diet" of a varied therapeutic program including small

[35] H. Ashley Weeks, "Youthful Offenders at Highfields," Ann Arbor: University of Michigan Press, 1963: Lloyd W. McCorkle, Albert Elias, and F. Lovell Bixby, "The Highfields Story," New York: Holt, Rinehart and Winston, Inc., 1958.
[36] Joachim P. Seckel, "Experiments in Group Counseling at Two Youth Authority Institutions," Sacramento: State of California, Department of the Youth Authority, 1965.
[37] Joachim P. Seckel, "The Fremont Experiment: Assessment of Residential Treatment of a Youth Authority Reception Center," Sacramento: State of California, Department of the Youth Authority, 1967.

group therapy, large group forums, work assignments at the clinic school classes and field trips.

Unfortunately, the experimental outcome was not extremely impressive when compared to regular institutional handling. In a 2-year follow-up after parole, the experimental group and control group showed no statistical significant difference in either recidivism or seriousness of post-release offenses.

(7) *The Fricot Ranch Study.*[38]—The design of this project also involved random assignment of boys (ages 8 to 14) into either a 20-boy experimental lodge or a regular 50-boy living unit. The experimental unit was planned to provide both intensified contacts between group supervisers and wards and to offer other therapeutic experiences.

Participation in the intensified program had a delaying effect upon recidivism, so that treated wards stayed out of more trouble, longer than did the control subjects. But by the end of a 3-year follow-up period, about 80 percent of both treated and control boys failed on parole.

COMMUNITY TREATMENT PROGRAMS

The one area where some significant gains in effective rehabilitation have been made is in the community treatment programs. The rather recent development in corrections has centered around the treatment of offenders in the community rather than in a correctional institution.

In community treatment efforts being tried in California, the delinquent youths spend several hours a day in an institution (similar to Highfields) receiving counseling and other aids. However, the youths remain in the community and live at home, so this program is an alternative to incarceration. Youths in the experimental groups have been compared to matched control subjects who have been institutionalized. For example, experimental subjects from community treatment efforts in Stockton and Sacramento, Calif., who have been on parole for 15 months show a parole violation rate of 29 percent compared to a violation rate of 48 percent for the control group cases.[38a] These results, modest as they are, suggest that community treatment might be an effective alternative to institutionalization.

Not only the Nation, but also its correctional and judicial agencies have been overwhelmed by the problem of responding to crime and juvenile delinquency. From all the above, it would appear unlikely that to continue to expand conventional correctional programs and hope for a reduction in the problem of delinquency is absurd. The inability of the agencies to handle the problem is reflected in: (*a*) the continued, inexorable rise in rates of law violation, (*b*) the high levels of recidivism generally, and (*c*) the maintenance of high levels of recidivism even among those who have been exposed to what appear to be competent well-operated correctional programs.

Some tentative leads can be suggested from these experiences. First, we must remember that whatever it entails, correction or rehabilita-

---

[38] Carl F. Jesness, "The Fricot Ranch Study," Sacramento: State of California, Department of the Youth Authority, 1965.

[38a] Department of the Youth Authority, "The Status of Current Research in the California Youth Authority," Sacramento: State of California, 1966, pp. 22–27.

tion is something that ultimately will, and must, be determined in natural settings of the community and by community standards. In the commonsense everyday world what we expect of correctional activity is that the traditional type of offender will be able to reenter the community and behave. Behaving in this sense means, first, that the individual not violate the law. Second, and stated more positively, it is anticipated that the person will assume some of the attributes of a legitimate identity, taking on one of the many forms of acceptable educational, occupational, family, political, and cultural roles.

It is in this regard that we begin to see some of the difficulties faced by correctional activities as they are presently constituted. For one, most so-called correctional activities isolate and segregate the offender from the community. This is true not only of incarceration, but also for much of community-based correctional efforts as well. In the case of the community response (of police and courts), the problem we encounter is the stigma that can result from correctional procedures, this stigma having as a potential consequence the further locking in of the young person into a troublesome role.

A second factor to be dealt with here is that the forces which generate and shape deviant careers lie within community institutions, and especially in the areas of education and work. When the rehabilitative effort is organized in a manner such that it segregates itself from these community activities, highly centralized juvenile court probation, and other correctional services may leave the individual correctional worker with little systematic and meaningful access to school, employment, recreational, or other community agencies. While the individual correctional worker may have individual contacts, his ability to influence the policy of other organizations for his client-offenders is negligible.

Yet, it may be precisely these organizations that provide the most meaningful resource for rehabilitation, and even the settings which give some positive meaning to this term. For most who function in legitimate roles, central to their identity will be the character of their work (and their feelings of competence and meaning that flows from work), how they stand in school (doing well in school yields social and personal rewards that go far beyond simple academic performance), and the extent to which they feel some potency to effect decisions influencing their lives—to list some of the more fundamental community experiences. The centrality of work, education, recreation, participation in politics, and other community activities for maintaining persons in legitimate roles suggests that these experiences might play a critical role in rehabilitative procedures.

If correction requires adjustment to community standards, if many of the factors which create the problem of youthful deviance lie inside various community institutions, and if the potentially more potent corrective experiences lie in community settings, then the inescapable conclusion is that there must be more aggressive development of community-situated efforts at correction. This will mean more than creating ways for offenders to remain in the community to work through their difficulties with counselors, probation or parole officers. What will be required will be alternative institutional arrangements, structural changes in other words, which extend new options for educational, work, recreational, and political involvement. The need for the latter in dealing effectively with those offenders involved in youth protest movements seems inescapable. The central task is to provide meaningful opportunities to delinquents for success in normal community social and economic roles. Our next task, then, is to specify the location, rationale, and shape, of such structural changes and to determine how to beef up resources so the delinquents can truly be rehabilitated.

In all this, of course, it should be recognized that basic social prevention of delinquency is more desirable than its cure after it is present. But to combat the major forces which contribute to delinquency, such as unemployment, poverty, racism, and inadequate educational systems, we would have to undertake difficult and not easily accepted legislative programs—programs aimed at a fundamental transformation of our society. Thus, for example, the employment situation facing most delinquents can be altered significantly only if a full-employment economy is established, accompanied by new patterns of occupational and educational training for the deprived which recognize that present and future society emphasizes credentials. Thus, new credentialling mechanisms (linking the worlds of work and education) would have to be a basic component of any such employment strategy.

C. Some Possible Foci of Community-Based Programs for the Delinquent

In addition to broad-range programs aimed at the wider social forces operating to create delinquency, we can suggest a series of more specific, limited steps aimed at deliquency itself which can be undertaken in local neighborhoods:

1. DEVELOPMENT OF RESPONSIBLE AND RESPONSIVE COMMUNITIES

There seems to be a clear need to encourage and facilitate the assumption of responsibility for correctional tasks at the local community level. The correctional process utilized in the United States suffers from its isolation and segregation from the rest of the community and its institutions. It typically applies resources which are too little and too late. Kim Nelson has noted:

There is general consensus in both professional and academic circles that American communities are relatively impotent in developing indigenous programs for the prevention of crime and delinquency. Community leadership appears all too willing to delegate (or default) its responsibility for dealing with antisocial behavior. Eventually that responsibility is assumed by large public agencies which take jurisdiction over the offender only after he has been defined as a lawbreaker by judicial action. Although extremely expensive, these services (probation, institutions, and parole) never seem to catch up with the need. They come too late to be "preventive" in the most desirable sense of the word. Moreover, the policies are controlled from political and administrative centers far removed from the "grassroots" of city and neighborhood where delinquency and crime originate through obscure and complex processes.[39]

---

[39] E. K. Nelson, "Community Approaches to the Prevention of Crime and Delinquency," Los Angeles: Youth Studies Center, University of Southern California, 1961, p. 1.

One problem identified by Nelson is the tendency for correctional programs to retreat from the community. Kobrin observes that it is not uncommon for correctional programs:

* * * whatever their initial intention or resolve, understandably tend to move away from direct contact with the delinquent and his milieu. Distance is achieved by interposing institutional forms between workers and delinquents, as in programs of formal and official treatment, or by dealing with the delinquent as a person arbitrarily abstracted from his social environment, as in programs based on individual therapy. This kind of evolution is comprehensive in the former type of retreat because the delinquent arouses anger and resentment in the law-abiding person, who consequently is hard put to form a sympathetic identification with him. Retreat from the milieu of the delinquent is even more under-standable, for nothing would seem more unrewarding than to attempt to put aright the social disorder of the delinquency area.[40]

In the past it has proven expedient, then, both for the correctional system and for the community, to segregate and isolate the offender from the community. As a consequence, correctional agencies are not responsive to neighborhood and community social organization, and are unable to articulate effectively with such local organizations. It is precisely this neighborhood level of organization, however, that can play such a central role in programs of reintegration and correction. Kobrin argues that the inference is unavoidable that effective correctional activities must somehow become activities of the residents constituting the natural social world of the offender. He notes, further, that effective community action will require a substantial involvement of local residents:

* * * Here another commonplace of sociological observation suggested that people support and participate only in those activities in which they have a meaningful role. The organized activity of people everywhere flows in the channels of institutions and organizations indigenous to their cultural traditions and to the system of social relationships which defines their social groups. Consequently one could not expect people to devote their energies to enterprises which form part of the social systems of groups in which they have no membership * * *.[41]

In the Chicago area project, Kobrin observes that effective involvement of the community in a correctional program (in this case a prevention program aimed at delinquency) was achieved through direct utilization of community residents in the program. He felt that this program offered the following advantages:

It became quickly evident, however, that, for cogent reasons, the employment of qualified local residents offered advantages in the establishment of such programs. In the first place the indigenous worker usually possessed a natural knowledge of the local society. Second, he was hampered by none of the barriers to communications with residents for whom the nonresidents, especially those identified with "welfare" enterprise, tended to be an object of suspicion and hostility. Third, his employment was a demonstration of sincere confidence in the capability of the area resident for work of this sort. Fourth, he was more likely than the nonresident to have access to the neighborhood's delinquent boys and therefore to be more effective in redirecting their conduct. Fifth, his employment represented a prime means of initiating the education of the local population in the mysteries of conducting the welfare enterprise.[42]

A major problem experienced with such programs to date, however, is that their capacity to integrate delinquent and near-delinquent youth

---

[40] Solomon Kobrin, "The Chicago Area Project—A 25-Year Assessment," "The Annals of the American Academy of Political and Social Science" (March 1959), 322, p. 28.
[41] Ibid., p. 23.
[42] Ibid., p. 24.

into the larger society's institutions of education and work has been minimal. As with official correctional agencies themselves, such programs lack the "leverage" sufficient to alter the broader institutional arrangements which continue to shut out vast numbers of deprived youth.

Yet, the several advantages that accrue to this kind of program should not be ignored nor interpreted narrowly as pertaining only to lower class sum communities. Delinquency is spreading throughout our class structure and can be found in rich and poor, urban, suburban and rural settings. Whatever the setting, individuals at differing levels also are likely to have more "natural" access to offenders than workers attached to the correctional system (that is, the contact of the resident need not be identified as coming from the correctional system), and the involvement of residents at differing status levels serves equally well to orient the community to the "mysteries" of the correctional enterprise.

2. THE INVOLVEMENT OF YOUTH

A second task for correctional strategies is to develop mechanisms within the community for the integration of youth into the mainstream of activities and decisionmaking affecting certainly their own lives, but also the wider community as well. The need for such mechanisms arises out of the changes in the role of young persons in the modern day, and how these changes have served to isolate the young.

This Nation has gone through a rapid transition from a relatively underdeveloped country to one that is highly urbanized and technologically oriented. Among the many consequent changes has been the alteration of the status and position of youth within the society. Perhaps it can be put most simply by stating that more young persons are staying in school for much longer periods of time.

But we pay some prices for the specific ways we have chosen to educate our young. Our model of education makes two fundamental problematic assumptions: (a) youth should be segregated (for an increasingly long period of time) from the rest of the community in order to be educated, and (b) youth while they go through the process of education shall play a passive role, one which virtually demands that they be denied access to roles of responsibility and authority either in the school or the community. While some defense of these assumptions might be attempted where the students are very young children, the extension of these ideas to groups whose ages run well beyond physical maturity is less defensible, especially in light of the what now appears to be the resultant costs.

Stating the proposition most directly, many youth do not feel that they belong to, or make any difference to, the communities where they live. Coleman once suggested that when we find persons behaving irresponsibly, it may be that they have no opportunity to be responsible.[42a]

While youth generally have few opportunities for responsible and meaningful participation in the communities and institutions where they live and work, the problem is especially acute for those identified as "problems." Our existing model of correction is centrifugal rather than centripetal. Our correctional techniques, such as "special adjust-

---

[42a] S. Coleman, "Adolescent Society," Glencoe, Ill. : The Free Press, 1961, p. 316.

ment classes" (or schools), court referral, or institutionalization as they are presently constituted serve to isolate the offender and make him exceptionally vulnerable to the power of the community, at the same time to sever any potential for him to influence decisions affecting himself or anyone else. The resultant feelings of isolation and lack of belongingness can be viewed as one of the fundamental aspects in the low stake in conformity that characterize problem youth. The situation can be viewed as an illustration of a vicious circle where isolation and nonbelongingness contribute to a low stake in conformity and then problematic behavior, which is responded to by segregative and stigmatizing procedures which verify, heighten, and aggravate the sense of isolation and nonbelongingness.

This issue is not easy to resolve. On the one hand we are not about to tolerate flagrant and persistent violations of law. Thus, we can anticipate the continued operation of the criminal justice process, which carries with it the realization that where other corrective techniques fail, institutionalization will be employed. Put in another way, youth will and should be held accountable for their actions. On the other hand, if correction can be granted as a desirable goal, and if a lowered stake in conformity is a basic part of the problem, then it would seem reasonable to attempt the development of mechanisms which heighten a sense of belongingness.

3. DEVELOPMENT OF NONLEGAL INTEGRATIVE PROCEDURES

The evolving theory of juvenile court and correctional practice is leading to two trends: (*a*) the narrowing of juvenile court jurisdiction, and (*b*) the development of corrective resources outside the justice-correctional system. The first of these has come about as a result of concern for the procedural rights of children:

The original humanitarian philosophy of the juvenile court was believed to require a significant change in the manner in which courts determined which children to deal with and how to deal with them. The formalities of criminal procedure were rejected on the ground that they were not needed in juvenile court proceedings and that they would be destructive of the goals of those proceedings. In their place was to be substituted a wholly informal and flexible procedure under which by gentle and friendly probing by judge, social worker, parent, and child, the roots of the child's difficulties could be exposed and informed decisions made as to how best to meet his problems. Informality in both procedure and disposition thus became a basic characteristic of juvenile courts.[43]

As alternatives to legally based correctional processes are developed, it becomes important to consider the nature of protections or guarantees that are built into new correctional procedures. Thus, for example, the Crime Commission report is concerned with the voluntary nature of the child's involvement:

Referrals by police, school officials, and others to such local community agencies should be on a voluntary basis. To protect against abuse, the agency's option of court referral should terminate when the juvenile or his family and the community agency agree upon an appropriate disposition. If a departure from the agreed-upon course of conduct should occur, it shoud be the community agency that exercises the authority to refer to court. It is also essential that the dispositions available to such local organizations be restricted. The purpose of using community institutions in this way is to help, not to coerce, and accordingly it is

---

[43] "The Challenge of Crime in a Free Society," op. cit., p. 229.

inapproprate to confer on them a power to order treatment or alter custody or impose sanctions for deviation from the helping program.[44]

Or somewhat later:

It is essential that acceptance of the Youth Services Bureau's services be voluntary; otherwise the dangers and disadvantages of coercive power would merely be transferred from the juvenile court to it. Nonetheless, it may be necessary to vest the Youth Services Bureau with authority to refer to the court within a brief time—not more than 60 and preferably not more than 30 days—those with whom it cannot deal effectively. In accordance with its basically voluntary character, the Youth Services Bureau should be required to comply with the parent's request that a case be referred to juvenile court.[45]

But saying that the alternative programs should not be coercive still does not indicate what it should be. We must then shift concern to the second and implied task: That of developing alternative programs outside the justice-correctional system. It is possible that a community-based agency such as a youth service bureau might serve as the conduit whereby the legally-based correctional system, as it becomes more restrictive in its own activities, can influence the development of institutional programs in schools, employment training agencies, or in recreatonal or other service agencies. It can be viewed, then, as a wedge whereby the correctional system can evolve and implement procedures of system advocacy, that is, efforts to alter the way in which various key bureaucracies relate to and involve youths.

4. DEVELOPMENT OF POSITIVE CAREER FLOWS

A fourth task of correctional programs is to serve as a system advocate for the development of mechanisms by means of which individuals who occupy illegitimate roles may more easily assume legitimate identities. This requires: (a) An understanding of how systems generate and sustain illegitimate and legitimate identities, and (b) a theory about how new mechanisms might be created to move individuals from illegitimate to legitimate roles.

Regarding the first, present evidence suggests that the school setting is central in the contemporary world for establishing the character of the adolescent identity. As our society has become more technologically oriented, the educational achievements of an individual have, and will increasingly come to be a basic determinant of his adult status. Success in negotiating one's way through school becomes, then, a condition for most of later life success.

But not all flow equally well through the educational experience. Most important for our present purposes is the observation that delinquency is concentrated especially among the academically unsuccessful. We must therefore consider what it is that contributes to academic performance.

When we examine this question, it is possible to come to the interesting conclusion that present (and from this perspective seriously deficient) educational theory virtually requires the presence of unsuccessful students and thus, perhaps, assures delinquency.

What leads to this curious, and certainly controversial conclusion? First, inspection of nearly all primary and secondary schools will re-

---

[44] *Ibid.*, p. 224.
[45] *Ibid.*, p. 225.

veal some form of ability grouping or tracking. Undergirding these mechanisms is a theory about intellectual ability, this theory posing a relative unidimensional, if not simplistic, notion of ability which divides young persons into smart and dumb categories. Such notions of ability might be defensible if: (a) they bore some strong relationship to abilities required in adult life (adult activities, including work require such a much wider range of operating abilities that we have all encountered academically bright people who are in fact incompetent or academically dull persons who are competent), and (b) they did not have the consequence of denial of opportunity and the generation of deviant behavior.

Second, these notions of ability cannot function without having a range of ability, including both bright and dull persons. The category of bright makes no sense whatsoever without a comparative dumb category.

Third, the range of abilities included is exceedingly narrow, having to do with particular forms of intellectual functioning (such as memorization and mathematical reasoning). Thus rather than having a wide range of ability options, and a consequent search and exploration of the individual's capacities, the task of the school instead is to evaluate the student within a given and rigid set of notions about ability.

Fourth, organizational "flows" through educational institutions into the external world develop in response to the existing theories of ability. Much of the actual meaning of education for the student derives from these flow mechanisms. For the successful student, the "sense" to be made out of a course in math, physics, or biology is that it is necessary in order to go "on to college." Why he is there, and what he does while he is there, in other words, is understood in light of where it fits into the total educational flow the student is currently experiencing and is anticipating.

Fifth, these organizational flows are relatively rigid once developed. A recent study in Michigan, for example, found that only 7 percent of high school students changed their track position between the sophomore and senior year.[46]

Sixth, the rationale of low track position contributes to a sense of alienation and degradation. A number of conditions are relevant here. One lies in the fact that low track position means that the occupant's adult occupational future is restricted, that is, that the flow probably will not lead to much success. Another is that in the immediate status system of the high school, dumbbell courses carry their own stigma. Thus, it is no wonder that recent research studies have shown that delinquency is much more likely to occur among the academically unsuccessful without regard to their social class background.

What can the basic preventive and correctional programs do about this problem? Implied is the need for such programs to serve as a systems change agents to create new kinds of education-work flows. These flows must provide adolescents:

    (a) A chance to be somebody, that is, they must move into economically rewarding positions.

---

[46] Walter E. Schafer, Carol Olexa and Kenneth Polk, "Programed for Social Class: Tracking in High School," *Trans-Action* (October 1970) 7, 12: 39–46, 63.

(*b*) A chance to become competent and to experience the feeling of competence.

(*c*) Opportunities to participate in roles which yield a sense of contribution, that is, that out of what they do they obtain a feeling of meaningful participation and contribution.

(*d*) Experience which yield a sense of belonging, that is, that they are part of the institutions and communities where they study, work, and live.

(*e*) Supportive counseling services: (1) to overcome psychological residues of earlier failure and delinquency experiences and (2) to provide supports necessary to deal with the strains imposed by new experiences.

5. MECHANISMS FOR REDUCTION OF YOUTH-ADULT CONFLICT

As problems which center around youth protest activities become more and more visible, so then does it become necessary to develop techniques for handling the resultant conflicts. Often, communities and institutions are caught unaware and unprepared for the situations posed by youth protest. Mechanisms have not been developed in advance to carry out any process of negotiation, arbitration, or youth involvement in decisionmaking. Youth can be expected to continue to express their opinions, and to want to demonstrate and organize around their positions. The challenge to the adult community then becomes one of providing ways whereby the organizing can follow constructive, rather than destructive, lines.

6. INDIVIDUALLY ORIENTED COUNSELING SERVICES

A final task of correctional efforts is to provide counseling or treatment for individuals in a setting outside the traditional correctional agencies. It was this function that the Crime Commission had in mind as the major thrust of an agency such as the Youth Service Bureau:

A primary function of the Youth Services Bureau thus would be individually tailored work with troublemaking youths. The work might include group and individual counseling, placement in foster homes, work and recreational programs, employment counseling, and special education (remedial, vocational). It would be under the Bureau's direct control either through purchase or by voluntary agreement with other community organizations. The most significant feature of the Bureau's function would be its mandatory responsibility to develop and monitor a plan of service for a group now handled, for the most part, either inappropriately or not at all except in time of crisis.[47]

D. Some Implementing Mechanisms for Specific Antidelinquency Programs

How might we begin to translate these goals into actual programs? There are two general ways to proceed that can be offered. One is to identify specific program mechanisms, the second is to identify a particular pattern of delinquency and how it might be dealt with. What we shall do here is to suggest three kinds of program mechanisms: Youth service bureaus, educational and employment demonstration programs, and community and youth development demonstration pro-

---

[47] "The Challenge of Crime in a Free Society," op. cit., pp. 224–225.

grams. Then, we shall use one illustration of how programs might be developed around a particular kind of delinquency, in this case, inner-city delinquency.

1. YOUTH SERVICE BUREAUS

It is difficult to suggest one form of programing that is comprehensive enough to encompass all the program foci we have outlined. One framework within which many of these might be accomplished, however, is the Youth Service Bureau. Such an agency was given particular emphasis by the Crime Commission. The Commission report recommended the following:

> There should be expanded use of community agencies for dealing with delinquents nonjudicially and close to where they live. Use of community agencies has several advantages. It avoids the stigma of being processed by an official agency regarded by the public as an arm of crime control. It substitutes for official agencies organizations better suited for redirecting conduct. The use of locally sponsored or operated organizations heightens the community's awareness of the need for recreational, employment, tutoring, and other youth development services. Involvement of local residents brings greater appreciation of the complexity of delinquents' problems, thereby engendering the sense of public responsibility that financial support of programs requires.[48]

The Commission then recommended that:

> An essential objective in a community's delinquency control and prevention plan should therefore be the establishment of a neighborhood youth-serving agency, a Youth Services Bureau, with a broad range of services and certain mandatory functions. Such an agency ideally would be located in a comprehensive community center and would serve both delinquent and nondelinquent youths. While some referrals to the Youth Services Bureau would normally originate with parents, schools, and other sources, the bulk of the referrals could be expected to come from the police and the juvenile court intake staff, and police and court referrals should have special status in that the Youth Services Bureau would be required to accept them all.[49]

In the Crime Commission description, the most clear-cut functions to be carried out are those of providing: (a) nonlegal intervention alternatives, and (b) individual counseling services. Such agencies may also be designed to include additional program components as well. For example, a Youth Service Bureau type program presently operating in the East Tremont section of the Bronx in New York City is diverting juveniles out of the juvenile justice system at an early stage. It is also providing such juveniles with an advocacy directed type of counseling service rendered by staff drawn from the immediate neighborhood where the program is situated.

In addition, however, the program also aims to: (a) develop conflict resolution procedures for the settlement of local adult-youth disputes operating in the East Tremont section of the Bronx in New York City through the use of residents trained as "forum judges," and (b) involve the local community itself in the study and assessment of how well various institutions serving the community (such as schools, courts, and probation) actually meet the needs of local children and youth. The program states its assessment goal in the following manner:

> Often effective control over the institutions which affect the lives of economically and politically disadvantaged youths rests in the hands of agency represent-

---

[48] Ibid., pp. 223–224.
[49] Ibid., p. 224.

atives who may lack a clear understanding of the needs of the poor. The study of what are called "'institutional dislocations" in the modern ghetto, therefore, becomes central in this approach. In New York City, this involves the study of public institutions such as schools, courts and probation services. It also involves the study of private institutions such as charitable agencies, community centers, and churches which were set up to serve a particular urban population at a particular moment in history (in the instance of East Tremont these institutions were predominantly Jewish and Catholic) ; with the advent of the Puerto Rican and Negro newcomers who replaced the earlier ethnic groups, these institutions are often ineffective or nonexistent because of the very different needs and interests of the new groups.

A central issue, therefore, in relation to institutions both in the public and private sector, is the involvement of the new residents in defining their own needs in a way that makes sense to them, and in their influencing the policy of the institutions on which their welfare depends. The prevention and correction of delinquent behavior, are seen as directly related to the issue of social change; that is, the creation of new institutions in a way that makes it possible for the current urban poor to pursue the welfare of their children effectively.[50]

Funded by public moneys, the Bronx program is operated by a private, nonprofit corporation, as a parallel system to the existing juvenile justice system serving the area. In similar ways, the Youth Service Bureau can serve as the link between the correctional and educational systems, with the schools providing new kinds of legitimate career flows, while the correctional program (located in the Bureau) provides funds, supportive services, and program monitoring.

In such functioning, the Bureau can be seen as operating at two levels. At one level it becomes the advocate of the individual young person working with him to find a "slot" in an educational or vocational program providing counseling where necessary, and being available for general support. This we can term the individual-advocacy function of the Bureau.

At a very different level, the Bureau is concerned with changing the institutional ways of relating to youth. Such changes might include: altering juvenile court procedures to provide for more nonlegal dispositions working with employment agencies to create new job roles and training opportunities for young persons, or working with schools in the development of more positive career flows. Here the Bureau would function as a systems-advocate. Both individual and systems advocacy are implied if the many needed program facets of such bureaus are to be developed.

There are many other possible ways of developing meaningful programs of delinquency prevention and control. Some alternatives might include:

2. EDUCATIONAL AND YOUTH EMPLOYMENT DEMONSTRATION PROGRAMS

It has been argued that one process of importance in sustaining, if not creating, delinquency is the locking-out of problem youth from entry into rewarding educational and employment experiences. It would follow, then, that a primary focus of some experimental or demonstration activity should be located in school and work training agencies. While we should be willing to examine many possible approaches to such training, some consideration might be given to the

---

[50] "Neighborhood Youth Diversion Program" City of New York: Unpublished action grant application, funded by New York State Office of Crime Control Planning under the Omnibus Crime Act, effective October 1970.

desirability of providing youth with ((1) new career flows by creating
the opportunity for them to work as tutors and teacher aides (other
roles could be developed in such human service agencies as health, welfare, recreational, or housing agencies) ; (2) opportunities to serve as
consultants to the agencies and the community on youth problems as
they emerge; and (3) involvement in various mechanisms for assessing
and relating local institutional functioning to perceived community
needs.)

3. COMMUNITY AND YOUTH DEVELOPMENT DEMONSTRATION PROGRAMS

The position has been elaborated that a major problem faced by the
juvenile corrections system is its isolation and segregation from both
the youth and the communities it is assumed to serve. This isolation is
such a fundamental problem in its own right that experimentation
with ways of integrating correctional activities into the wider community deserve to be given serious consideration. Thus, on a demonstration basis, a juvenile court might experiment with methods for
involving local residents not only in the decision councils of the court,
but in the work of the court itself, both as volunteers and perhaps as
paid paraprofessionals.) Certainly, it would make some sense for
schools, courts, and communities to experiment with procedures for
the reduction of youth-adult conflict, such as the creation of arbitration boards. The issue here is that while ultimately the needed strategy
may encompass a number of different functions, in the short range
especially it may be important to experiment with programs that are
organized around a more concentrated focus.

Obviously, the implementing mechanisms outlined above represent
only an initial list for guiding the introduction of new orientations
into specific antidelinquency programs. Local communities, program
operators and planners, and others may easily expand the number and
type of implementing mechanisms suggested.

4. AN ILLUSTRATION OF PROGRAM DEVELOPMENT AROUND A PARTICULAR DELINQUENCY PROBLEM—INNERCITY DELINQUENCY [51]

Special delinquency problems will require more specific program
directions. One illustration is the problem of delinquency in the ghetto,
which will require consideration not only of youth and their situation,
but the wider social, economic, and political pressures operating in
this environment. On the level of the local ghetto, greatly enlarged,
targeted programs clearly need to be established for a variety of purposes, including the provision to all disadvantaged minorities of a
means for their communities to support necessary local services. From
region to region, from city to city, from neighborhood to neighborhood,
the needs are so widespread that no one group among the poor, on one
neighborhood among a large city's many slums, should be given pref-
erential treatment.) The discussion here will be about new types of
welfare programs (and their delivery systems which seem particularly
suited to two tasks: (1) meeting the goal of a fair distribution of re-

[51] Adopted from John M. Martin, Joseph P. Fitzpatrick, and Robert E. Gould, M.D., "The
Analysis of Delinquent Behavior: A Structural Approach," New York: Random House,
1969, ch. 5.

sources on an intracity basis, as these might be allocated for the purpose of doing something significant about urban delinquency; and (2) developing and administering in the most efficient manner neighborhood welfare programs specifically designed to prevent and control delinquency among slum children and youth) The complex and difficult problem of maintaining a fair distribution of resources on a regional or intercity basis would have to be resolved by other means which will not be considered here.

The identification of high-priority delinquency areas within a particular city is an ecological problem. Using police or court records and other population data, the most seriously disadvantaged neighborhoods with the highest concentrations of official delinquents can be plotted and described by any agency, public or private, interested in doing the job.

Once high-priority neighborhoods have been identified, new types of locally based welfare and service programs might be mounted in such areas. These locally based programs would have four general purposes. First, they would be designed to meet a number of the self-defined reality needs of ghetto youth and at the same time act to prevent the spread of alienation and the outbreak of serious delinquency among such youth.

Second, these programs, if administratively situated outside the system of criminal justice in the so-called private sector of welfare, could be used to divert local youth out of the official system when they got "in trouble." Thus modern ghetto dwellers could follow the lead presented by the Jews, Irish Catholics, and other earlier immigrant groups who developed their own large-scale private welfare systems which served to divert their children and youth from the courts, public training schools, and reformatories of earlier days(Such local programs might not only help local youth in some worthy welfare sense, but they might also, quite literally, be used, wherever feasible, to keep local youths out of official trouble by taking them out of the hands of overworked police youth bureaus and precincts, off the overcrowded dockets of juvenile courts, and otherwise out of the official processes of justice.)

Just such a mechanism for local communities could be found in the form of local youth services bureaus. Such bureaus could be situated in comprehensive neighborhood community centers and might receive juveniles, both delinquent and nondelinquent, referred by the police, the juvenile court, parents, schools, and other sources. Linked with juvenile court policies designed to narrow the court's jurisdiction to more serious offenders and to policies designed to dispose of as many cases as possible without official adjudication, such bureaus could deal much more informally with many local adolescents defined as deviant.

Initially, then the parent structures operating such services in local communities might best be situated administratively outside of the network of public agencies. Sponsored and operating to a maximum extent by local community residents, such services would be offered in the private welfare sector, but not by those groups and organizations which now run things in private welfare. Ideally, the new services would be run by those sectors of the Nation's population whose members most often inhabit urban slums and whose children and youth most often are arrested, sent to court, and committed to correctional institutions. In plain language, this means that in Washington, D.C., Chicago, New

York City, Boston, and scores of other cities, north and south, the blacks, Puerto Ricans, and other presently disadvantaged groups in the ghettos of these communities would develop the capacities to direct, operate, and staff the new local services.

This leads to the third purpose, which could be served by local, privately controlled welfare services to ghetto youth. Such service delivery systems could themselves become increasingly important bases of institutionalized power for presently disadvantaged groups, which could use these service structures and the taxes which would support them to help create their own welfare enterprises. Following an argument advanced by Frances Piven and Richard Cloward, private agencies of this order would be as much political as social welfare institutions, inasmuch as they would serve as organizational vehicles for the expression of the group's viewpoints on social welfare policy and also as the means for other forms of political association and influence.[52] Once developed, the strength of these new welfare organizations, working in combination with similar local and communitywide enterprises in education, health, religion, and other fields, could be used by the disadvantaged to improve their own general bargaining position vis-a-vis other, more established, interest groups. It is the enhancement of this bargaining position and the consequent enrichment and emphatic modification of institutions and practices that offers the key to social change in the ghetto. The accomplishment of this kind of change is the goal of those who would take a structural approach to delinquency and related social problems.

This general course of action has been followed in the past, and remains the case today, in New York, for example, with the Catholics, Jews, and also, of course, with the white Protestants. The political advantages to be gained by today's disadvantaged groups through the development of their own, privately controlled, tax-supported welfare delivery systems cannot be matched by launching new programs and continuing old programs for the disadvantaged through long-established agencies, either public or private, particularly where the recipients of service exercise little or no voice in policy. Put bluntly, the issue is one of control and influence : who is going to run what for whom? And consequently, who is going to profit politically, psychologically, economically, and in many other ways from the enterprise?

Fourth, and in the long run of prime importance, such an agency could provide the framework for opening new educational and employment channels. To advance their programs of youth development ultimately these agencies must integrate their activities with school and employment agencies which control access to legitimate career lines. If the task is not to be limited to that of making people "happy though poor," then ways have to be specified for giving people an opportunity to be nonpoor. Poverty is only partly a power problem. Since for most nonpoor, money comes from their occupational role, the critical mechanisms must in the end deal with education and training issues, and, of course, the careers themselves. Then, the youth involved will in fact have the chance to "be somebody," to feel a sense of success, to feel they have something to contribute, to feel that they

---

[52] Frances Fox Piven and Richard A. Cloward, "The Case Against Urban Desegregation," Social Work, 12 : pp. 12-21 (January 1967).

belong in the school and the community. The rationale should be self-evident. Given true responsibility, irresponsibility is unlikely. We are highly unlikely to burn or destroy those things that are "ours."

Fifth, success in preventing delinquency and rehabilitating delinquents will require the development of service delivery systems which are more comprehensive and more effective than presently exist in most communities. This will require flexible, noncategorical funds and an exceptional degree of cooperation among local, State, and Federal agencies.

E. Some Concluding Thoughts

Juvenile delinquency is very much a part of the contemporary scene. If present trends continue, we can expect it not only to increase, but to spread increasingly into more advantaged groups. At the same time, we can anticipate the continued rise in protest-related delinquency.

What will be crucial is our collective response to this problem. One set of choices available will continue to isolate and alienate young people, and aggravate the set of conditions that lock persons into problematic roles. Another set would ask how can we involve and integrate young people generally, and problem youth in particular, into the mainstream of community life.

The issue is not delinquency, but the kind of society in which we wish to live: is it be divisive or integrated, centrifugal or centripetal. Many of our current mechanisms for dealing with "problems" (of all types) are inherently divisive: the problems involve other people not us, the solution is their problem, not ours. Unfortunately the solutions we develop heighten the difference, and by labelling and tracting often cast people farther outside the pale of ordinary life. As a consequence, we have become traumatized by our inabilities to deal with the major polarities that constitute the facts of contemporary life in America: rich versus poor, black versus white, powerful versus powerless, and central to the present discussions, old versus young, and "good" versus "bad."

How can we bind ourselves together? This, it would seem, is the question we must ask as we seek to address contemporary delinquency. How can we build delinquency prevention and control activities that involve people, young and old, poor and nonpoor, black, brown, and white, in a common and integrated effort to deal with the problem? It is this that has led to our emphasis here on community and youth development. It seems to us that many youth, especially problem youth, have precious few opportunities to be "anybody," to feel that they contribute to the communities in which they live, that they control their own futures. Adults of various kinds, too, have become isolated from existing agencies mandated to deal with delinquents and delinquency.

If isolation is a fundamental part of the problem, then integration might be considered as part of the solution. What we have suggested are ways of involving youth and adults in programs of community and youth betterment that will build the stake of young people in conformity. The premise is deceptively simple: The more you have to lose, the less likely you are to risk deviant behavior. The more responsibility you exercise, the less attractive is irresponsibility.

A related issue concerns priorities—public and private. Even unlimited involvement of youth in trouble or near trouble will not lead far less public agencies and private organizations provide resources to give the disadvantaged, troubled youth the nutrition, health, educational, training and related services on a timely and intensive enough basis to solve their problems and enable them to enter the mainstream of our economy. The dominant fact of our antidelinquency programs to date has been that they have been starved for resources adequate enough to develop and demonstrate effective strategies.

The ultimate stakes are enormous. At issue is literally our ability to live together in communities governed and bound by law.

JOBS FOR YOUTH

(A discussion paper for the 1970 White House Conference on Youth,
by Herbert C. Morton, February 1971)

I. Introduction

More than 3 million young Americans begin testing the job market
each year in search of their first employment experience.

Most of them are 16 to 19 years of age—either pupils seeking summer and part-time jobs, or high school graduates and dropouts usually
seeking full-time employment.

A somewhat smaller number are 20 to 24 years old, primarily college
students who have been able to postpone going to work and veterans
who went into military service before they had work experience.

A still smaller number are 14 and 15 years old and are seeking summer jobs and part-time work permitted by the child labor laws.

Many of these young people find the transition into the world of
work painfully difficult. They are thwarted by serious obstacles, such
as their own lack of education, skills, and self confidence—the lack of
information about job opportunities and the unavailability of counseling—the decline in the number of common labor jobs and other
entry-level jobs largely resulting from technological change—the distance between home and workplace—and discrimination against minority groups and the inexperienced. Some teenagers are unable to find
jobs after prolonged search; some find dead-end jobs only. Discouraged
or disillusioned, some turn away from regular employment as a way of
life. That the majority of young Americans make the transition reasonably well is not much solace for the one in five who does not.

The problems of adjustment are reflected in the persistence of high
unemployment among teenagers—three to five times as high as unemployment among adults during the 1960's. Youth unemployment, as
these figures suggest, has emerged as a special problem that is identi-
fiably distinct from the broader goal of full employment for the
economy as a whole. It has triggered efforts to make the Nation's educational system more responsive to the needs of youths who do not go to
college and to strengthen manpower programs that will provide work
experience and training for the disadvantaged. Since 1962, for example, when the Manpower Development and Training Act was passed,
expenditures for manpower activities have gradually risen to more
than $3 billion a year, with more than a third of the funds going to

(139)

programs for youths 21 and under. But more resources and a better understanding of the best ways to use them are still badly needly.

The purpose of this paper is to help provide background information for a discussion of ways to improve job prospects for youth. The paper will review some characteristics of young jobseekers, the probable nature of job markets in the 1970's, and recent experience with programs to remove barriers to employment. Finally, it will indicate some of the alternatives that need to be considered in determining how to achieve further gains during the decade of the 1970's.

The phrase "further gains" seems fully warranted. The catalog of problems suggested above should not be allowed to obscure the achievements of the 1960's when the economy provided far more jobs for young people than during any previous decade. About 2 million new jobs were generated for teenagers 16 to 19—an increase of 50 percent over the 1950's. Moreover, steps were taken against discrimination. Special programs for the disadvantaged were introduced. If the task of solving the employment problems of the young seems immense today, it appears so partly because we have raised our sights. Educational and earnings targets that might have been acceptable 25 years ago or 10 years ago simply won't do any longer.

II. The Job Seekers

The decade of the 1960's was a period of extraordinary change in the size and characteristics of the youth population.

THE YOUTH POPULATION IN BRIEF

One of the most widely publicized facts about young people was the increasing numbers of them. Between 1960 and 1970, the number of people in the 16 to 24 age group increased by about 50 percent, from about 22 million to 32 million, and the number in the civilian labor force rose from about 11½ to 17½ million. (See table 1.)

Less publicized, but noteworthy, was the increase in the numbers going to school, attributable in part to the success of programs to encourage school attendance. Among 14- to 17-year-old youths, school enrollment rose from about 86 percent to about 95 percent. College enrollment soared from 3.6 million to more than 7 million—to 30 percent of the 18 to 24 age group.

Of particular interest to manpower analysts was the change in the proportion of youths working or looking for work—the labor force participation rate. Overall, it declined for 16- to 24-year-old youths during the 1960's. But this generalization masks two opposing trends. On the one hand, the rate for young men declined, owing in part to increased school attendance and uncertainty about the draft, which discouraged many from job hunting in the months preceding induction. On the other hand, the participation rate for young women increased as an expanding economy offered more opportunities for employment.

TABLE 1.—GROWTH OF YOUTH LABOR FORCE AND TRENDS IN UNEMPLOYMENT RATES, 1950–70

Year	Civilian labor force (thousands)		Unemployment rate		Ratio of teenage rate to rate for adults 25 and over
	16 to 19	20 to 24	16 to 19	20 to 24	
1950	4,216	7,307	12.2	7.7	2.8
1951	4,105	6,594	8.2	4.1	2.9
1952	4,063	5,840	8.5	4.6	3.5
1953	4,026	5,483	7.6	4.7	3.2
1954	3,976	5,476	12.6	9.2	2.7
1955	4,093	5,666	11.0	7.0	3.1
1956	4,296	5,940	11.1	6.6	3.4
1957	4,276	6,068	11.6	7.1	3.4
1958	4,260	6,271	15.9	11.2	2.8
1959	4,492	6,413	14.6	8.5	3.3
1960	4,840	6,703	14.7	8.7	3.3
1961	4,935	6,953	16.8	10.4	3.1
1962	4,915	7,082	14.6	9.0	3.3
1963	5,138	7,473	17.2	8.8	4.0
1964	5,390	7,963	16.2	8.3	4.3
1965	5,910	8,258	14.8	6.7	4.6
1966	6,557	8,409	12.7	5.3	4.9
1967	6,519	9,010	12.9	5.7	4.9
1968	6,618	9,305	12.7	5.8	5.5
1969	6,970	9,879	12.2	5.7	5.5
1970	7,246	10,583	15.3	8.2	4.7

Sources: Handbook of Labor Statistics, 1972; Monthly Labor Review, March 1970.

For policymakers, the most troubling development was the persistence of high unemployment. To be sure, youth unemployment did decline. But it didn't decline enough, given the rapid expansion of the economy and the sharp decline in total unemployment rates. The annual rate of unemployment in the 16 to 19 age group failed to drop below 12 percent: the rate was 25 percent and higher for black youths. By comparison, the rates for all adults declined to 3.3 percent during part of 1969—and for black adults it dipped below 6 percent. The teenage unemployment rate—which had been two and a half times, the rate for adults 25 and over in 1948 and three times the adult rate in 1963—climbed to more than five times the adult rate in 1969.

What will the 1970's bring?

CHART 1. CHANGES IN THE YOUTH LABOR FORCE, AGES 16-19

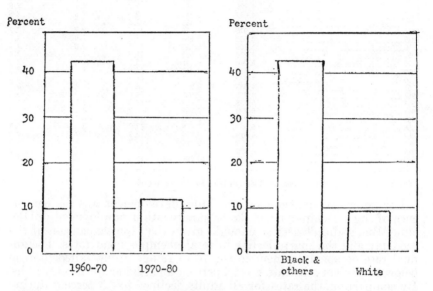

The number of youths will continue to increase—but at a slower rate (chart 1). The most rapidly expanding group will be young adults 25 to 34. As a result the 16 to 24 age group will be a smaller proportion of the population. A good estimate is that the teenage labor force will grow at the rate of about 100,000 a year, compared to the annual average increase of 250,000 for the 1960's and the 20- to 24-year-old labor force will grow at the rate of 300,000 a year instead of 450,000. A projection showing the size and characteristics of the youth population in 1980 is shown in table 2. (This projection assumes a very slight decline in labor force participation rates for men and a leveling off of the rate for 16- to 19-year-old women and a slight rise for women 20 to 24 years of age.)

TABLE 2.—POPULATION, LABOR FORCE, AND LABOR FORCE PARTICIPATION RATES, BY COLOR, SEX, AND AGE, 1960–80

Color, sex, and age	Total population, July 1			Total labor force, annual average			Labor force participation rate, annual average (percent)		
	Actual		Projected,	Actual		Projected,	Actual		Projected,
	1960	1968	1980	1960	1968	1980	1960	1968	1980
TOTAL, ALL RACES									
16 years and over	121,817	137,659	166,554	72,104	82,272	100,727	59.2	59.8	60.5
White:									
Both sexes, 16 years and over	109,279	122,889	146,919	64,210	73,166	88,634	58.8	59.5	60.3
Men:									
16 years and over	53,408	59,527	70,997	44,119	47,708	56,374	82.6	80.1	79.4
16 to 19	4,763	6,328	7,300	2,801	3,707	4,193	58.8	58.6	57.4
20 to 24	4,905	7,028	9,117	4,370	5,993	7,599	89.1	85.3	83.3
Women:									
16 years and over	55,871	63,362	75,922	20,091	25,457	32,260	36.0	40.2	42.5
16 to 19	4,630	6,090	7,061	1,853	2,612	2,935	40.0	42.9	41.9
20 to 24	4,842	6,847	8,897	2,215	3,691	5,110	45.7	53.9	57.4
Negro and other races:									
Both sexes, 16 years and over	12,538	14,770	19,635	7,894	9,106	12,093	63.0	61.7	61.6
Men:									
16 years and over	6,011	7,010	9,336	4,814	5,322	7,238	80.1	75.9	77.5
16 to 19	635	971	1,325	361	489	702	56.8	50.4	53.0
20 to 24	648	948	1,479	569	795	1,196	87.8	83.9	80.9
Women:									
16 years and over	6,527	7,760	10,299	3,080	3,784	4,855	47.2	48.8	47.1
16 to 19	645	972	1,313	208	336	514	32.2	34.6	39.1
20 to 24	705	965	1,504	343	560	881	48.7	58.0	58.6

Source: Bureau of Labor Statistics, Special Labor Force Report 119 (1970), table 4.

At the same time there will be an important change in the racial composition of the labor force. During the 1970's the number of Negroes age 16 to 24 in the labor force will increase at a rate twice as fast as the rate of increase in the number of whites (51 percent for blacks between 1968 and 1980 compared to 24 percent for whites). Although blacks account for only about 12 percent of the total population, they will account for nearly 30 percent of the total increase in the number of youths 16 to 19. Clearly these figures underscore the importance of intensifying efforts to combat discrimination and to compensate for economic and educational disadvantages of youth in minority groups.

WHERE TEENAGERS FIND JOBS

Most teenagers find jobs in the less skilled occupations, though by the ages of 18 and 19 a noticeable number of them begin to move up the occupational ladder.

As shown in table 3, about half of the boys age 16 to 19 are blue collar workers, employed mostly as nonfarm laborers and operatives. A fourth are in service jobs. About 7 percent, however, are draftsmen and foreman, and a few are in professional and technical jobs.

About 40 percent of the girls are white collar workers, primarily in clerical and sales occupations. Nearly 35 percent are in the service sector, primarily in household and waitress jobs.

EMPLOYMENT EXPERIENCES OF GRADUATES AND DROPOUTS

The prevailing belief that better educated young people are initially more successful in the job market is supported by data on employment for high school graduates and dropouts.

TABLE 3.—OCCUPATIONS OF TEENAGERS, JANUARY 1971

[In thousands]

Occupation	Male, 16 to 19 years	Female, 16 to 19 years
Total, all occupations	2,937	2,468
White-collar workers	608	1,391
Professional and technical	74	62
Managers, officials, and proprietors	50	10
Clerical workers	264	1,022
Stenographers, typists, and secretaries	4	273
Other clerical workers	259	750
Sales workers	220	296
Retail trade	166	278
Other sales workers	54	18
Blue-collar workers	1,487	225
Craftsmen and foremen	222	16
Carpenters	18	2
Construction craftsmen, except carpenters	41	
Mechanics and repairmen	83	1
Metal craftsmen, except mechanics	17	1
Other craftsmen and kindred workers	59	11
Foremen, not elsewhere classified	5	2
Operatives	618	174
Drivers and deliverymen	103	6
Other operatives	515	168
Durable goods manufacturing	150	44
Nondurable goods manufacturing	94	80
Other industries	271	45
Nonfarm laborers	647	35
Service workers	638	828
Private household workers	15	311
Service workers, except private household	623	517
Protective service workers	9	
Waiters, cooks, and bartenders	150	248
Other service workers	464	269
Farmworkers	203	24

Source: "Employment and Earnings" (February 1971), table A-18.

CHART 2. EMPLOYMENT EXPERIENCE OF CLASS OF 1969

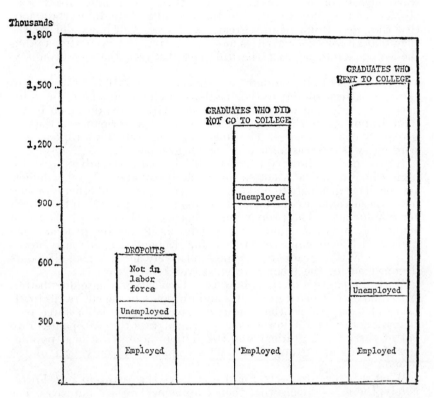

A BLS study of the class of 1969 provides detailed data (see chart 2). About 1.3 million high school graduates of 1969—nearly half of the entire class—did not go on to college. In October of that year more than 1 million of them were in the labor force. About 900,000 were employed—mostly in office work, sales work, and semiskilled jobs—and 100,000 unemployed. The unemployment rate—graduates, out of work and looking for a job—was 11.4 percent.

The number of dropouts during the year ending in October 1969 was estimated at 660,000. This is the number of young people between the ages of 16 and 24 who had left school during the preceding 12 months. About half of them had jobs, about one in 10 was unemployed, and the remaining four in 10 were neither unemployed nor working.

Clearly, the dropouts are less inclined to look for work during the first year after leaving school and if they look for work are less successful in finding it. The labor force participation rate of dropouts was 61 percent, compared to 79 percent for graduates, and the unemployment rate was 16.8 percent, well above that for graduates.

It would be incorrect, however, to attribute this difference solely to differences in educational attainment between the two groups. The average age of the dropouts is lower. More of them are 16 and 17 and are barred by Federal and State laws from some occupations or are required to comply with certain procedures that put additional paperwork burdens on employers. Moreover, their youthfulness itself is an obstacle; an employer is less inclined to hire them for certain jobs that they may think require greater maturity. And like older youths they find alternative activities more attractive. But even after taking these points into account the difference between the two groups is substantial.

An analysis of all graduates and dropouts in the 16 to 21 age group shows a pattern similar to the one that was found among those graduating or dropping out in a single year. Graduates do much better than dropouts, and the difference between the performance of the two groups widens with age. The unemployment rate for dropouts—14 percent—was twice as high as it was for graduates.

It is also clear, however, that for black youths the advantage of a high school diploma is not so immediately apparent. It takes longer for the black graduate to find a job. Discrimination and other obstacles offset the advantages of education during the first months of the search for employment. The proportion of blacks in the class of 1969 who found jobs was the same for graduates as it was for dropouts—50 percent. (The unemployment rate for dropouts was actually lower than it was for graduates because relatively more school dropouts dropped out of the labor market as well.)

With the passage of time, however, the black graduate does better. A comparison of black graduates and dropouts in the entire 16- to 21-year-old group shows the graduates have a higher labor force participation rate and a lower unemployment rate than dropouts. Two out of three black graduates in the civilian-noninstitutional population for this age group found jobs, compared to only half of the dropouts.

What are the prospects for dropouts as the years go by? Fortunately, there is evidence that their employment record improves. The labor force participation of dropouts increases in adulthood and their unemployment declines. The difference in job holding between the two groups narrows and so does the gap in earnings. In this context, the manpower problem can be viewed as the task of telescoping the time elapsing between leaving school and acquiring the attitudes and skills necessary to hold a job. The number of those who never become employable is relatively small.

How does the experience of college students and graduates compare with that of high school dropouts and graduates?

About 1.5 million of the 2.8 million high school graduates in 1969 went on to college, virtually all of them full time, and one out of three entered the labor force. Over the decade of the 1960's, the labor force participation rate of college students increased substantially, from 26 percent for the class of 1959 to 35 percent for the class of 1969, which may be attributable largely to higher costs of education and increasing job opportunities.

The unemployment rate for college students was 11.4 percent, the same as it was for graduates who didn't go on to college. The rate for Negroes and other minority group members in college was three times as high as that for whites, however (30 percent versus 9 percent), about the same as it was for graduates who didn't go on to college.

VETERANS IN THE LABOR FORCE

One out of four men 20 to 24 years of age during the first half of 1970 had served in the Armed Forces. Collectively, these veterans differed from others in the same group in that a higher proportion of them had jobs and a smaller proportion were in school. The employment status of the 20 to 24 age group is summarized below:

	Veterans, 20 to 24	Nonveterans, 20 to 24
Civilian noninstitutional population	1,746,000	4,913,000
Percentage of noninstitutional population employed	81.9	71.3
Labor force participation rate	90.6	78.6
Unemployment rate	8.7	7.3

Source: Bureau of Labor Statistics, "Special Labor Force Report 126," table 2.

The key distinction—the big difference in labor force participation rates—is attributable to several factors. First, the veteran was not affected by uncertainty over his draft status, which discouraged many other young men from seeking work. Second, he knew that if he failed to find a job he could draw unemployment compensation, whereas nonveterans without employment experience could not. (Benefits averaging $48 weekly were paid to 177,000 veterans returning to civilian life in 1969.) The availability of unemployment compensation also made it easier for the veteran to shop around for a job instead of taking the first offer. Third, he was aided by special programs of counseling, education, training and placement—beginning with information programs that were offered in Vietnam and at separation points in the United States that sought to tell servicemen about the benefits to which they are entitled. More than 400,000 veterans were enrolled in college and 200,000 in other educational classes in mid-1969. At the same time about 40,000 were enrolled in on-the-job training.

Black and white veterans had almost identical labor participation rates, but the blacks suffered much more unemployment—averaging 10 percent during 1969 and the first half of 1970 compared to 5.1 percent for white veterans. More black veterans sought employment in the public sector and a substantially higher proportion—nearly 16 percent—found jobs in Government compared to 9 percent of the white veterans. Whereas 2.5 percent of the white were self-employed, only 0.7 blacks were self-employed. Among nonveterans on the other hand, there was no difference between white and blacks in the proportion working for Government.

By 1971 the number of Vietnam veterans exceeded 4 million, and servicemen were returning to civilian life at the rate of 1 million each year, severely testing counseling, training, educational and placement resources.

III. The Job Market

During the 1960's the real output of the American economy expanded at an average rate of more than 4 percent a year. The number of persons employed increased by about 13 million. The output of almost every major industry in the economy increased; the exceptions were coal mining, wooden containers, leather tanning and industrial leather products. The fastest growing industries—reflecting the rapid rate of technological innovation and an accelerated rate of capital investment—were electronic components and accessories; radio, TV, and communications equipment; office and computing machines; plastics and synthetics; drugs, cleaning and toilet preparations. Among occupations, opportunities for white collar workers increased much more rapidly than for blue collar workers.

During the 1970's many of the patterns and trends of the 1960's are likely to continue. Generalizations by decades are, after all, more a matter of political pedagogical convenience (like scheduling the census and White House youth conference at decennial intervals) than a reflection of underlying economic change, which has a rhythm of its own and is also subject to outside jolts. But cumulatively the demographic changes, the rapid growth of the service industries, the shift toward white collar occupations, and growing demand for more highly trained and highly educated employees—all apparent during the 1960's—will continue to affect youth employment during the current decade.

The following discussion of the market for jobs in the 1970's is based on the 1980 projections of the Bureau of Labor Statistics, but are presented in broad strokes without the careful qualifications contained in the full study. The Bureau's estimates of the number of jobs in each industry and occupation are the end products of a carefully worked out sequence of projections. It begins with an estimate of the gross national product, based on projections of the labor force, assumptions about the rate of unemployment, and trends in hours worked and output per man-hour. The demand for this potential output by consumers, business, government, and foreign buyers is then determined. Detailed requirements for raw materials, fuel and power, semiprocessed goods, transportation, business services and so on by industry are then estimated, and these in turn, lead to estimates of employment and occupational distribution. Underlying the projections are a number of broad assumptions, namely, that the Vietnam conflict will come to a halt and military spending will continue to decrease as a proportion of national expenditures, that the rate of technological advance will be about the same as in the 1960's, and that attitudes toward work will remain fundamentally unchanged.

The slowdown in economic activity during 1970, which occurred after the projections were made, has altered the chances of achieving some of the projections—at least in the early years of the decade—but over the decade the estimates provide useful indicators of changes in employment by industry and occupation.

What do the government's projections for 1980 tell us about the economy's requirements for manpower a decade hence?

Overall, if the economy grows at an average rate of about 4.3 percent a year in the 1970's with unemployment at a level of 4 percent, or under, we can expect:

About 4 million new jobs will have to be filled each year.

About three out of five of these job openings will be for replacements of workers who have retired or died.

About two out of five jobs will be new ones created as a result of the economy's growth.

Along with meeting the replacement and growth needs the Nation's labor force will have to adjust to changes in output reflecting changing technology and tastes. In calculating the overall job openings transfers among occupations cancel out, but in terms of training, mobility and so they must be kept in mind.

Among the major sectors of the economy, construction, services, and government are expected to provide the greatest rate of growth in new jobs. Trade and finance (insurance and real estate), manufacturing, transportation, communications, and public utilities sector will grow somewhat more slowly. Employment will continue to decline in agriculture, forestry, fisheries, and in mining.

Comparing white collar and blue collar jobs, the rate of new jobs will be substantially greater for white collar occupations than for blue collar occupations. Among the white collar occupational groups, the rate of increase will continue to be fastest among profressional and technical employees.

In considering the employment problems of the youths of the 1970's a central question is the occupational mix of the job market. Assuming relatively full employment, where will the new jobs be? How can one be prepared to fill them?

Two types of changes are distinguished in the following discussion: (1) the rate of growth in the number of jobs in each occupation and (2) the occupations that will provide the greatest number of jobs. Some of the fastest growing occupations, such as computer programing, will still provide relatively few jobs, and some slow growing occupations, such as teaching, will continue to offer substantial employment opportunities.

The need for professional and technical employees will be increased by more than 50 percent. The number of such employees will increase from 10.3 million in 1968 to 15.5 million in 1980. The only group requiring more workers will be clerical, where employment is projected at 17.3 million. By 1980, one worker in six will be a professional and technical employee, a reflection of the rapid technological development within the country.

The growth in the estimated demand for professional workers is another indication of the relationship between educational attainment and occupational opportunity. During the 1968–80 period there will be 777,000 net job openings annually for professional and technical workers. But there will be substantial differences within this group.

The most rapidly expanding fields will be those related to computer technology—programers (projected to increase by 129 percent) and systems analysts (projected to increase by 183 percent).

The slowest growing professional field on the other hand will be elementary school teachers (projected to increase at only slightly over 3 percent) and secondary school teachers (projected to increase by 14 percent).

Yet there will be far more teaching jobs to be filled each year (56,000 elementary and 40,000 secondary) than programing or systems analyst jobs (23,000 and 27,000, respectively). (Appendix, table A, compares occupations with the greatest percentage and number of job changes.)

The second most rapidly expanding group of occupations is the service work group, which is expected to grow 40 percent between 1968 and 1980—increasing from 9.4 to 13.1 million jobs. There will be an average of 752,000 service job openings each year through the 1970's. The most rapidly expanding field within the group will be the health services. It will also provide the most jobs: 100,000 a year for hospital attendants and 48,000 for practical nurses.

The demand for clerical workers is expected to increase by 35 percent over the 1968–80 period, from 12.8 million to 17.3 million. The annual number of job openings in these occupations will be 911,000, the greatest for any group. Here again it is important to recognize that the most rapidly expanding group in this field—electronic computer operating personnel—is not the field which will have the most job openings. It will provide about 20,000 openings a year—not much different from the annual openings for bank tellers, shipping clerks, office machine operators, or telephone operators. The greatest number of job openings will continue to be for stenographers and secretaries—about 237,000 jobs a year (and an increase of 37 percent over the period).

The number of sales workers is expected to increase by 29 percent, from 4.6 million to 6 million, providing 263,000 openings each year, an increasing proportion of them for part-time work. The most rapidly expanding field will be manufacturers' salesmen, while the greatest number of job openings will be in retail trade—about 150,000 annually.

The number of craftsmen, foremen, and kindred workers will increase by 22 percent, from 10 million to 12.2 million. The number of job openings is expected to be 396,000 per year. Among the building trades, there will be 39,300 jobs for carpenters, 19,500 for plumbers and pipefitters, 23,200 for painters and paperhangers. The demand for excavating and grading and machinery operators will increase more rapidly than for the others, and will provide 16,200 openings each year. The most rapidly expanding repair service will be for business machine servicemen, but the most jobs will be for motor vehicle mechanics, about 26,500 a year. The number of composing room jobs for printers will decline.

The number of jobs for managers, officials and proprietors will also increase by 22 percent—from 7.8 million to 9.5 million, with 380,000 new openings a year.

Semiskilled occupations, which up to now have provided more jobs than any other group, will grow at a slower rate than the average for all groups and by 1980 will be providing fewer jobs than the clerical group. The demand for operators will rise slightly, increasing from 14 million in 1968 to 15.4 million in 1980, providing 426,000 job openings each year, including 58,600 for truck drivers. Among the manual occupations, the most rapidly expanding field will be for welders and oxygen and arc cutters, which provide 23,000 new jobs a year.

The declining demand for unskilled workers is reflected in estimates that the number of nonfarm laborers will decline by about 50,000 workers over the period, to 3.5 million. Replacement needs will be for only about 60,000 new jobs a year. The number of farmworker jobs will decline from 3.5 million to 2.6 million, with replacement needs at only 25,000 a year.

IV. Programs To Promote Employment

When their public schooling ends, large numbers of youths do not read well enough, cannot express themselves effectively enough, and cannot perform simple arithmetic calculations with sufficient reliability to make their way in the world of work. Local school testing programs and selective service qualifying tests indicate that one out of five young people are not literate enough to advance beyond unskilled employment. In a technological society in which perhaps only one job in 20 is for the unskilled—and in which the proportion is shrinking—their employment prospects are dim indeed. Jobs will be increasingly scarce and advancement beyond entry level unlikely unless they are given additional help.

Even if one concedes that in the long run the task of providing basic education is one for the public school system—with additional resources for the disadvantaged who need special help—it is clear that in the short run there is much to be done by other public agencies and by private employers. For that reason, basic education is included in the Job Corps, Neighborhood Youth Corps, JOBS and other programs sponsored by the Department of Labor, as well as in transition programs for war veterans. (And an adult basic education program is being offered by the U.S. Office of Education to the estimated 24 million adult Americans with less than an eighth grade education.) Moreover, it is quite possible that, irrespective of gains made in public education, an alternative to the public school system may continue to be needed for some young people who have been discouraged or intimidated by classroom instruction. Indifferent or rebellious in an academic environment, they may be more readily motivated when they see the relationship of education to employment opportunity in a work-training program. Because it is related to the acquisition of other job skills and because it is so widespread, basic education is viewed not as a separate program but as a component of virtually all training and development programs for young people, whether the program is designed to equip enrollees in special skills, give them work experience, or provide income.

VOCATIONAL EDUCATION

Vocational education has been part of a bridge to two worlds. It has offered a direct path to employment, similar to apprenticeship, or on-the-job training, for both youth and adults. At the same time, it has been part of the public school system, which has the broader responsibility of educating young people for citizenship. Trying to succeed in both worlds, it has encountered more than its share of criticisms and difficulties. In recent years it has been undergoing substantial change—particularly the programs in secondary schools, which account for over half of vocational enrollment.

The Federal budget treats vocational education as an education expenditure. (It classifies as manpower programs only those activities that are outside normal educational processes, gives service for periods less than a year, provide training and job opportunities for nonprofessional jobs and are directed primarily at the disadvantages.) Nevertheless, because of its close similarity to some manpower programs it warrants mention in this discussion.

Historically, the principal role of vocational education has been to provide readymade workers for local industry, or at least well-trained learners ready to step in with little additional training. In big urban comprehensive schools with adequate resources—and in the big-city vocational high schools—vocational programs have been successful, if the criterion is job placement. Graduates get jobs and their unemployment rate is well below that of other high school graduates who do not go on to college. However, smaller schools, especially in rural areas have often offered little choice—usually only agricultural and homemaking courses that did not reflect the shift in labor market opportunities. Moreover, even urban schools with substantial vocational offerings generally limited enrollment to pupils with the greatest aptitude; thus, many youngsters who perhaps could have benefited most from vocational courses were unable to take them.

During the 1960's, increasing concern with disadvantaged youth led to a recognition that more resources are needed for vocational education and that schools ought to take a broader view of the purpose of vocational education. The conventional measure—number of job placements—has also been challenged. It has been pointed out that a pupil's interest in a vocational field can be broadened to include general educational skills, concepts, and attitudes that are important in the world of work. Instruction should be directed primarily to these needs of the individual young person rather than to the narrow occupational requirements of local industry. In view of the continuous change in skill requirements for industry, a number of critics (particularly economists) have stressed the importance of the breadth of training that will enable workers to adapt more readily to changing opportunities.

In their efforts to upgrade the level of instruction, vocational educators have put special stress on the need to end the bias of the school system. In their view, American education has been too preoccupied with training young people for further schooling rather than with training them for employment and citizenship. As a result, vocational courses have been looked down upon, and pupils taking vocational courses have typically been regarded as inferior to those enrolled in college preparatory work. If vocational education is to succeed both in imparting work skills and in achieving its general educational objectives, this prejudice must be eliminated.

Apart from the broad questions of purpose and emphasis, there are a number of problem areas related to the instructional program itself.

A frequent criticism has centered on alleged obsolescence—equipment that is out of date, teachers who are out of touch, and curriculums that have not been adapted to new occupations and new industrial demands. Even if one concedes that the skills taught in vocational courses are basic—and that these basic skills haven't changed so much—or that replacements will be needed even in declining occupations, there seems little question that teachers and curriculum have not been responsive enough to changes in the labor market.

Not surprisingly, another problem for vocational education has been financial. Vocational classes cost about twice as much to operate as do academic classes of the same size. The costs of providing a balanced program are relatively much higher in smaller schools where equipment cannot be used as intensively and efficiently.

What has been done in recent years to cope with some of these problems related to the purpose and quality of vocational education? Legislatively, most important was the enactment of the Vocational Education Act of 1963 (amended in 1968) which provided a commitment of additional resources and embodied the broader view that vocational education should put more stress on importing general skills and work habits.

Recent program developments warranting particular attention include the efforts to combine work experience and education. Under one approach, the student may simply be released from school part time to find a job, for which he gets some credit. The other—usually called part-time cooperative education—requires the school to help find the job and to supervise the students work. About 250,000 students have been involved in the cooperative programs in 1968 and perhaps 100,000 in the other. Part-time cooperative students reportedly have had the best placement records, job satisfaction, and job ability, but it's uncertain whether this finding tells more about pupils who elect such a program than about the value of this program compared to others.

Another trend has been the increasing emphasis on developing effective placement services in schools that are in closer touch with industry and sensitive to the varied needs of pupils.

Under the impetus of the 1963 legislation, enrollment in vocational education courses has increased rapidly. After relatively slow growth during the 1950's total enrollment in vocational education jumped from 4.1 million in 1962 to more than 7.5 million in 1968. Secondary school students account for well over half of the total enrollment. Nearly one out of four pupils were enrolled in office occupations while about one in 10 was enrolled in agricultural programs.

Establishment of the National Advisory Council on Vocational Education by the Vocational Education Amendments of 1968 has helped focus public attention on the field that has long been needed.

Members are appointed by the President and charged with advising the Commissioner of Education, they report annually to the Secretary of Health, Education, and Welfare. In its third report issued in September 1970, the Council focused on the needs of the disadvantaged and specifically endorsed (1) the trend toward part-time employment as part of the educational curriculum, (2) the role of the school as an employment agency, especially in disadvantaged neighborhoods, and (3) taking a cue from Job Corps experience the establishment of residential schools for those who need to be separated from their homes and neighborhoods.

APPRENTICESHIP

Compared to the lack of consensus on the purpose and role of vocational education, the objective of apprenticeship training is clear enough. Apprentice programs are designed to train craftsmen for the trades—primarily for the building trades, printing, and metalworking trades. In the building trades particularly, the view has prevailed that the proper way to enter the trade (though not the most used path) is through a formal apprenticeship program.

Nor is there much debate about the payoff of apprenticeship training. Apprentices find jobs—and generally lifelong work—as journeymen in the trade. A relatively high proportion become foremen, and in certain trades such as plumbing, metals, and electrical trades a substantial number become independent contractors. How much of the success of apprentices can be attributed to selection and how much to the training programs is not readily answerable.

Questions arise, however, over estimates of the number of apprentices needed, the length and scope of specific programs, admission to programs or, to put it the other way around, discrimination against minority groups and, overall, whether apprenticeship training is the best way of preparing workers for the needs of a rapidly changing technological order.

First, how does apprenticeship rate among the ways of entering an occupation.

Despite the historic recognition given formal apprenticeship as the natural and legitimate path to journeyman status, most workers approach the skilled trades by other routes: by informal apprenticeship, by vocational schools, by learning the trade in a nonunion sector or in military service or in another industry, or by working up from a helper's status. Three out of five workers probably enter "apprenticeable" trades without any formal training. Fewer than 1 in 5 complete a formal registered apprenticeship program, and the rest get a job after dropping out of a formal program or after taking an unregistered program or vocational training.

In recent years the number of persons participating in apprenticeship programs has been increasing—from 278,000 in 1967 to 331,000 in 1969; the estimate for 1970 is 355,000. The number of persons completing training also increased substantially, totaling more than 37,000 a year in 1967 and 1968, compared to an average of about 26,000 in the preceding 5 years.

The relationship of apprenticeship to total supply of workers can be illustrated as follows. During the 1960's, the number of completed apprenticeships in the construction trades has generally been between 16,000 and 20,000 a year, averaging about one-third of the total average annual number of job openings during the period. During the 1970's, the number of job openings in the building trades is expected to be about 126,000 a year. Thus, even in these occupations in which apprenticeship programs have had their greatest strength, apprenticeship must expand significantly to hold just the proportion of entrants as in the 1960's. The number of apprenticeships completed in recent years is shown in the accompanying table.

TABLE 4.—COMPLETED APPRENTICESHIPS, 1955–68, TOTAL AND SELECTED TRADES

Year	Total [1]	Construction	Metal working	Printing
1955	24,795	13,444	3,617	1,435
1960	31,727	16,656	4,986	1,675
1965	24,917	16,201	3,770	1,565
1968	37,287	20,263	6,916	2,124

[1] Includes miscellaneous trades not shown separately.

Source: Manpower Report of the President, 1970. Table F–18.

From time to time studies have indicated that great increases in apprentice training are needed to meet replacement needs and expansions of trained personnel in certain expanding areas. Such estimates have generally assumed that apprenticeship would be or should be a much more traveled road than it is, or has been in the past. Fears of disastrous shortages have not been borne out because of the alternative ways of getting started in a trade.

The question has been raised whether changing technology has made it possible for persons with less training to perform on the job and has also reduced the number of the all-around workmen needed by industry. In terms of the requirements of industry, is there any reason to expect a growing demand for apprenticeship? Or should there be greater efforts to encourage other paths to the building trades, printing, and machinist jobs.

Apprenticeship has persisted in certain trades characterized by a high degree of unionization and small firms which are individually unable to provide training and assurance of steady employment, and high turnover. Journeymen have less attachment to an employer than to an industry. The future of apprenticeship thus appears to be linked to the persistence of the present structure of the labor market in these trades.

In discussions over the future magnitude of apprenticeship programs, the options are likely to be a little more or about the same. But discussions over the composition of the program are likely to be more sharply focused on assistance to veterans and opportunities for members of minority groups. Black workers have been under-represented in some trades, for example, and especially under-represented in the highly skilled jobs. In 1969 about 15,000 out of 200,000 apprentices registered under Federal programs were from minority groups, an increase of 4,000 during the year, but still an under-representation. In early 1971 the Department of Labor proposed new regulations to promote equal opportunity in the selection of apprentices for skilled trades and crafts. The new regulations require that registered apprenticeship programs take affirmative action through aggressive recruitment of minority youths; passive nondiscrimination will not be enough. Apprenticeship programs provide a path to highly skilled, better-paying jobs for those who have long been held back by discriminatory practices.

THE JOB CORPS AND OTHER INSTITUTIONAL TRAINING

The Jobs Corps was started in 1965 by the Office of Economic Opportunity to teach and train disadvantaged youth in new surroundings far removed from the ghetto environment. It offered basic education, vocational training, recreation and work experience in improvised residential centers—old military bases, hospitals, and hotels—generally located in rural areas. Most were conservation centers run by the Departments of Agriculture or Interior, stressing remedial education for functional illiterates as well as work experience. Several large urban centers were operated by private firms to train the more literate youths in skills that would lead to employment in urban areas. A few centers were also provided for women and operated by private or nonprofit groups.

During the 1965–June 1969 period, enrollments totaled nearly 250,-000; for 1969 they were 53,000. About three out of four enrollees were male youths averaging 17 years of age; of those old enough to be eligible for the draft, three out of five had failed the qualifying tests for educational, physical, or other reasons. Fewer than a third were white.

The Jobs Corps encountered difficulties from the outset as a result of enrolling too many youths too fast before a program had been properly developed and tested. It ran into heavy fire from the Congress and had a difficult time trying to prove its worth.

A major attempt to evaluate experience was built into the program from the beginning. Studies within the program and by outsiders sought to identify successes and failures and determine whether benefits outweighed costs. Experience proved difficullt to assess, however, and despite a substantial volume of research, the central issue of whether Jobs Corps experience had any longrun beneficial effect on future earnings and employment experience remained unresolved. The various studies, although contradictory in many respects, did tend to agree that there is a measurable difference between those who stayed in the program for 6 months or more and those who participated only a few months or weeks. They also confirmed the usefulness of residential centers for certain youths who had been unable to learn in blighted and disruptive environments. On the other hand, high dropout rates in the first 30 days after enrollment suggested that many centers were probably located too far from home and in remote areas that were uncongenial to many youths. Many centers proved less self-sufficient than intended. Moreover, they were too far away from businesses that might provide job opportunities.

Among other questions posed by the Job Corps experience, one stemmed from the age of the participants. Since most were 16 and 17 years old, age itself was an obstacle to employment. Thus some interim role—such as further training—seemed to be needed. Another question stemmed from its expense. Since the Job Corps provided room and board, it was a high cost operation which put it at a disadvantage when compared with less expensive programs—unless it could demonstrate that it has a definable role quite distinct from other programs and could identify the youths who can profit most from its special advantages.

On July 1, 1970, the Job Corps was transferred to the Department of Labor, wholly revamped, and integrated into the Department's overall manpower program. Fifty-nine of the least effective and most remote centers were closed and 30 smaller new centers that would accommodate about 25,000 persons were planned in cities or nearby. The relocation of the centers is intended to make it possible to coordinate Job

Corps programs with other manpower programs. A few small residential centers are for youths with serious personal problems; these centers will have no training facilities but will enroll the youths in work-training programs in the community.

Institutional training was also provided under the Manpower Development and Training Act. Seventy MDTA training centers have been established in which occupational skills are taught and remedial education provided, but without residential facilities. In the first 3 years after passage of the MDTA enrollment in institutional training programs increased rapidly, but declined after 1966 as other manpower programs were developed. About two out of three persons trained has been disadvantaged. About a third of all trainees have been enrolled in shortage occupations.

JOBS, PUBLIC SERVICE CAREERS, AND OTHER OJT

Private business launched a different approach to reduce hard core unemployment in 1968 in response to a Presidential request. Under the leadership of the newly formed National Alliance of Businessmen, employers in 50 cities joined in the job opportunities in the business sector (JOBS) program which reversed the usual sequence of events. If offered a regular job first and then supplemented it with remedial education and training in the belief that this approach would give a better incentive to the disadvantaged. An initial goal of 100,000 jobs by June 1969 was established, and it was exceeded. On-the-job training had long been part of the manpower program but the enlistment of well-organized private initiative was new.

Beginning in 1969, Federal funds were made available to reimburse employers for training costs. More than 80,000 trainees were enrolled under the Government contract program by January 1970, about half of them 21 years of age or younger; seven out of eight were Negroes or Spanish Americans. In addition, about 300,000 were employed by private firms without Government subsidy.

The program was expanded in 1970 to additional cities and greater stress was placed on upgrading workers already employed but in dead-end jobs. Enrollment of 600,000 disadvantaged persons is the target for June 1971.

The retention rate has been above 50 percent in the JOBS program, which is good compared to other manpower programs. It is about the same as the usual turnover rates for entry level jobs in private industry, which may be considered a substantial achievement since the JOBS program is generally controlling the kinds of applicants that personnel offices have historically been turning down.

How this program will fare when economic growth is sluggish is not clear. Certainly it will be difficult to maintain the program's momentum when firms are slashing payrolls. A related question is whether there will be an increasing tendency for employers to "cream" the ranks of the unemployed, hiring the more qualified rather than the hard core. This could be considered less of a criticism of the program than recognition that JOBS must be part of a broader approach that includes other programs for the hard-core.

For small firms that cannot provide the full range of services that characterize JOBS programs, a JOBS optional program continues the job training efforts originally established under the MDTA.

The JOBS program has attracted particular interest because it is the first major program that has enlisted the private sector, which, after all, accounts for five out of six jobs in the American economy. Moreover it is the first large-scale Federal program for the poor that stresses hire first, train later, an approach that has won support because it avoids the letdown that occurs when disadvantaged youth are trained in an institutional setting and are unable to find employment after the training is completed.

A counterpart to the JOBS program, the Public Service careers program was started in 1970 to provide employment in rapidly expanding governmental agencies, especially State and local governments. In recent years, employment opportunities in the public sector have been expanding twice as fast as those in the private sector. From 1950 to 1970, employment in State and local governments increased from 4 million to about 9.5 million. Entry into these jobs has been difficult, however, particularly for disadvantaged young people who have found civil service requirements an insurmountable barrier. Moreover, they have had little encouragement from State and local agencies. Hard pressed to finance the growing demand for education and other public services, States and localities have not had the funds to establish training programs of their own.

Like the JOBS program, the PSC program provides funds to governmental agencies for training and services such as health and education that are needed to help disadvantaged workers adjust to the world of work. Salaries and fringe benefits are paid by the agency providing the job. Like the JOBS program, PSC also puts the newly hired disadvantaged on the payroll first as a regular full-time employee and then introduces the training program.

Five approaches to the encouragement of public employment have been designed. The first stresses entry level jobs and opportunities for upgrading of current employees in State, county, and local governments. The second enlists the cooperation of other Federal agencies in encouraging the employment of disadvantaged under ongoing grant-in-aid programs for education, hospital care, pollution control, and so on. Again, the disadvantaged would be enrolled in regular jobs that qualify them for the same retention rights as other employees, and supplemental funds would be provided to cooperating agencies to defray costs of training, education and special services. The third approach incorporates the new careers program that was started by the Office of Economic Opportunity to help overcome the shortage of subprofessional personnel in health and welfare occupations. The fourth approach calls for cooperation with the Federal Civil Service Commission in making it easier for the disadvantaged to enter Federal employment and to advance beyond entry level positions. An applicant may be hired for a maintenance or service job on the basis of an interview rather than a qualifying examination, and, after a probationary period, could be made a regular employee in the agency without further testing. Apprenticeship opportunities will also be expanded in

Government agencies. The fifth approach offers temporary subsidized jobs to persons who have completed training but who are unable to find employment.

All of these programs are open to persons 17 years old and over except the new careers program which has a minimum age requirement of 18. Persons in other manpower programs will be informed of PEC opportunities and encouraged to transfer when it is advantageous to do so. In its 1971 budget proposal the Department of Labor requested funds to provide 86,000 training opportunities for PSC (compared to 103,000 for the JOBS program). Three-fourths of the funds would be provided from appropriations for the Office of Economic Opportunity.

On-the-job training for veterans has become increasingly important, with funds for fiscal 1972 estimated at $200 million, four times the sum spent in 1969. This program is administered by the Veterans' Administration.

NEIGHBORHOOD YOUTH CORPS AND WORK SUPPORT

The Neighborhood Youth Corps was ostensibly set up under the Equal Opportunity Act to provide education and training for disadvantaged youths. It also sought to provide work experience and income. The operation of the program was delegated to the Department of Labor.

The NYC tried to reach youths 16 to 21, through three programs: A summer program, a part-time program for youths going to school, and a full-time program for youths out of school.

As a training program, the out-of-school Youth Corps was much less ambitious than, say the Job Corps. It provided fewer training resources and its counseling and training activities were limited. Most of the money went directly to enrollees and because of the minimum investment in training the cost per person was lower than it was in the Job Corps, the program became more of a device to alleviate poverty than as a device to prepare disadvantaged youth to adjust to a work environment. The in-school and summer programs provided badly needed income for the poor, helping to keep youngsters from dropping out of school and keeping them usefully occupied in the summer, which became increasingly important in the wake of the urban riots of the late 1960's.

Total enrollment has increased from 138,000 in 1965 to more than 500,000, accounting for about half of first-time enrollments in work and training programs administered by the Department of Labor during the year 1969 and one-third of the year's budget. Over the 5-year period, about three out of five enrollees have been in the Neighborhood Youth Corps.

The summer program became an increasingly large part of the Youth Corps over the 5 years, accounting for seven out of 10 participants. The out-of-school and part-time in-school programs were slowly cut back to about half of the peak enrollments of 1966 and 1971.

The focus of the out-of-school program, which was originally aimed at the entire 16 to 21 age group, has been redirected during 1969 and 1970 toward 16- and 17-year-old youths on the assumption that the

Job Corps and other programs are more suitable for older youths. What the younger group needs is prevocational training and education and a more sustained program. The length of the training period is thus being extended from less than 6 months to more than a year. The in-school program's training component is also being strengthened.

In the 1972 budget, NYC is clearly identified as a work support program—is contrasted with the training programs—along with Operation Mainstream and the concentrated employment program. Whereas NYC and CEP are primarily for urban youth, Operation Mainstream provides work for the chronically unemployed in rural areas.

EMPLOYMENT SERVICES

The system of public employment offices, established in 1933 and revised and modified on several occasions since then, is potentially a key component of the job placement effort. Its operations are complicated by the fact that it is responsible for administration of the unemployment compensation program as well as for counseling and placement. Some observers have recommended that these two functions be assigned to separate agencies.

Public employment offices are operated by the States with Federal financial support and in accord with Federal regulations. In recent years, these offices have made about 6 million placements a year outside of agriculture, mostly in domestic and other personal service, in construction labor, and in other unskilled work. Relatively few skilled workers or white collar workers have obtained jobs through the employment service. Overall, only about a fourth of the jobs in the private sector are filled through the statement employment offices since employers are able to fill most jobs directly.

One of the difficulties in the placement operation of the Federal-State employment system is the conflict between welfare and economic objectives. On the one hand, the employment service has been under pressure to find jobs for the disadvantaged. On the other hand, it has encountered objections from employers who complain about having to interview many patently unqualified candidates.

Since 1968 the Manpower Administration has been experimenting with the use of computers to improve job placement services of State employment security offices throughout the country. First it developed a computerized job bank experimentally in Baltimore. Brief descriptions of all known local job openings were obtained. Then the list of openings was updated every night by deleting filled jobs and adding new openings. The revised job list was printed out and distributed the next morning to counselors and placement interviewers—not only those in the employment service office, but also those in nonprofit community agencies. The resulting increase in the volume of activity and success of the experiment led to an expansion of the program. By the end of 1970 the Labor Department's job banks were operating in about 60 of the Nation's largest cities, with the target of 100 by mid-1971.

The second step—a long range one—is the development of a job matching system which will make it possible to match job applications with job openings, rapidly and efficiently. This is a long-range objective that will not be achieved on a wide scale until after extensive testing of several alternative approaches being tried in a number of States.

The job bank gives the worker access to many more job openings and gives the employer a potentially larger group of applicants to select from. It offers increased opportunities for expanding the scope, magnitude, and effectiveness of public employment services.

MINIMUM WAGES AND OTHER PROTECTIVE LEGISLATION

The States have long sought to protect young people from hazardous jobs, overwork, and unduly low pay. Twenty-eight State child labor laws had been enacted before 1900. The Federal Government has also regulated youth employment since 1938. Today, both State and Federal laws must be observed, and where they apply to the same situation, the more restrictive standard prevails.

Most States restrict the employment of youths up to the age of 16, and require school attendance to the same age. From State to State, provisions vary widely, especially with regard to special exemptions for employment of minors under 16. Under Federal law—principally the Fair Labor Standards Act—16 is also the minimum age for employment generally, but 18 is the minimum age for a number of hazardous occupations ranging from coal mining to wrecking and demolition. Youths 14 and 15 years of age can work in certain occupations under certain conditions.

Federal law also provides for certification programs under which students and learners can work at wages below the established minimum wage for specified periods of time.

As an obstacle to employment, Government regulation differs from the other obstacles discussed in this paper: It is an intentional obstacle, not an unwanted byproduct of prejudice and discriminatory practices, imperfections in the labor market, or the inadequacies of the job seekers. Society has decided that up to a point other goals related to health and education are more important than the work experience and income. Thus, in general, there is no evidence of any serious effort to do away with these protective provisions.

But opinions differ over specific provisions, especially over the level of the minimum wage. A number of economists have argued that any governmentally imposed minimum wage interferes with the efficient operation of the labor market and it leads to unemployment since workers whose output isn't worth the minimum rate won't be hired. Supporters of minimum wage legislation concede that at some level a minimum wage rate would deter employment, but they argue that it is possible to raise the rate for the poorest paid workers without having an adverse effect on employment—and indeed Congress takes the probable impact of an increase into account when it periodically revises the minimum wage law. Many empirical studies of the impact of past changes in the minimum wage have been conducted but the results aren't conclusive.

During the 1960's, as the rate of unemployment among youths failed to decline as rapidly as the rate among adults, the minimum wage issue was raised again in a new light. It was suggested that minimum wages might be inhibiting the employment of youth even if it had not affected adult employment, and that the minimum rate for youths ought to be lower than the rate for adults.

The question was studied in considerable detail by the Bureau of Labor Statistics. Its report attributed the youth unemployment problem to a number of factors—the growing proportion of teenagers in the civilian labor force, the difficulties in accommodating job requirements to school schedules, the decline in the number of agricultural jobs, higher costs of training, the draft, dissatisfaction among employers over teenage absenteeism and performance on the job, State and Federal restrictions on hours of work and hazardous occupations, as well as the minimum wage.

The report indicated that a separate rate for youths might be desirable, but that little responsibility for past employment problems could be attributed to the minimum wage. Nor was there much evidence to suggest that Government regulation is a significant barrier to youth employment, although the redtape associated with obtaining learner and student certificates may explain why these programs were underutilized.

V. THE POLICY FRAMEWORK

Manpower planning for the 1970's must take into account a number of questions, including the following:

1. What are the dimensions of the youth employment problem at the beginning of the 1970's?

2. What have we learned from the manpower programs of the late 1960's that will help us choose among alternative ways of providing remedial education, training, work experience, counseling, and so on during the 1970's?

3. How much is being spent and what is the likelihood that greater resources will be available in the years ahead to assist young people who need help in making the transition to the world of work?

SOME PRELIMINARY CONSIDERATIONS

Quantitative data relating to the first question above are reasonably accessible and convincing. Parts one and two of this paper show clearly, for example, that the growth rate of the youth population has slowed down. Although there will be more youths 16 to 24 years of age during the 1970's they will constitute a smaller proportion of the total population than during the late 1960's. Youth employment, like adult employment, will continue to depend primarily on the level of economic activity. Projections of job requirements for the 1970's, made on the basis of reasonable assumptions, identify the industries and occupations that will offer the greatest employment opportunities. Guidance counselors and manpower planners have useful data to work with. The projections also point up declining opportunities, such as the steadily falling demand for unskilled labor. The case for more education and training is persuasive. The demographic and economic data provide some basis for optimism in planning youth manpower programs, optimism that must be tempered by a recognition of some less tangible difficulties related to the attitudes of many young people.

When we direct our attention away from the demographic and economic basis and begin to assess attitudes and mood we find elements of greater uncertainty. Clearly large numbers of affluent youth are questioning many aspects of American life, and ghetto youth are more assertive of their rights; unwilling to settle for jobs that do not provide for advancement or security. Patience has worn thin. Tempers are shorter. Demands are greater. Other ills of society—crime, drugs, environmental deterioration, impatience with the war—all these have vastly complicated the problem of motivating and training young people for gainful employment. Whatever efforts are made to improve manpower programs, the outcome will inevitably depend in some measure on the success of other programs to deal with the Nation's economic and social malaise and the revitalization of public faith in the intent, will, and competence of government.

Having thus taken account of the setting in which manpower programs operate, we are ready to ask: What progress can be made in easing the transition to work by training, counseling, and related activities? Where should the money go? More for JOB's and less for Job Corps? Or vice versa? More for Neighborhood Youth Corps, or less? And so on.

After more than 5 years of experience, one might hope that the answer would be clear—that we could say, with a fair degree of certainty, that one program is better than another—or that the costs and benefits of individual programs can be toted up. When the poverty programs were initiated in the midsixties rather extensive efforts were made to obtain information that would make it possible to answer such questions. Continuing evaluation of programs was undertaken and a number of studies have been made. The results have been rather ambiguous, however. What has been demonstrated chiefly is that the job of evaluation is an extremely difficult one.

How do you measure the differences in employment experience between Job Corps graduates, trainees, and others who haven't trained? And after having established some comparative data how do you make sure that the differences are properly attributable to the training program itself and not to the conditions that led to the selection of particular young people to enter the Job Corps program? Is a program to be judged solely by the results that are quantifiable—increased earnings, for example—or should weight be given to intangibles such as a reduction in delinquency?

Or if you compare two programs, such as Job Corps and Neighborhood Youth Corps, and discover that the cost per Job Corps trainee is far higher than the cost per enrollee in NYC, can you conclude that taxpayers get more for their money from NYC? (Differences in unit costs are illustrated in table 5.) Or should one attempt more sophisticated analysis that tries to take into account the training achievements under the Job Corps training program that will lead to greater lifetime earnings for the the Job Corps trainee.

Nevertheless, at the beginning of the 1970's a consensus was developing on several issues: (1) Greater interest in jobs first, and training later, (2) a persistent recognition of the need to couple remedial education programs with training and work experience, (3) an elevation in the status of vocational education, (4) reorganization of manpower programs to provide better coordination and more flexibility, and (5) a willingness to increase emergency expenditures during periods of economic slowdown. The following exercise in estimating costs take these into account. The first discussion of the alternatives follows the categorical approach which has guided manpower programs since they were introduced. Then the administration's revenue-sharing approach is considered.

TABLE 5.—UNIT COSTS OF MAJOR PROGRAM APPROACHES IN 1970 [1]

Approach	Man-year unit cost estimate	Average duration of en- rollment (years)	Participant unit cost estimate
On-the-job-training	$1,900	0.55	$1,050
Institutional training	2,800	.54	1,500
Rehabilitation	1,150	1.17	1,350
Postschool work support	3,800	.51	1,950
Subtotal postschool	1,850	.78	1,400
In-school work support	1,600	.28	450
Total	1,800	.58	1,050

[1] Based on man-years of service. Includes State and local share, if any. Excludes child care components. All dollar amounts rounded to nearest 50.

Source: Special Analyses, Budget of the United States Government, fiscal year 1972, table J–10.

BUDGETARY ALTERNATIVES: CATEGORICAL APPROACH

How much is being spent for youth manpower programs, how many youths are being helped, and what are some budget alternatives for the future?

The budget that was submitted to the Congress for fiscal year 1971 provides a starting point for our discussion. It recommended $93.3 billion for major social programs, including $3.2 billion for manpower programs (defined as programs that operate outside the educational system and are intended primarily for the disadvantaged—thus excluding vocational education but including vocational rehabilitation). This sum represented a 50-percent increase in 3 years: in 1968 manpower outlays totaled over $2 billion, as shown in chart 6. (These figures are from the Government's Special Analyses, fiscal year 1971 and are not consistent with the presentation of the revenue-sharing budget for 1972.)

The number of new enrollees in manpower programs is expected to increase to 2.1 million in 1971 (compared to 1.5 million in 1968), including 452,000 in vocational rehabilitation programs.

Of more than 1.2 million enrollees in programs other than rehabilitation, an estimated 40 percent were estimated to be 21 years of age or younger.

A crude first approximation from the foregoing figures suggests that in 1971 the Government proposed to spend about $1.1 billion for on-the-job training, institutional training, work support programs, job placement and related manpower activities to help 650,000 youths in the 16 to 21 age group make the transition to the world of work.

TABLE 6.—FEDERAL OUTLAYS AND INDIVIDUALS SERVED BY PROGRAM, 1968–71

[Outlays in millions of dollars, individuals in thousands]

Program	Outlays				New enrollees [1]			
	1968 actual	1969 actual	1970 estimate	1971 estimate	1968 actual	1969 actual	1970 estimate	1971 estimate
Vocational Rehabilitation	281	351	478	530	330	368	432	452
Employment Service	312	317	350	380	([2])	([2])	([2])	([2])
Job Opportunities in the Business Sector/On-job training	68	104	192	346	107	136	156	202
Manpower Development and Training Institutional training	203	197	205	212	140	135	148	152
Neighborhood Youth Corps in-school and summer	198	182	212	215	374	429	445	427
Concentrated Employment Program	68	140	189	212	54	127	152	155
Work Incentive Program	0	33	138	199	0	81	133	180
Job Corps	318	258	180	192	65	53	47	49
Neighborhood Youth Corps out-of-school	143	106	100	121	94	74	37	59
On-the-job-training for veterans	5	49	92	115	19	49	65	80
Other programs [3]	490	488	566	714	331	309	338	370
Total	2,086	2,225	2,702	3,236	1,514	1,761	1,953	2,126

[1] Estimated new enrollees during a fiscal year, less overlap due to persons served more than once.
[2] Enrollment not applicable.
[3] For some programs enrollment data are not applicable.

Source: Special Analyses, Budget of the United States Government, Fiscal year 1971, table J–1.

Chart 3. Expansion of manpower programs, 1962-71

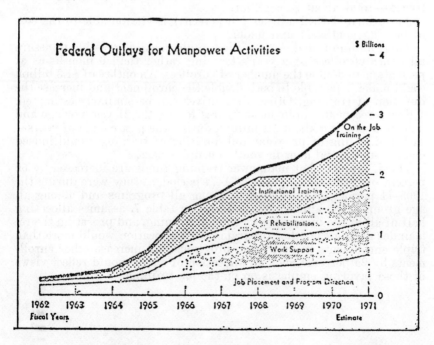

Federal Outlays for Manpower Activities

Source: Special Analyses. Budget of the United States, Fiscal Year 1971, p. 134.

ILLUSTRATIVE CATEGORICAL OPTIONS, 1972–74

Looking beyond 1971, what is the range of alternative program changes. In simplified form, here are some of the options.

First, suppose that no substantial increases in manpower funds are forthcoming. If policymakers should decide that youth employment programs deserve higher priority despite the shortage of funds, they can shift the present allocation of funds in favor of young people. In recent years about 40 percent of the funds go to persons 16 to 21. This percentage might be increased to 50 percent or 60 percent to give youth greater assistance under existing budgets. An allocation of 60 percent of the funds for youth would make it possible to raise annual new youth enrollments to about 1 million.

Second, suppose that funds for the training components of manpower programs were increased by 50 percent over the next 3 years—as they were during the past 3 years—how might the programs for youth be expanded? The additional funds could be used either to increase the average length of training or to increase the number of youths enrolled in the programs, as noted below.

Government-budget analysts estimate the average duration of enrollments in training programs at slightly over 6 months.

Proposed outlays for the institutional training, on-the-job training, and work support components of the manpower programs alone—after deduction for rehabilitation, research, and various support activities—total about $1.6 billion.

An estimated $640 million (40 percent) is attributable to the cost of helping youths 21 and under.

Thus, an additional $640 million might make it possible to assure all youth enrollees of a year's training rather than 6 months as at present, or to double the number of enrollees. An outlay of $1.3 billion could make it possible to both double the enrollment and increase the duration of training. Other alternatives can be similarly estimated.

Given recent unemployment figures for youths 21 years or age and under—averaging about 1.1 million during the past couple of years—such a doubling of program and duration of training would indeed make a substantial dent in youth unemployment.

Third, suppose that manpower training funds are increased by 50 percent over the next 3 years 1971–74 period, as they were during the 1968–71 period, and distributed among all programs and among all age groups. One alternative, budget I in table 7, assumes allocating half of all of the increase to on-the-job training, and prorating the remainder among the other programs. This allocation would more than triple enrollments in on-the-job programs and increase other enrollments by 25 percent. Such an allocation of funds would reflect views, of those favoring emphasis on on-the-job training.

TABLE 7.—ALTERNATIVE HYPOTHETICAL BUDGETS FOR 1974

[Outlays in millions of dollars, enrollees in thousands]

Program	Budget I [1]		Budget II [2]	
	Outlay	Enrollees	Outlay	Enrollees
Vocational rehabilitation	$669	556	$669	556
Employment service	487	(³)	487	(³)
Job opportunities in the business sector/on-the-job training	1,165	675	1,165	675
Manpower development and training institutional training	279	187	279	187
Neighborhood youth corps inschool and summer	282	525	645	1,281
Concentrated employment program	279	191	636	465
Work incentive program	258	221	258	221
Job Corps	242	60	242	60
Neighborhood youth corps out-of-school	163	72	363	177
On-the-job training for veterans	149	98	149	98
Other programs	881	455	881	455
Total	4,854	2,940	5,664	4,175

[1] Assumes a 50-percent increase in total manpower funds over 3 years, in constant dollars. Half of the total increase is allocated to JOBS and related on-the-job training. The remainder of the dollar increase is distributed proportionately among other programs. Figures are projected from table 6, using 1971 as a base.
[2] Assumes a 75-percent increase in total funds, with the additional 25 percent in funds allocated among NYC and CEP programs (items 5, 6, 9).
[3] Enrollees figures not applicable.

Note: In both budgets, 40 percent of the funds would go to youths 16 to 21.

Fourth, assume a 75 percent increase in funds (rather than 50 percent) with the additional 25 percent allocated to the Neighborhood Youth Corps and concentrated employment program. This alternative, shown as budget II in table 7, might be proposed on the assumption of a large reduction in military expenditures and a slowdown in economic activity that fostered backing for work-support programs rather than expansion of training programs.

Whether the public could be convinced that (*a*) youth employment indeed deserves this priority in manpower programs, especially during a period of high adult unemployment, (*b*) that investment in manpower programs is a better investment than a comparable expenditure for vocational education or other types of programs to combat poverty, (*c*) that the expansion of facilities could actually be achieved, and (*d*) that enrollees would join the programs and stay in—all these questions are beyond the scope of this exercise. What has been suggested here only is a way of facing up to alternatives. For more than 2 years there has been considerable talk about what to do with the "fiscal dividend" that would result from the attainment of peace in Vietnam and the continued growth of the economy. The dividend still has not materialized but the hope for it need not be abandoned.

DECENTRALIZATION, AND THE REVENUE-SHARING OPTION

A crucial issue in the planning of future manpower programs is the amount of discretion to be given to local areas. The Department of Labor has been urging that greater flexibility be given to State and local officials in determining how much should be spent for various types of institutional training programs, for example, or work support, or on-the-job training programs. In the past, Congress has specified the amount to be spent for each program within these broad categories. In the future what the Manpower Administration would prefer is a more flexible approach that would enable local areas to design and operate programs that would be more responsive to needs of participants and the employment opportunities. The choice among institutional training, on-the-job training, work support and so on would be made locally.

Such flexibility and delegation of authority to States and localities was recommended in the Manpower Training Act proposed to the Congress in 1969. The act also sought to consolidate the funding of programs administered by the Department of Labor, including those funded by the Office of Economic Opportunity, to eliminate overlap and duplication. In addition, it sought to establish a nationwide computerized job bank system based on recent trial efforts in selected cities. As enacted by Congress in 1970, however, the bill was unacceptable to the President, who vetoed it largely because of the type of public service job program included in it.

Similar objectives are being sought in the legislation proposed this year. The administration's 1971 proposal incorporates manpower into the $16 billion revenue-sharing program. Of this total, $11 billion would go for so-called special revenue sharing. The money would be earmarked for six broad areas—including $2 billion for manpower, an increase of about one-third over current spending levels. (Table 8 shows manpower outlays for all Federal agencies, including the Department of Labor's revenue sharing component.) About $6 out of $7 would be apportioned among the States by a statutory formula, that takes into account labor force, unemployment, and the number of low-income individuals. The remainder would be allocated by the Secretary of Labor for special projects. The States and localities would determine the allocation of the funds they receive among programs in accord with local needs. All governmental units receiving funds would be required to publish an annual statement of program objectives and proposed expenditures for the year ahead along with a report on the preceding year's activities.

The act also includes a "trigger mechanism" that would provide additional funds for training and jobs in areas of high unemployment when national unemployment rises to 4.5 percent or more for 3 consecutive months. It also provides authority to create public service jobs during periods of slack economic activity, provided that they be recognized as "transitional opportunities" limited to 2 years. To meet current needs the administration has proposed creation of 200,000 jobs for welfare recipients.

In his manpower message to the Congress the President called the 9-year-old commitment to manpower programs a good idea, but said that the programs had become "overcentralized, bureaucratic, remote from the people they mean to serve, overguidelined, and far less effective than they might be in helping the unskilled and disadvantaged."

He added that it was essential to recognize that the job market "is really thousands of interacting but separate markets spread all over the economic and geographic map of the United States, and . . . that the 'labor force' is actually 87 million individual men and women with a wide diversity of training needs."

TABLE 8.—FEDERAL OUTLAYS FOR MANPOWER PROGRAMS BY ADMINISTERING AGENCIES

[Outlays in millions of dollars]

Agency and program	1969 actual	1970 actual	1971 estimate	1972 estimate
Office of Economic Opportunity	293	30	32	33
Department of Defense	24	21	19	19
Department of Health, Education, and Welfare	534	659	877	999
Department of Housing and Urban Development	(¹)	6	29	36
Department of the Interior	24	33	39	39
Department of Justice	2	3	4	6
Department of Labor:				
Special revenue sharing for manpower training:				
Existing authorities ²	837	1,056	1,331	1,375
Additional amounts				153
Work incentive training	26	67	97	155
Employment service	293	325	344	363
Computerized job placement	5	6	26	28
ES labor market information	19	21	23	24
BLS labor market information	9	9	10	11
OFCC and age discrimination	1	1	3	4
Program administration and other	87	108	151	134
Subtotal, Labor	1,276	1,592	1,985	2,247
Veterans Administration	90	141	237	281
Equal Employment Opportunity Commission	9	12	18	25
Total	2,313	2,563	3,314	3,758

¹ Less than $500,000.
² These include JOBS, Public Service Careers, MDTA institutional training, Job Corps, NYC, Operation Mainstream, and CEP.

Source: Special Analyses, 1972, table J–11.

CONCLUDING THOUGHTS AND UNANSWERED QUESTIONS

This review of program alternatives began with some questions about the effectiveness of manpower programs. In concluding, it seems appropriate to reemphasize this fact, and to elaborate on it. Present programs are operating despite a number of gaps in our knowledge and despite some questionable assumptions about youth behavior. Indeed, it is just likely that the budgetary aspects of youth employment problems are the easiest to define. It has been much more difficult to determine how well programs work and whether they are worth the cost than whether they can be financed.

One of the biggest gaps in knowledge was recognized several years ago—the need for data about how young people adjust over time. How do they proceed from their first job experience to a secure place in the world of work? Most research has measured the composition of the work force, the unemployed, at particular points in time. The evolution of the work life of selected individuals had not been charted. About 5 years ago a million-dollar study or so-called longitudinal study of a group of young people was started and it will be concluded during 1971.

Researchers have also pointed to the need to know more about how different kinds of young people conduct their job hunts—the wages they expect, the length of time they are willing to look, the sources of information they use, the wages they expect, and their attitude toward legitimate work.

Questions have been raised, too, about the inferences that sometimes are drawn too readily from availability data. Are the frustrations encountered in looking for a job merely demoralizing or do they provide young people with a useful learning experience? Is a high rate of turnover among young poeple a discouraging note or is it a natural reflection of the urge to experiment and a healthy evidence of the opportunities provided by a free labor market?

The avowed purpose of manpower programs is to increase employment opportunities for the disadvantaged and to improve the performance of the economy by eliminating skill shortage, by increasing productivity and facilitating the movement of workers to jobs. During the 1963–70 period billions of dollars were spent on manpower training programs and several million enrollees received assistance in some form. The value of that assistance—by how much did it improve employment opportunities and by how much did it improve productivity in the economy cannot be measured. But so long as youth employment problems persist, determined efforts must be made to see that the existing programs pay off or are modified in the light of new experience. That success is not assured, does not make the goal less important.

A NOTE ON SOURCES

In preparing this background paper I have drawn freely not only on Government documents but on published studies by a number of participants in public programs and independent observers and scholars. In particular, the Princeton symposium on youth unemployment and Edward Kalachek's study of the youth labor market were especially helpful. Among the Government documents, a number of studies by the Bureau of Labor Statistics were indispensable, as were the manpower reports of the President and the analyses of the Federal budget.

The major sources are listed below:

U.S. GOVERNMENT PUBLICATIONS

Special Analyses, Budget of the United States, fiscal year 1971 Part II, Section J (GPO 1970)
Special Analyses, Budget of the United States, fiscal year 1972
U.S. House, Hearings before a subcommittee of the Committee on Appropriations, 91st Congress, 2d Session, Subcommittee on Departments of Labor and Health, Education, and Welfare, Part 5 Department of Labor (May 1970)
U.S. Department of Labor, Manpower Administration
Manpower Report of the President, for years 1963 through 1970
U.S. Manpower in the 1970's: Opportunity and Challenge
U.S. Department of Labor, Bureau of Labor Statistics
The U.S. Economy in 1980. A Summary of BLS projections by Maxine G. Stewart (Bulletin 1673, 1970)
"The U.S. Labor Force: Projections to 1985," by Sophia C. Travis, Monthly Labor Review, May 1970. Represented as Special Labor Force Report 119.
"Vietnam War Veterans transition to civilian life," by Elizabeth Waldman, Monthly Labor Review, November 1970. Reprinted as Special Labor Force Report 126.
Youth Unemployment and Minimum Wages, prepared under the direction of Thomas W. Gavett (Bulletin 1657, 1970)
Employment and Earnings (monthly)
Monthly Labor Review
Handbook of Labor Statistics (annually)

OTHER SOURCES

Kalachek, Edward, "The Youth Labor Market," Wayne State University, Institute of Labor and Industrial Relations, Policy Papers on Human Resources and Industrial Relations, No. 12, January 1969

Kershaw, Joseph A. "Government Against Poverty" (Washington: The Brookings Institution, 1970)

Lêvine, Robert A. "The Poor Ye Need Not Have With You: Lessons from the the War on Poverty." (Cambridge: The M.I.T. Press, 1970)

Levitan, Sar. "The Great Society's Poor Law" (Baltimore: John Hopkins, 1969)

Piore, Michael J. "On-the-Job Training of Disadvantaged Workers," in Public-Private Manpower Policies, edited by Arnold R. Weber, Frank H. Cassell, Woodrow L. Ginsberg (Madison, Wis.: Industrial Relations Research Association, 1969)

Strauss, George. "Apprenticeship: An Evaluation of the Need," Employment Policy and the Labor Market, edited by Arthur M. Ross (Berkeley and Los Angeles: University of California Press, 1965)

"The Transition from School to Work," A Report Based on the Princeton Symposium, May 9–10, 1968. Research Report Series III, Industrial Relations Section, Princeton University

"Vocational Education," Report of a conference sponsored by the Brookings Institution, published as a supplement to the Journal of Human Resources, vol. III, 1968.

APPENDIX TABLE A.—EMPLOYMENT AND AVERAGE ANNUAL OPENINGS IN SELECTED OCCUPATIONS, 1968 AND PROJECTED 1980 REQUIREMENTS

Occupations	Employ-ment 1968	Require-ments 1980	Percent change, 1968–80	Average annual openings, 1968–80 [1]
Total	75,920,000	95,100,000	25	3,990,000
Professional, technical and related workers	10,325,000	15,500,000	50	777,000
Business administration and related professions:				
Accountant	590,000	720,000	43	33,000
Personnel worker	110,000	155,000	43	6,900
Public relations worker	100,000	165,000	64	8,800
Engineering	1,100,000	1,500,000	40	53,000
Health service occupations:				
Dentist	100,000	130,000	30	4,900
Dental hygienist	16,000	33,500	109	2,400
Medical laboratory workers [2]	100,000	190,000	90	12,800
Physician (M.D.'s and D.O.'s)	307,000	469,000	53	20,800
Radiologic technologist	75,000	120,000	60	7,300
Registered nurse	660,000	1,000,000	52	65,000
Speech pathologist and audiologist	18,000	33,000	83	2,300
Natural scientists:				
Chemist	130,000	200,000	56	8,800
Physicist	45,000	75,000	64	3,200
Life scientist	170,000	245,000	41	9,900
Oceanographer	5,200	9,700	85	500
Teachers:				
Elementary school teachers	1,230,000	1,270,000	3.3	56,300
Secondary school teachers	940,000	1,065,000	14	40,000
College and university teachers	286,000	395,000	38	17,000
Technician occupations:				
Engineering and science	620,000	890,000	43	31,000
Draftsmen	295,000	435,000	48	15,300
Other professional and related workers:				
Lawyer	270,000	335,000	23	14,500
Librarians	106,000	135,000	¹29	8,200
Mathmetician	65,000	110,000	60	4,600
Pilot and copilot	52,000	114,000	117	1,800
Programer	175,000	400,000	129	23,000
Social worker	160,000	270,000	67	15,700
Systems analyst	150,000	425,000	183	27,000
Managers, officials, and proprietors	7,776,000	9,500,000	22	380,000
Clerical workers	12,803,000	17,300,000	35	911,000
Bank clerks	400,000	512,000	29	29,500
Bank tellers	230,000	337,000	46	20,000
Bookkeeping workers	1,200,000	1,500,000	19	78,000
Cashiers	730,000	1,110,000	51	69,000
Dental assistant	100,000	150,000	50	9,000
Electronic computer operating personnel	175,000	400,000	129	20,400
Office machine operators	325,000	460,000	39	25,000

See footnotes at end of table.

APPENDIX TABLE A.—EMPLOYMENT AND AVERAGE ANNUAL OPENINGS IN SELECTED
OCCUPATIONS, 1968 AND PROJECTED 1980 REQUIREMENTS—Continued

Occupations	Employ- ment 1968	Require- ments 1980	Percent change, 1968-80	Average annual openings, 1968-80 [1]
Clerical workers—Continued				
Receptionists	240, 000	400, 000	66	30, 000
Shipping and receiving clerks	370, 000	465, 000	25	15, 400
Stenographers and secretaries	2, 650, 000	3, 650, 000	37	237, 000
Telephone operators	400, 000	480, 000	21	28, 000
Typists	700, 000	930, 000	37	63, 000
Sales workers	4, 647, 000	6, 000, 000	29	263, 000
Automobile salesmen	120, 000	145, 000	21	4, 400
Insurance agents and brokers	410, 000	480, 000	17	16, 200
Manufacturers' salesmen	500, 000	735, 000	47	32, 000
Real estate salesmen and brokers	225, 000	270, 000	20	14, 200
Retail trade salesworkers	2, 800, 000	3, 460, 000	24	150, 000
Security sales men	135, 000	170, 000	24	7, 400
Wholesale trade salesworkers	530, 000	695, 000	30	25, 200
Craftsmen, foremen, and kindred workers	10, 015, 000	12, 200, 000	22	396, 000
Building trades:				
Bricklayers	175, 000	230, 000	33	7, 600
Carpenters	859, 000	1, 075, 000	24	39, 300
Electricians (maintenance and construction)	430, 000	575, 000	34	20, 400
Excavating, grading, and road machinery operators	285, 000	425, 000	49	16, 200
Painters and paperhangers	439, 000	560, 000	39	23, 200
Plumbers and pipefitters [3]	330, 000	475, 000	44	19, 500
Mechanics and repairmen:				
Air conditioning, refrigeration, and heating mechanics	100, 000	140, 000	40	5, 000
Airplane mechanics	135, 000	230, 000	70	9, 700
Appliance servicemen	205, 000	260, 000	27	8, 800
Business machine servicemen	115, 000	200, 000	74	8, 500
Industrial machinery repairmen	175, 000	220, 000	25	7, 550
Motor vehicle mechanics	825, 000	1, 000, 000	21	26, 500
Television and radio service technicians	125, 000	145, 000	16	3, 000
Printing: Compositors and typesetters [4]	190, 000	180, 000	−5	3, 200
Operatives	13, 955, 000	15, 400, 000	19	425, 000
Driving occupations:				
Local truckdrivers	1, 200, 000	1, 450, 000	22	37, 000
Over-the-road truckdrivers	640, 000	800, 000	25	21, 600
Other manual occupations:				
Assemblers	785, 000	850, 000	8	26, 000
Gasoline service station attendants	400, 000	475, 000	16	10, 900
Inspectors (manufacturing)	585, 000	635, 000	8	19, 200
Welders and oxygen and arc cutters	480, 000	675, 000	41	23, 000
Nonfarm laborers	3, 555, 000	3, 500, 000	−2	60, 000
Service workers	9, 381, 000	13, 100, 000	40	752, 000
Private household workers	1, 700, 000	1, 980, 000		121, 000
Food service workers:				
Cooks and chefs	670, 000	900, 000	33	48, 000
Waiters and waitresses	960, 000	1, 240, 000	28	67, 000
Health service workers:				
Hospital attendants	800, 000	1, 500, 000	88	100, 000
Licensed practical nurses	320, 000	600, 000	88	48, 000
Personal service workers:				
Barbers	210, 000	260, 000	24	12, 800
Cosmetologists	475, 000	685, 000	43	38, 000
Protective service workers:				
Firefighters	180, 000	245, 000	34	7, 700
Municipal police officers	285, 000	360, 000	28	15, 000
Other service workers: Building custodians	1, 100, 000	1, 460, 000	33	80, 000
Farmworkers	3, 464, 000	2, 600, 000	−33	25, 000

[1] Growth and replacement openings; does not include transfers.
[2] Includes medical technologist, technician, and assistant.
[3] Also called—operating engineer (construction machinery operations).
[4] Also called—composing room occupations.

Note: Percent increase based on unrounded estimates.
Source: The U.S. Economy in 1980 (A Summary of BLS Projections), Bulletin 1673, U.S. Department of Labor, Bureau of Labor Statistics.

BACKGROUND PAPER ON

DAY CARE AND PRESCHOOL SERVICES: TRENDS IN THE 1960's AND ISSUES FOR THE 1970's

By Ronald K. Parker and Jane Knitzer

INTRODUCTION

For a variety of reasons, a burgeoning interest in the creation of an effective network of child care and child development services is now manifest in the United States.

Experts stress the importance of a child's early years upon his development (Bloom, 1964; Birch, 1969), and they have demonstrated the positive value of early education programs (Parker, Ambron, Danielson, Halbrook, and Levine, 1970).

Spokesmen for low-income groups are calling for a more thoughtful and broad commitment to the needs of the young, the poor, and minority children.

Many others, such as the women's liberation movement, are generating a demand to aid working mothers by providing child care and child development.

Opinions vary, overlap, and conflict as to the nature of the goals for child-care services.

For some, the goals would involve the creation of a high quality developmental program accessible to a broad range of children.

Others project the implementation of a network of multiple services with actual, not just theoretical, linkages among programs, with responsive mechanisms for monitoring the individual child's experience, and with defined accountability of the provider to the consumer.

Still a third group would intend simply to furnish more facilities for child care on a temporary basis or for assisting mothers to do better the important task of rearing children in their early years.

With such a multiplicity of goals, the challenge to child-care planners is great. Different goals, stemming from different definitions of the problem, dictate different strategies for achieving results.

This document has been prepared for presentation to the 1970 White House Conference on Children by Dr. Ronald K. Parker, Graduate Center, The City University of New York, and by Dr. Jane Knitzer, Department of Human Development and Family Studies, Cornell University, as a basic "perspective" paper.

It provides an overview of the issues in developing a more extensive child-care network. Its purpose is: (1) to examine and communicate knowledge as to existing child-care and preschool services, (2) to summarize some of the major pragmatic and theoretical problems that are 1970's inheritance from the 1960's--problems that will have to be met during the 1970's, and (3) to pose some critical options for policy decisions.

It must be recognized in passing that the discussion of day-care and preschool programs faces obstacles because child care is generally applicable to children under age 16, whereas preschool services apply to children under age 6. Despite the age differences involved, and except for actual programming, many of the parameters for discussion, conceptually, are the same. Where possible, day care for children under age 6 will be examined separately.

Many qualified individuals contributed generously of their time, their knowledge and their perspectives to this work. The thanks of the authors go to each of them, with special thanks to Mr. Leo Fishman, Office of Child Development; Mr. Richard Emery, Office of Management and Budget; Mr. Harley Frankel, Office of the Undersecretary, HEW; Mrs. Marjorie Elsten, Office of Child Development; Mr. Martin Berdit, University Research Corporation, Washington, D. C.; and Dr. Michael S. March, on loan from the Office of Management and Budget to serve as Senior Research Consultant to the 1970 White House Conference on Children and Youth, who provided general guidance for the paper.

CHAPTER ONE

AN ASSESSMENT OF
PAST AND PRESENT PRACTICE

A. Rationale for an Early Childhood Focus

Both scientific and humanitarian reasons have been
advanced for focusing resources upon a child's development
during his early years. The scientific reasons (particularly
during the early years) are evident from certain basic and
applied research, and, generally, this research data can be
used as rationale for a firm commitment to the total development of the young child.

First, the importance of early environment in
promoting the maximum growth and development of a child is
becoming increasingly clear from published findings of basic
research (Hunt, 1961, Chapter 4). Findings from many areas
of the behavioral sciences suggest that a child's intellect,
physique, and personality develop most rapidly during his
first five years of life (Hunt, 1970). Environmental
experiences occurring during this formative period will
substantially influence his later health, motivation,
intelligence, self-esteem and social interaction. Even
though some genetic constraints exist across all of these
areas of development, these environmental influences can
either enhance or impede development. Thus, it would seem
far easier to plan a positive program of development during
the early years than to mount a costly, sometimes ineffective,
program of remediation at later ages. There is convincing
documentation, for example, that an inadequate health and
nutritional program for young children can affect their
subsequent capacity to learn (Birch, 1970; Ricciuti, 1969).
Deprived of an adequate diet, the child may not only develop
health complications, but may have difficulties in school.

Second, the behavioral sciences have provided evidence
that the quality of cognitive and linguistic stimulation
during infancy and preschool years affects later learning
skills. For example, a child deprived of certain learning
opportunities, which promote the attainment of the preacademic

skills, will probably have difficulty with the early school grades (Schaefer and Aaronson, 1971; Palmer, 1971). In the areas of affective and social development, a rather strong case exists for the importance of a child's early years in developing self-esteem and interpersonal relationships (Coopersmith, 1970).

Applied research data, however, are equivocal about the effectiveness of early intervention efforts. This doubt can be extended to the effectiveness of many child-care programs, since many child-development programs have shown evidence of three major weaknesses.

First, many programs have had poorly conceptualized curricula. Inferior curriculum conception stems from two causes: (1) the development of preschool curricula without the necessary research foundation or with ignorance of available research data and (2) the unwillingness of most early educators to make their curricula explicit.

Second, many programs have been poorly implemented. Poor implementation generally evolves from inadequate training, and from embryonic delivery systems that have potential (Nedler, 1971), but nevertheless remain undeveloped.

Third, the inferior evaluation of intervention programs has indicated three problem areas, namely, conceptual, psychometric, and scientific. Without an adequate statement of curriculum and a specification of the curriculum objectives, it is difficult to design or conceptualize a sensitive evaluation. The psychometric problem exists because the few means for measuring program impact have limited utility (e.g., I.Q. test). Scientifically, evaluation efforts have been handicapped by the conceptual and psychometric limitations as well as the failure in most cases to apply even elementary knowledge of experimental design when evaluating preschool programs (e.g., random assignment of children to treatment groups, and adequate comparison groups).

In those cases where programs were well funded, clearly conceptualized, accurately implemented, and appropriately evaluated, we have attained a variety of positive benefits (Hawkridge, et al., 1968; Parker, et al., 1970(e)). Only in the last three years, for example, have we developed the minimum knowledge necessary to provide a good preschool curricula which can gain a variety of objectives spanning all areas of child development (see p. 16). This does not

mean that we do not need additional programs nor does it
mean that we are now effective in implementing high quality
programs on a mass scale. The critical point is that the
expertise and strategies to foster positive child development
do exist. With adequate resources, effective training and
delivery systems can be built.

Next, there are the humanitarian reasons for focusing
upon intervention during the child's early years. Basically,
these reasons center around the facts: (1) that all children
deserve a minimally acceptable quality of life from
conception, and (2) that, if parents are unable to provide
such quality, for whatever reason, it becomes a governmental
responsibility to undertake it. In a word, no child should
be denied good health care, adequate nutrition, affective
support, interesting and challenging environment, and
appropriate experiences to facilitate his maximum growth and
development. In its sphere, this conclusion is as valid as
any scientific or economic argument ever presented.

President Nixon, recognizing the importance of these
early years, called for a "national commitment to providing
all American children an opportunity for healthful and
stimulating development during the first five years of life. . ."
He continued--

> We have learned, first of all, that the process of learning
> how to learn begins very, very early in the life of the
> infant child. Children begin this process in the very
> earliest months of life, long before they are anywhere
> near a first grade class, or even kindergarten, or play
> school groups. We have also learned that for the children
> of the poor this ability to learn can begin to deteriorate
> very early in life, so that the youth begins school well
> behind his contemporaries and seemingly rarely catches
> up. He is handicapped as surely as a child crippled by
> polio is handicapped: and he bears the burden of that
> handicap through all his life. It is elemental that, even
> as in the case of polio, the effects of prevention are
> far better than the effects of cure.[1]

Based upon these considerations, the following generalizations can be suggested: (1) we have an obligation to develop

---

[1] Press release of President Nixon establishing the
Office of Child Development, April 9, 1969.

methods to help children whose cognitive, linguistic, physical,
social and affective development are likely to be constrained
by their environment, (2) we have much of the knowledge
necessary to define appropriate methods of help, and (3) the
cost of developing a child-care network to make possible such
a response, while great, is less costly than it would be if
we engaged in later remedial or rehabilitative programs.

Not everyone shares this point of view, but there are
signs of an emerging consensus about the importance of the
early childhood years. Parents, increasingly interested in
organizing better services for their children, professionals
involved with child development, political representatives,
and the general public have manifested their concern through
traditional ways, and by forming new special-interest
organizations.

Given these concerns, and the scientific and humanitarian reasons previously cited, this paper will focus on
child-care and preschool services. At the same time, it
will present, for those who will help shape future policies,
a brief overview of some of the major foci that might be
incorporated into an early childhood network. This network
could include the following types of services:

1. Homecare services designed to help the
    family build a child development focus
    into relationships with the child. Programs
    such as those that disseminate resource
    information to the mother and/or father about
    child rearing to encourage parents to give
    their children access to programs such as
    Sesame Street, and bring visiting aides and
    services to the home, would fall into this
    category (Whitney and Parker, 1971).

2. Organized preschool experiences designed
    to provide the child with the cognitive,
    linguistic, affective and social stimulation
    now deemed important for future development.
    These can be incorporated either into half-day
    or full-day programs (e.g., Karnes, 1971).

3. Organized childcare services oriented both
    towards the developmental needs of the child
    and the needs of the mother. Thus a network
    would ideally support a night child-care center,

a drop-in center which a mother might use
in an emergency or simply intermittently,
as well as the more familiar forms of
service, namely, family and group care
(e.g., Whitney, 1970).

4. Comprehensive Childcare Service Centers
designed as resources for parents; as
detection centers for actual or potential
health, nutritive or similar problems
demanding remediation; and, ideally, as
facilities for handling such problems, or,
at least, helping the community develop
appropriate resources (e.g., Parent-Child
Centers).

The linkage system between services, the recruitment
and training of staffing personnel, the extent of parental
involvement in program development and program control, and
the auspices (public, private, or cooperative) will vary
appreciably from community to community. Options for new
approaches will grow. These areas are merely presented as
a backdrop for considering: (1) the current network and
(2) appropriate policy perspectives and goals for the 1970's.

B. Child-Care Arrangements: An Overview

In discussing child-care arrangements, a central
concern is the overall patterning of child-care arrangements.
This includes both ad hoc solutions in which the child is
cared for by a relative, friend of the mother, or is simply
left alone, and more formal situations. Three surveys of
the child-care arrangements made by working mothers provide
background for discussing this question.

Between 1960 and 1964, Ruderman (1968) gathered data
in seven communities characterized by varied size,
socioeconomic and racial composition, rates of maternal
employment, and geographic region. Low and Spindler (1968)
took a national sample in 1965. In addition, the Massachusetts
Committee on Children and Youth (1966) surveyed six major
cities and forty-seven rural and suburban towns prior to 1966.
TABLE I (following) presents the data in summary form. The
distributions recorded during the first five years of the
1960's (i.e., pre-Head Start) are strikingly similar.

TABLE I

COMPARATIVE DISTRIBUTIONS OF CHILD-CARE ARRANGEMENTS BY PERCENT[1]

Type of Care	Ruderman	Total %	Spindler & Low	Total %	Mass. Comm. on Children	Total %
Care in Home		63		45.5		59.6
Father	23		14.9		23.3	
Relative	17		21.2[2]		19.2	
Sibling	12				8.7	
Other	11		9.4		8.4	
Care Outside Home		23		15.7		18.7
Child Looked After Self		7		8.1		14.3
Group Care		4[3]		2.2		6.0[4]
Other		3		28.5		1.4
Mother worked only during school hours			13.0			
Mother looked after child at work			15.0			
Unspecified			.5			

[1] See Appendix C for original tables from which composite data drawn: n.b.-- Ruderman and Mass. data based on number of arrangements; Low and Spindler on percent of children. This means data are not strictly comparable since some children are involved in multiple arrangements.

[2] Low and Spindler categories make it impossible to separate sibling from relative--21.2% is composite.

[3] Ruderman included day-care centers and recreation facilities in group care, respectively, 3 and 4%.

[4] Mass. included full-time centers and nursery school in group care, respectively, 3.9 and 2.1%.

The contrast between the percentage of children cared for in homes (63.0%, 45.5%, and 59.6%, respectively) and those in group facilities (4.0%, 2.2%, 6.0%) is startling.[2] Moreover, in every instance, a higher percentage of children look after themselves (7.0%, 8.15%, 14.3%) than are in group care. A pattern parallel to the national sample, i.e., the seven-community sample across states, and the within-state survey, gives the data considerable weight.

These data also suggest a question for future policy determination. If a more adequate child-care network is in fact a goal, should we increase the availability of group facilities or should we also design programs directed toward upgrading the quality of informal care? This is an especially relevant question because, regardless of the extent of our commitment to developing a network of organized care facilities, the extent and the coordination of outreach services to advise and assist mothers in their homes on the complex task of early child care thus becomes a significant matter.

C. Day Care and Preschool Capacity

It is clear that during the past decade, there has been an increase in formal facilities available for preschool children. TABLE II documents both an increase in the number of licensed day-care facilities over the past ten years (from a capacity of 183,400 in 1960 to 638,000 in 1969),[3] and a dramatic increase in preschool facilities.

The day-care data are particularly noteworthy. First, the percentage of privately owned facilities is consistently

---

[2] Estimates suggest there is an equally large, if not larger, network of unlicensed facilities.

[3] While there are no compiled estimates, it seems that in the past two years, there has been a burgeoning of new day-care programs (many unlicensed) under the auspices of community-based agencies, parental groups, etc. Data from the State of Washington suggest that, in a five-county area, the number of day-care centers increased from 82 to 102 from July 1969 to July 1970. In New York City over the past year, at least 22 centers were started. In Appalachia, a six-state project is under way to stimulate new programs for preschool-age children.

TABLE II

TRENDS OVER LAST DECADE: DAY CARE AND PRESCHOOL CAPACITY

Licensed Day-Care Facilities, 1960-1969

	1960[1]		1967[2]		1969[3]	
	Number of Facilities	Number of Children	Number of Facilities	Number of Children	Number of Facilities	Number of Children
Day Care Centers						
TOTAL	4,426	141,200	10,400	393,000	13,600	518,000
Public	310	52,244	400	22,600	230	34,700
Voluntary	1,239	16,944	2,600	113,900	4,100	178,000
Proprietary	2,877	72,012	6,900	239,300	7,600	266,000
Unreported	---	---	500	17,500	170	39,300
Family Day Care						
TOTAL	13,600	42,200	24,300	81,900	32,700	120,000
Public	680	No Data	800	2,500	2,500	8,000
Voluntary	136		400	1,300	550	2,100
Proprietary	2,784		18,400	63,900	27,700	102,000
Unreported	---		4,700	14,200	1,950	7,900
TOTAL CENTERS	18,026	183,400	34,700	474,900	46,300	638,000

TABLE II—Continued

Preschool Enrollment, 1964-1969

Age Group	1960	1964[4]		1969	
		Numbers	% of Population Served	Numbers	% of Population Served
3 year old	Not available	181,000	4.3	315,000	8.7
4 year old		617,000	14.9	880,000	23.1
5 year old		2,389,000	58.1	2,755,000	68.9

[1]Kadushin, A. Child Welfare Services, 1967 (Chapter 8).

[2]Child Welfare Statistics, Children's Bureau, Table 13, Statistical Series #92, U. S. Government Printing Office.

[3]"Licensed or Approved Day Care Centers & Family Day Care Homes by Auspices and Capacity, March 1969" (Provisional), from OCD, xeroxed.

[4]Hurd, Gordon. Preprimary Enrollment Trends of Children Under Six, 1964-1968, Tables 2, 3, 4 and October 1969 (in press). (No data available prior to 1964; n.b., population decreased in all age categories, percentage served increased.)

higher than the public facilities, despite the involvement
of the U. S. Government in the last half of the 1960's.
Second, rough analysis suggests a yearly increase of about
50,000 children in licensed group facilities, and the number
of day-care homes appears to be increasing even more rapidly.

At the same time the total percentage of children
actually served remains small, particularly at age levels
three (8.7%) and four (23.1%). (See **TABLE III.**) No
systematic data recording the extent of programs for children
under three exist, but all evidence suggests that only an
infinitesimal number are served. In part, this is probably
due to the concern of many child-development specialists
about the impact of group care upon the infant,[4]/and, in
part, because infant care demands more staff, more equipment,
etc.

At ages three and four, at least in 1969, minority
group children received a somewhat larger proportion of
available services. This seems to reflect the increase in
public (federal) funds for anti-poverty programs. For the
child five and over, however, this finding no longer holds.
Federal funds have not been so widely used to stimulate
development of kindergarten programs.

As **TABLE II** suggests, we do better in providing
preschool services than we do in providing day care services.[5]/
An optimistic estimate for day-care services would cite under

[4]/Many of the studies from which the concern stems
were conducted in the 1930's on samples of children in
institutional settings, not in settings designed with a child-
development focus, and involving temporary separation, not
permanent separation, from parental figures. More recent data,
using this latter model, seem to indicate that both child and
parent can benefit from this type of experience (Caldwell,
1969). Currently, best estimates suggest that about a dozen
well-developed programs for infants are in use throughout
the country with an equal number in various stages of
development. In addition, approximately thirty parent-child
centers are operative, providing the opportunity to focus on
prevention of environmental deficit rather than upon simply
engaging in remedial efforts.

[5]/The data in **TABLE II** are not strictly comparable
as the day-care estimates include school-age children as well.

TABLE III

ESTIMATES OF NUMBERS OF PRESCHOOL CHILDREN
SERVED IN 1969 BY RACE AND AGE--INCLUDES
ONE-HALF DAY AND FULL DAY HEAD START
(Numbers in Thousands)

	Total Eligible	Enrolled	% Enrolled Out of Total Eligible	% Enrolled Full Day Out of Total Eligible
TOTAL--				
Ages 3-5	11,424	4,325	37.8	5.1
White	9,522	3,604	35.7	3.9
Non-white	1,902	721	37.8	11.1
Negro	1,626	654	37.7	12.0
Age 3	3,614	315	8.7	3.1
White	2,998	243	8.1	2.2
Non-white	616	72	11.7	7.3
Negro	565	67	11.9	7.4
Age 4	3,809	880	23.1	4.7
White	3,173	691	21.8	3.5
Non-white	636	189	29.7	10.8
Negro	575	175	30.4	11.3
Age 5	4,001	3,130	78.2	7.0
White	3,351	2,670	79.7	5.8
Non-white	650	460	70.8	15.0
Negro	586	412	·70.3	15.1

Source: Adapted from Preprimary 1969 October Enrollment
Data, NCES, Tables 1 and 9 (in press). (N.b.,
population estimates differ slightly from 1969
estimates in Appendix although both based on
Census data.)

10% of children in the three to five age group receiving
services; the percentage of younger children receiving
services is infinitesimal. Overall, the estimated figure
of children receiving services is between 2% and 3%.[6]
Currently, no state has the capacity to serve more than 6%
of the conservatively estimated population needing services.[7]
(See APPENDIX G.)

D. Enrollment Patterns: Socioeconomic
   Status in Day Care and Preschool

For the relatively small group of children who are
served, utilization of organized facilities is clearly
dependent upon economic and racial factors. TABLE IV, for
instance, documents a pattern geared to economic levels
during the last five years. Usually, the proportion of
children served each year increases within each income
group; in addition, for each year, the lower the income,
the smaller the percentage of eligible children enrolled.
Thus, we can observe a familiar pattern in the delivery of
human services. The affluent are able to purchase services;
the poor go without. An income pattern emerges, as the
more affluent can and will purchase services which are
available in the "open market." However, the rate of
increase in the percentage enrolled has been significantly
greater in the lower income groups in the last half of the
1960's.

---

[6] It is not possible, with any accuracy, to assess
the percentage of unmet needs for special groups of
children--i.e., the Indians, migrants, handicapped, etc.
There is no reason to believe the pattern is any better
than the overall national patterns and in some instances
it is likely to be worse.

[7] Many states are becoming deeply interested in
Day Care. Rhode Island has set up a statewide legislative
committee, backed by the Governor. New York State has
just passed a Youth Facilities Improvement Act to stimulate
construction (although no funds have yet been released),
and the Governor has said that public properties (state)
can be used for day-care facilities. A state-by-state
inventory of new approaches would be productive.

TABLE IV

PERCENTAGE OF 3-5 YEAR OLDS ENROLLED
BY INCOME (1964-1969)

Year	Under $3,000	$3,000-4,999	$5,000-7,499	$7,500 & Over
1969	23.4	24.2	30.6	41.1
1968	23.4	25.8	28.4	40.3
1967	21.2	26.0	29.0	38.5
1966	19.3	21.3	29.0	37.8
1965	14.4	21.0	26.3	37.4
1964	15.1	19.8	25.8	37.2

Source: Adapted from Hurd, G., Preprimary Enrollment
Trends of Children Under Six (1964-1968),
Table 1, 1969, and Hurd, G., Preprimary
Enrollment (October 1969), Table 3-A (xeroxed).

Moreover, as is clear from TABLE III,[8] a consistently
higher percentage of minority-group children are in full day
care than white children. This pattern, based on 1969 data,
corroborates the pattern Ruderman (1968) found earlier in the
decade. On the basis of her survey in seven communities,
she concluded that organized day care is typically for the
low-income, one-parent, or minority-group child. She also

[8] Enrollment patterns in Poverty and Non-poverty
metropolitan areas with populations over 250,000 is consistent
with TABLE III. (See APPENDIX F.) Corroboratively,
kindergarten utilization patterns, in a survey conducted
in the fall of 1968, suggest that the higher the income,
the more likely the child is to be enrolled in kindergarten
(Jaffe, R. and Jaffe, E., 1969, TABLE XVI, p. 26).

concluded that nursery school enrollment tends to be for the white middle-class child. In these cases, a pattern is evident since the low-income or minority groups receive federal services.

Certain implications of these data must be considered. In the first place, since a widespread concern with child development is relatively new, many of the existing day-care programs (excluding the full-year, full-day Head Start programs, and special demonstration programs) may primarily serve custodial functions.

It also means that the children from low-income backgrounds have only their peers for models. From the Coleman Report (1968), which found that a mixed socioeconomic peer group is a critical factor in improving the school performance of older low-income children, it can be inferred that the potential cost to children is great. Likewise, for middle- and upper-income children, exposure to peers from other backgrounds can lead to an important learning climate.

Most important, the consequences of continuing and expanding such patterns of segregation according to socio-economic status (and thus, often, race) deserve the most careful attention. Without a concerted effort, there appears to be real danger that the long-term consequences will be reinforcement of a permanent "underclass" or caste. This can develop regardless of new child-care models and regardless of the expressed goals of such models. The issue is particularly crucial because, in planning an extended network of child care, we face a choice of developing directions which can either undercut or reinforce stratification.

E. Quality of Existing Programs and Models

In an earlier section, we noted evidence of expertise and the employment of strategies which can foster positive child development during the first five years. There is no systematic evaluation of the quality of existing child-care-program models. Some high-quality programs have been developed by universities, educational research and development centers, regional educational laboratories, and private companies. A series of recent handbooks summarize the best child-development programs for infants and preschoolers (Parker, 1970(a); 1970(b)). Additionally, Parker (1971) prepared a comparative analysis of thirteen

promising preschool curricula. These preschool programs
were selected on the basis of clear conceptualization,
written materials, empirical evaluations, and degree of
exportability. However, conclusions that high-quality
programs can be developed become meaningless unless the
national perspective is also discussed. In general, the
national perspective indicates much room for improvement.[9]
Many child-care programs are custodial and lack planned
programs to foster positive development. Or, child-
development programs are at least a decade behind advanced
efforts in child-care programs. The situation in school-age
child care (i.e., after-school day care for children between
6 and 16) is critical because, in general these programs
fail to meet even minimally acceptable standards for
high-quality child development (see Parker, 1970(c), for
a discussion of school-age programs).

The issue, therefore, is to design and develop a
delivery system so that the advances in infant and preschool
programming can reach field practice. Implicit in this
concern is the need for adequate budgets and sophisticated
training programs. Additionally, in school-age programs,
the need for extensive development of new programs continues
to exist.

F. The Role of the Federal Government

In assessing child-development services currently
available, and the trends over the past ten years, the role

---

[9] Using a criterion derived from nine indices rated
by observers, Ruderman (1968) assessed the quality of the
day-care centers and nursery facilities sampled selectively
in the seven communities in her survey. She found that, in
general, the higher quality centers were voluntary. The
lower were proprietary. Prescott-Jones (cited in LaCrosse,
1970), on the other hand, from a more recent examination of
commercial Los Angeles centers, found no difference in the
quality of programs offered in proprietary and non-profit
centers. (See Featherstone, 1970, for corroborative evidence.)
She also found that proprietary centers tend to be more
responsive to parents' needs than public centers. Responsive
in terms of scheduling, etc., not in terms of parental
involvement when that term is used to mean involvement in
the decision-making process.

of the Federal Government is quite significant. This role
has had an impact on the number of children served (from
4,900 in 1965 to 440,100 in 1971, not including half-day
Head Start or ESEA). (See APPENDIX K.) More significantly,
the Federal Government has had an impact on making visible
the need to develop a network of child-care facilities to
the population-at-large, as well as to appropriate agencies
and non-Federal officials.

     In this context, a brief historical synopsis is
appropriate. Generally, development of services for young
children has reflected response to crises. The Civil War,
for example, triggered a spurt of child-care facilities. In
the Twentieth Century (until recently), the greatest impetus
for day-care facilities for all children, and preschool facilities for young children, was in response to a double crisis,
namely the economic depression that preceded World War II
and that war itself. In the 1930's, under the Works Progress
Administration (WPA), Federal monies were made available for
group care for children. In 1941, Congress passed the Lanham
Act (the Community Facilities Act) making monies available for
operation and construction of day-care facilities. Under
pressure of wartime need, expansion proceeded at a rapid
rate. It is estimated that at the end of 1945 day-care
facilities were serving 1,600,000 children.[10]

     Two points about the Lanham Act have implications
for the 1970's: first, this network was established with
great speed, and, second, the administrative structure was
developed just as rapidly.

     Lanham Act monies for preschool services were
administered through the Office of Education. The Children's
Bureau managed a greater part of the money for day care.
The ideological and political ramifications of that policy
decision are still very real. Ideologically, the focus
clearly was not on comprehensive child development, but
rather on vague program goals with a custodial emphasis.
Politically, the decision set the pattern for fragmented
administration of services to children, and for the
inculcation of vested self-interest among personnel in
program maintenance and expansion.

-----

[10]Bradbury, D. E. Five Decades of Action for
Children: A History Re: Children's Bureau, U. S., Drew,
1962.

The goal of the Lanham Act was to release women to meet wartime labor needs; the needs of children apparently were secondary. With a few major exceptions, day-care services ceased with the halt in Federal funds,[11]/ and no one thought about sustaining a new network of services.

For the greater part of two decades, the Federal Government did not become significantly involved with services for children other than through the Aid to Dependent Children Program (ADC). In 1962, Congress amended the Social Security Act to include day care as a child-welfare service, and it allocated some special funds.

In 1965, Head Start, begun under the scope of the Economic Opportunity Act, turned the national spotlight on the needs of preschool children from low-income families. This illuminated the needs for educational services, for medical services, for adequate nutrition, and for significant parental involvement. Head Start, in fact, has provided the basic model of programs for compensatory/preventative intervention.[12]/

Again during 1965 (under Title I of the Elementary and Secondary Education Act (ESEA)), funds were made available to school systems to meet the needs of disadvantaged children. A number of districts used those monies either for programs for preschool children or for training staff personnel who would work with those children. In 1967, authorization for Child Welfare Services was shifted to Title IV, Part B of the Social Security Act. Annually, this has provided about

---

[11]/ For an interesting account of the political struggle to keep New York City day-care centers operative, see Mayer, A., Day Care As An Instrument Of Social Policy (mimeographed, Columbia University School of Social Work, 1965). Only one state, California, assumed responsibility for continuation of the centers.

[12]/ While evaluations of the impact of Head Start on the individual participant have been mixed, there is no question but that its impact upon the awareness of the school system to the needs of the very young child has been positive. It has been positive, too, as to the parents of the Head Start participants, many of whom had become sensitized to new possibilities for themselves, their children, and their communities.

$6-1/2 million to the states for staff, administrative or operative costs, licensing programs, or the purchase of day-care services.[13] That same year, also under Title IV, the WIN (Work Incentive Program) program was established. AFDC (Aid to Families with Dependent Children) funds also became available for day-care services. APPENDIX M provides a summary of Federal involvement.

In 1968, the School Lunch Act (SLA) was amended to make grants available for food and kitchen equipment in day-care centers. That same year, the Handicapped Children's Early Education Assistance Act was enacted, providing support for experimental programs for handicapped preschoolers. In 1969, the Concentrated Employment Program (CEP) was developed to coordinate manpower programs with expenditures allowed for day care.

By 1970, estimates from congressional hearings cited over sixty different federally supported programs which were involved, to varying degrees, with child care. These programs created, in effect, a fragmented, confused national commitment. Lazar (1970(b)) describes over two hundred Federal programs for young children. In fact, in 1970, an effort to examine systematically different day-care programs and different preschool programs has led to a series of projects focusing on research rather than large-scale expansion. These include day-care models, Parent and Child Centers, and Head Start Planned Variation.

During the past year, no major new legislation directly affecting child-care or preschool services was passed. However, as an incentive to private-sector involvement, the Taft-Hartley Act was amended to authorize bargaining for a combined union-management trust fund for child-care centers. The bargaining provision is not mandatory, so the impact on supply of facilities cannot yet be appraised.

In addition, several pieces of legislation are pending that could appreciably affect the availability of options for day care, and for a child-care network. The most visible of these, the Family Assistance Plan (FAP),

---

[13]Title IV, Part A, requires 25% state matching funds, and therefore is not always utilized. In Appalachia, in an interesting precedent, a private foundation has provided the state's share of matching funds.

provides for day-care money for children of the poor. Most
recent estimates suggest that during the first year (if FAP
passes), some 472,000 children could be served. A third of
these will be preschoolers; two-thirds will be school-age
children. Since many of the children will be shifted from
existing WIN or Child Welfare slots, the number of new
children served will be only a small percentage since most
of the total recipients are already served under Federal
programs.

There are also legislative proposals with broader
foci such as the Comprehensive Child Development Act (the
Brademas-Dellenback bill). A proposal also has been
introduced by Senator Russell Long for creating a Federal
Child Care Corporation that will guard and administer a
revolving trust fund to be used to finance a child-care
network.

Among these new legislative proposals, the most
far-reaching is the Brademas-Dellenback bill. It would
outline the following priority strategy:

1. preschool services for the economically
    disadvantaged,

2. day care for all children under age fourteen,

3. parent education, and

4. services for all children not already
    covered.

As this is written, the bill rests in committee.

A revealing pattern emerges, if the range of current
Federal involvement in day-care and preschool programs is
carefully analyzed. In 1969, it was estimated that in all
relevant Federal programs, some 623,000 children were served,
and most of these came from low-income families (see TABLE V)
Authorizations for these services are usually embedded in
bills with other goals (either relating to the provision of
welfare services, or educational enrichment services). The
one provision responding only to day care, Title V, Economic
Opportunity Act, has never received authorization for
specific funding.

In addition to this pattern, different mandates for
the program make it difficult to set up effective linkage

TABLE V

ESTIMATED NUMBERS OF CHILDREN SERVED IN
PRESCHOOL AND DAY CARE NON-EXPERIMENTAL
FEDERAL PROGRAMS, 1969[14]

Age Groups and Program	Full Day	Part Day	Total
Infant			
Parent-Child Centers	2,600		2,600
Preschool			
Head Start	75,000	142,000	217,000
ESEA		342,000	342,000
Other	35,700		35,700
School Age		26,000	26,000
TOTALS	113,300	510,000	623,000

[14] For data sources, see APPENDIX K.

systems. Thus, while Head Start requires comprehensive
services, for example, Title I of the Elementary and
Secondary School Act does not.[15] Yet both programs respond
to children drawn from the same general population. Programs
that have Federal money for day care are expected to use the
Federal Interagency Day Care Standards as guidelines (these
require comprehensive components), but the extent to which
the guidelines are actually implemented is unknown.[16]

Monies directly related to staff training are minimal.
The problem of providing monies or incentives for facilities
(either construction or renovation) has not yet been directly
legislated in any significant way.[17]

In summary, over the past thirty years, the U. S.
Government has developed services for children based on the
needs of three target groups. During World War II, the
focus was on child services for working mothers--all working
mothers, not just mothers from low-income groups. In the
last half of the 1960's, with Head Start and ESEA-Title IV
monies, priority shifted away from the needs of mothers to
the needs of a selected group of children, principally those
economically, educationally and, to a large extent, physically
deprived.

Now, as previously indicated, we seem to be in a
stage of transition, and there is a great deal of interest
in defining an alternate target group, namely, poor or

---

[15] Some 90% of the children in Head Start receive
medical examinations, and 50% have access to counseling
services.

[16] In fact, the standards are open to much criticism
and are currently being revised. Reference to these are not
included in many of the pending comprehensive bills.

[17] Monies for Model Cities Programs can be used for
day-care facilities, but there are no estimates as to what
extent this resource has been utilized. Small Business
Administration provides limited loans to profit-making
groups for day care. (Senator Percy has introduced an
amendment to the FAP legislation providing for construction
monies; construction monies are also provided in the
comprehensive child-development bills (see **APPENDIX N**).)

low-income mothers unable to work because they lack child-care facilities.[18]

At the same time, there appears to be another trend struggling to gain legitimacy. That trend is best described as a thrust toward having the Federal Government make a policy and monetary commitment to a comprehensive network of child-service facilities. These facilities should include educational, medical and/or remedial components and be available to a broad range of children. The Brademas-Dellenback bill discussed earlier grows out of this orientation. APPENDIX N summarizes the bills.

G. Summary

The majority of children involved in child-care arrangements are cared for in informal settings, without formal programs or trained staff.

For those utilizing organized facilities, three major trends over the past decade are discernible:

1. an increase in the number of formal child-care facilities distributed in relatively stable proportions among private, non-profit and public auspices;

2. an increase in the extent of Federal involvement in providing funds for day-care and preschool services.

Federal involvement in preschool and child care is directed primarily at serving children of the poor. In

---

[18] In 1967, the WIN program made a start in this direction followed by CEP in 1968. FAP enlarges on the same theme. It should be noted that there are many unpublished, serious critiques of the WIN program within the Federal Government, and some are incorporated in the First Annual Report of the Department of Health, Education and Welfare Services to AFDC families. Among the most telling are that the program merely takes day-care slots from other children, that the services cease when the training ceases, that the quality monitoring has been poor. The training aspect for the mother has also many serious drawbacks, including the unavailability of jobs once training is completed.

actual numbers, only a small percentage of this group is reached. Some of the programs have been initiated primarily to serve the needs of the working, or potential working mother, if training and jobs were available. Others have a child-development thrust. Still others are grounded in providing social service.

The third trend:

3. a two-pronged pattern reflecting economic and racial stratification: fewer poor children proportionately are enrolled in any kind of service than children from affluent families; white children are more likely to be enrolled in preschool programs; and minority-group children are more likely to be enrolled in day-care programs.

There appear to be several reasons why preschool and child-care services are so discriminatory and so minimally developed:

First, it has long been popular opinion that young children should not be separated from their parents. Within this framework, child care has been seen as an undesirable child-rearing practice.

Second, it has only been relatively recently that child-development specialists have been able to spell out convincingly the adverse implications of not focusing on early child development.

Third, until fairly recently, the particular needs of poor children for early childhood services have not been so highly visible (nor for that matter have the needs and rights of their parents).

Fourth, the trend for women to become a more substantial part of the labor force has increased need for day care.

In 1969, for instance, it was estimated that of 30.5 million working women, 2.1 million had children under age 3; 2.1 million had children between ages 3 and 5; and 7.4 million had children between ages 6 and 17.

In 1980, it is estimated that 5.3 million working women will have children under 5 years of age (see APPENDIX I).

These figures include increasing numbers of working
women who are the sole providers for their families, and
women whose earned income makes the difference between a
family living in poverty or in marginal security.[19] Of the
former, 1968 data suggest some 5 million families were
included, and these involved some 900,000 families living
on less than the poverty standard of $3,600 for a family of
four.[20]

Until recently, however, there has been minimal
demand for universally available child-care or preschool
services. This appears to be changing. The Gallup Poll of
July 13, 1969, suggests that 64% of a national sample
supported using Federal funds for child care. Women's
Liberation has made 24-hour-a-day, consumer-controlled day-
care centers a major part of its plank. Recent data from
a Department of Labor survey suggests that of the non-working
population who would like to work, 39% cannot because of home
responsibilities, including the lack of day-care facilities.[21]
A survey conducted in New York City holds that 6 out of 10
welfare mothers with preschool children would prefer to work
if day-care facilities, and jobs, were available.[22] Both
Ruderman (1968) and Cochran (1966) included questions in
their sample about interest in more day-care facilities, and
responses indicate much interest. Assuming that the expression
of demand is probably understated because many women do not
include day care as a viable alternative since it is not
available, strong trends toward organized support are highly
significant.[23]

---

[19] Fleisig (1969) estimates that the presence of the
wife in the labor force reduces poverty (based on $3,600
standard for a family of four by a factor of 2.7 among blacks
and 3.6 among whites).(See APPENDIX J.)

[20] Background Facts on Women Workers in the United
States, U. S. Department of Labor, 1970.

[21] Idem.

[22] Podell Study, Reported in Hearings on H.R. 16311
(FAP), April 29, 30 and May 1, 1970.

[23] There is also increasing awareness that this country
lags far behind other western and non-western countries in the
provision of services for children. In the USSR, for example,
day-care facilities (including temporary facilities for seasonal
farm workers) served in 1963 some 7.4 million children (Madison,
1968).

CHAPTER TWO

PLANNING FOR THE 1970's:
ISSUES AND OPTIONS

Assuming a national commitment to support an expanded
and more effective network of child-care services in the
1970's, two fundamental questions arise:

1. What are the priorities in the development
   of an effective network of services?

2. What are the critical parameters of an
   effective network of services?

A. Child-Care Services for Whom?

Generally, as discussed in the preceding chapter,
there are four distinct groups of children which could be
defined as needing a range of child-care services, namely,
(1) low-income children caught in a cycle of poverty and often
of racism, (2) children who are physically or emotionally
handicapped, (3) children of working parents, and (4) all
children up to age sixteen irrespective of personal status
or family background. Obviously, there is overlap among the
respective groups, but the extent of overlap is unknown.

Rationales to support the development of services
for each group vary. For each, however, supporting arguments
have strength. For the child who is disadvantaged either
because of income or minority status, the contention is that
high-quality child-development services will compensate for
poor environmental conditions such as malnutrition or health
neglect. Additionally, the mother dependent on public
assistance may be freed for employment if adequate child-care
services are provided for her children. This is the premise
of the day-care component of the Family Assistance Plan.

Theoretically, the physically- or emotionally-
handicapped child can be provided with a necessary healthful

environment to help overcome physical handicaps or to learn
to cope with his emotional difficulties. The desire to
provide preschool and child-care services for handicapped
children is generally predicated upon the child's right to
be treated, as far as possible, like any other child and,
upon the premise that preliminary training and rehabilitative
efforts may make it easier for both the child and his family
to cope with handicaps. In current practice however,
preschool programs and day-care centers have not been
equipped to deal effectively with the needs and problems
of special populations. Knowledge of problems of the
handicapped exists, but, at present, methods for dealing
with such problems within a national child-care network are
largely lacking.

For children of working parents, a variety of good
reasons can be offered for providing child-care services.
Lacking readily accessible child-care facilities, women are
deprived of opportunities for seeking work, and thus they
lose a fundamental right. Equality for women in employment,
training, and advancement is, of course, a right legally
protected by the Equal Pay Act of 1963 and the Civil Rights
Act of 1964, although the former applied to only half the
jobs in the country. Most recently, the proposed Equal Rights
Amendment, now under debate, is an additional example of the
thrust toward equal rights and opportunities for women.
According to the U. S. Civil Service Commission, no individual
or group has charged that lack of suitable child-care
facilities is discriminatory; however, such a charge may be
imminent as a focal point in the Women's Liberation Movement.
From the employer's perspective, some evidence has been
gathered to suggest that there are corporate economic benefits
if child-care services are provided for female employees.
Business reasoning is that when mothers are comfortable with
their child-care arrangements, their productivity may increase
while absenteeism decreases. In unions, particularly those
composed primarily of women, the demand for child-care
services as an additional fringe benefit may indeed become
a base for bargaining with management.

For the fourth group needing child-care services,
the belief is that all children can benefit from developmentally
oriented services. For a young child, kindergarten is
available in nearly every state, and the trend is toward
early education beginning at age three. Proposed services
range from part-time "convenience" services for non-working
mothers to the parent-child center approach of providing

child-care and parent-involvement programs for infants. The complex family and vocational patterns of contemporary society demand an institutional response to family and child needs, with the particular kind of service dependent upon a wide range of needs.

TABLE VI summarizes the best estimate of the numbers of children involved in each age category. The data are mainly based on 1969-1970 figures.

At present, some of the data are very tentative, and we meet the needs of only a minority in each eligible group; thus, projections for 1975 and 1980 have not yet been made. Overall population projections are indicated, however, in APPENDIX B.

Data on economically disadvantaged children are based on a poverty index which selects as a cutoff point an income of approximately $3,600 for a family of four. Undoubtedly, there are at least an equal number of children living in "marginal" poverty. The Census Bureau has cited 9.8 million children as existing in poverty. Among all children under age six, 15.3% are living in poverty; among all those between ages six and seventeen, 13.5% are existing in poverty. (See TABLE VII.)

TABLE VII also documents the fact (by now painfully familiar) that, as compared to white children, a larger percent of children from black and other minority-group populations live in poverty. In terms of actual numbers, however, the numbers of black and white children living in poverty are about equal. The table does not include other non-white children.

There are no estimates of the number of children of working mothers broken down by exact age of child.[1] Bureau of Labor Statistics data suggest that, of working women with children under age eighteen (some 11.6 million as of March 1969), 50.7% had children between ages six and seventeen; 30.4% had children under age six (and possibly other older children), and 25.7% had children under age three (and

---

[1] See Appendix H for breakdown of children by state, but not by age categories.

TABLE VI

ESTIMATES OF POTENTIAL DAY CARE
POPULATIONS (1969 Figures)
(In Millions)

Age	Economically Disadvantaged[A]	Working[B]	Physically or Emotionally Handicapped[C]	All Children[D]
0-5	3.3	5.8[1]	2.0[1]	22.0
6-14	6.5	15.0[1]	3.9[1]	37.3
TOTALS	9.8	20.8	5.9	59.3

[1]No breakdowns by age for the totals of children of working mothers and handicapped children exist. Therefore, the numbers were derived by assuming one-third of the children are under age 6, two-thirds between ages 6 and 14. This is roughly consistent with both the percentages in the categories of disadvantaged and all children.

Sources: [A]Census Bureau Data: Available in White House Children's Chart Book. N.b.: 6-14 estimate in this case is for 6-17.

[B]Unpublished data from OCD xeroxed breakdown by state in 1969 of number of children with working mothers outside the home.

[C]Unpublished data (dated May 1970) from Office of Education, Bureau of Educationally Handicapped (xeroxed). Total compiled from breakdown by state which is sometimes based on ages 5-17, sometimes 0-21.

[D]Current Population Reports, Series P-25, March 1970. (For detailed age breakdown see Appendix A.)

NOTE: Accurate age breakdowns for the handicapped do not exist; Census Bureau cannot provide specific figures for children in poverty areas under 3 and between 3 and 5; while we know how many working women have children under 6 and between 6 and 14, we do not know exactly how many children are involved at different ages. Therefore, this table should be read as a very rough estimate.

possibly other older children).[2/] The same problem, lack of
adequate data by age, negates any discussion of the number of
handicapped children. Personnel in the Bureau of the
Handicapped use, as a rough guide, the estimate that about
10% of the children identified in each state as handicapped
are under age six. More reliable data, however, are clearly
lacking.[3/]

TABLE VII

CHARACTERISTICS OF CHILDREN LIVING IN POVERTY

	% of Total Age Group Below Poverty Level	% of Total Age Group in Female-headed H.H.
Children Under 6:		
Total	15.3	65.3
White	10.5	59.2
Black	41.0	72.6
Children 6-17:		
Total	13.5	50.3
White	9.5	40.3
Black	38.8	66.2

Source: Children's Chart Book prepared for the White
House Conference on Children and Youth, 1970.

[2/]Source: U. S. Department of Labor, Bureau of Labor
Statistics: Monthly Labor Review, May, 1970.

[3/]Gathering data for this paper has been very difficult
because of the lack of reliable, comparable information. While
there is some information on number of children either eligible
for service, or actually served by age and race, more specific
population breakdowns do not exist for particular groups of
children. Thus, we are unable to report how many handicapped
children under age 6 live in this nation, just as we are unable
to determine how many Indian or Mexican-American children
there are. (Hopefully, when the 1970 Census material is
available, some of this will be corrected.) It should also
be noted that even when data on programs do exist, the data

These data, coupled with the total population figures for all children, define the universe of potential eligibility for preschool and child-care services, and can serve as a framework for priority decisions.

B. Financing Child-Care Service

The cost and who shall pay it

At present, the consensus among those actively engaged in trying to determine the cost of child-care services is that there is no reliable answer to the question of how much different patterns of service would cost; this applies to both initial and operational costs. Moreover, those estimates that have been made are limited by highly variable factors such as geographic region; efficiency of administrative management; [4] differential salary scales; [5] length of time

---

often must be pieced together because they are gathered under different auspices. Even within the Federal Government there is no one data-gathering system that applies to all federally funded programs for children. This makes an overall view very difficult to describe with any specificity. It is beyond the scope of this paper to deal with the issues involved in developing a useful data-information system. At the same time, it must be noted that the lack of information imposes serious restrictions not only on detailed assessment, but also detailed planning and goal setting.

[4] Regarding the issue of central management costs, size of center appears important. Universal Education Corporation has decided that the trade-off point between size and cost efficiency is for one 60-child center to serve as the administrative head of four other 60-child centers. Thirty-child centers are thought to be inefficient to manage and operate. Romper Rooms, Inc., planned for 100-child capacities. Other analysis also suggests that a critical factor in profit is plant utilization--the more ancillary programs that are developed (adult education, remedial services, etc.), the better it is (Ref.: Personal Communication, F. Chitister, Romper Rooms).

[5] There is no comprehensive analysis of current salary scales of starting personnel for child-care centers. There are, however, tabulation of salary ranges by states of consultants on foster care and licensing child-welfare supervisor, and child

system operative; size of system, etc.[6]

Typically, analyses exist for individual day-care centers with between 20 and 30 children. California, however, has compiled estimates showing the distribution of total state expenditures by category, including staff, instructional supplies, etc. These appear in APPENDIX O.

With the foregoing reservations as background, the following summary of current cost information is noteworthy.

Estimated costs of meeting the Federal Interagency Day Care Standards for a 30-child care center are $57,000, or $1,900 per child, with teachers' salaries pegged at $7,250, assistants at $5,250, and aides at $3,500.[7] Information from the State of Maryland, on the other hand, estimates the total cost of a 30-child center at $32,073, or $1,069 per child.[8] Rough estimates from the Indian and Migrant Programs Division of the Office of Child Development hold that costs for full-day, full-year Head Start programs range from $1,024 to $1,589 per child.[9]

---

welfare worker. The ranges respectively are $6,900-$17,460; $3,600-$17,403; $2,400-$14,100 (State Salary Ranges, January 1, 1970, DHEW Office of State Merit Systems).

[6]"California Data" documents a decrease in hourly cost per child from $2.51 in 1965-1967 to $1.98 in 1968 to $1.91 in 1969, with further decreases projected. Whether this affects quality control is not discernible from the data. California's Compensatory Preschool Education Program at a Glance, Part II, 1970.

[7]Unpublished Government document prepared by OEO and consultant from Rand Corporation, Table 5, 1969.

[8]Projected Annual Budgets: State Department of Social Services, Baltimore, Maryland, xeroxed, May, 1968.

[9]Indian and Migrant Program Review Summary. Indian and Migrant Programs Division unpublished data, 1970.

For after-school programs, the quality program average
is usually set within the $600-$800 range.[10] Estimates for
family day-care homes vary considerably. The Day Care and
Child Development Council of America suggests that the cost
of operating family day care is higher than operating a day-
care center. Reports from experienced operators, however,
reflect an opposite trend, namely that the cost of setting
up family day care is less than the cost of setting up center
care.[11] Apparently no one has yet estimated the cost of a

---

[10] Communication to Staff of Senate Finance Committee
by L. Feldman, Executive Director of Day Care and Child
Development Council of America (mimeographed in LaCrosse,
1970) actual figure--$634. Standards and Costs for Day Care,
DHEW/OCD, mimeographed, no date. Table IV, Before and After
School and Summer Care, $310 is figure for minimum service,
$653 for acceptable or desirable. Mushkin, S., Urban Institute,
Washington, D. C. (Data published in Compact, 3, (6) Dec.
1969, Educational Commission of the States, Denver.)

[11] This poses a provocative problem. Most professionals,
practitioners or model developers alike, concern themselves
primarily with day-care centers. Rarely do they advocate
family day care as a first choice. If this cost pattern is
accurate, the implication is that once again, professionals
may be using their expertise for programs for the few and
ignoring the quality of programs for the many that will develop
with or without their efforts.
There are some innovative efforts to take family day
care seriously and to attempt to upgrade the quality of the
experience of the child. Particularly interesting is the
concept of the Block Mother in Providence, Rhode Island, which
was built into the WIN program in that city as well as in the
New York City Family Day Care Careers Program. While in New
York the program has been well received, there are some
serious limitations that defeat the ultimate goal of upgrading
child care. Thus, for instance, there is the fact that women
who care for the children are not treated as workers; they do
not receive a regular salary, nor wage benefits, but are paid
according to the number of children present. This is
tantamount to penalizing specially trained women if the child
they care for is sick. Ultimately it means that the woman's
own child is deprived; a most striking case of double
jeopardy.

day-care center with satellite family day-care homes. But
cost data are soon expected from Appalachia, and from
Pennsylvania where plans are developing for the establishment
of such models.

Of available estimates, only one systematically breaks
down the cost of component services. Lazar's annual budget
(1970(a)) for operating child-care programs for preschool
children in Appalachia provides the following breakdown for a
high-quality program and its components. Not including
building costs, the cost of a child-development program was
determined as $3,000 per child, per year--plus $350 for a
health component (however, 5% of the children will need $700
for health), $300 for family service, $250 for parent education
and $750 for training per staff member. These reported costs
seem to be reliable inasmuch as an adequate data base was used
to derive them.

Cost data from the Day Care and Child Development
Council of America provide estimates of annual costs per child
for food, medical services, limited counseling, and
developmental programs. TABLE VIII reflects the breakdown
as made by the authors on the basis of the Council's data.

TABLE IX reflects some rough estimates of overall
operating costs in child care for different population groups.
The estimates merely suggest a range. How accurate they may
prove to be will depend upon factors that cannot be predetermined.
The figures reflect combined Federal and non-Federal resources.

Initial costs are difficult to determine. Renovation
and construction costs vary widely depending upon land taxes,
building codes, labor costs, etc. Estimates made under the
auspices of the Bank of America suggest a range of $37,380 to
$53,825 for a center with 30 children, although this is
considered low in view of the increases in current land costs.

Estimates from Romper Rooms, based in the East, put
construction costs, land costs and initial equipment costs
at about $125,000, with $145,000 estimated for a 100-child
care center. The $125,000 estimate breaks down as follows:
$2,000-$2,500 for land; $80,000-$100,000 for a building for
100 children; $5,000 for site preparation; $10,000-$15,000
for initial equipment and $5,000 for outdoor equipment.
Included is the cost of audio-visual equipment for training
and monitoring of programs.

TABLE VIII

COMPONENT ESTIMATES AS PERCENTAGE (%)
OF ANNUAL COST, PER CHILD

	Family Day Care	Center	After School
Food	7.4%	11.0%	18.9%
Medical	1.0	1.0	not incl.
Limited Counseling	1.5	1.6	not incl.
Developmental	3.5	4.0	12.4
Staff	72.0	66.0	54.0
Training	7.4	6.2	7.8
Other	7.2	10.2	6.9
Total	100.0	100.0	100.0

Source: Adapted from tables incorporated into communication to Staff of Senate Finance Committee by L.
Feldman, Executive Director of Day Care and
Child Development Council of America (mimeographed
in LaCrosse, 1970). After school component
includes summer care. Developmental expenses are
for supplies, materials and equipment.

TABLE IX

OPERATING COST ESTIMATES BASED ON FOUR
CONDITIONS OF NEED (1969 Figures)[1]

Age Group	Cost per Child Used for Estimate	I Economically Disadvantaged[2]		II Working Mothers		III Handicapped		IV All Families	
		Children (In Millions)	Cost (In Billions)	Children (In Millions)	Cost (In Billions)	Children (In Millions)	Cost (In Billions)	Children (In Millions)	Cost (In Billions)
0-2	$2,500	1.6	$4.0	2.9	$7.3	1.0	$2.5	10.4	$26.0
3-5	2,000	1.6	3.2	2.9	5.8	1.0	2.0	11.6	23.2
6-14	600	6.5	3.9	15.0	9.0	3.9	2.3	37.3	22.4
TOTALS			$11.1		$21.9		$6.8		$71.6

[1]
Table based on Table VI: See note on p. 30 for inaccuracies re population estimates. When numbers are not broken down by ages 0-2/3-5, total figure is divided in half. (This is consistent with general population trends.)

[2]While precise data are not available on the family circumstances of the children in the poverty group (I), statistics presented by the President's Commission on Income Maintenance Programs in its Background Papers (U.S. G.P.O (1970) pp. 144-148 and by Mollie Orshansky in the Social Security Bulletin, March 1968, pp. 3-32 indicate the followin regarding children under 18 living in poverty (figures are derived from various data for 1965,1966,1967): Slightly less than 40% lived in some 1-1/2 million families headed by females. In these families headed by females the head worked full year or part year in slightly over half of families; and nearly half of the families were receiving public assistance. The remaining 60% of the children in poverty lived in about 2.3 million families headed by males, of whom about 5/6 worked full year or part year and less than one-fifth were aided by public assistance.

Note: Groups I through III overlap, e.g., some of the economically disadvantaged families in I also have working mothers included in II, etc.

Estimates made by the Office of Child Development suggest a wide regional variability in total initial construction costs--from $180,596 in Anchorage, Alaska, to $94,952 in Memphis, Tennessee. Costs in New York City are estimated at $151,788. These cost data apply to a 100-children center. They stem from estimated corrected cost per square foot derived from a national average of $23.50. APPENDIX P presents projected costs for 1971 and 1972.

Questions relating to start-up costs essentially concern the provision of facilities, and therefore are tied to an array of complex options. In the first place, is it better for the Government to provide incentives for renovation or for new construction? If monies are provided for renovation, will they in the long run, simply have to be buttressed by new construction monies? OCD estimates suggest that renovation may save as much as 50% of funds granted by the Federal Government. However, in many cases, monies may be provided for construction. Does this necessitate coping with many building codes, especially regarding building materials? If such problems are not solved first, will facilities become so costly and inflexible that they will be unable to accommodate children with a full range of needs?

In terms of a rapid increase in the number of facilities, what implications would develop if the Government required that space for day care be provided before Government construction loans were made available? What kinds of tax provisions could spread the cost of building facilities over a suitable span of time, and what would the consequences be in terms of distributing the cost burden between private and public sectors? What are the management and logistic problems of large-scale day-care expansion in America? Unfortunately, the authors have been unable to find analyses of these implications and questions. At most, there seems to be interest in developing easily deployed models for centers; what is lacking is an overview of issues involved in developing facilities as they relate to a larger complex of choices.

The question of cost analysis is usually posed in relation to cost benefit; assessing actual cost in relation to benefit cost in the case of child-care service would be very difficult, both conceptually and practically. In the first place, benefits would be unusually difficult to estimate. For example, what impact would child-care facilities have on the labor force? Could an early network, acting partly as a health radar system, prevent higher medical costs in the future? Ultimately, how many children will remain in school longer because of the educational components in child care, and, as youths and future adults, therefore be much less likely to depend upon public welfare?[12]

Secondly, we have no direct way to assess child care in terms of psychological benefits to children, families, and communities. Assumptions can be made about an increased sense of competence and similar considerations. But assumptions are unreliable in financial equations. Most importantly, in terms of human resources, there are hidden costs in not developing a network of child care. We lack a politically convincing way of measuring and communicating these hidden costs.

Dilemmas of financing

As **TABLE IX** illustrates, without question, funding expanded child-care and preschool services will be costly. A significant question follows: how shall such a network be financed? The principal options appear to be:

1. Use only public funds (all Federal or some combination of local, state and Federal) allocated from general tax revenues, or from a special child-care trust fund;

2. Use some combination of public and private funds.

The chief difficulty with the former is the absence of available funds, both in our current tax structure and our national priorities. Thus, choosing this option would probably mean that only a limited number of those in need could be served; this might also, for political reasons, increase pressures to spend allocated funds in a random fashion instead of in a sufficiently concentrated way to have impact.

---

[12] Preliminary evidence from Appalachia suggests children in preschool programs are less likely to drop out of school earlier than non-enrolled children. (Appalachian Education & Economic Development Report III, 1969.)

Selecting the second option might lead to development of a more extensive child-care network, particularly if many organizations from the private sector can be included (industries, unions, etc.). Regarding this option, however, there is need to guard against unrealistic expectations of enthusiasm from the private sector; their interest in setting up child-care facilities may depend upon particular incentives from the Government, particularly those incentives which would increase profits.[13] Profit-making may not always be consistent with quality. Furthermore, unless there are special incentives, most private-sector involvement may be geared to the needs of the middle-class and affluent child.

There is a real dilemma regarding incentives. Financing guidelines must be structured to meet the needs of the private sector and also protect consumer rights, particularly rights of the low-income consumer. This latter idea includes the consumer's right to determine the nature of her child's daily experience; the right of the low-income parent to have the same quality and range of services for her children as those available to children from wealthier families; parental rights to share in shaping policies for the child-care center.

Potentially, there are both ideological and practical tensions between the needs of the two groups. Business needs efficiency and rapid decision making. Parents, particularly those whom society has usually deprived chances to develop competence and skills, need opportunities to grow at their own pace, and from their mistakes. A vital issue for the 1970's may be solving the "if, how, and when" of these two sets of conflicting needs.

Specific financing options

Until now, the grant system has been the major Federal mechanism for funding human service programs. It has been either project oriented or categorical. There are recent proposals to explore the effectiveness of a consolidated project grant/vendor payment system, designed: (1) to capitalize on the strengths of the grant system (such as its proven effectiveness in developing services more rapidly), (2) to

---

[13] Even industries who employ primarily women may find it more profitable, especially where there is a ready supply of labor, to tolerate absenteeism or rapid turnover.

minimize its weaknesses, such as "grantsmanship," and (3) to provide the consumer with a greater range of options. The mechanism would operate as follows:

1. Grants would be used to stimulate new programs and, therefore, would be for parts of a network, such as construction, training, etc.

2. Vendor payments would be used to provide operating funds. Funds would be allocated to states. Parents without adequate income to pay for services would receive vouchers (with Federal involvement on a sliding scale), and they would use these vouchers to enroll their children in the service program of their choice. The voucher system, it is thought, might stimulate competition, thus resulting in development of new centers, or the closing of inadequate ones; it also might protect the parent's right to make decisions about his child's experience.

3. If a voucher system could not support a center, as in rural areas, grants would be available to supplement operating funds.

4. Theoretically, all approved centers would be open to all parents. Centers would be filled on a first come, first served basis. Centers would have the right to charge more than the Federal amount allocated for each child.

It is difficult to predict the operational success of this mechanism. Clearly, it is based upon the operation of a strong marketing apparatus. Whether or not this system could exist, particularly in low-income communities, and whether or not it would protect the right of the poor to have quality programs, similar to those for the more affluent, remains to be seen.[14]

_____

[14]The G. I. Bill is often used as an example of a successful vendor payment system, but in that system, a range of quality institutions already existed. In child care, this is not the case, nor do children have the geographic mobility of adults.

C. The Question of Auspices

Traditionally, existing child-care services have been operated under private or welfare auspices: preschool services have been identified with the private nursery, the public school system, and recently, as in Head Start, with community-based agencies.[15] Currently, there is debate about the role the schools might play in day care and the role of others such as community-based groups and a broad segment of the private sector. Here are some of the strengths and weaknesses of each:

> Day Care with a Welfare Service Base: The child welfare focus is essentially an outgrowth of a foster care, or action in loco parentis. This network may have difficulty meeting demands and requirements for child care with a developmentally oriented approach.
>
> The School: While the school would presumably be in a position to facilitate educational needs, its operations would have to be restructured to meet time requirements for a full-day or even day/night service. On the other hand, all schools have recreational facilities and various non-educational resources. Hence, schools might be particularly suitable for after-school care if remaining on the school grounds were suitable to the children.
>
> Community-Based Agencies: Establishment of child-care services under the auspices of a community-based agency might result in a high level of consumer involvement and a high regard for consumer needs. At the same time, a community agency might have difficulty identifying facilities that met licensing standards and providing resources necessary for high-quality programs.

In addition to these options, there is a possibility of developing, within the local community, a comprehensive child-service center or family center with multiple components,

---

15/Today, growing numbers of "underground" child-care centers are developing, either as cooperative ventures or linked to community-action groups.

including preschool and child care. In effect, setting up such a multi-service center with a child/family focus would develop a new structure for child-care services.[16]

The question of auspices is, of course, related to funding. Funding priorities under different auspices might be set legislatively or administratively, or all options might be equally supported by the present funding system.

D. The Challenge of Quality

Consumers of child-care service as well as child-development specialists are becoming increasingly concerned with program quality so that the question of competence may be as significant as the question of cost distribution. The issues of training, manpower, and licensing regulation therefore attain great importance.

Training and manpower

There are no hard projections of the number of personnel needed to establish a network of child-care facilities, but rough estimates can be useful. These estimates are based on the quantities of eligible children in the previously cited categories.

Based on 1969 figures, some 7 million personnel would be required to meet all the needs of all children at child-care facilities. Accommodating children of the economically disadvantaged and the working mothers, alone, would require some 3 million personnel (see TABLE X). While accurate figures are unavailable on the numbers currently involved in early childhood care, estimates from data suggest there are less than 250 thousand. [17]

---

[16] There are currently some 30 parent-child centers operating across the country. If the model proves to be successful, it might model the type of service center specified here.

[17] Estimates from the National Center for Educational. Statistics indicate 1,516 prekindergarten and 55,509 kindergarten teachers were involved in public school systems in the fall of 1968. (Kahn, G., and Hughes, W., Local Public School Systems, Fall 1968, Table K, p, 17, March 1970.). No summary data are available on day-care and preschool personnel, licensed or unlicensed. Head Start data for 1968 suggest a total full-year staff of between 20,000 and 25,000 people.

TABLE X

PROJECTIONS FOR MANPOWER NEEDS BASED ON 1969 POPULATION
FIGURES UNDER FOUR CONDITIONS OF SERVICE
(In Millions)

Age of Child	Staff to Child Ratio	I Economically Disadvantaged		II Children of Working Mothers		III Handicapped		IV All Families	
		Children	Staff	Children	Staff	Children	Staff[1]	Children	Staff
0-2	1:4	1.6[2]	.4	2.9	.7	1.0[2]	.3	10.4	2.6
3-5	1:7	1.6	.2	2.9	.3	1.0	.1	11.6	1.7
6-14	1:15	6.5	.4	15.0	.9	3.9	.3	37.3	2.5
TOTALS[3]		9.8	1.1	20.8	1.9	5.9	.7	59.3	6.7

[1]Ratios for all conditions the same; although actually child/staff ratio for severely handicapped may have to be higher, many handicapped children are absorbed in regular programs.

[2]When numbers not broken down by ages 0-2/3-5, total figure divided in half. (This is consistent with general population data.)

[3]Totals do not take into account hours day-care facility open and consequent need for additional staff, therefore reflect conservative estimate.

NOTE: Table derived by authors; ratios do not include ancillary manpower; administrative staff, remedial staff, etc. Numbers of children based on Table VI which in turn has only partially validated figures. Categories overlap, as noted in Table IX.

This implies that developing a network of child-care services essentially means developing a new corps of human service personnel, with career lines and patterns for both professionals and non-professionals; for new careers, this includes provision for non-professional career advancement.

Finding personnel should not be too difficult. The Department of Labor's Monthly Review notes that shortly we will have a surplus of teachers.[18] With re-training, some of them might be able to work with preschool-age children. The non-working poor who are available for work, provide an untapped and potentially valuable resource, especially if the Family Assistance Plan becomes a reality. High-school students, school drop-outs, foster grandparents, and parental volunteers, might all be useful if sufficient funds and training programs are available.

At the same time, developing a new career field poses several challenges. First, child care has generally not been considered a high-prestige job. The erroneous misconception that anyone, without special training, can handle children leads to many unfortunate consequences. Perhaps a clear-cut formulation of goals with ensuing statements of specific areas of productivity can demonstrate not only the need for skill and knowledge but also indicate that child care is productive and intrinsically challenging.

Secondly, the tendency for conflict between professional and non-professional roles can become aggravating. Without special effort, there will be very few jobs, and there will be highly unrealistic career development opportunity available for low-income people.[19]

---

[18] Hedges, J. N. "Women Workers & Manpower Demands in the 1970's," Monthly Labor Review, June 1970.

[19] The Statement of Principles of the Child Development Day Care Handbook (Parker, 1970(e)) takes this position: "We advocate the concept of consumer control in order to bring about economic and social change. A system of child care enables people to seek jobs, training and other experiences which serve as a way out of economic poverty. . . . We recognize that the development of child care programs creates a new industry with jobs and economic opportunities. We believe that the consumers of these programs should have the greatest access to the immediate economic benefits and

Thirdly, there are no clear role definitions or methods for developing competent child-care workers. There is some exploration of appropriate models, but in building a new field, it is important to evaluate procedures and to maintain flexibility about what works and what is desirable.[20]

Given such parameters, the question of training strategy appears to be just as important as previous issues. Consequently, this brief overview of the current training situation is appropriate.

In this discussion, "training" is used generically to include both initial, in-service, and supplementary training experiences. In this area, there are three basic questions: (1) How many people are being trained annually (this has implications for the speed with which we can expand a child-care network in the next few years)? (2) What is the quality of training? (3) What are the strengths and weaknesses of the training models that currently exist?

First, estimates of the number of people trained annually are limited. Data from the National Center for Educational Statistics suggest that 3,816 degrees were conferred in 1966-1967 in early childhood education.[21] Cross-checking with other sources suggests this is a low estimate, but how low is unknown. Latest summary data on Head Start hold that 74% of the full-year Head Start personnel in 1968 had some training experiences compared with 57% in

---

opportunities created by this burgeoning child care industry." (p. 15, draft version.)

The argument is, of course, buttressed by the acknowledged need for the minority-group children to see minority-group adults in a wide range of roles, both professional and non-professional.

[20] See, for example, report of National Conference on Curricula for the Career Ladder in the Child Caring Professions, May 20-23, 1969.

[21] Silverman, L. J., Metz, S. Selected Statistics on Educational Personnel, U. S. DHEW National Center for Educational Statistics, 1970, Table 19.

1966.<u>22</u>/ Miller (1969) has estimated that probably some
5,000 individuals now receive training annually. Until hard
data are substituted for conjecture, there is no reason to
question his estimate.

Our <u>second</u> concern--the quality of training--poses
the most disturbing problems when one considers our present
status. In general, the quality of training is very poor
across all types of training but it is extremely poor when
provided on an in-service basis (where most "training"
actually takes place for the majority of child-care personnel).
This state exists for three reasons: ·

1. the specific objectives of training have never
   been clearly identified;

2. the methods to attain objectives such as the
   use of multimedia materials have never been
   developed; and,

3. the few promising training models have never
   been empirically evaluated.

Several papers have attempted to provide overviews and the
implications of their conclusions are frightening. Katz,
after a review of the available data, commented:

No matter how we would wish to construe the "ideal"
and the "ought," the quality of teacher performance
in the majority of our preschool settings today is
such that it potentially threatens the very goals
which have stimulated its recent expansion. (p. 8, 1969)

Miller, in a review for the National Laboratory on Early
Childhood Education, summarized his appraisal of the
situation thus:

. . . the field of early childhood education has
experienced a phenomenal growth which is continuing.

<u>22</u>/In 1968, 11% of the full-year staff attended
eight-week, university-sponsored training; 63% lectures,
movies or demonstrations on child development, and 48% training
and teaching preschool children. About 15% of the staff
attended adult education classes after being employed by Head
Start (Part D, Staff Member Information, Report on Head Start,
1970).

The proliferation of programs has created a crisis in
staffing. The problem has been met by using inadequately trained personnel. Training capabilities
have lagged far behind demonstrated need.[23] Those
training programs which are being developed probably
reflect little understanding or conversance with the
inner city and its people. The meager resources
available for the development of training programs
appear to be distributed on the basis of inappropriate
criteria.[24], [25] (p. 18, 1969)

Third, with reference to training models, in the 1960's
a variety of strategies were developed for persons without
university connections. These were largely the result of
Head Start program needs in addition to the traditional

---

[23] Federal investment in training for early childhood
has been minimal. . . . For FY 1971 Educational Professions
Development Act (EPDA) has $5 million dollars to
distribute for training. (Estimates are that the money will
serve some 4,000 people, at an average cost of $1,250.) Some
monies from the Scheuer Amendment are involved in training
early-childhood workers, although how many people are
involved is unknown.

[24] More optimistically, it should be noted that there
are signs of change in training institutions, particularly
in the directions of consolidating training resources and
making greater efforts to match training programs with real
needs. (See, for example, the plan of the Puget Sound area
in Washington State.)

[25] Training costs are variable depending on location
and level of personnel. As indicated, EPDA averages for
FY 1970 pegs the sum at $1,250 per trainee. Analysis of
Head Start Supplementary Training Grants Nationally suggests
a range per training from $121 to $982, with an average cost
of $592.18. These figures apply to both professional and
non-professional training. Different cost figures for
different levels of training are not available. (Data from
list of Regional Grantees for Contract 4215, xeroxed,
HEW.)

university-based programs.[26] Thus, there was development
of summer training programs, of special institutes and
workshops, and of patterns for in-service training.

Over the years, Head Start training models have
become more complex and more lengthy as it became clearer
that condensed training programs do not provide adequate
background for high-level or even adequate staff performance.
Currently, in-service training experiences are filtered
primarily through Regional Training Officers (RTO) and
consulting contracts for Supplementary Training Programs;
their purpose is to provide Head Start staff with opportunities
to gain both related training, and marketable credentials for
job mobility.[27]

Based on information from persons involved in training
programs, it appears that many fundamental problems in
training are similar to problems previously cited in developing a network of child-care services. There has been a
growth of patchwork training programs lacking linkages and
clear directives about responsibility. Thus, for example,
it is unclear whether, (1) RTO's and outside consultants in
Head Start serve the same population, (2) whether one is or
should be responsible for training trainees, (3) under what
conditions efforts could be better coordinated, etc.

Furthermore, there has been no continuous evaluation
of the impact of training efforts, or assessment of the most
effective methods for developing competence in child-care
workers. It would seem unwise to continue on this route at
an expanded rate.[28]

---

[26] It is not the purpose of this paper to describe
specific training models but rather to summarize mechanisms
for delivering training and upgrading experiences to large
numbers of people.

[27] In 1969, some 7,000 people were involved in
Supplementary Head Start Training from 65% of the full-year
Head Start grantees. We do not, however, have any satisfactory empirical data demonstrating the effectiveness of
these training programs.

[28] The EPDA administrators are taking a stand by
requiring all training programs, whatever the level, involve
work with real children; that professionals and non-professionals

In addition, under current pressures to set up a
training network, little hard thought is given to the question
of selecting appropriate trainers and consultants, and what,
if any, special training or experience each should have. For
several reasons, this concern may become important in the
1970's. Until recently, both consumers and program operators
seemed to assume that professionals were the only qualified
consultants.[29] However, this idea may prove to be incorrect,
since non-professionals may prove equally valuable in terms
of actual experiences which can enrich the professional's
contribution.[30], [31]

---

be trained together, and that jobs exist for non-professionals
after training is completed. At the same time, there is no
sign that other agencies involved with training will make the
same demands.

[29] There is actually less and less likelihood that this
pattern of the past will continue. In the more organized
communities, groups are refusing consulting services if they do
not feel their needs are met, or if the consultant groups do
not have minority representation in high-level positions. It
is likely that, in the next few years, this trend will be
accelerated.

[30] Unfortunately there is no systematic exploration of
the pay-off in terms of human or program development of different
"mixes" of consultants. Some programs have used non-professionals
as catalysts, and consultants in setting up new programs, but the
efforts are rarely reported except by direct communication.

[31] The idea of setting up a national registry of consultants has been proposed by several groups (e.g., those working
with Title I, the Joint Commission of the Mental Health of
Children). The concept might well be applicable to all early
childhood development programs with a registry channeled through
whatever local coordination units exist--the 4C's, the Child
Development Councils proposed by the Joint Commission, vendor
payment agencies, etc. Such a strategy might provide an effective
way to enable inexperienced groups to connect with a wide range
of talents acceptable to them, and thus would facilitate more
rapid network development. This might be particularly effective
if tax deductions were legislated for time donations for individuals with incomes above a certain level; and with those below
that level compensated with money or coupons for course credit.
As far as the authors know, no contract has been awarded for a
feasibility study or the development of a model registry.

In summary, the design and implementation of quality training is certainly one of the most important goals of the decade. Not only is there a need of competent, results-oriented personnel for new programs, but also, a need to meet turnover problems caused by the inconstancy of Federal funding and the hardship of working in the inner city.

Finally, there are equally critical issues which are part of larger manpower career development dilemmas, and which, until confronted more effectively, will hold back positive change in the child-development field. These will be noted briefly, since it is not possible to discuss them in detail within the limits of this paper. One example is the problem of insuring a match between job training and job availability; another is the problem of implementing career development programs. In Head Start, for instance, when people have moved up in job levels, it has typically been for circumstantial reasons, such as job vacancies, rather than promotions upward on operative career ladders.[32] For most non-professionals, vertical mobility exists only in the realm of the hypothetical. In addition to these examples, there is the problem of credentials. Attention to this has been spotty at best, and, on a large scale, of questionable impact. An overall strategy or incentive system to move both states and universities toward more flexible, realistic patterns has yet to be defined.[33] Until the "lock-out" function of credentials is modified, the possibility of developing a field with real job rewards (both psychological and economic) is in question.

Licensing and setting standards

The fundamental purpose of licensing is to insure that minimal standards are met, and that the child is protected. The licensing process can also be seen as a means for upgrading programs and educating consumers and program personnel about reasons for supporting high standards. To insure that minimal standards are met, the licensing agency must have recourse to legal procedures and actions. It should also have a sufficiently

---

[32] Under Scheuer funds, monies are available to implement new careers in those preschool programs that operate within school systems (i.e., when the civil service system is in effect).

[33] Pressures toward open enrollment appear to be mounting. This, albeit indirectly related is positive--in New Jersey as a consequence of an experiment at Camden College, the New Jersey

large, well-trained staff to follow up on significant licensing
deviations, and to provide training to child-care practitioners.

The most recent data suggest that there is some form
of state regulation of child care in all but one of the 54
states. In 46 states, the welfare agency has the primary
responsibility; in the others, either the Department's of
Health or Education, or a combination, are involved.

Since 1962, 18 states have enacted new or substantially
improved day-care legislation. The coverage, however, is
uneven.

Generally, different standards are required for
different types of care, i.e., home, family-group and center
day care.34/ Several states have, or are now working on,
regulations to cover the provision of infant care. Legal
standards and their requirements usually deal with safety
issues, space measurements, health codes, staffing ratios and,
sometimes, even program components. In addition, most state
licensing agencies develop a parallel body of recommended
standards to stimulate higher quality programs.

There are many problems inherent in licensing which
are attributable to such factors as the understaffing of
licensing agencies, the lack of power to issue provisional
licenses, or the ability to deviate under special circumstance
from prescribed regulations. Thus, even where there are
appropriate facilities, the ability to deliver service is
restricted. Furthermore, demoralizing delays in obtaining
licenses, particularly for community groups, encourage the
operation of unlicensed centers. In addition, local communities,

---

State legislature passed a law stating that any person over
19 could attend a community college with or without a GED
(General Equivalency Diploma) or high school diploma and
after 12 hours of credit are completed, will be said to have
a high school diploma.
     There is also evidence of growing interest in the
problem at the state level. Thus, for instance, Texas is
examining its credentialing requirements. Several other states
are showing interest as well.

     34/ Standards are generally defined by the licensing
agency, although they may be spelled out in legislation as
well.

municipalities or agencies may sometimes set contradictory
regulations making the process of meeting requirements even
more complex and time-consuming.[35/]

Some approaches to change are being explored. Under
the aegis of the Federal Government, a model licensing code
will be created shortly. Obviously, there is need to examine
the rationales, within respective states, cities and
individual agencies, for supporting particular legal requirements. This is a slow process.

A new organizational structure is also under
consideration. Currently a licensing agency is required to
coordinate visits of the multiple agencies involved in
inspections. This is a difficult task. As an alternative,
it may be possible to develop inspection teams composed of
individuals from appropriate agencies which would work from
a central child-based setting. In any event, the community
licensing procedure often seems to act as a deterrent, rather
than an incentive, on efficiency in programs.

Finally, there is an additional factor involving
Federal guidelines. In 1968, the Federal Panel on Early
Childhood wrote the Federal Interagency Day Care Requirements.
They are now being rewritten because of unfavorable criticisms.
The question of staff ratios is of primary interest, since
they affect not only program impact, but also program cost.
The criticized Inter-agency Guidelines required a ratio of
one adult to every four children. Even the carefully
monitored (LaCrosse, 1970) research programs described
elsewhere in this document have ratios of about 1:8. California
has a 1:10 ratio requirement. In the absence of hard data,
experience seems to suggest a need for increasing the Federal
ratio requirement. Presumably, what is most important is the
quality of staff-child interaction. Perhaps efforts to provide
for the child should be developed in the direction of requiring
high-quality programs only.

[35/]A California Task Force report cites one situation
in which the fire department declared a yard latch to be un-
suitable because it was too high for the children to reach in
case of fire. Another department declared that the latch was
so low that children could run into the street. (California
Women: A Report of the Advisory Committee on the Status of
Women, 1969.) New York City took approximately one year to get
a fully equipped, licensed nursery school relicensed as a day-
care center. During that time, none of the space was utilized
(Personal Communication, Esther Cole).

E.   Coordination and Linkage

Another consensus suggests that one of the critical
problems in implementing effective child-care services
involves the need to develop new strategies which insure
coordinated planning and service efforts, both within and
across governmental agencies and within individual
communities.

Coordination of services is a two-fold problem. At
one level, coordination confronts a fragmented administrative
bureaucracy. At another, it contends with the social fact
that there are no consolidated national goals for inspiring
public response to children's needs. Furthermore, we have
yet to decide what services ought to be Government supported
and thus available to all children as a basic right, and
what services will remain available for specific, more affluent
segments of the population.

There is valid reason for criticizing Federal agencies.
As compared to other social intervention programs, including
preschool and child-care efforts, the Federal Government until
recently has not exploited or used planned-policy incentives
to channel child-care-service efforts. It has not solved the
problem of administrative fragmentation. It has not developed
adequate methods for gathering information about who is served,
or how effectively and at what costs they can be served.[36]

---

[36] There appear to be two fundamental needs to resolve
this: (1) Develop a basic data-gathering system for all programs (across, not just within) agencies. There are signs now
that within-agency plans are underway to develop information
systems, but the comparability of information is being left to
chance. (2) Coordinate Federal resources with other existing
sources of knowledge (NEA, NAEYC, etc.) and to establish
research priorities that realistically meet the needs of planners.
Until fairly recently, most research efforts have been focused
on the impact of demonstration models, with the exception of
Head Start evaluation. We know little, however, about the impact
of less formally designed programs on children, and still less
about how to institutionalize, on a large scale, basic effective
demonstration models focusing around the needs of children.
Moreover, it is unlikely that without incentive from the Federal
Government, such information will become available because, for
the most part, professional researchers are more interested in
creating new models than in exploring the kinds of parameters
defined here.

While the Federal weaknesses pose a substantial problem, it is possible to draw from it some specific issues that are particularly relevant in developing a child-care-service network. For example, regarding planned-policy incentives, should all Federal programs for children be required to meet a set of uniform guidelines incorporating, for instance, required continuity of service? Such an instrument would be intended to compel communities to plan for sequential programs; this might include articulated, rather than haphazard, linkages, ranking priorities for service, utilization of in-service training, and/or Federal resource program banks.

Coping with administrative fragmentation appears to be unusually difficult. As indicated earlier, Federal programs responsive to children's needs are distributed through many agencies, most of which do not have primary responsibility to children. Unfortunately, up to now, there has been no systematic documentation of cost. Perhaps such a study should be commissioned. We now know, however, that only in rare cases do conceptually sequential programs flow sequentially to individual children, or to individual communities.[37] Obviously, such bifurcation cuts sharply into the dollar value of Government money being spent, not to mention the cost to the child.

In 1968, an Interagency Federal Panel on Early Childhood was established to facilitate coordination. (This is the panel that wrote the Federal Interagency Day Care Requirements.) The origination of such a panel, however, does not alone solve the problem. Both within and outside the Federal Government, structures without authority and funds lack impact. In July 1969, the Office of Child Development (OCD) was created and mandated to act as an advocate for the needs of all children, to coordinate existing efforts, and to articulate Federal priorities and goals for children. Political reality dictates,

---

[37] Efforts to map overlap in geographic concentration of Title 1 and Follow Through in several cities reveals, not surprisingly, little parallel concentration. While a similar pattern as to Head Start and Follow Through has not been documented, it has been examined. Estimates suggest that, of the many children served under one type of Head Start, only a small percentage (some 200,000) children had Head Start experiences several years in succession. If continuity of experience is important, as most data indicate, this means that current monies are not being used to provide the greatest payoff.

however, that while OCD may develop more effective ways to monitor new programs, it will have a difficult time restructuring those programs already established within different agencies.

In addition, the Brademas-Dellenback bill builds an alternate approach. That bill includes a provision to supplant separate authorities for relevant programs across various agencies: Head Start (EOA), migrant day-care authorizations; Titles IV-A and IV-B of the Social Security Act pertaining to child-welfare services. Whether or not such a solution is politically feasible remains to be seen.

Whatever the approach, it is clear that there is need for an effective mechanism to implement coordinated child-care services. It is equally clear that whatever method is adopted, it should be flexible enough to be modified in the light of experience.

A real Federal push to set up an effective, comprehensive network of services for children demands detailed planning and incremental goal setting (target populations and rates of expansion, for instance). Currently, these are difficult to attain for two fundamental reasons, namely, (1) realistic goal setting is impeded because critical information is lacking, widely scattered, or noncomparable, and (2) the requisites for planned strategy conflict with the political process, which involves rapidly shifting commitments, funding uncertainties, etc.

Currently, primary interest is concentrated upon activating mechanisms with a child-oriented focus. Thus, there is considerable interest in the potential impact of the 4C's (Community Coordinated Child Care) program as a linking mechanism. The objective underlying the 4C's concept is to develop a representative community body to focus all energies and community groups upon sharing resources.

Currently, over 300 communities have 4C's in some stages of development. Five states have 4C's at the state level. At least four are in cities with populations over 250,000. Some 24 of the 4C's have been designated as pilot projects and are being carefully monitored by the Federal Government. Of these, 21 have received funding. Participation in the 4C's is voluntary although the goal of each council is to reflect a mixed community group with one-third of the group being parents. Response to the program, despite the minimal funding involved, speaks well for the search within communities for a satisfactory approach to more adequate delivery of service.

Hence, when legislation mandating a more comprehensive and extensive network is passed, the 4C's concept may prove to be an important system for effective implementation. At the same time, it should be pointed out that linkage between state and local levels is not mandatory although sometimes, due to pressure from the communities and state interest, linkage is made. Lack of clearly articulated coordination may ultimately undercut the effectiveness of the 4C's, particularly if the trend to allocate monies to states rather than directly to local communities increases.

Moreover, a horizontal strategy may reinforce rather than diminish local hostilities. Currently, the 4C's concept has not become rigid. It may yet evolve into a suitable mechanism, particularly if new Federal funds are clearly directed to those communities adept at coordination. The procedure may be particularly appropriate for middle-sized communities; alternative methods may be more suitable in larger communities.[38]

Basically, it is clear that sophisticated mechanisms for the delivery of service in the 1970's need to be developed. As yet however, neither approach nor methodology for evaluation of these systems exist. But a three-year study exploring alternate models has been awarded, and hopefully will stimulate new thinking when completed.

It is also clear that in any mechanism, effectiveness is determined by the interplay of several individual groups such as parents, minority-group children, and professionals, often with a vested interest in maintaining the status quo.

To serve children, a fundamental challenge in the 1970's may involve decisions on whether or not a consensus on

---

[38] The Joint Commission of the Mental Health of Children has proposed a mechanism similar to the 4C's concept, but with municipal as well as state and local arms. Both the 4C's and the Joint Commission models call for National Advisory Councils. While the Joint Commission model has not been tested, conceptually it has both strengths and weaknesses as do the 4C's. How it will function in actuality remains to be seen. (For a critique, see Knitzer, 1970.)

on goals can be worked out in the face of these competing
perspectives. The need for resolution is particularly great
for two reasons: (1) there is no effective lobby to act as
an outside monitor for the needs of children as, for example,
the National Welfare Rights Organization is becoming for
welfare recipients and (2) since monetary resources for a child-
care network are minimal at this time, and likely to remain
minimal as compared to other funding, it is vital that ways
be established to get the most leverage from available monetary
and non-monetary resources.

F. Summary

This chapter has identified a growing demand for child-
care and preschool services, and has described some of the
issues that relate to the current lack of an effective supply
system, including:

Clear goals for a comprehensive child-care and child-
development program are lacking. These objectives
should answer such questions as whether society
should be responsible only for the disadvantaged or
should it make a universal commitment to the needs
of all children?

Current sponsoring auspices include child-welfare
services, educational systems, community-based or
consumer groups, and segments of the private sector.
Services under each aegis have different emphases,
and different goals ranging from primary concern
about freeing the mother for work, to stimulating
positive development in the child.

An effective financing mechanism is also lacking.
Public funds are inconstant and, within the current
national priority system, inadequate to support a
massive implementation network although they are
useful in stimulating the development of demonstration models. Private-sector involvement has not
been proven clearly profitable, and forces for profit
may at times conflict with service needs. Groups
most in need of services are least able to pay for
them. No alternative mechanism has been defined to
provide a continuing source of revenue, although
such programs as child-care corporations are
contemplated.

There are underdeveloped plans: (1) to channel
resource personnel into child care, (2) to train
a new corps of paraprofessionals and professionals,
(3) to increase the supply of new or renovated
facilities, and (4) to monitor the effectiveness
of the programs.

There is inefficient utilization of existing
resources, both program and financial, and coordinating mechanisms are inadequate or non-existent
both within the Federal Government and in the
community-at-large.

Complex licensing processes do not always meet the
goals of protecting the child and upgrading services.

In the body of this chapter we have examined the
options for dealing with some of these problems.

CHAPTER THREE

SUMMARY OF CONCLUSIONS:
AGENDA FOR THE SEVENTIES

This document has concentrated upon examining the
trends, issues, and options in child care, and the
organization of a data base to determine an agenda for the
1970's in child-care and preschool services. This chapter
summarizes the material and draws conclusions from our
examination and appraisal.

A. Trends, Issues, Options in Child Care

In summary, the trends and issues involved are these,
classified in order of importance to the public interest:

1. Funding.--Absence of an effective financing
mechanism is the single most important consideration in developing a national network
of high-quality child-care services. Available
public funds are woefully inadequate to meet
current needs, and substantial private - sector
financing seems unlikely until such time as
public funds enable private corporations to make
a reasonable profit.

2. Delivery.--Creation of effective training and
delivery systems is the second most important
consideration in developing a network to
implement child-care services on a national
level. Implied in this concern is staffing,
training, monitoring, and administering
evaluation systems that not only will enable
the best of current knowledge to reach the field
but will also stimulate the creation of new
knowledge, through research, so as to improve
the best of current practice.

3. Coordination.--The necessity to utilize limited
resources efficiently dictates the development

of a workable multilevel (national, state, local)
coordinating mechanism. The 4C's Model,
theoretically, appears promising as such an
effective mechanism of coordination. Numerous
practical problems have confronted it in practice,
however, and they must still be overcome.

4. Quality.--Standards and licensing procedures for
child-care services must focus on insuring that
high-quality child-development programs are
provided for children. These procedures should
not be established in a complex, rigid framework
lest they impede the activation of good programs.

5. Priorities.--The population groups of children to
be served in child-care facilities must be clearly
identified. Possible options range from
accommodation of minority-status children or
subgroups of children from poor families to a
national commitment to meet the needs of all
children.

6. Sponsorship.--Current sponsoring auspices include
child-welfare services, educational systems,
community-based organizations, consumer groups,
and segments of the private sector. Services
under each aegis may have different emphases,
and different goals ranging from custodial care
in order to free the mother for employment, to
programs designed to stimulate positive development
of the child with parental involvement.

Options for dealing with each of the issues have been
discussed in the body of the text.

B. Conclusions Emerging From Our Examination

On the basis of the material presented in this document,
the following conclusions may be drawn:

1. Need.--Approximately 5% of the children under age
six receive full-day care service, and 30% have
some preschool experience. Only 2% of children
between age six and age fourteen receive any form
of child care. These services cover children of
widely diverse backgrounds and geographical

locations, and they often disclose a poor match
between those for whom services are most needed
and those to whom they are most readily available.

2. _Focus_.--Though the national trend is toward
providing more day-care services, no medium
exists, at present, to insure that a comprehensive child-care program will be originated.
Existing programs, in many cases, are fragmented,
lacking in quality control, and more harmful
than beneficial to children. The problem would
be compounded were a national expansion of the
present child-care program to occur. The focus,
rather, should be on an integrated network of
child-care services to meet the multiple needs
of various consumers.

3. _Knowledge_.--There are no adequate information
systems for determining, accurately, the number
of children served by various child-care services,
the quality of their service, the components of
such services, and a cost/benefit analysis of these
components from this standpoint of impact on the
child, his family and the community itself.
Moreover, a lack of support exists for enlarging
the reservoirs of our current knowledge through
basic and applied research. We would be ill
advised to expand child-care services nationally
without clear provision for increased research
funds, and accompanying processes which would
guarantee that advances in knowledge will be
transformed into practical application.

4. _Plan_.--Since no comprehensive, countrywide child-
care program now exists, the nation stands before
the opportunity to plan policy and structure for
the development of a network of child-care services focused upon the attainment of multiple
goals, namely, to facilitate maximum child
development, to free mothers for employment who
want to work, and to provide jobs for a host of
citizens.

C. Essentials in an Agenda for the Seventies

Our mandate requires that we outline the major decisions that the United States must face as its leaders prepare
an agenda for the nation's next decade. Specifically, the
following decisions must be made:

1. Funding.--The three high-priority questions
    related to funding are:

    a. What are the appropriate roles of the
        Federal, state and local governments
        in bearing the cost of various child-care
        services? More specifically, which
        options are most viable, ranging from
        total Federal support to Federal and state
        cost-sharing, to total consumer support?

    b. What level of funding should be provided
        to ensure high-quality programs? The
        current average costs contemplated in
        pending legislation (e.g., the Family
        Assistance Plan) do not specify adequate
        funds to support high-quality programs.

    c. What would be revealed by an accurate
        cost-benefit analysis of the various
        components (e.g., health, nutrition, child
        development, etc.) of child care? Do the
        positive benefits accruing to the child
        also have economic impact by improving
        health, for example, or demolishing poverty
        cycles, improving academic skills, and
        increasing employability?

2. Planning.--If an improvement of existing child-
    care services, or an expansion of present services,
    is a goal for the Seventies, plans must be drawn
    for the development of adequate facilities,
    delivery systems and coordinating mechanisms.
    Additionally, we must consider the timetable of
    phasing the various efforts over the next ten
    years. For example, what are the implications
    of slow rather than rapid expansion?

    a. Facilities.--Child-care facilities, currently,
        are a national disgrace because most of them

do not satisfy licensing standards. Nor has
enough productive consideration been given
to the design and use of space in the
facilities which meet state licensing standards. Too often, building space is converted
into a child-care site without employing
standards of excellence as criteria. What
if our public schools were housed in available
renovated space?

b. Delivery Systems.--Only through sophisticated
delivery systems can we insure adequately
trained personnel and high-quality programs.
Such national programs as Head Start are still
suffering because adequate delivery systems
were not developed prior to national expansion.

c. Coordination.--The necessity for efficient
utilization of limited resources dictates the
need for development of a successful system
of program coordination.

3. Focus.--Several interrelated questions are posed
and discussed here:

a. What type of program settings should be
developed? Within a setting, which program
models should be used? A decision must be
made as to what proportion of available
resources should be invested in center-based
care, in home care, or in a combination of
center and home care. A determination must
also be made as to which programs are most
effective for which children in these three
settings. This acknowledges the obvious
fact that numerous objectives exist across
programs, and that one must strive to find
the program most closely matching objectives
and child-family needs.

b. What level of quality should be provided
across child-care settings? This document
discussed the advantages and disadvantages
of programs with objectives ranging from
custodial programs to high-quality developmental programs. If the focus is on high-
quality programs, monitoring systems are

needed to help the local staff improve their
program. Other monitoring systems are needed
to insure that program standards are indeed
met. The Seventies may well be the decade
that will hold program operators accountable
for the quality of their programs.

4. <u>Priorities</u>.--The fundamental question is essentially:
   Which population groups are to be served? The
   range of potential consumers has been discussed
   in the text.

5. <u>Sponsorship</u>.--The issue of program control at
   Federal level is critical. Will the new programs
   of child care be under the Office of Child
   Development, a natural heir if President Nixon's
   definition of the agency stands firm, or shall
   these programs be administered by another Federal
   agency.

   Sponsorship at the local level remains a serious
   question. The role of the state leadership in
   allocation of funds and resources must be defined
   at the administration level. Four groups seem
   likely to be involved--the community, the schools,
   the welfare departments, and the private sector.
   The advantages and disadvantages of each of these
   groups sponsoring child care in America must be
   given depth study against the background of
   Federal funding and national planning.

6. <u>Knowledge</u>.--While important advances have been
   made in child-development programs, the text
   delineates the urgency of expanded support for
   research so that it may broaden the knowledge
   base and, consequently, improve child-care services.

7. <u>Implications</u>.--Lastly, the most important of all
   agenda items for the Seventies is to weigh carefully the implications of the decision of the
   1970 White House Conference on Children and Youth
   for the remainder of this Century.

It is hoped that the data presented in this document
will assist the White House Conference on Children and Youth,
thus contributing to the successful outcome of that significant
assembly.

APPENDICES

I. Population Data

    A. Comparative Population by Age--1960, 1969.

    B. Population Estimates and Projections by Selected Age Categories--1960, 1969, 1975, 1980.

II. Information Related to Child Care Arrangements and Day Care and Preschool Services and Needs

    C. Original Data for Table I.

    D. Day Care Utilization by Age.

    E. Regional Variability in Percent of Eligible Population Served--Pre-primary, Day Care, Kindergarten.

    F. Percent Enrollment in Poverty and Non-poverty SMSA's--1969.

    G. Day Care Facilities by States: Capacity as Percentage of Combined Numbers of AFDC Children and Children of Working Mothers--1969.

    H. Numbers of AFDC Children and Children of Working Mothers Under Fifteen--1969.

    I. Chart, Percentage of Working Mothers--1960-1980.

    J. Cumulative Income Distribution of Families with Husband and Wife Present by Race and Female-headed Households.

    K. Federal Expenditures and Numbers of Children Served--1960-1971.

    L. Type of Day Care.

III. <u>Federal Issues</u>

    M. Summary of Major Programs for Day Care and Pre-school Services.

    N. Summary of Selected Pending Legislation.

IV. <u>Cost Data</u>

    O. Trends in Distribution of California Expenditures--1965-1968.

    P. Estimates of Construction Costs for 100 Child Centers in Several Cities.

APPENDIX A

TOTAL UNIVERSE (1969) OF CHILDREN POTENTIALLY ELIGIBLE
FOR CHILD CARE/CHILD DEVELOPMENT SERVICES
(In Thousands)

Age	1960	1969
Under 5	20,321	17,960
Under 1	4,112	3,495
1 year	4,106	3,419
2 years	4,099	3,543
3 years	4,016	3,643
4 years	3,988	3,867
5-9 years	18,692	20,827
5 years	3,954	4,050
6 years	3,820	4,119
7 years	3,787	4,198
8 years	3,649	4,295
9 years	3,482	4,164
10-14 years	16,773	20,518
10 years	3,481	4,167
11 years	3,473	4,157
12 years	3,574	4,143
13 years	3,507	4,037
14 years	2,739	4,014

Source: U. S. Dept. of Commerce, Bureau of the Census,
Current Population Reports, Series P-25, #441,
March 19, 1970.

APPENDIX B

POPULATION ESTIMATES AND PROJECTIONS--CHILDREN 0-14
(In Thousands)

	1960[A]	1969[A]	1975[B]	1980[B]
Infancy (0-2)	12,317	10,448	11,195	12,756
Pre-school (3-5)	11,958	11,560	10,652	11,823
School Age (6-14)	31,512	37,294	31,000[1]	32,593

[1] For age 9 and above Series P-25, #381 provides only one combined projection for all four population models for 1975.

Source: [A]U. S. Dept. of Commerce, Bureau of the Census, Current Population Reports, Series P-25, #41, March 19, 1970.

[B]Ibid., Series P-25, #381, Dec. 18, 1967; projections from Series D, Table 14, pp. 89-91.

n.b.: Series D--estimates are lowest of four series projected, but may still be higher than actual numbers. (Births in 1969 are actually lower than projected.)

APPENDIX C

CHILD CARE ARRANGEMENTS: NUMBER AND
PERCENT DISTRIBUTION OF CHILDREN BY
TYPE OF ARRANGEMENT AND EMPLOYMENT
STATUS OF MOTHER
(In Thousands)

Arrangement	Total		Children of Full-time Working Mothers		Children of Full-time Full-time Working Mothers	
	Number	Percent	Number	Percent	Number	Percent
TOTAL	12,287	100.0	8,315	100.0	3,072	100.0
Care in own home by	5,592	45.5	4,099	40.3	1,493	37.6
Father	1,828	14.9	1,144	13.8	684	17.2
Other relative	2,607	21.2	2,013	24.2	595	15.0
Under 13 years	91	0.7	53	0.6	37	0.9
13-15	479	3.9	344	4.1	135	3.4
16-17	552	4.5	405	4.9	147	3.7
18-64	1,044	8.5	862	10.4	183	4.6
65 years and over	440	3.6	348	4.2	92	2.3
Nonrelative who only looked after children	581	4.7	429	5.2	153	3.8
Nonrelative who usually did additional household chores	575	4.7	513	6.2	62	1.0
Care in someone else's home by	1,933	15.7	1,637	19.7	296	7.5
Relative	953	7.8	801	9.6	153	3.8
Nonrelative	979	8.0	836	10.1	143	3.6

APPENDIX C--Continued

Arrangement	Total		Children of Full-time Working Mothers		Children of Full-time Working Mothers	
	Number	Percent	Number	Percent	Number	Percent
Other arrangements:						
Care in group care center	265	2.2	239	2.9	27	0.7
Child looked after self	994	8.1	800	9.6	194	4.9
Mother looked after child while working	1,594	13.0	575	6.9	1,020	25.7
Mother worked only during child's school hours	1,847	15.0	917	11.0	930	23.4
Other	63	0.5	50	0.6	13	0.3

Source: Low, S. and Spindler, P., National Survey, 1968, Tables A-1, A-3.

APPENDIX C(A)

CHILD CARE ARRANGEMENTS: PERCENT DISTRIBUTION
OF CHILDREN OF FULL-TIME WORKING MOTHERS BY
TYPE OF ARRANGEMENT AND AGE OF CHILDREN

Arrangement	Total	Under 6 Years			6-13 Years		
		Total	Under 3	3-5	Total	6-11	12-13
TOTAL	100.0	100.0	100.0	100.0	100.0	100.0	100.0
Care in own home by	49.3	47.2	46.0	48.1	49.9	52.6	43.1
Father	13.8	10.3	9.5	10.8	15.3	15.5	14.9
Other relative	24.2	18.4	18.6	18.3	26.4	27.0	24.9
Under 16 years	4.7	1.0	0.6	1.3	6.5	6.7	5.9
16 years and over	19.5	17.4	18.0	17.1	20.0	20.4	19.0
Nonrelative who only looked after children	5.2	9.3	8.7	9.7	3.3	4.1	1.1
Nonrelative who usually did additional household chores	6.2	9.2	9.1	9.3	4.9	5.9	2.3
Care in someone else's home by	19.7	37.3	41.7	34.3	12.1	14.6	5.9
Relative	9.6	17.6	22.0	14.8	6.2	6.9	4.3
Nonrelative	10.1	19.6	19.8	19.5	5.9	7.7	1.5
Other arrangements:							
Care in group care center	2.9	7.7	4.8	9.7	0.7	0.8	0.4
Child looked after self	9.6	0.3	0.2	0.3	13.8	9.6	24.2
Mother looked after child while working	6.9	6.7	6.4	6.9	7.1	7.0	7.3
Mother worked only during child's school hours	11.0	0.5	---	0.8	15.7	14.8	18.2
Other	0.6	0.4	1.0	---	0.7	0.7	0.8

Source: Low, S. and Spindler, P., National Survey, 1968, Tables A-1, A-3.

APPENDIX D

DAY CARE UTILIZATION BY AGE

	0-3 (%)	3-5 (%)	6 and over[1] (%)
Low and Spindler[2]			
Part-time Working Mothers	0.9	1.5	0.2
Full-time Working Mothers	4.8	9.7	0.7
Cochran and Robinson[3]	1.5	5.8	0.7

Source: [1]Low and Spindler data use age break of 0-3, 3-5, 6 and over; Cochran and Robinson use age break of 0-2, 3-6, 7 and over. Therefore, data are not strictly comparable.

[2]Low, S., Spindler, P., Child Care Arrangements of Working Mothers, Tables A3 and 5 (1968).

[3]Cochran and Robinson, Day Care For Children in Massachusetts (1966), Table 10.

66-385   443

APPENDIX E

REGIONAL VARIABILITY IN PERCENT OF
ELIGIBLE POPULATION SERVED

	Northeast	Northcentral	South	West
1969 Pre-primary[1]				
3 year old	8.9	5.2	9.1	12.9
4 year old	29.7	17.6	20.0	28.1
5 year old	75.1	79.3	47.6	80.2
Day Care: 1965[2]	1.3	0.4	3.5	3.1
Kindergarten Enrollment[3]	95.4	76.0	35.0	90.0

Source: [1]Hurd, G., October 1969 Pre-primary Enrollment
Data, Table 8-A (in press).

[2]Low, S. and Spindler, P., Child Care Arrangements of Working Mothers (1968), Table A-60.
Based on number of children for whom arrangements made--not potentially eligible population.

[3]Jaffe, R., Jaffe, E., Survey of Available
Public and Private Kindergarten, Fall, 1968,
Table 13, p. 28 (1969).

APPENDIX F

1969
PERCENT ENROLLED IN SMSA's OVER 250,000
(October 1969)

	POVERTY SMSA's % ENROLLED	NON-POVERTY SMSA's % ENROLLED
Total--3-5 Years	33.5	40.5
White	29.9	39.9
Non-white	37.0	44.1
Negro	36.3	49.1
Total--3 Years	8.3	12.1
White	3.2	11.4
Non-white	13.2	16.9
Negro	12.8	17.4
Total--4 Years	26.4	29.2
White	18.3	27.3
Non-white	31.5	42.1
Negro	31.0	44.3
Total--5 Years	65.3	76.0
White	65.8	76.4
Non-white	64.8	72.6
Negro	64.7	71.1

Source: Adapted from National Center of Educational
Statistics October 1969 Report on Pre-primary
Enrollment--from xeroxed Table 7 (in press).

APPENDIX G

DAY CARE FACILITIES BY STATES

State	Combined Day Care & Family Care Facilities[1]	Combined AFDC & Children of Working Mothers By State, 1969[2]	% Children Who Could be Served By Existing Facilities
Alabama	11,142	675,030	1.6
Alaska	585	42,072	1.4
Arizona	16,314	319,557	5.1
Arkansas	4,569	344,072	1.3
California	24,062	4,205,782	.6
Colorado	no data	424,682	no data
Connecticut	12,692	610,560	2.1
Delaware	4,082	103,823	3.9
District of Columbia	6,679	233,259	2.9
Florida	22,047	1,243,896	1.8
Georgia	28,076	973,293	2.9
Hawaii	8,180	140,650	5.8
Idaho	836	132,315	.6
Illinois	22,972	2,166,074	1.1
Indiana	6,413	924,702	.7
Iowa	4,514	521,422	.9
Kansas	6,272	432,369	1.5
Kentucky	7,556	552,807	1.4
Louisiana	9,869	663,618	1.5
Maine	1,189	182,158	.7
Maryland	32,516	742,235	4.4
Massachusetts	24,132	1,173,949	2.1
Michigan	3,920	1,547,900	.3
Minnesota	7,574	680,982	1.1
Mississippi	219	474,910	.1
Missouri	11,416	855,847	1.4
Montana	1,329	128,166	1.1
Nebraska	1,608	284,834	.6
Nevada	2,886	100,231	3.4
New Hampshire	4,840	140,753	3.4
New Jersey	15,621	1,396,832	1.1
New Mexico	739	200,418	.8
New York	135,580	4,138,032	3.3
North Carolina	12,375	1,008,919	1.2

APPENDIX G--Continued

State	Combined Day Care & Family Care Facilities[1]	Combined AFDC & Children of Working Mothers By State, 1969[2]	% Children Who Could be Served By Existing Facilities
North Dakota	251	110,529	.2
Ohio	3,714	1,801,811	.2
Oklahoma	9,984	469,905	2.1
Oregon	4,527	369,452	1.2
Pennsylvania	10,556	2,306,109	.5
Rhode Island	1,361	316,351	.4
South Carolina	9,318	511,518	1.8
South Dakota	140	128,781	.1
Tennessee	25,490	781,395	3.3
Texas	52,417	1,980,153	2.7
Utah	3,411	204,411	1.7
Vermont	940	80,922	1.2
Virginia	13,100	861,210	1.5
Washington	18,924	605,614	3.1
West Virginia	1,046	299,105	.4
Wisconsin	3,924	805,892	.5
Wyoming	863	65,090	1.3

[1]Licensed or approved Day Care Centers and Family Care Homes, March 1969 (provisional).

[2]AFDC Children and Children of Working Mothers by State, 1969, mimeographed with WIN date by State (from OCD, xeroxed).

APPENDIX H

CURRENT UNIVERSE OF NEED--1969--BY STATE[1]

	Children Under 15 on AFDC	Children of Working Mothers
United States	4,309,040	35,408,880
Alabama	70,140	604,890
Alaska	4,632	37,440
Arizona	30,567	288,990
Arkansas	25,832	318,240
California	643,132	3,562,650
Colorado	38,582	386,100
Connecticut	52,470	558,090
Delaware	12,563	91,260
District of Columbia	23,829	209,430
Florida	120,696	1,123,200
Georgia	114,513	858,780
Hawaii	13,120	127,530
Idaho	8,295	124,020
Illinois	240,254	1,925,820
Indiana	40,182	884,520
Iowa	38,212	483,210
Kansas	31,059	401,310
Kentucky	77,787	475,020
Louisiana	116,058	547,560
Maine	18,358	163,800
Maryland	82,355	659,880
Massachusetts	117,439	1,056,510
Michigan	145,070	1,402,830
Minnesota	43,332	637,650
Mississippi	73,600	401,310
Missouri	84,817	771,030
Montana	7,656	120,510
Nebraska	18,074	266,760
Nevada	6,631	93,600
New Hampshire	5,033	135,720
New Jersey	147,272	1,249,560
New Mexico	29,598	170,820
New York	653,772	3,484,260
North Carolina	72,919	936,000
North Dakota	6,399	104,130

APPENDIX H--Continued

	Children Under 15 on AFDC	Children of Working Mothers
Ohio	16,391	1,785,420
Oklahoma	56,895	413,010
Oregon	32,582	336,960
Pennsylvania	241,059	2,065,050
Rhode Island	22,681	293,670
South Carolina	28,308	483,210
South Dakota	9,441	119,340
Tennessee	78,225	703,170
Texas	126,873	1,853,280
Utah	18,381	186,030
Vermont	7,212	73,710
Virginia	49,230	311,980
Washington	49,864	555,750
West Virginia	48,725	250,380
Wisconsin	52,412	753,480
Wyoming	3,080	62,010

[1]AFDC Children and Children of Working Mothers By State, mimeographed with WIN data by State, 1969 (from OCD, xeroxed).

APPENDIX I

THE NUMBER OF WORKING MOTHERS WITH YOUNG CHILDREN WILL CONTINUE TO RISE
(Labor Force Status of Mothers 20 to 44 Years of Age, With Children Under 6 Years, 1960-67,[1] and Children Under 5 Years, Projected to 1980[2])

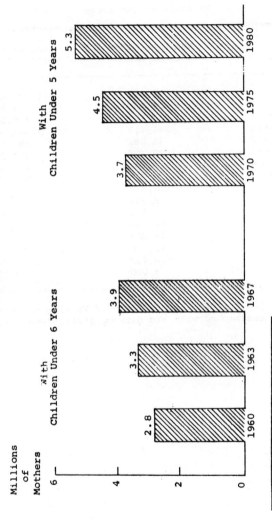

Millions of Mothers

With Children Under 6 Years

With Children Under 5 Years

1960: 2.8
1963: 3.3
1967: 3.9
1970: 3.7
1975: 4.5
1980: 5.3

[1]Data are for March of each year.

[2]Projections for children under 6 years of age are not available.

Source: U.S. Dept. of Labor, Bureau of Labor Statistics: Special Labor Force Report #49, March 1960, March 1963, or projections to 1980 #94 for March 1967. Chart from Working Mothers and The Need for Child Care Services, U.S. Dept. of Labor, June 1968.

APPENDIX J

CUMULATIVE INCOME DISTRIBUTION OF FAMILIES WITH BOTH
HUSBAND AND WIFE PRESENT, BY RACE
(Male Head: Married, Wife Present)

Total Money Income	White			Negro		
	Total	Wife in Paid Labor Force	Wife not in Paid Labor Force	Total	Wife in Paid Labor Force	Wife not in Paid Labor Force
Number (000)	39,821	14,134	25,687	3,113	1,565	1,553
Percent--						
Under 1,000	1.1%	0.4%	1.5%	2.6%	0.8%	4.3%
Under 1,500	2.3	0.7	3.2	6.0	2.8	9.0
Under 2,000	4.2	1.2	5.9	10.2	4.8	15.4
Under 2,500	6.6	2.0	9.2	15.8	7.7	23.7
Under 3,000	8.7	2.9	12.0	19.9	10.0	26.9
Under 3,500	11.3	4.2	15.4	25.5	13.8	37.0
Under 4,000	13.9	5.8	18.5	29.7	17.2	42.0
Under 5,000	19.5	9.9	25.0	40.3	27.0	53.4
Under 6,000	26.8	15.7	33.1	51.7	37.3	65.9
Under 7,000	35.1	22.2	42.3	60.5	46.8	73.7
Under 8,000	44.3	30.2	52.2	69.1	56.0	81.8
Under 9,000	53.2	39.1	61.1	75.7	64.9	86.1
Under 10,000	61.0	47.9	68.3	80.6	71.2	89.5
Under 12,000	74.2	64.7	79.6	88.4	82.0	94.3
Under 15,000	86.2	82.0	88.7	94.7	91.5	97.3
Under 25,000	97.1	97.4	97.1	99.2	98.6	99.3
Under 50,000	99.5	99.7	99.6	99.9	99.7	99.6
Residual	0.4	0.3	0.4	0.2	0.1	0.4
Median Income ($)	8,629	10,232	7,783	5,854	7,333	4,693
Mean Income ($)	9,710	11,094	8,949	6,856	8,175	5,528

Source: U. S. Dept. of Commerce, Bureau of the Census,
Current Population Reports, Series P-60, No. 59,
"Income in 1967 of Families in the U. S.,"
U. S. GPO, Washington, D. C., 1969, Table 10,
pp. 32-38.

APPENDIX J(A)

CUMULATIVE INCOME DISTRIBUTION OF
FAMILIES HEADED BY WOMEN, HUSBAND
NOT PRESENT--BY RACE

Total Money Income	White	Negro
Number (000)	4,008	1,272
Percent--		
Under 1,000	7.4%	11.1%
Under 1,500	11.9	19.3
Under 2,000	17.9	27.1
Under 2,500	24.3	39.8
Under 3,000	29.4	49.7
Under 3,500	35.3	59.5
Under 4,000	40.6	55.5
Under 5,000	51.2	76.1
Under 6,000	61.2	83.8
Under 7,000	70.3	89.4
Under 8,000	77.9	92.3
Under 9,000	83.2	94.6
Under 10,000	87.0	96.2
Under 12,000	92.1	98.2
Under 15,000	95.7	98.9
Under 25,000	99.1	99.9
Under 50,000	99.8	100.0
Residual	0.1	0.0
Median Income ($)	4,879	3,015
Mean Income ($)	5,823	3,676

Source: U. S. Dept. of Commerce, Bureau of the Census,
Current Population Reports, Series P-60, No. 59,
"Income in 1967 of Families in the U. S.,"
U. S. GPO, Washington, D. C., 1969, Table 10,
pp. 32-38.

APPENDIX K

CHILDREN SERVED AND FEDERAL EXPENDITURES FOR CHILD CARE, 1960-1971[1,2]
(In Millions)

	1960[4]		1965		1969		1970		1971	
	Children	Cost	Children	Cost	Children	Cost	Children	Cost	Children	Cost
Full Day Pre-school										
Head Start			300	.5	75,000	75.0	90,000	97.0	90,000	98.0
OEO Local Initiative					1,000	1.0	1,000	1.0	1,000	1.0
AFDC Non Win					7,800	5.6	15,900	11.4	19,500	14.0
AFDC Win					4,100	1.2	26,500	19.1	65,300	47.0
CWS[3]			4,600	4.6	20,300	6.2	22,300	6.2	24,600	5.2
Migrant					1,500	1.9	2,000	2.5	2,300	2.2
CEP					1,000	1.0	2,200	2.2		
Subtotal			4,900	5.1	110,700	91.9	159,900	139.4	202,700	168.4
After School										
CWS					15,500	2.8	31,900	5.8	39,000	7.1
WIN					10,500	3.0	68,100	12.3	168,000	30.2
Subtotal					26,000	5.8	100,000	18.1	207,000	37.3
Experimental										
PCC					2,600	4.9	4,050	5.6	4,500	6.9

APPENDIX K--Continued

Experimental

	1960		1965		1969		1970		1971	
	Children	Cost	Children	Cost	Children	Cost	Children	Cost	Children	Cost
Head Start					1,800	.5	6,500	7.0	10,500	12.5
Day Care (OCD/OEO)					400	.9	5,400	3.0	15,400	21.0
Subtotal					4,800	5.3	15,950	15.6	30,400	40.4
TOTAL			4,900	5.1	141,700	103.0	275,850	173.1	440,100	246.1

[1]Based on latest data available from Bureau of the Budget (January 19, 1970). Other estimates from government sources differ, especially around WIN figures.

[2]Chart does not include one-half day Head Start or ESEA.

[3]Number of children reflect Federal and non-Federal effort.

[4]None of programs listed were funded in 1960.

APPENDIX L

TYPE OF DAY CARE
HOME CARE--PRIVATE ARRANGEMENT

Distinguishing Characteristics:

1. Child remains in his own home
2. Child caregiver comes into child's home
3. Parents pay caregiver directly

Variations:

1. Caregiver frequently is also a housekeeper
2. Caregiver may be private agent or member of a
   commercial service

Advantages for Family Life:

1. Child remains in familiar, secure place
2. Convenience: flexible hours, no frantic, early
   morning packing up the child
3. Economical for large family
4. Family can be together
5. Caregiver can be important addition to family

Disadvantages for Family Life:

1. Expensive for small family
2. Anxiety about selecting caregiver
3. Anxiety about whether caregiver will be reliable
   in showing up and dependable in service
4. Lack of uniformity in capacities of caregivers,
   some may have poor talent for child rearing
5. Caregiver may be outsider to the neighborhood

Additional Services Needed to Assure
 Optimum Child Development:

1. Occupational licensing of caregivers
2. Training programs for caregivers
3. Temporary child care help when needed, including
   neighborhood assistance
4. Information and referral service for parents

APPENDIX L(A)

TYPE OF DAY CARE
HOME CARE--AGENCY PROGRAM

Distinguishing Characteristics:

    1. Child remains in his own home
    2. Child caregiver comes into child's home
    3. Parents obtain child care as part of an agency
        service

Variations:

    1. Caregiver may be part of a home-teaching program
        for child, siblings and parents
    2. Home care may be related to a comprehensive
        parent-child service from a center
    3. Care may be supplemented by visits from health
        or home economics specialists, teachers, social
        workers, etc.

Advantages for Family Life:

    1. Child remains in familiar, secure place
    2. Program brings enrichment to family
    3. Family can be together; cross-age group
    4. Convenience for family to stay at home
    5. Specialized services available through agency
    6. Especially useful for large families

Disadvantages for Family Life:

    1. Caregiver may be outsider to neighborhood
    2. Uneconomical for one child
    3. Families may resist agency intervention

Additional Services Needed:

    1. Occupational licensing of caregivers
    2. Training programs for caregivers

APPENDIX L(B)

TYPE OF DAY CARE
PRIVATE FAMILY DAY CARE

Distinguishing Characteristics:

    1. Child goes to caregiver's home
    2. Care is in family setting in neighborhood home
    3. Arrangement is made privately between parents
        and caregiver

Variations:

    1. Size and composition of family group may vary
    2. Caregiver may have children of her own

Advantages for Family Life:

    1. Child remains in familiar neighborhood with
        caregiver of his parent's liking
    2. The nearness of the neighborhood home makes for
        convenience
    3. Flexibility of hours and work schedules is
        possible
    4. Child has new teaching experiences that he
        wouldn't have at home
    5. Economical for one or two children
    6. Useful for full-time, part-time, and irregular
        employment
    7. Children of all ages can be accommodated

Disadvantages for Family Life:

    1. Uneconomical for large families
    2. Anxiety about selecting and keeping the caregiver
    3. Lack of uniformity in capacities of caregivers;
        some may have poor talent for child rearing
    4. Arrangement sometimes lack stability

Additional Services Needed to Assure Optimum
  Child Development:

    1. Licensing program
    2. Neighborhood consultation, training
    3. Health visiting
    4. Information and referral service
    5. Home teaching programs

APPENDIX L(C)

TYPE OF DAY CARE
AGENCY FAMILY DAY CARE

Distinguishing Characteristics:

1. Child goes to caregiver's home
2. Care is in family setting
3. Agency supervises placement of child and agency
   pays caregiver

Variations:

1. Size and composition of family group may vary
2. Caregiver may have children of her own
3. Combined home/day care teaching

Advantages for Family Life:

1. Provides service, quality of care and accounta-
   bility--agency provides complete service for
   parents, children, and caregiver, including
   certification and training of caregivers,
   supervision of placement, and social services
   for parents
2. Especially useful for parents who need
   professional help
3. Supports provided for stable arrangements
4. Give careful attention to the family situation
   for child
5. Flexibility of hours, services
6. Children of all ages can be accommodated

Disadvantages for Family Life:

1. Some parents avoid agencies
2. Parents have less autonomy in selecting caregiver

Additional Services Needed:

1. Licensing
2. General education in child care and child
   development

APPENDIX L(D)

TYPE OF DAY CARE
CENTER CARE AS PRIVATE FACILITY

Distinguishing Characteristics:

    1. Child goes to a group care facility
    2. The facility is supported by fees

Variations in Setting:

    1. Private commercial day care
    2. Church operated; parents cooperative
       (frequent use of volunteers)
    3. Industry--located and operated
    4. University--located, non-profit service

Advantages for Family Life:

    1. Stability of setting
    2. Auspicies may be familiar for parents
    3. Clientele may be acquainted and have things
       in common
    4. Potentially capable of providing care during
       any work shift of day or night

Disadvantages for Family Life:

    1. Distances are generally less convenient
    2. Expensive for large families
    3. Hours may be restricted
    4. Standards not uniform; may be high or low

Additional Services Needed to Assure
  Optimum Child Development:

    1. Licensing of facility
    2. Occupational licensing for staff
    3. Program consultation and promotion of
       standards for child care programs
    4. Health service
    5. Social services available
    6. Continued education and training for staff

APPENDIX L(E)

TYPE OF DAY CARE
CENTER CARE SUPPORTED BY COMMUNITY AGENCY

Distinguishing Characteristics:

1. Child goes to center
2. Center is supported by fees plus public funds
3. Program accountable as a community service

Variations in Settings:

1. Could be neighborhood based
2. Could be located at place of work
3. Could be mobile unit for migrant labor

Advantages for Family Life:

1. Stability of setting
2. Has trained staff and professional direction
3. Offers enriched child development programs
4. Has adequate number of staff
5. Is in best position to offer comprehensive day
   care service
6. Is able to provide or obtain specialized professional services for children and parents
7. Setting can become a cultural center for
   neighborhood and family life.
8. Setting has economic ability to tide the family
   over temporary inability to pay the fee and to
   apply a sliding-fee scale
9. Capable of providing care during any work shift
   of the day or night

Disadvantages for Family Life:

1. Distances are generally less convenient, especially when centers are fewer and larger
2. Some centers are too large
3. Requires more investment in administration
4. Hours and program constraints make use of the
   center sometimes difficult
5. Relatively unfeasible for large families to use

Additional Services Needed:

1. **Licensing of facility**
2. **Occupational licensing**

APPENDIX M

MAJOR PROGRAMS FOR DAY CARE OR PRE-SCHOOL SERVICES

Program	Legislative Authority	Administering Agency	Services	Federal Share
		General Funds		
Work Incentive Program (WIN)	Title IV-A, Social Security Act (as amended, 1967)	HEW	Funds for the years arrangements for mothers in job training	1st year--80% After 75%
Concentrated Employment Program (CEP)	Title I-B, Economic Opportunity Act, 1964	DOL-MA	Same as above[1]	100%
Aid to Families With Dependent Children (AFDC)	Title IV-A, Social Security Act (as amended, 1967)	HEW SRS CB	Monies for day care services or direct payments to AFDC recipients for day care[1]	75%
Child Welfare Services (CWS)	Title IV-B, Social Security Act (as amended, 1967)	HEW SRS CB	Grants-in-aid to states for provision of day care services: some monies for training, research[1]	66-2/3%

APPENDIX M--Continued

Program	Legislative Authority	Administering Agency	Services	Federal Share
General Funds				
Head Start Full Year--Full Day Full Year--1/2 Day Summer	Title II, Economic Opportunity Act, 1964	HEW OCD	Comprehensive early childhood services emphasis on child 3-5	80% Local share In cash
Parent Child Centers	Title II, Economic Opportunity Act, 1964	HEW OCD	Comprehensive early childhood services emphasis on child under 3 (and family)	80% Local share Cash or kind
Model Cities	Title I, Demonstration Cities and Metropolitan Development Act, 1966	HUD MCA	Funds for Day Care as part of general neighborhood improvement[1]	
General Programs Focusing on Special Target Groups				
Aid to Educationally Deprived Children in Low-Income Families	Title I, Elementary and Secondary Education Act, 1965	HEW OE	Funds for instruction, training of staff	100%

APPENDIX M--Continued

Program	Legislative Authority	Administering Agency	Services	Federal Share
General Programs Focusing on Special Target Groups				
Assistance for migrant[2] and seasonal farm workers	Title III-B, Economic Opportunity Act, 1964	OEO	Comprehensive services for farm workers, including Day Care[1,2]	100%
Assistance for Handicapped Children	Handicapped Children's Early Educational Assistance Act, 1968	OE	Demonstration Programs	90%
Funds for Components of Child Care Services				
Food Services	National School Lunch Act (as amended, 1968)	DOA	Food-Milk	Cash Payments
Health Services Migrant Health	Migrant Health Act of 1962	HEW PHS	Health Service	No fixed ratio approximately 60% Federal

APPENDIX M--Continued

Program	Legislative Authority	Administering Agency	Services	Federal Share
		Funds for Components of Child Care Services		
Pre-school or School Health Program	Title V, Social Security Act (as amended, 1967)	Health Services and Mental Health Administration	Range of medical/dental services	75%
Staffing Foster Grandparents	Title I, Economic Opportunity Act, as amended	HEW SRS AOA	Employs low-income persons over 60 to work with youth	90%
Training, Professional/Non-professional	Educational Professions Development Act, 1967	OE	Training grants to institutions	
		Legislation of Potential Impact		
Day Care Funds	Title V-B, Economic[3] Opportunity Act	Not designated	Funds to public or private non-profit agencies for Day Care	90%

APPENDIX M--Continued

Program	Legislative Authority	Administering Agency	Services	Federal Share
		Legislation of Potential Impact		
Incentives to Unions	Labor-Management Relations[4] Act (as amended, 1969)	Management	Authorizes collective bargaining to set up joint trust funds for financing Day Care	50% for Union sponsor

[1]Services described part of a larger array of services not directly involving Day Care.

[2]Proportion of funds spent on Day Care sharply reduced from 75% in 1966 to 5% in 1969.

[3]No funds have ever been appropriated.

[4]Bargaining not mandatory, difficult to assess impact.

Source: Adapted from Table (p. 35) in Hearings on Headstart-Child Development Act Bill, Part I, August 4, 5, 6, 1969, and Congressional Record Chart, Congressional Record, February 7, 1970.

APPENDIX N

SUMMARY OF MAJOR PENDING LEGISLATION ON
COMPREHENSIVE CHILD CARE SERVICES

Head Start Child Development Act (S2060)--Mondale	Pre-school and Day Care services for children 0-5; services for expectant, nursing mothers; priority for low-income families; participation by non-low-income families who pay fees authorized. Ninety percent Federal funding, with waiver options; funds for facilities, training, technical assistance. Student loans with forgiveness clause authorized; parent participation required.
Comprehensive Pre-school Education and Child Day Care Act, 1969 (H.R. 13520)--Brademas[1]	Pre-school and Day Care services for children 0-5 and Day Care for school-age children; priorities for (1) low-income families, (2) 3-5 year-old children in all families, and (3) children of all working mothers. Eighty percent Federal funding for low-income programs. For other programs funding levels from 30%-50% over time. Aid for renovation and construction, training programs. Some parent participation, parents one-third of State Commission membership.
Comprehensive Head Start Child Development Act, 1970 (H.R. 16572)--Dellenback[1]	Pre-school and Day Care services for children 0-5 and Day Care for school-age children. Parent education for low-income adolescent girls and expectant mothers. Child development programs for Federal employees. Priorities, (1) low-income children, (2) Day Care, (3) parent education, and (4) other children. Federal share--80%. Construction and training monies. Mortgage insurance. Parent participation authorized--not

APPENDIX N--Continued

	required. Repeals separate authorities for various anti-poverty programs.
Comprehensive Head Start Child Development Act, 1970 (S. 3480)--Prouty	Identical Bill save for minor administrative modifications.
Family Assistance Plan, 1970 (H.R. 16311)--Mills	Authorizes only Day Care programs-- no pre-school. Priority for families receiving (or past recipients of) Family Assistance. One hundred percent Federal funding assistance for renovation, training and technical assistance. No provisions about parental involvement.
Federal Child Care Corporation Act, 1970 (S.4101)-- Long	Bill calls for establishment of three-member board with responsibility to oversee provision of, or provide Child Care services. Priority-- children of working mothers or mothers in work training programs and children served under Title IV, S. S. Act. Board responsible for planning, investment of funds, setting up revolving fund, issuing bonds. Board advised by National Advisory Council on Children (up to 15 members), Secretaries of HEW, HUD, LABOR, and twelve appointees by the Board.

---

[1]H.R. 19362, sponsored by Brademas, Dellenback and a bi-partisan group of House members, is a "clean bill" combining features of H.R. 13520 and H.R. 16572.

Source: Adapted from Comprehensive Analysis, Selected Legislation Affecting Early Childhood Program and Day Care; OCD, April 8, 1970.

APPENDIX O

PROPORTIONS OF EXPENDITURES
CALIFORNIA STATE PRE-SCHOOL PROJECTS
(1966-1968)

	1966-67	1967-68
Teachers--including in-service training	30.8	35.75
Aides	16.0	15.50
Other Certified Personnel	5.5	4.75
Capital Outlay	12.5	4.75
Institutional Supplies	5.0	2.75
Administrative Expenses	2.5	2.75
Food	6.4	8.75
Rental	4.8	2.25
Health	3.3	4.00
Transportation	5.8	8.00
Maintenance and Operation	3.7	2.50
Fixed Charges	3.7	5.25

Source: Adapted from Table II-III, California's
Compulsory Pre-school Educational Program
at a Glance. Report and Recommendations,
Part II, Sacramento, California, April, 1969
(mimeographed).

APPENDIX P

PROJECTED COSTS FOR FUTURE CONSTRUCTION OF
CHILD CARE CENTERS FOR 100 CHILDREN
(Based on 7.25% annual increase in costs)

City and State	1970	1971	1972
Anchorage, Alaska	$180,596	$193,689	$207,731
Phoenix, Arizona	115,856	124,256	133,264
Los Angeles, California	124,020	133,011	142,654
San Francisco, California	140,660	150,858	161,795
Denver, Colorado	111,696	119,794	128,479
Washington, D. C.	111,696	119,794	128,479
Atlanta, Georgia	104,364	111,930	120,045
Chicago, Illinois	127,920	137,194	147,141
Indianapolis, Indiana	115,596	123,977	132,965
Boston, Massachusetts	123,812	132,788	142,415
Detroit, Michigan	136,760	146,675	157,309
Kansas City, Missouri	111,696	119,794	128,479
Albuquerque, New Mexico	111,436	119,515	128,180
New York, New York	151,788	162,793	174,595
Fargo, North Dakota	110,344	118,344	126,924
Cleveland, Ohio	140,920	151,137	162,094
Philadelphia, Pennsylvania	118,924	127,546	136,793
Memphis, Tennessee	94,952	101,836	109,219
Dallas, Texas	103,636	111,150	119,208
Seattle, Washington	125,736	134,852	144,629

Source: Fishman, L., Constructing FAP Child Care
Facilities, OCD, xeroxed August, 1970.

BIBLIOGRAPHY

AFDC Children and Children of Working Mothers by State. Mimeo-
     graphed with WIN data by State, 1969 (from OCD,
     xeroxed).

Appalachian Education and Economic Development. Report #III,
     Early Childhood Education: Summary and Recommendation
     of the Education Advisory Committee to the Appalachian
     Regional Commission (unpublished).

Background Facts on Women Workers in the United States. Women's
     Bureau, Wage and Labor Standards Administration, U. S.
     Department of Labor, 1970.

Birch, H. G., Gussow, J. Dye. Disadvantaged Children; Health
     Nutrition and School Failure. New York: Harcourt, Brace
     & World, 1970.

Bloom, Benjamin. Stability and Change in Human Characteristics.
     New York: John Wiley and Sons, 1964.

Caldwell, B. Educational Child Care for Infants and Young
     Children. New York: Holt, Rinehardt & Winston, 1971.

California's Compensatory Pre-school Educational Program at a
     Glance. Report and Recommendations, Part II, Sacramento,
     California, April, 1969 (mimeographed).

California Women. Report of the Advisory Commission on the
     Status of Women, May, 1969.

Child Welfare Statistics 1967. Children's Bureau Statistical
     Series, #92, Children's Bureau, 1968.

Cochran, L. E., Robinson, C. W. Day Care for Children in
     Massachusetts. Massachusetts Committee on Children
     and Youth, Monograph #2, 1966.

Coleman, J. Equality of Educational Opportunity. U. S. Govern-
     ment Printing Office, Washington, D. C., 1966.

Congressional Record. February 9, 1970, H700-727, 91st Congress, 2nd Session.

Coopersmith, S. Pre-school Education and Affective Development. University of California, Davis, 1970 (mimeographed).

Dellenback, J. "Report on Programs for Early Childhood." Congressional Record. April 2, 1970, E2762-E2767.

"Estimates of the Population of the United States by Age, Race and Sex, July 1, 1967, to July 1, 1969." Current Population Reports. Series P-25, #441, March 19, 1970.

Featherstone, J. "The Day Care Problem, Kentucky Fried Children." New Republic. September 12, 1970.

Fishman, L. Cost of Construction of FAP Child Care Facilities. Memo prepared for Office of Child Development, August, 1970.

Fishman, Leo. Study of Federal Policy Toward Child Care and Child Development Programs. Draft, 1970.

Fleisig, H. Provision for the Care of the Children of Working Mothers in Tompkins County. Unpublished paper, Cornell University, 1969.

Flynn, John C. Head Start Supplementary Training: From Aloofness to Commitment. Washington University Research Corporation, 1969.

Gertler, D. Preprimary Enrollment of Children Under Six, October, 1967. National Center for Educational Statistics, U. S. Government Printing Office, 1968.

Hawkridge, D. G. Foundations for Success in Educating Disadvantaged Children. Final Report, American Institute for Research in Behavioral Sciences, Palo Alto, California, December, 1968.

Head Start Careers Bulletin. Vol. 1, #5, April/May, 1970 (National Institute for New Careers, University Research Corp.).

Head Start Career Development: A Pause for Reflection. University Research Corporation, Washington, undated (mimeographed).

Head Start Staff Statistics, Staff Statistics, Staff Member Information, Part D. No date (mimeographed).

Hearings Before the Senate Subcommittee on Education on H.R. 13520.
Nov. 18, 20, Dec. 1-4, 9-11, 16, 1969; Feb. 21, 23, 25,
26, March 2-4, 1970.

Hedges, J. N. "Women Workers and Manpower Demands in the 1970's."
Monthly Labor Review, June 1970, Department of Labor,
pp. 19-29.

Hunt, J. McV. Intelligence and Experience. New York: Ronald
Press, 1961.

Hunt, J. McV. Chapter I in The Young Child in America, E.Grotberg (Ed.)
U.S. Govt. Printing Office, Office of Economic Opportunity,
Washington, D.C., 1971.

Hurd, G. Highlights from October 1969 Survey of Preprimary and
Primary Enrollment. Data from xeroxed Tables, Final
Report in press, 1970.

Hurd, G. and Nehrt, R. Preprimary Enrollment of Children Under
6, October 1968. NCES, 1969 (OE 20079-68). U. S.
Government Printing Office, Washington, D. C.

Hurd, Gordon. Preprimary Enrollment Trends of Children Under 6,
1964-1968. NCES (OE 16001). U. S. Government Printing
Office, Washington, D. C., February, 1970.

Hurley, R. Poverty and Mental Retardation: A Casual Relationship.
New York: Vintage Books, 1969.

Indian and Migrant Program Review Summary. Indian and Migrant
Programs Division, unpublished data, 1970.

"Information Sheet on Federal Assistance for Day Care Programs."
Prepared by Office of Child Development, September, 1969.

Jaffe, R., Jaffe, E. Survey of Available Public and Private
Kindergarten Services, Fall, 1968. (OEO supported contract #B89-4569, unpublished document).

Kadushin, A. Child Welfare Services. New York: Macmillan Co.,
1967.

Katz, L. G., Weir, M.A. Help for Teachers in Preschools: A
Proposal. National Laboratory on Early Childhood
Education, ERIC Clearinghouse, 1969.

_____. Staffing Schools: Background Information. National Laboratory on Early Childhood Education, ERIC Clearinghouse, 1969.

Knitzer, J. Advocacy and the Children's Crisis. Albert Einstein College of Medicine, unpublished paper, 1970.

LaCrosse, R. Day Care: Effects and Affects. California Pacific Oaks College, 1970 (draft manuscript).

Lansburgh, T. "Day Care of Children." Article prepared for the Encyclopedia for Social Work, 1970.

Lazar, I. Annual budget for the Appalachian Regional Commission, 1970 (a).

_____. Federal programs for young children. Appalachian Regional Commission, 1970 (b).

_____. "Organizing Child Development Programs." Appalachia. Vol. 3, #4, January, 1970 (c).

Licensed or Approved Day Care Centers and Family Day Care Homes, by Auspices and Capacity. March, 1969 (provisional) (data from OCD, xeroxed).

Low, S., Spindler, P. G. Child Care Arrangements of Working Mothers in the United States. Children's Bureau Publica- #461: USDHEW and USDOL, 1968.

Madison, B. Q. Social Work in the Soviet Union. California: Stanford University Press, 1968.

Mayer, A. G. (with Kahn, A. J.). Day Care as a Social Instrument: A Policy Paper. School of Social Work, Columbia University, January, 1965.

Miller, J. O. An Educational Imperative and its Fallout Implications. National Laboratory of Early Childhood Education, July, 1969.

Moore, Winifred A. Some Aspects of Day Care Licensing at the State Level. New York Child Welfare League of America, October, 1957.

National Conference on Curricula for the Career Ladder in the Child Caring Professions. May 20-23, 1969, Pittsburgh, Pennsylvania.

Nedler, S. A Developmental Process Approach to Curricula Design. In R. K. Parker Ed. Conceptualizations of Preschool Curriculum. Boston: Allyn & Bacon, 1971.

Number of Children Receiving Child Care Under the Work Incentive Program, December, 1969, by State (Data from OCD, xeroxed).

Palmer, F. Minimal Intervention and Intellective Change at Age Two and Three. In R. K. Parker Ed. Conceptualizations of Preschool Curricula. Boston: Allyn & Bacon, 1971.

Parker, R. K. (Ed.). Child Development/Day Care Handbook-- Infancy. Draft version, 1970(a).

_____. Child Development/Day Care Handbook--Preschool. Draft version, 1970(b).

_____. Child Development/Day Care Handbook--School Age. Draft version, 1970(c).

_____. Child Development/Day Care Handbook--Training. Draft version, 1970(d).

_____. Child Development/Day Care Handbook--Principles. Draft version, 1970(e).

Parker, R. K., Ambron, S., Danielson, G., Halbrook, M., Levine, J. Overview of Cognitive and Language Programs for 3, 4 and 5 Year Old Children. Southeastern Education Laboratory, Monograph #4, 1970.

Parker, R.K. (Ed.). Conceptualizations of Pre-School Curricula. Boston: Allyn & Bacon, 1971.

A Plan for a Comprehensive Day Care Training Program to Serve the Puget Sound Region in Washington State. (No author, mimeographed, 1970. Plan developed with cooperation of Washington State Department of Social and Health Services, Division of Public Assistance Licensing, State Office of Vocational Education.)

"Population Estimates and Projections." Current Population Reports. Series P-25, #441, March 19, 1970, U. S. Department of Commerce.

Projected Annual Budgets: State Department of Social Sciences. Baltimore, Maryland. Xeroxed, May, 1968.

Rand Corporation. Report on Day Care. Untitled, unpublished, in-house document. Office of Economic Opportunity, 1969.

Ricciuti, H. Malnutrition, Learning and Intellectual Development: Research and Remediation Invited Address. American Psychological Association, September, 1969.

Riggan, W. Day Care: Paper Written for Bureau of Budget. November 18, 1969 (unpublished).

Rosenberg, B. "Facts About Day Care." Prepared by U. S. Department of Labor, October, 1969 (WB 70-23).

Ruderman, F. A. Child Care and Working Mothers: A Study of Arrangements Made for Daytime Care of Children. New York: Child Welfare League of America, 1968.

Schaefer, E. and Aaronson, M. Infant Education Project. In Parker, R. K. Ed. Conceptualizations of Preschool. Curricula. Boston: Allyn & Bacon, 1971.

Services to AFDC Families: 1st Annual Report of DHEW Under Title IV-A, SSR, Government Document, 1970.

Southern Regional Educational Board. "Objectives for Families and Communities." Draft, July 1, 1970 (unpublished, no author).

Special WIN Child Care Report (Auer, 1928, Tr-300-2). Information and Management Sciences, Auerbach Corp., P.A. 1970.

State Day Care Licensing. Prepared by Children's Bureau, Social Rehabilitative Service, Department of Health, Education and Welfare for 4th National Conference of Commissions on the Status of Women, August, 1970. Xeroxed, Office of Child Development.

State Salary Ranges, January 1, 1970. DHEW, Office of State Merit Systems.

Sugarman, Jule M. The Future of Early Childhood Programs: An American Perspective. Draft, undated.

Title V, 2nd Year Report Coordination of State and Federal Pre-school Programs., Bureau of Pre-school Educational Programs, California, 1970 (mimeographed).

Whitney, D. C. Educational Day Care: A Comprehensive Early Education and
    Day Care Program. New York: Universal Education Corporation, 1970.

Whitney, D. C. and Parker, R. K. A Comprehensive Approach to
    Early Education: The Discovery Program. In Parker, R. K.
    Ed. Conceptualizations of Preschool Curricula. Boston:
    Allyn & Bacon, 1971.

Wilner, M. "Unsupervised Family Day Care in NYC." June, 1969,
    in The Changing Dimensions of Day Care. New York:
    Child Welfare League of America, 1970.

BACKGROUND PAPER ON HEALTH

FOR THE 1970 WHITE HOUSE CONFERENCE

ON CHILDREN AND YOUTH

November 1970

by Richard W. Dodds, M.D., F.A.A.P.
Office of the Assistant Secretary
    for Planning and Evaluation
Department of Health, Education,
    and Welfare

This paper presents essential facts and information on health among children and youth. Its purpose is to enable the Conferees at the White House Conference to assess the status of health programs and services and to judge national needs and priorities in this area for the 1970-1980 decade.

INTRODUCTION

Health is much more than just the absence of disease for it also includes a positive physical, mental and social well-being. The commitment which a nation makes to specific activities which it labels as "health activities" is only a small part of what that nation does to contribute to the health of its citizens.

Thus, whatever a nation does well, which contributes positively to its being, also contributes to its health. Though this approach is too broad to be manageable, it sets the perspective in which health should ultimately be viewed. Many activities of a society bear strongly on the health status of the people such as nutrition, housing, sanitation, income, jobs, pollution control, and education.

Other papers are being written for the Conferees of the White House Conference. These other papers such as Food and Nutrition, Handicapped Children, Drugs, Family Planning, and Education have important contributions to the understanding of the health status of the children and youth of our country.

This paper will seek to avoid duplicating the content of other papers but will explore current estimates of health status, the utilization of health care, expenditures, present programs and possible goals and alternatives for the next decade.

Health requires attention to both the small specific items and the large long term concerns; it is not one or the other. If we turn our attention too exclusively to one part, another part starts to slip away. And so to serve the health of the "whole child" we must do the specific things well and still give continuity and coordination to the collectivity of all our health activities. Thus, we must give attention to very specific areas such as immunization status and yet also watch on a broad scale the distribution, cost, quality, organization, supply and financing of medical care.

ISSUES AND PROBLEMS

Our nation makes major efforts to achieve health for our children
and youth. Although there are problems, it is important to remember
that quite a lot is already being done. We spent $8.4 billion on
health for people 0-18 years of age in 1969. An estimated 45.6 million
people age 0-16 received 240 million physician visits in 1967. Infant
mortality rates are declining, especially the neonatal mortality rates
among American Indians. However, serious health problems remain
among the children and youth of the United States.

I. There is evidence of poor <u>health status</u> among infants,
children, and youth in the United States. Although our
life-saving and health-saving capabilities are increasing,
when society's health care services neglect a child in
the early and middle years of childhood, society continues
to pay the costs of resulting handicaps or preventable
death for years. The performance of our society in
achieving adequate health status for children and youth
is less adequate than it should be.

II. If we view lack of <u>access</u> to medical care as a social
disease, the epidemiology of this disease reveals
wide inequities in access among children and youth by
race, income, place of residence, educational level,
age, and social class.

III. There are deficits in the <u>supply</u> of medical care which
result from absolute deficits and from maldistribution.
Supply of care is limited in absolute terms, but this
is aggravated by maldistribution of manpower, facilities,
and services.

IV. There is maldistribution of <u>ability to purchase</u> medical
care. Children in poor families have little health
insurance and few out of pocket resources with which
to purchase care.

V. The way in which money is spent on health care and the
way in which the purchased services are organized and
delivered affects the total amount, the access, the
quality, and the cost of the outputs of the health
care system. How should health services for children
and youth be organized and delivered? What outputs
should be sought? What should the various levels of
government and the private sector do in the organization and delivery of care? Among others, the roles of
physician assistants, prepaid group practice, health
maintenance organizations and the balance of preventive
care vs. treatment are at issue.

VI. What quantifiable health goals are attainable over
the next decade for children and youth? Should these
be expressed in units of services delivered, numbers
of people reached, specific categorical disease programs,
or increments of health status?

VII. To what extent are non-medical investments in such
things as nutrition, education, housing, income, and
pollution control more beneficial to the health status
of children and youth per unit of cost than investments in personal health services?

VIII. At what costs could we remedy these deficits in the
financing, supply, organization and delivery, distribution, and control of categorical diseases? If a less
universal solution for the deficits is desired, how
should we subdivide the population and the programs in
order to identify situations where limited funds would
maximize the benefits over the costs?

The distribution of health services resembles
a patch work of covered and uncovered areas. There is a marked
inequity in the level of health status among children and youth in
poor families versus those in middle and high income families.
Only 20% of poor children are covered by hospital insurance, but
83% of children in high income families are covered. Though 76%
of children have some form of hospital insurance, 100% of those
over 65 years old are covered. 21.4 million of the children
under 17 never see a physician each year, and another 24.3 million
see physicians a little but not enough.

Infant mortality in the U.S.A. is higher than in some other
industrially-developed countries. However, the international
differences are less important than the differences in infant
mortality which exist among social classes and among different
states within our own country. The infant death rate is twice as
high among blacks as among whites, 2.7 times higher among Alaskan
natives, and 1.4 times higher among American Indians.

Good health status, life expectancy, and access to health services
are very unevenly distributed among our people. Immunization status is
inadequate for several diseases; we have outbreaks of 9-day measles,
diphtheria and polio this year. Chronic bronchitis in children 0-5
years of age, hepatitis, syphilis, gonorrhea, malaria and suicide in
youths are rising disproportionately fast compared to the rest of the
population. Accidental death and psychiatric disease remain massive
problems. The diseases with which poverty is associated are widely
prevalent.

There are many options and alternatives possible for us to
attack these problems. New institutions such as neighborhood
health centers, comprehensive child care centers, hospital-based
group practices and school-based group practices can be started.
The productivity of child care physicians can be increased with
pediatric nurse practitioners or other physician assistants,
so that more children can be cared for. Comprehensive family-
centered whole-child care can be sought as the standard or we
can attack on a categorical disease by disease basis. We can
elect to give all children, the poor, the disadvantaged, the
very young, the minority or the rural and central city children
and youth the highest priority. We can aim for the highest, the
optimal, the adequate, or the lowest level of medical care for
our children and youth. We can choose to emphasize prevention
over treatment or vice versa. The choices are up to us; even if
we try to make no choice, that still turns out to be a choice.

ASSESSMENT OF HEALTH STATUS

Industrialized nations have been experiencing a decline in death rate for over 200 years; the graph below shows this for England and Wales.

Source No. 1

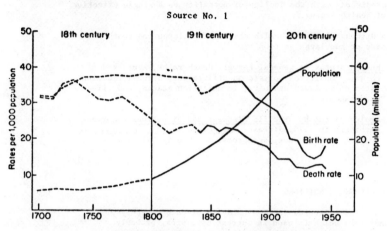

Population, birth rate and death rate: England and Wales.

Health services have only contributed to the very latest parts of that declining curve. It is important to remember that most of the decline from 1740-1920 came as a result of environmental changes rather than personal health services. Improvements in nutrition, housing, education, income, sanitation, refrigeration of food, and clothing caused death rates to fall. These changes in the environment reduced the exposure to disease and increased the resistance of humans. Although the virulence of some diseases may have decreased as well, the primary cause was improvement in the environment and the resistance of the human host.

Society must realize that if it wishes to purchase additional health status as measured by death rates (as opposed to purchasing the feeling of being cared for or reductions in severity or duration of non-fatal disease), it might wish to give higher priority to accident prevention, nutrition, housing, sanitation, income, and education.

Thus when we try to assess the health status of children and youth, we must look at both death rates (mortality) and the duration and severity of fatal and non-fatal illness (morbidity). We must look at acute conditions which are so important in children because of the influx each year by birth of new susceptibles into the population. We must look at the rising importance of the morbidity of chronic conditions with the decline of mortality as a single effective measure of health status.

This discussion of the health status of children and youth will consist of two large sections:

A. health status in general terms: death rates, acute and chronic conditions, physician utilization, disqualification rates of military recruits, immunization status, and life expectancy.

B. health status by specific diseases and situations: current outbreaks in 1970, diseases among poor people, malnutrition, suicide, adolescence, accidents, and mental illness.

ACUTE AND CHRONIC CONDITIONS

We can find no trends in the incidence of each category of acute conditions which is used in Current Estimates, probably because these categories lump many diseases together; and even massive changes in one disease may be hidden. A later section of this paper will deal with trends in several specific diseases.

The proportion of children under 16 and their percentage of the acute conditions incurred has been essentially stable:

	Source No. 2 1961-62	Source No. 3 1968
% of population age 0-16	33%	34%
% of total acute conditions suffered by those 0-16	49%	46%
No. of acute conditions among those 0-16	199,347,000	184,571,000
No. of people age 0-16	60,815,000	67,006,000

In 1963, children ages 0-16 accounted for 35% of the population and 16% of those with one or more chronic conditions. Furthermore, 20% of children under 16 (i.e., 13,087,000 of them) had one or more chronic conditions.

National estimates are available of the number of children
in 1960 and the projected number in 1970 who have handicapping
chronic conditions. Children's Bureau publication No. 427 reported:

	1960 (in thousands)	1970 (in thousands)
Epilepsy (under 21)	360	450
Cerebral Palsy (under 21)	370	465
Mentally Retarded (under 21)	2,180	2,720
Eye Conditions needing specialist care including refractive errors (5-17)	10,200	12,500
Hearing Loss (under 21)	360-725	450-900
Speech Defects (5-20)	2,580	3,270
Cleft Palate - Cleft Lip	95	120
Orthopedic (under 21)	1,925	2,425
Congenital Heart Disease	About 25,000 born each year of whom 7,000 die in the first year	
Emotionally Disturbed (5-17)	4,000	5,400

About 12% of children of school age are in need of special education
because of handicapping conditions. Visual acuity develops to
nearly adult levels by 7 years of age. Failure to treat strabismus
(a crossed eye) in childhood causes amblyopia (loss or dimness of
vision) which is found in 2% of young men examined for military
service. About 7% of children enter school with a hearing loss;
this percentage rises to 9% by fifth grade and 12% by high school.
Otologists estimate that 50% of hearing problems result from
medically treatable conditions. However, in the area of chronic
dental caries only 5% of the population escape. The average number
of carious teeth per child is 0.36 at age 5, 4.77 at age 10, and
10.65 at age 15.

A search was made for trends among chronic diseases, as well, in unpublished data from the National Health Survey for 1962-1966. The eleven chronic diseases of highest rank order in prevalence were looked at in two age brackets: 0-5 years and 6-16 years. Only "chronic bronchitis" in the 0-5 age group showed a marked upward trend. The chart below shows the essentially stable prevalence of several chronic diseases and the up-trend of chronic bronchitis.

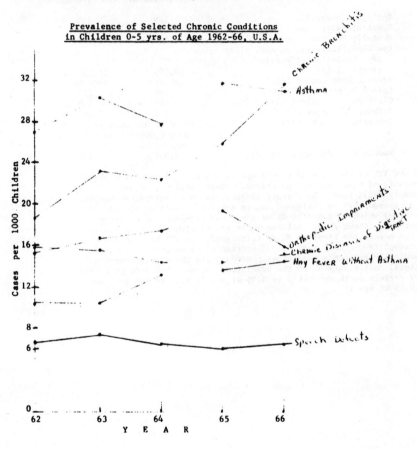

Prevalence of Selected Chronic Conditions
in Children 0-5 yrs. of Age 1962-66, U.S.A.

Source No. 4

The 1968 population breakdown was: Source No. 5

Age	Number	
0-6	22,698,000	
6-16	44,308,000	67,006,000
17-24	23,938,000	
17-24 (employed)	14,082,000	
Total All Ages	195,392,000	

(a) Children under 6 years old each averaged 3.2 acute
     conditions, 10.1 days of restricted activity with
     these, and 4.3 bed disability days. Furthermore
     among each hundred children (age 0-6 yrs.) 29.9 were
     injured (over two-thirds of the time in the home) and
     they lost 62.3 days of restricted activity recovering.

(b) Children 6-16 years old averaged 2.5 acute conditions,
     8.5 days of restricted activity with these, 3.8 bed
     disability days, and 4.9 days lost from school. Among
     each hundred (age 6-16 yrs.): 1.6 were injured by
     moving motor vehicles, 12.9 in the home, and 16.3
     elsewhere. These accidents among each 100 children re-
     quired 157.3 days of restricted activity to recover.

(c) Out of 67,006,000 children under 17 years old 3.3%
     (i.e. 2,252,000) had chronic conditions severe enough
     to limit their activities.

(d) These 67 million children under 17 required 4,047,000
     hospitalizations averaging 5.6 days per stay. In fact
     246,000 children received 2 hospitalizations and 63,000
     received 3 or more hospitalizations. Children under 17
     years lost 668,541 restricted activity days and 300,785
     bed disability days.

(e) Youths between 17 and 24 years of age (23,938 million
     in number) received 3,687,000 hospitalizations averaging
     5.6 days each in short-stay hospitals. 278,000 youths
     received 2 hospitalizations and 63,000 received 3 or more
     hospitalizations. These youths lost 259,169 restricted
     activity days, 114,823 bed disability days, and 67,000
     work days.

UTILIZATION

In 1968, among those under 17 years old, 9.8 million had not
seen a physician in a year, 8.7 million had not seen one in 2-5 years,
and 739,000 had never seen one. Among youths 17-24 years old, 2.9
million were a year, 2.6 million were 2-5 years, and 113,000 were
a lifetime since their last physician visit. These youths had an
average of only 1.7 visits each to dentists in 1968.

In 1967, 4.4 million children (18.7%) under 6 years never
saw a physician even once during the year and another 19% only
had one physician visit. Furthermore, 17 million children (59.2%)
between 6-16 years saw no physician, and 25.9% more only had one
visit. Children 0-16 years averaged only 1.3 visits to a dentist
in the year.

In 1968 a larger proportion of children and youth were un-
insured for hospital costs and for surgical costs than any other
age group. Thus 24.9% of those under 17 years and 25.4% of those
17-24 years of age had no surgical insurance. Similarly 23.7% of
the 0-17 years group and 23.9% of the 17-24 group had no hospital
insurance. This compared with 16.4% among those 25-44 years of age
and 0% among those over 65 years. Hospital insurance covers only 20%
of children in low-income families (under $3000 per year), although
it reaches 83.3% of children in high-income families (over $10,000/yr).

In 1964, 350,000 children and youth under 20 years of age
accounted for one third of all persons in outpatient psychiatric
clinics. In 1965, persons under 24 years of age accounted for
21% of first admissions to State and county mental hospitals.
The absolute numbers and the rate of mental illness under 15
years of age has been rising for a number of years.

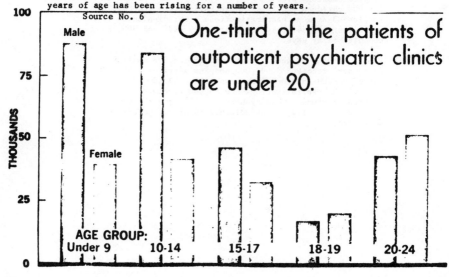

Among those children already receiving care 4.2 million age 0-5 lack 21.0 million visits/year and 8.5 million (also age 0-5) lack 25.5 million visits/year.** The national health survey in 1962 revealed that, with respect to dental care among school age children (5-14 yrs.), 50% of all children and 70% of black children had never seen a dentist.

Source Nb. 7

For the age 15-24 group

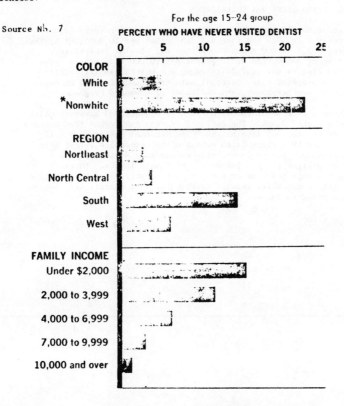

PERCENT WHO HAVE NEVER VISITED DENTIST

COLOR
White
*Nonwhite

REGION
Northeast
North Central
South
West

FAMILY INCOME
Under $2,000
2,000 to 3,999
4,000 to 6,999
7,000 to 9,999
10,000 and over

---

*   Please see the footnote about the context for using data
    by race on page 16.
** See chart on page 50.

Let us now look at trends and present status in maternal death
rates, rate of prematurity, infant mortality, and life expectancy
among children and youth. Then, let us expand the analysis of these
categories by race, income, and urban-rural location.

MATERNAL DEATH RATES and PREMATURITY

Approximately 60 years ago 100 mothers died for every 10,000
pregnancies. In 1967 the rate was 2.8 deaths per 10,000 live births.
The rate is 2.5/10,000 among Caucasians but remains four times
greater among non-whites at 10 deaths per 10,000 live births. The
excessive risk of maternal death among non-whites has its origin
in lack of prenatal care, maternal malnutrition during and throughout life before pregnancy, and unplanned or unwanted pregnancy.

Toxemia is a major complication of pregnancy and presents major
risk of maternal death. The national average for deaths from toxemia
is 6.2 deaths/100,000 live births. The National Research Council
has concluded that there is no evidence that excessive weight gain
causes toxemia. But we do restrict weight gain during pregnancy
hoping to prevent toxemia and we restrict salt intake. There is
growing evidence that one or both of these practices is contributing
to our infant mortality rates. Death rates from toxemia are, however,
very sensitive to income:

Income	Deaths by Toxemia/100,000 live births
	Source No. 8
High	3.8
Medium	5.9
Low	11.9
Total Average	6.2
The State with Lowest Income Per Capita	30.2
The State with Second Lowest Income Per Capita	21.0

Toxemia is a special hazard for young pregnant girls. The fertility rate among women 15-44 years old has sharply dropped from 122.9 per 1000 women in 1957 to 87.8 in 1967. In 1960 there were 25.196 million girls age 10-17 and 189,188 pregnancies occurred under 18 (rate = 0.0075). In 1965, 29.486 million girls age 10-17 had 196,372 pregnancies (rate = 0.0066). Age of menarche continued to fall to an average age now of 13 years. Preteen adolescence, preteen pregnancy, and preteen parenthood are emerging and will be discussed later as a specific problem. Pregnant girls under 17 have nutritional requirements for the growth and development of their own bodies which are in excess of the requirements of the pregnancy which they and adult pregnant women experience. These additional nutrient demands increase the risk of pregnancy under 17. Fetal loss and infant mortality increase when the mother is under 17. A study among girls who were under 16, pregnant, and poor showed 43.6% were on "poor diets" and 20% ate no more than two meals per day.

In 1964, 8.3% of live births in the U.S.A. were premature or immature. The percentage of prematures was 7.5% among Caucasians and 16% among non-whites. In 1965, 18.7% of low birth weight babies were born to mothers under 15 years of age. Since 1960 the proportion of newborns weighing less than 2500 gm (the definition of low birth weight for full term newborns) has been increasing. There is some evidence that prenatal care is actually decreasing, rather than increasing, among the poor in our ghettos.

INFANT MORTALITY

The infant mortality rate in the U.S.A. has decreased considerably since 1930. It has declined from 27 deaths (under 1 year of age) per 1,000 live births in 1958 to 21.8 deaths per 1,000 live births in 1968. Provisional information indicates the 1969 rate was near 20.7. Since 1966 the infant mortality rate among non-whites has been declining twice as fast as among whites.

Source Nos. 9 & 10

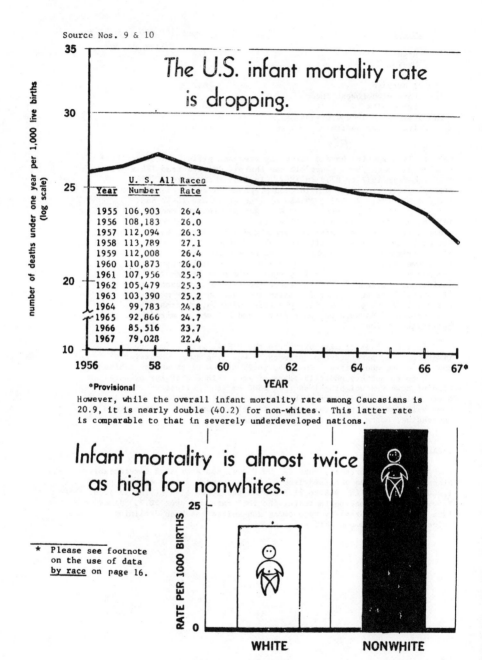

The U.S. infant mortality rate is dropping.

number of deaths under one year per 1,000 live births (log scale)

	U. S. All Races	
Year	Number	Rate
1955	106,903	26.4
1956	108,183	26.0
1957	112,094	26.3
1958	113,789	27.1
1959	112,008	26.4
1960	110,873	26.0
1961	107,956	25.3
1962	105,479	25.3
1963	103,390	25.2
1964	99,783	24.8
1965	92,866	24.7
1966	85,516	23.7
1967	79,028	22.4

YEAR

**Provisional

However, while the overall infant mortality rate among Caucasians is
20.9, it is nearly double (40.2) for non-whites. This latter rate
is comparable to that in severely underdeveloped nations.

Infant mortality is almost twice as high for nonwhites.*

RATE PER 1000 BIRTHS

* Please see footnote
on the use of data
by race on page 16.

WHITE   NONWHITE

INFANT DEATH RATES
INDIAN AND ALASKA NATIVE, AND U.S. ALL RACES
Source No. 11

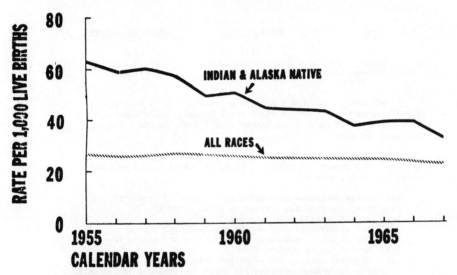

Between 1955, when the Indian Health Service opened under HEW, and
1967, the infant death rate among Indians and Alaska Natives declined
48% while the rate for all races declined 15%. The rate among Alaska
Natives remains more than 2.0 times the rate for all races and the
Indian rate is 1.4 times higher. The Indian Health Service has made a
major impact on perinatal mortality which accounts for most of the
massive improvement. The remaining preventable infant mortality among
Indians is after the perinatal period when the infant has left the
hospital and returned home.

		Indian and Alaska Native		Rates per 1,000 Live Births Indian		Alaska Native	
	Year	Number	Rate	Number	Rate	Number	Rate
	1955	1,065	62.5	936	61.2	129	74.8
	1956	1,066	59.4	900	56.1	166	87.0
	1957	1,136	60.4	989	58.2	147	80.2
	1958	1,123	58.0	989	56.7	134	69.0
	1959	1,016	49.5	870	46.7	146	76.7
Source No. 12	1960	1,064	50.3	914	47.6	150	76.3
	1961	961	44.4	827	42.3	134	64.0
	1962	967	44.2	827	41.8	140	66.8
	1963	972	43.6	864	42.9	108	50.7
	1964	856	37.6	747	35.9	109	54.8
	1965	872	39.0	740	36.4	132	65.4
	1966	822	39.0	722	37.7	100	51.4
	1967	666	32.2	571	30.1	95	55.6

Within a single large city, infant mortality varies from 27/1000 among the lowest socioeconomic groups to as little as 16/1000 among the higher groups.

Neonatal mortality varies severely with age, race, and the number of pregnancies before age 20.

	Source No. 13	
age	white mothers	non-white mothers*
20-24	32.1	46.5
under 15 yrs.	15.9	25.3
5th pregnancy under 20 yrs.	NA	127.6 !!!

If all states had infant mortality rates as low as Utah (19.7), 23,000 infants who die before their first birthday would survive. If the U.S.A. had the rate of the Netherlands (14.8), 40,000 infants per year would be spared.

The United States ranked 13th of 40 countries in infant mortality in 1966. Many things contribute to this, according to the National Research Council, such as:

(a) excess pregnancy rate among girls under 17 (poverty)
(b) short interval conceptions in girls under 17
(c) lack of prenatal care (poverty)
(d) lack of adequate diet during pregnancy AND throughout life up until pregnancy; both are very important. (poverty)
(e) smoking during pregnancy
(f) excessive restriction of weight gain during pregnancy -- especially among underweight women and pregnant adolescents.

During the next 10 years the Public Health Service expects the infant mortality rate in the Netherlands to continue to fall to 9.4 (in Sweden 10.7).

*FOOTNOTE ON THE USE OF DATA BY RACE:

It is important to realize that the data for racial differences show that the origin of the differences is environmentally imposed on the non-white people, not genetic in origin. The percentage of prematurity in pregnancies among low socioeconomic class black people is 23.3%, but improvement in environment lowers this to 5.3% ** among high socioeconomic black people.

** Max Seham, "Poverty, Illness, and the Negro Child," Pediatrics, Vol. 46, No. 2, August 1970, p. 306.

Fewer data are available on the health status of youth 17-24
years of age than are available for children 0-16. There is almost
no access to data on health status of young women 17-24 because
nothing exists which is comparable to the preinduction medical
examination done by the armed services on young men 17-24. The
National Center for Health Statistics is conducting a Health
Examination Survey of Youth ages 12-17 which includes both sexes.
However, the information gap on women 17-24 will remain. The
health status of youth will be discussed later with regard to
specific diseases. The section on military disqualifications which
follows applies only to young men.

DISQUALIFICATION RATES OF YOUTHS EXAMINED FOR MILITARY SERVICE

In 1968, 96.6% of all draftees examined for military service for
the first time were given a preinduction examination. A total of
42.1% were disqualified. The rate of disqualification for reason
of "mental requirements" has fallen from 18.6% in 1965 to 9.5% in
1968. This is because lower standards for acceptable trainability
were set; and draftees with psychosis and psychoneurosis are now
acceptable if cured or compensated in normal life.

The percentage disqualified for medical reasons is the largest
category and rising fast. In the graph below we see that disqualifications in the "medical only" category rose from 21.8% in 1968
to nearly 40% at the end of 1968.

DISQUALIFICATIONS ON PREINDUCTION EXAMINATIONS BY DISQUALIFYING CAUSE
1958-1968

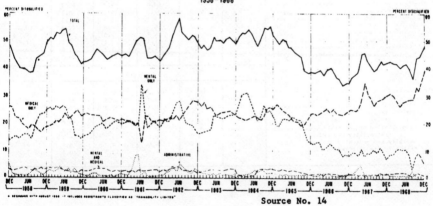

Source No. 14

The following table shows the breakdown by races. Among whites the "medical only" disqualifications rose from 23.7% in 1965 to 32% (average for all of 1968). Among Negro draftees the "medical only" disqualifications rose from 10.1% to 16.4%

Source No. 15

HEALTH OF THE ARMY SUPPLEMENT

--RESULTS OF THE PREINDUCTION EXAMINATION OF DRAFTEES FOR MILITARY SERVICE, BY ETHNIC GROUP: PERCENT
July 1950 through December 1968

Results of examination	Jul 1950 through Dec 1968	1968	1967	1966	1965	Jul 1950 through Dec 1964
	Total					
Examined..	100.0	100.0	100.0	100.0	100.0	100.0
Found acceptable............................	60.2	57.9	59.3	62.4	56.0	62.4
Disqualified..............................	39.8	42.1	40.7	37.6	44.0	37.6
Administrative reasons...................	1.2	0.9	1.5	1.2	1.3	1.2
Failed mental requirements only, total...	15.3	9.5	9.3	10.9	18.6	15.8
a. Failed mental tests..............	12.0	8.0	7.0	8.9	10.7	13.9
b. Trainability Limited.............	3.3	1.5	2.3	4.0	7.9	1.9
Mentally and medically disqualified......	2.5	1.8	1.4	1.5	2.3	3.1
Medically disqualified only.............	20.8	29.9	28.5	24.0	21.8	17.5
	White (~ Non-Negro)					
Examined..	100.0	100.0	100.0	100.0	100.0	100.0
Found acceptable............................	63.9	59.7	60.8	64.8	60.3	66.6
Disqualified..............................	36.1	40.3	39.2	35.2	39.7	33.4
Administrative reasons...................	1.2	0.8	1.3	1.2	1.3	1.2
Failed mental requirements only, total...	10.3	6.2	6.6	7.6	12.9	10.4
a. Failed mental tests..............	7.8	5.2	4.9	4.5	6.8	9.1
b. Trainability Limited.............	2.5	1.0	1.7	3.1	6.1	1.3
Mentally and medically disqualified.....	1.9	1.3	1.1	1.1	1.8	2.4
Medically disqualified only.............	22.7	32.0	30.2	25.3	23.7	19.4
	Negro					
Examined..	100.0	100.0	100.0	100.0	100.0	100.0
Found acceptable............................	38.1	45.8	49.9	42.5	29.2	38.8
Disqualified..............................	61.9	54.2	50.1	57.5	70.8	61.2
Administrative reasons...................	1.4	1.1	2.4	1.6	1.1	1.4
Failed mental requirements only, total..	45.1	31.5	27.1	39.2	54.0	45.4
a. Failed mental tests..............	36.6	26.7	20.7	27.1	35.3	40.3
b. Trainability Limited.............	8.5	4.8	6.4	12.1	18.7	5.1
Mentally and medically disqualified.....	5.8	5.2	4.0	4.2	5.6	6.7
Medically disqualified only.............	9.6	16.4	16.6	12.5	10.1	7.7

IMMUNIZATION STATUS

Immunization data for the age 0-19 years population reveal
several trends in different directions ... some dangerous.

Immunity against polio has slipped. The percentage of our
people age 1-4 yrs. who are fully immunized has fallen from a high
of 87.6% in 1964 to 67.7% in 1969. The percentage of age 1-4 years
who have never had any polio immunizations has risen from 9.9% in
1965 to 10.2% in 1969. There have been 5 cases of paralytic polio
type I, one death and 8 suspect cases in Texas among migrant families
in 1970, but this should not be construed as a national outbreak.

We are holding steady in aggregate percentages of our population with DPT immunity. From 1964 to 1969 the aggregate percent
immunized has stayed in the range of 76% to 77.9%. The percent
who have never had any DPT shots has declined from 14.1% in 1962
to 7.2% in 1969. But the aggregate numbers conceal blocks of our
population who are severely under-immunized. There are significant
outbreaks of diphtheria in Chicago, Phoenix, and Texas. The United
States has experienced 2.8 times as many cases of diphtheria in
1970 as for the same portion of 1969.

We are experiencing a new outbreak of 9 day measles (rubeola)
in 1970. We have already had more than double the measles in 1970
that we had in 1969. From 1966 to 1969 our aggregate immunity
(derived both from natural infection and measles immunizations)
rose from 51% to 66.9% of the population, age 1-4 years; but it is
apparent that even the latter is an inadequate level of herd immunity
to prevent an outbreak. The percent of children age 1-4 years who
have received measles vaccine has increased from 24% to 61.4%, and the
percent obtaining natural immunity by actually contracting the disease
fell from 20.5% to 8.3%.

However, if we look at immunization status among age 0-19 years
instead of age 1-4 years, DPT/DT immunization percentage is very much
lower (54.8% vs. 77.4%) among the older age group. On the other hand,
polio and measles immunization is lower among the 1-4 age group.
From the following data table for ages 0-19, we can see that non-
white people in the central cities, poor people in both central and
non-central cities, poor people in both central and non-central
large cities, and people in center parts of small cities are the
most severely underimmunized.

Source No. 16

1969 Immunization Survey (Age 0-19 years)

Population Category	Polio [a]	DPT/DT [b]	Measles [c]	
Total Caucasian -------	82.3	57.4	74.2	LEAST PROTECTED
Total Non-White -------	68.6	40.7	61.8	
Total U.S.A. ----------	80.2	54.8	72.2	
Cauc. Central Cities --	79.3	54.6	70.8	LEAST PROTECTED
Non-White Cent. City --	67.2	39.5	65.7	
Other SMSA ------------	83.0	59.3	75.0	
Non-SMSA --------------	81.1	53.7	71.6	
Lg. Cent. City Poverty -	68.6	42.3	65.5	LEAST PROTECTED
Lg. Cent. City Non-Poverty --------------	78.2	51.3	70.8	
Lg. Non-Cent. City Poverty --------------	78.0	49.9	68.6	
Lg. Non-Cent. City Non-Poverty ----------	83.3	60.1	75.8	MOST PROTECTED
Small Cent. City ------	76.8	55.2	68.8	
Small Non-Cent. City --	80.6	58.7	72.8	

A serious argument exists as to whether some programs such as immunizations should stand alone or should be combined in comprehensive care. The Vaccination Act was allowed to expire with the expectation that comprehensive care would pick up and maintain immunization status. Most of us would favor an ideal system of family-centered comprehensive care which integrates preventive, acute, and chronic care. But in the short run it may be necessary to have separate immunization programs in order to prevent disease outbreaks, until the time comes when comprehensive care can reach everyone.

(a) To be considered immune either 3 oral polio vaccine (OPV) doses or 3 intramuscular polio shots (IPS) are required.

(b) To be considered immune 4 or more doses of diphtheria-pertussis-tetanus (DPT) or diphtheria-tetanus (DT) are required.

(c) To be considered immune either a history of clinical 9-day measles or a measles shot is required.

LIFE EXPECTANCY

Lastly, we can suspect health shortcomings when some of our population have markedly reduced life expectancy. The current Vital Statistics of the U. S. reports that the life expectancy of a newborn is:

Source No. 17	Life Expectancy (in years)			
	1970	1960	1955	1950
all U.S.A. newborns	70.5	69.7	69.5	68.2
Caucasian newborns	71.3			
non-white newborns	64.6			

SPECIFIC DISEASE TRENDS AND SPECIAL HEALTH SITUATIONS

A search for disease trends was made among the reportable diseases tabulated in Morbidity and Mortality and in its Annual Supplement. The diseases in the table below are not related to each other, except that they have all shown recent upturns in incidence, and they affect children and youth.

The Problem	The Illness	Cases in 1st Six Months of 1970	1969	5-year Average 1965-69
Uneven Distribution of DPT Shots	Diphtheria	186	70	79
Waning Interest in Measles Shots	9-day Measles (Rubeola)	39,051	17,928	
Returning Vietnam Servicemen	Malaria	1,748	1,316	994
Drugs & Drug Abuse	Serum Hepatitis	3,582	2,604	
Change in Sexual Mores	Syphilis	8,664	7,824	
	Gonorrhea	/Total cases in 1968 = 288,694/		

Source No. 18

DIPHTHERIA

Diphtheria is a disease of autumn; therefore, at the time of writing this paper the period of peak incidence is yet to come, but we already know that 1970 will be an outbreak year. Diphtheria had been falling in incidence until 1968, the last outbreak year (260 cases, 60% of cases between ages 1 and 9). 82% of cases are under 15 years old. 80% of cases in patients over 20 years old and a majority of cases between 5 and 14 years are in females. The incidence is 7 times greater among non-whites than among whites.

HEPATITIS

Drug addiction among youth(and spreading to pre-teen children) is
a major contributor to the increase in serum hepatitis and to tetanus
because of the injection of drugs into veins. 67% of 4,829 cases of
serum hepatitis in 1968 were in youths between age 15 and 24 years.
Drug addiction and lawnmower injuries account for 12% of all tetanus
cases among youth and adults.

MALARIA

The incidence of malaria has increased 76% over the average of
1965-69, primarily because of returning Vietnam servicemen who acquire
the disease in Southeast Asia. Nine deaths with acute malaria were
reported in 1969. Servicemen who donate blood without knowing or
revealing past malaria have accounted for passively transferred
malaria acquired by the recipient of the blood.

MEASLES

Seven of the nine major geographical areas of the United States,
80% of the States, and both urban and rural areas report increases
in nine-day measles (rubeola). The U.S.A. is by mid-1970 21,000
cases over the total for all of 1969. The incidence of encephalitis
is one per 1,000 cases and two-thirds of those with rubeola encephalitis are left with some residual neurological damage. Hence,
we have had 21 encephalitis cases (14 with permanent damage) more
in the first half of 1970 than in all of 1969. But since effective
immunization exists, all cases of rubeola encephalitis are "in excess."

VENEREAL DISEASE

The following data for syphilis and gonorrhea show that venereal
disease has the highest incidence among youth 20-24 years old:
(Of course, there is a massive undercount of VD cases and these figures
are artifically low.)

Age (years)	1966 Incidence per 100,000 Syphilis	Gonorrhea
15-19	22	436.1
20-24	48	992
25 and over	11	136

Source No. 19

Syphilis is highest among 20-24 year olds.

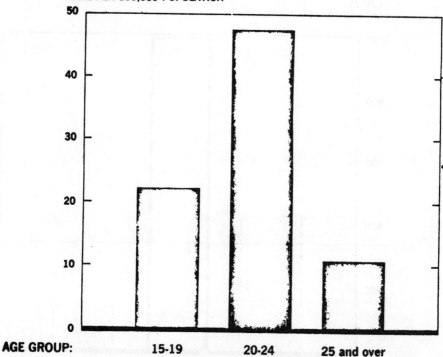

RATE PER 100,000 POPULATION

50		
40		
30		
20		
10		
0		

AGE GROUP: 15-19   20-24   25 and over

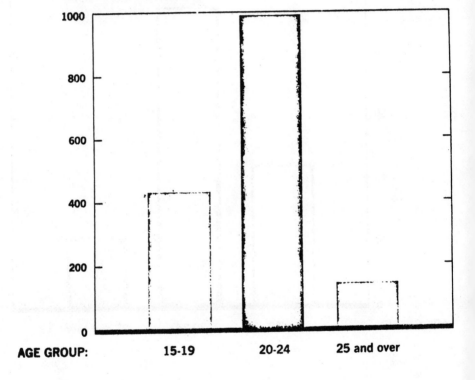

302

Gonorrhea is also highest among 20-24 year olds.

RATE PER 100,000 POPULATION

AGE GROUP: 15-19   20-24   25 and over

In 1966 when syphilis dropped for the first time in a decade, gonorrhea increased by its greatest amount in a decade (8%). Nearly 1% of all 20-24 year olds have gonorrhea, and youths 15-19 years are three times as likely to have the disease as persons over 25.

Effective treatment and prevention is available for venereal disease. We know that a massive post-World War II public program against VD reduced the incidence by half.

DISEASES OF POVERTY

There are a number of diseases which are very important because they are indicators of poverty among children. They are tuberculosis, untreated middle ear infections (otitis media), iron-deficiency anemia, lead poisoning, impetigo, and malnutrition. Tuberculosis is 7-9 times more common among non-white children, 8 times more common among Indians, rampant among migrant families compared with the rates among white children.

Age	TB cases in whites (1968)		TB cases in non-whites (1968)
0-4	1479		1068*
5-14	1417		1377*
15-24	2391	Source No. 21	1924*

* Note that the 10% of the population which is non-white has 35-50% of the tuberculosis.

Untreated middle ear infections are virtually universal among Indian and migrant children, and this condition is extremely common among central city children. Wherever poverty exists, the incidence of iron-deficiency rises sharply among children. The primary sources of iron in the diet (meats, egg yolk, and the commercial ironized infant cereals) are not eaten by these children. The iron deficient child is more susceptible to infections and is more irritable and hard to live with. For lack of soap and water and clean household surroundings impetigo of the skin follows poverty among children. Each of these diseases has some importance in its own right, but together they are indicators of poverty where the whole health maintenance system has failed for some of our people.

MALNUTRITION

Malnutrition interfers with defenses against infectious diseases, increases mortality from the usual childhood diseases, and damages the child's nervous system and intelligence. At birth the brain is growing at the rate of 1-2 mg. per minute. The growth of the brain is so fast that its rate is comparable to some tumors. It is the massive growth of the infant's brain which pushes the skull from inside to grow in size itself. When the brain doesn't grow, neither does the skull size. At this rate of growth the brain is very sensitive to even temporary shortage of essential nutrients. A temporary shortage can cause a permanent decrease in the intelligence of the child. The following graphs show that across ages 6-11 years, taller children on the average make fewer errors in certain kinds of intellectual function. The same is true for well-nourished urban children over poorly-nourished rural children.

The August 1966 supplement to Pediatrics (Vol. 38) reported both temporary and permanent damage to neurointegrative brain function as a result of protein-chlorie malnutrition. There is both intellectual damage and organic neurological damage. The study observed three kinds of neurointegrative function (visual-kinesthetic, haptic-kinesthetic, and visual-haptic) among Guatemalan children and found in the graphs below that intellectual function was better in tall rural children (the better nourished group) than in the shorter rural children and was better in urban children (the better nourished group) than in rural children.

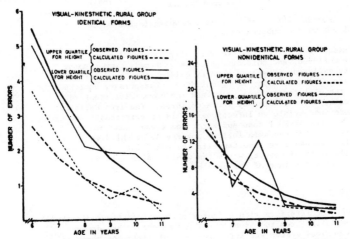

Empirical and theoretical developmental curves for visual-kinesthetic integration in two groups of rural children at extremes of height. (Judgment of identical forms)

Empirical and theoretical developmental curves for visual-kinesthetic integration in two groups of rural children at extremes of height. (Judgment of nonidentical forms)

Source No. 22

305

Source No. 23

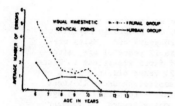

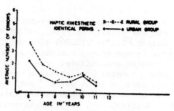

Comparison of the age-specific error curves for visual-kinesthetic intersensory organization of rural children and upper social class urban children.

Comparison of the age-specific error curves for haptic-kinesthetic intersensory organization of rural children and upper social class urban children.

What is the nutritional status of our children and youth? Dr. Charles U. Lowe, as Chairman of the Committee on Nutrition of The American Academy of Pediatrics, had estimated that:

(a) In 1965, 13.9 million children under 15 years of age (24% of the total under 15) lived in poverty. OEO estimates that the average person in poverty can purchase only 1680 calories per person per day.

(b) Based on a Columbus, Ohio, study, it is estimated that 1.5 million children in the U.S.A. have daily food intake of less than 80 calories per kg, a value "which is well below the ideal."

(c) 2½ to 3 times as many children are underweight or short (as defined by one standard deviation below the mean) as are heavy or tall (one standard deviation above).

SUICIDE

Suicide and use of psychiatric care are increasing among children and youth. In 1964, out of 990,000 people in psychiatric out-patient clinics 350,000 were under 20 years old. Males predominate in use of psychiatric care up to 17 years of age, afterwhich females predominate. Also, 21% of first admissions to State and county mental hospitals are under 24 years old, and 5/6's of them are between 15-24 years. But the admissions under 15 years old are increasing in numbers and rate faster than the 15-24 age group. Suicide, too, is progressively moving toward the younger age groups. The rates of suicide among all males age 15-24 have turned sharply up since 1960.

Death rate for suicide, White, Male, United States, 1910-1964.

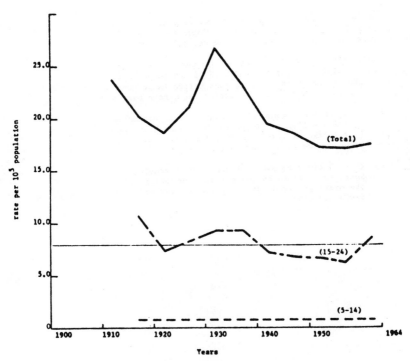

Source No. 24

Among non-white males (15-24) the suicide rate now exceeds the
rate for non-whites of all ages.

Death rates for suicide, Nonwhite, Male, United States, 1910-1964.

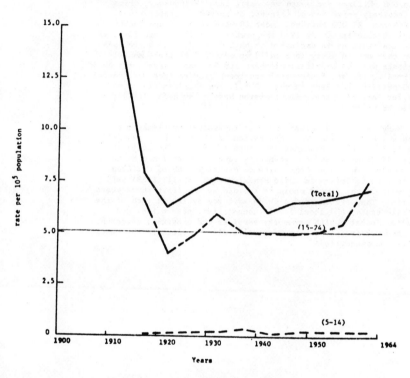

Source No. 25

There are 10 million people 24 and under in the United States who
are in need of help from mental health workers. In 1966 the NIMH
estimated that 1,400,000 children under 18 needed psychiatric care,
but only 400,000 received it. Nearly a million children and youth
in need of psychiatric care in 1966 did not receive treatment.

The risk is that for lack of psychiatric care many of these
disturbed children and youth may drift into delinquency, crime,
progressively worse mental illness, or custodial institutions.
In 1966 over 27,000 children under 18 were in state and county
mental institutions. By 1970 the number of children age 10-14 in
these institutions is estimated to have doubled. One survey has
shown that one in every four children admitted to state mental
hospitals will be hospitalized there for 50 years. For every child
admitted to private residential treatment centers (national capacity
8,000 children per year in the U.S.A.), ten children are turned
away for lack of space. Eight states have no such facilities,
public or private.

Many say that we create most of the social problems of our
youth which we so deplore. Prevention of ill health is generally
more fruitful than treatment and rehabilitation. The basis for
mental development and competence is largely established by the
age of six. The Joint Commission on Mental Health of Children
in its report "Crisis in Child Mental Health" (Fall, 1969) said
that much of the damage could be avoided in the first three years
of life. They recommended a child advocacy system at each of the
Federal, state, and local levels; supportive, preventive, and
remedial mental health community services and programs; research;
and manpower training. The Commission did not estimate the costs
of its recommendations.

ACCIDENTS

Accidents of all kinds (motor vehicle and others) are the
leading cause of death in all age groups from 1-24. Home accidents
predominate in ages 1-4, and motor vehicle accidents predominate in
ages 15-24.

In ages 1-4, accidental deaths exceed pneumonia or congenital
malformations 3 to 1. The bar graph below shows the relationship
of accidental deaths to other causes by age. Accidents are even
more destructive as cause of disability, both temporary and permanent.

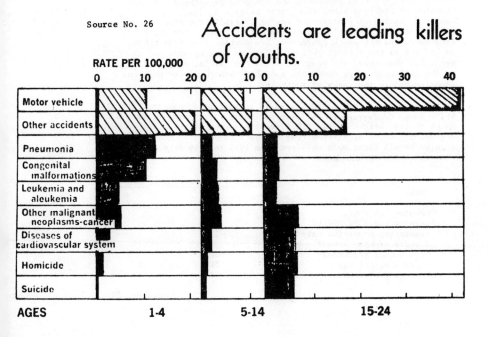

PROLONGATION OF ADOLESCENCE

Good childhood nutrition has been associated with the
steadily falling age of pubarche (i.e. the onset of sexual
maturity). The average age of menarche is now 13 years, and
most pediatricians have seen 9-10 year old girls with menstrual
periods. In the latter, the early adolescent growth spurt starts
at 7½ to 8 years of age. Childhood is thus shortened physiologically
and only partially shortened psychologically. Adolescence becomes
lengthed both by younger pubarche and also the by older age at
which youth are finally assimilated into adult society. Pre-teen
adolescence, pre-teen pregnancy and pre-teen parenthood are now
emerging as problems along side their teenage equivalents.
The prolongation of adolescence may be a significant contributor
to the intense frustration which youth feel today. The child
conference and the youth conference are divided from each other
at the end of the twelfth year of life. We must be sure to
recognize that there are youth problems (VD, drugs, pregnancy)
in the childhood years under 13, and there are childhood problems
(immaturity) in the years of youth.

Pregnancy in the United States is an appropriate subject for this
White House Conference on Children and Youth. For example, in 1967,
54.4% of live births in the U.S.A. were to women 24 years old
and under. 82.7% of first-births are born to women 24 and under.
A third of all first born children from 1964 to 1966 were conceived outside of marriage:

women	% pregnant at the time of marriage
white	20.0
non-white	42.0
earning $10,000/yr.	8.2
earning under $3,000/yr.	37.5
elementary education only	21.2
3 years of high school	31.6
high school graduates	20.7
3 years of college	18.1
college graduates	7.5

Source No. 27

EXPENDITURES FOR HEALTH

In 1969 the United States spent $63 billion on health. Public
funds accounted for 38% of this total. Out of the $63 billion spent
on health, $52.564 billion (Table 1) was spent on personal health
services. This discussion of health expenditures excludes research,
construction, and most education expenditures.

Children and youth are only a part of those totals. In 1969
personal health care expenditures on people age 0-18 years amounted to
$8.4 billion (i.e. 16% of the $52 billion total), shown in Table 1.
Public funds accounted for 26% of this $8.4 billion ($2.2 billion)
which was spent on children and youth. Public funds accounted for
72% of the $13.49 billion spent on personal health services of those
65 years of age and over.

In the latter years of the 1960's, health expenditures grew at
a rate of 12% each year.

The public fund share of health care expenditures for children
and youth remained stable, while the public share for all ages rose
from 25% to 38% and for those 65 and over rose from 31% to 72% in
the 1960's. The absolute amounts spent on children and youth grew,
but the proportion of the whole remained stable.

Table 2 shows that on a percapita basis we spend $101.96
on each person age 0-24 and $607.71 on each person 65 and over
for personal health care.

Children and youth age 0-18 receive more in physician services
than in hospital care, but the reverse is true for those 65 and over.

Consistently, from 1967 through 1969 children and youth age
0-18 received $3 of physician services for every $1 of dentist
services.

Table 4 shows $618 million in 1969 for Department of Defense
expenditures on health (0-18 yrs. group). This expenditure dwarfs
all other federal health programs for children and youth. Together
DOD and public assistance account for 77% of federal health expenditures for ages 0-18. However, State and local government spends most
heavily on public assistance with both school health and maternal and
child health close behind.

Tables 5, 6, and 7 show that the age group 0-5 is the only one
where more is spent on programs for indigent people than on programs

for non-indigent people. At all ages, 6-18, and 19 and over federal
health outlays are larger for non-indigent people than for indigents.
39.2% of children 6-16 never see a physician each year, whereas 18.7%
of children 0-5 never see a doctor. In absolute numbers there are 4
children age 6-16 for every one child 0-5 who never sees a physician
each year.

Comprehensive Health Planning program money for child health
services predominantly reaches indigent children. 93.3% of CHP
money for child health age 0-5 reaches indigents. 87.8% of OEO
apparently reaches only indigents. Both CHP and OEO fund neighborhood health centers.

94% of Maternal and Child Health money for ages 0-5 yrs. reaches
indigents through Comprehensive Child Care Clinics, Well Baby Clinics,
and M&I and C&Y Centers. 88% of MCH money for ages 6-18 reaches
indigents in the same way.

Seven tables of estimated health expenditure data follow
in Appendix A.

Table No.	Content (for all ages and 0-18 years)
1	1967,'68,69; Personal Health Care: what was purchased, divided into public and private.
2	Same as Table 1, except on a percapita basis
3	The Public expenditures part of Table 1 broken down into federal, state and local.
4	The federal, state and local expenditures divided among the various types of programs.
5	1969 federal health expenditures divided by Agency and its Sections, by indigent and non-indigent.
6	Same as Table 5, but for fiscal 1970.
7	Same as Table 5, but for fiscal 1971.

These tables cover personal health care, but they do not include construction or research expenditures.

PRESENT PROGRAMS

It is extremely difficult to get an overall view of health
programs for children and youth by private, local, state, and
federal categories. The section on health expenditures on pages
57-63 in this paper reports comprehensively on health dollars
spent by these categories.

Based on estimated federal health outlays which occurred in
fiscal 1970, the largest federal health programs for children and
youth are: (see table 5, p. 61)

(1) Medicaid (Social and Rehabilitation Services --
$455,981,000 in 1970, ages 0-18

(2) Medical Care of military personnel and their dependents,
Civilian Health and Medical Programs for United Services,
CHAMPUS (D.O.D.) -- $559,448,000 in 1970, ages 0-18.

(3) Maternal and Child Health (HEW-HSMHA) -- $144,072,000
in 1970, ages 0-18. Total MCH for all ages amounted to
$202 million.

There are other federal health programs which benefit children
and youth under:

Comprehensive Health Planning -- e.g. neighborhood health
centers under 314(e) funds
Health Services Research and Development
Mental Health
Indian Health Service
Office of Economic Opportunity -- e.g. neighborhood health
centers with the equivalent of over a 100 pediatricians
working there
Appalachian Regional Development Commission
Panama Canal Zone Authority
Federal Prisons (Justice Department)
Coast Guard (Department of Transportation)
U. S. Information Agency
Vocational Rehabilitation Administration -- includes young
people down to 14 years of age
Food and Nutrition Service, Department of Agriculture

Please see the expenditure tables on pages 57-63 for more information.
The tab titles on the expenditure tables for private, state, and local
health programs identify those programs.

With respect to federal programs Medicaid finances health care
for children but delivers it through the private system; CHAMPUS,
predominantly finances and delivers its own medical care to children
and youth in the military. Maternal and Child Health is a complex
program combining federal, state, and local financing and delivery
of health care; it will be discussed in detail here. Lastly, the
decade of the 1960's gave significant attention to programs for
mentally retarded children; this will be highlighted.

PRESENT PROGRAMS IN MATERNAL AND CHILD HEALTH

In fiscal 1971 the Maternal and Child Health financial plan provides nearly $222 million, which is up from $208 million in fiscal 1969.

The MCH program under Title V of the Social Security Act operates through formula grants to the States and project grants which provide direct services to mothers and children, research and training, and family planning services.

Source No. 28	Appropriations (in millions)		
Maternal and Child Health	1969 (actual)	1970 (actual)	1971 (request)
formula grants to states	105.959	108.000	118.600
project grants	74.971	75.825	83.030
research and training	15.188	14.885	17.085
program		3.071	3.109
total	196.118	201.781	221.824
family planning services	11.909	22.800	33.515

The 1962 Budget of the U. S. reports "actual expenditures for 1960" as follows:

Source No. 29	1960 (millions)
formula grants to states for maternal & child health	$17.442
formula grants to states for crippled children's services	15.873
state & local health services for children	0.774
research in child life and services for children	0.274
information for parents & others working with children	0.335
administration	0.276
Total	$34.974

In 1960 $33.5 million was actually appropriated for maternal and child health versus $202 million in 1970.

The goals of the Maternal and Child Health program are to provide:

(1) basic preventive maternal and child health services,

(2) case-finding, diagnostic, and treatment services to handicapped children, especially in rural areas,

(3) to respond to the serious deficiencies that exist in the quantity and quality of care received by poor children,

(4) to reduce infant and maternal mortality.

The States are now required to make MCH services available on a State-wide basis by 1975; federal assistance will be given to achieve this. High priority is also being given to the provision of family planning services.

Are these programs effective? We know that the infant mortality rate is falling, especially in the areas of high impact by MCH programs, as shown in the table below:

| | Infant Mortality Rate Per 1,000 Live Births | | | |
| | Calendar Year | | | |
	1965	1966	1967	1968 prov.
Nationwide..........................	24.7	23.7	22.4	21.7
Major maternity and infant care projects:				
New York City...................	25.7	24.9	23.9	23.1
Detroit........................	28.8	28.0	27.8	26.8
Dade County, Florida...........	27.7	23.7	23.2	21.5
San Juan, Puerto Rico...........	43.0	37.6	32.8	28.6

How adequate are these programs in reaching those in need? Out of 5 million women needing family planning services, 605,000 are reached by MCH programs. Some of the remainder are reached by other programs and the private sector. In the areas served by children and youth projects, surveys show that about 16% of the children living there become registered in the C&Y projects.

Formula Grants to States

The number of mothers and children reached by programs funded by formula grants grew significantly over the last decade. Since 1969, however, the number reached has not increased, except for family planning and dental services. A $9 million increase in FY 70 for family planning services and the newly proposed, and passed by the Senate, Office of Population Affairs represent new initiatives

in that area. The table below shows the number of mothers and
children reached by formula grants:

Source No. 30	1960* Actual	1969* Actual	1970 Estimate	1971 Estimate
Mothers receiving prenatal and post-partum care in maternity clinics	253,754	337,000	292,000	292,000
Women receiving family planning services	0	395,200	357,000	605,000
Public health nursing visits made on behalf of:				
Mothers	524,566	515,000	548,000	548,000
Children	3,331,171	2,326,000	2,524,000	2,524,000
Children attending well-baby clinics	1,480,377	1,301,000	1,639,000	1,639,000
Children receiving screening tests for:				
Vision	7,022,421	8,141,000	9,607,000	9,607,000
Hearing	4,311,874	4,693,000	5,698,000	5,698,000
Children immunized against:				
Smallpox		2,010,00		
Diphtheria		3,949,000		
Children receiving dental services		1,300,000		
Mothers receiving dental services		32,000		

* Data from MCH Trend Book per Mr. Don Trauger

    The 15 tables in appendix B of this paper are from the NCSS
Report MCH-1 (FY-69) entitled Statistical Summary of Cases Served
under Maternal and Child Health programs of state and local health
departments, fiscal year 1969.

The formula grants to the States also fund Crippled Childrens Services. These programs act to locate, diagnose, and treat children who are suffering from crippling or handicapping illnesses. In 1969 this program provided medical care to 490,000 children of whom:

220,500 had orthopedic handicaps
30,000 had congenital heart disease
82,000 had multiple handicaps

Until now the primary focus of the Crippled Children's Services program has been rural. Extension of the program to urban children is under consideration.

The Conferees are referred for more information to the separate paper on Handicapped Children which has been prepared for the White House Conférence.

Project Grants

The programs funded with project money focus their efforts on providing comprehensive medical care to poor and near-poor mothers and children who might otherwise not receive such services, particularly those who live in urban ghettos.

MATERNITY AND INFANT CARE projects now number 54 in operation and 2 more to open in 1971 in low-income areas. These projects provide comprehensive M & I care. Along with the Comprehensive Children and Youth Projects and the Neighborhood Health Centers (under OEO and 314(e) funds), the M&I Projects make is possible for community health organizations to develop new methods of reaching out to the people in slum areas. This decentralizes services into neighborhoods, reduces crowding in tax-supported hospitals by paying for care in voluntary hospitals, and establishes well organized systems of providing comprehensive health programs for case-finding, prevention, health supervision, and treatment. Such programs, for the most part, are being carried out in areas where there are few physicians in private practice and where existing clinics are grossly over-crowded. In these areas, the programs are creating new resources and changing existing methods of delivering health services in response to the needs of the people.

Examples of the services received under the M&I Projects are
as follows:

Source No. 31

	1969 Actual	1970 Estimate	1971 Estimate
Admissions for services:			
Mothers	115,000	128,000	130,000
Cumulative since start of program	480,500	608,500	738,500
Infants	43,100	46,000	48,000
Women receiving family planning services	86,500	93,000	95,000

In another effort to combat the high infant mortality rates, intensive
care projects have been started in which specialized care is given to
infants born at high risk (prematurely or with conditions detrimental
to their normal growth and development).

HEALTH OF SCHOOL AND PRESCHOOL CHILDREN. The "Children and
Youth" project grants support comprehensive health care for children
in areas where low-income families are concentrated. The program
provides screening, diagnosis, preventive services, correction of
defects, and aftercare (both medical and dental) to children who
would probably not receive such care because of their family's
low-income. Services are coordinated with the program of the State
or local health, education, and welfare departments and with related OEO programs.

The 58 health care centers for children and youth in operation
in June 1970, served areas in which about 2,250,000 children of
poor families live; by the end of FY 1969, 362,000 children were
registered for care. An additional 18,000 children will be receiving
preventive health services through this program by 1971.

During calendar year 1968:

-- 3,800 children were provided eyeglasses
-- 100,000 children received acute and episodic medical treatment
            before their first complete health examination
-- 125,000 children received a complete health examination
-- 130,000 children received dental care
-- 51,000 days of hospital care were given to 7,000 children.

Nearly all projects employ community workers in a variety of categories such as social work aides or assistance, nutrition aides, community health aides or assistants.

DENTAL HEALTH OF CHILDREN. The Child Health Act of 1967 authorized a program of special project grants to promote the dental health of children and youth of school or pre-school age, particularly in areas with concentrations of low-income families. The program includes preventive services, treatment, correction of defects, and aftercare.

Funds requested for 1971 will initiate the dental health program. It is expected to provide services for about 5,000 children from low-income families. The program will initially cover only first grade children. Ultimately, full coverage will be provided for all eligible children in grades 1 through 12. The advantage of the incremental approach is that less professional time is required to carry out preventive and early corrective measures than to correct neglected and advanced dental problems. As evidence of this, note that if you spend $100,000 on each of the following dental programs, the number of cavities prevented and the ratio of dollar benefits per dollar of cost.

Source No. 32

Program	Cavities Prevented or Restored	Dollar Benefits/ Dollar Cost
Fluoridation of Water	666,666	40/1
Hygienist Teaches Children Self- application of Fluoride	233,333	14/1
Hygienist Applies Topical Fluoride	59,999	3.6/1
Fluoride Dentifrice	25,600	1.54/1
Restorations (fillings)	16,666	1/1

Family Planning Activities

Family planning services, which enable women to decide the number
and spacing of children they wish to have, are essential to improving
the health of mothers and children. In the section on health status
this paper reported the increased infant and maternal mortality
associated with closely spaced pregnancies, pregnancies in girls
under 17 years of age, and large numbers of pregnancies in girls
under 20.

Current estimates indicate that there are about 5,000,000
women living in poverty or near-poverty who do not have access to
family planning services. These women, who make up the target group
of the National Center for Family Planning Services, and the new
Office of Population Affairs, have the greatest risk of high infant
and maternal mortality and the greatest chance of having mentally
or physically handicapped babies as described in the health status
portion of this paper.

State and local health departments as well as non-profit organizations are eligible to receive project grants for the purposes of
expanding existing clinics and creating new ones. At least the
following services must be offered by all clinics: contraceptives,
physical examinations, basic medical tests, and counseling.

The number of women receiving family planning services through
MCH programs is shown below:

Program	1969	1970 Estimate	1971 Estimate
Maternal and Child Health State Grant Program	(actual) 395,200	357,000	605,000
Maternity and Infant Care Project Grants	(actual) 86,500	93,000	95,000
National Center for Family Planning Services - Project Grants	(estimate) 150,000-300,000	650,000	800,000
Total	631,700-781,700	1,100,000	1,500,000

OEO estimates that by fiscal year 1971 it will reach 500,000 women
with its family planning services. Together MCH, OEO, NCFPS (National
Center for Family Planning Services), and OPA (Office of Population
Affairs) expect to reach 1.5 million of the 5 million needy women
estimated to require such care.

Present Programs in Mental Retardation

Another paper written for the White House Conference on Children and Youth covers handicapped children including crippled children and mental retardation. In early 1970, a distinguished Presidential Task Force on the Mentally Handicapped (covering mental retardation and the physically handicapped) was formed. The report of that Task Force has gone to the White House but at the time of writing this paper (September 1970) the report has not yet been made public.

Because of the existence of these other sources of information on mental retardation for the conferees, the discussion here will be brief.

As recently as 1954, maternal and child health activities for mentally retarded children and their families were extremely limited. In 1957 Congress increased the MCH appropriation $1 million and ear-marked it specifically for projects serving mentally retarded children. Formula grants to states were also increased for mental retardation. In 1965 training grants were started for mental retardation workers. In fiscal year 1970 these training grants to university-affiliated centers were increased $2.2 million, and 4 more centers were started.

The programs for the mentally retarded are for either prevention or basic and supportive care.

PREVENTION

The present preventive programs are aimed at MR research, rubella vaccine, maternal and infant care, phenylketonuria (PKU) screening, nutrition, family planning, reduction in exposure of children to lead poisoning, and genetic counseling of parents in cases of familial mental retardation.

Research provides the hope for the future through prevention and early treatment. The availability of Rubella vaccine (German measles) in 1970-71 should prevent a repetition of the estimated 9,000 retarded babies born as a result of the 1964 rubella epidemic. Rubeola vaccine (9 day measles) prevents 2 cases of permanent central nervous system damage for every 3,000 cases of rubeola prevented. The maternal and infant care projects prevent MR by improving the quality of pregnancies, deliveries, and follow-up care of the infant. Screening for PKU and other metabolic diseases which can cause MR are carried out in a majority of the States. One case of PKU is found per 10-20,000 screening tests. Dietary improvement prevents harmful effects of malnutrition on the development of children. Family planning research and services prevent some of the MR caused by closely-spaced pregnancies and excessively large numbers of pregnancies per woman. The environmental hazard of lead poisoning is a recognized cause of acquired mental retardation among children which can be prevented by housing code enforcement and clean up of lead paint in old, dilapidated housing.

322

SERVICES

Basic and supportive services in mental retardation consist of
screening and case finding , clinical diagnosis, treatment, crippled
children's services, and laboratory programs in the cytogetics and
biochemistry of mental retardation. In fiscal 1969, 43,000 children,
of whom one-third were under 5 years old, were reached with clinical
services through 235 mental retardation clinics around the country.
The 58 C&Y Projects also serve mentally retarded children. In 1966,
over 20,000 mentally retarded children received medical services under
the Crippled Children's Program. By the end of 1968, 20 programs of
cytogenetic and biochemical services had been approved.

Part C of the community mental retardation facilities program
has funded 385 projects which, when completed, will serve 102,500
persons. Part D has funded 476 projects to serve 136,500 persons.
The Community Resources Branch of the Division of Mental Retardation
in SRS cannot estimate the proportion of children and youth in the
service population of parts C and D. Part B has financed 18 university-
affiliated centers for mental retardation; 7 of these are completed
and 8 more will be completed in 12-18 months. It is estimated that
90% of the people served by university-affiliated centers are children
and youth under 24 years of age.

The total program for the mentally retarded in all age groups by
HEW is estimated at $607 million in fiscal 1971. This is almost
$40 million more than in 1970, and $18 million of that increase is
for services and grants. The complete funding is:

	(millions)
*Services, Research, Education, Rehabilitation ...	$370
SRS Income Maintenance	86
SSA Income Maintenance	151
Total	$607

The scope of the department-wide MR activities is described in a
report to the House Appropriations Subcommittee by the Secretary's
Committee on Mental Retardation.

This is only a brief overview of present programs in MCH and
Mental Retardation but the conferees are referred to the other sources
cited in the text for more information.

---

* This is from testimony by Mr. Creed C. Black to the Committee on
  Interstate and Foreign Commerce, June 9, 1970.

ESTIMATES OF UNMET NEEDS

In order to estimate needs we must choose an estimate of population for 1970, 1975, and 1980. The Bureau of the Census recommends Series E estimates which assumes the same mortality and immigration rates as the other series do but also assumes a fertility rate of 2.11 children per woman.

Series E Census Estimates (in millions)

Year	Age 0 to 13 yrs.	Age 13 to 25 yrs.	Total 0 to 25 yrs.
1970	50.494	44.475	94,969
1975	47.939	48.917	96.856
1980	47.135	48,940	96.075

The unmet health needs which children and youth have or will have in the decade ahead can be approached by looking at deficits in:

(A) Outcomes (i.e. deficits of health status)
(B) Inputs (i.e. deficits of health services, inadequate utilization rates)
(C) Categories (i.e. specific diseases and health situation needs)

These health deficits are each of two types for they each have some medical solutions and some non-medical (i.e. nutrition, education, income, housing, etc.) solutions.

There is certainly no adequate, single composite index of health status. We have discussed infant and maternal mortality, immunization status, rejection rates from military, and life expectancy within our society and cross-comparing our country with others. We can and should work to reduce our infant mortality to a level comparable to that of the Netherlands or Sweden. The deficits of health status are related to the causes of infant mortality:

(a) lack of health education to inform girls under 17 of the increased risk of becoming pregnant in that age group, of smoking while pregnant, excessive weight restriction, of short interval pregnancies, and large numbers of pregnancies under 20 years of age.

(b) lack of family planning services to make it possible for high risk women to avoid pregnancy and to space desired pregnancies.

(c) lack of adequate access to and utilization of prenatal medical care and hospital care at the time of delivery.

(d) malnutrition of women before and during their pregnancies.

Our health status deficits in immunization reflect our lack of emphasis
on prevention, continuity of care, and comprehensive maintenance
health care. There is serious argument as to whether the immunization
deficits cry out for crash immunization programs on a disease by
disease basis; or should the immunization deficits be viewed as consisting
of a lack of sustained continuous preventive care integrated with acute
and chronic illness care.

The rejection rates among military recruits reveal conditions
which were preventable or treatable earlier in the recruit's life.
Again, lack of effective access to continuing maintenance medical
care enters.

The racial, income, and socioeconomic status comparisons <u>within</u>
our population reflect non-medical deficits of housing, jobs, equal
opportunity, etc. as well as medical care deficits.

Some quantitative estimates of these "outcome types" of
deficits are presented below:

(a) women in poverty needing maternity care = 600,000, those reached
     publicly = 130,000, deficit is estimated at 470,000
     women needing maternity care.
(b) 5,000,000 poor or near-poor women without access to
     family planning services; 1.5 million may now be
     reached: 3.5 million remain.
(c) the 35-40% of central city, poor, or non-white children
     (0-19) who are inadequately immunized.
(d) the 17-25% of our most immunized child populations
     (age 0-19) who are inadequately immunized.
(e) the 43.6% of pregnant girls under 16 who are on
     "poor diets."
(f) such inadequate health status that 36% of white
     18 year olds and 62% of non-white 18 year olds must
     be rejected from service in the military.
(g) the 40% of children in families earning over $4,000/year,
     66% in families under $4,000/year, and 75% in families
     under $2,000/year who have never seen a dentist.
(h) the 50% (1.7 million) of children 2 years of age who
     have decayed teeth.
(i) the 3 decayed teeth on the average in each child at
     6 years of age (4.1 million) and the 11 decayed, filled
     or missing teeth per each 15 year old (4.16 million).
(j) the deaths of 40,000 infants per year because of our
     infant mortality rate is 22.1 per 1,000 live births
     instead of 14.8/1,000 as in the Netherlands. It should
     be noted that differences between the USA and the Netherlands
     in genetic stock, population density, cultural homogeneity,
     income levels, employment, and climate may make it impossible
     to achieve the same levels of infant mortality.

Unmet needs can also be estimated by "inputs" of health
services which we are failing to put into our system or failing
to distribute equitably among our people. A corollary of the
principle that medical care is a right rather than a privilege
is that there should be equal access to care for equal need.

Many children never see a physician each year -- even for
necessary acute care and/or necessary preventive care. Other
children see physicians some but in inadequate amounts. Both
represent deficits.

Actual household survey data for 1967 by the National Center
for Health Statistics revealed that 4.4 million (18.7%) of children
0-5 years of age never saw a physician at all in that year. There
is disagreement within pediatrics as to what is the necessary level
of physician visits under 6 years of age -- but it is certainly
not zero. Some say an average of 6 visits per year for the first
5 years of life; some say 10 visits per year counting sick and
well child care. I will use 6 and 10 as low and high estimates
in calculating the deficits which follow.

The 1967 survey, furthermore, revealed that 17 million (39.2%)
of children 6-16 years of age never saw a physician in the year.
Among those other children (6-16) who did see a physician the
rate of use in 1967 was 2.6 visits/year; I shall use this to estimate
deficits among those who did not see a physician.

If we assume the proportions of the child population reached
by medical care will continue roughly the same, we can estimate
deficits of physician visits for the years ahead using the Census
Bureau's series E projections in the tables on the next page.

DEFICITS OF PHYSICIAN VISITS ONLY AMONG CHILDREN
WHO NEVER SEE A PHYSICIAN EACH YEAR

Year	Age Group (yrs.)	Total Children (millions)	Assumed % Who Never See Physician	No. of Children Who See No Physician (millions)	Estimated Deficit of Physician Visits (in millions per year)			
					Each Age Group		Total Ages 0-16**	
					Low (missed 6 visits)	High (missed 10 visits)	Low**	High**
1967	(0-5)	23.7	18.7*	4.4	26.4	44.0	70.6	88.2
	(6-16)	43.3	39.2	17.0	44.2	Same		
1970	(0-5)	17.4	18.7	3.3	19.6	32.6	69.2	82.2
	(6-16)	48.9	39.2	19.1	49.6	Same		
1975	(0-5)	17.4	18.7	3.3	19.6	32.6	67.6	80.6
	(6-16)	47.4	39.2	18.5	48.0	Same		
1980	(0-5)	19.2	18.7	3.6	21.5	35.8	65.6	79.9
	(6-16)	43.5	39.2	17.0	44.1	Same		

* The percentage of children who never saw a physician in 1967 is that which the Survey of Physician Visits by the National Center for Health Statistics reported. For the purpose of this table, this percentage has been assumed to be constant from 1967 to 1980. Losses of child visits by vanishing general practitioners are accumulating faster than visits provided by new pediatricians are building up. Maldistribution of physicians continues to be a primary cause of lack of access to care for many children. Both of these factors would keep the % without access as high or higher than 1967. Against this is the 6.4% decrease in the child population from 67 million in 1967 to 62.7 million in 1980.

** For the purposes of this paper two levels of use of physician visits have been selected and labeled "low standards" and "high standards." These are based on opinions of some pediatricians that children require between 30 and 50 physician visits in the first 5 years of life (i.e. 6-10 visits/year). Children 6-16 use an average of 2.6 visits/year. Hence, "low standards" level is defined as 6 visits/year under 6 years of age and 2.6 visits/year over 6. "High standards" level is defined as 10 visits/year under 6 years of age and 2.6 visits/year over 6.

Thus, it can be seen that the deficits among these children decrease slightly over the next decade because of changes in total numbers of children and the age mix. But very substantial deficits are present throughout. Between 21-23 million children each year will not see a physician even once, when they could have used 65-82 million visits each year. The costs of fulfilling this unmet need can be estimated by assuming costs of $100,000 to train each pediatrician, $2,000 to train each pediatric nurse practitioner, and $8 per visit.

	Low Deficit* (65 mil. visits)	High Deficit* (82 mil. visits)
Using 9,280-11,700 Pediatricians:		
training cost	$928 mil.	$1,170 mil.
visit cost	520 mil.	656 mil.
Using 9,280-11,700 Pediatric Nurse Practitioners under Physican Supervision		
training cost	18.6 mil.	23.4 mil.
visit cost	520.0 mil.	656.0 mil.

In addition to the unmet needs of the children mentioned above, we know that in 1967 many children saw a physician at least once but not up to the normative and empirical standards already mentioned. So more deficits appear in the table on the next page:

_____

* These are available estimates of deficits and depend entirely on the assumptions spelled out in the text and in the footnote to the table on page 48.

DEFICITS OF PHYSICIAN VISITS AMONG CHILDREN WHO SAW PHYSICIANS

LESS THAN STANDARDS INDICATE

Year	Age Group (yrs.)	Total Children (mils.)	% of Children Who Under-used Physician	No. of Children Who Under-used Physician (mils.)	Deficits of Visits(mils.) by Age Group					Total Deficit (all ages 0-16)	
					(Age 0-5) Low Stds.		High Stds.		Age 6-16	Low Stds. (mils.)	High Stds. (mils.)
					Missed 5visits	Missed 3visits	Missed 9visits	Missed 7visits	Missed 1.6visits		
1967	0-5	23.7	19	4.5	22.5						
	0-5	23.7	36	8.53		25.6	40.5	59.7		66.1	118.2
	6-16	43.3	26	11.26					18.0		
1980	0-5	19.2	19	3.65	18.2						
	0-5	19.2	36	6.91		20.7	32.8	48.4		57.0	99.3
	6-16	43.5	26	11.3					18.1		

Thus, even among children who have some access to a physician we have deficits of 66-118 million visits in 1967 and 57-99 million visits in 1970. The costs of these deficits among children with access to care would be: (using the same assumptions from the cost table on page 59.)

	Low Deficit* (57 mil. visits)	High Deficit * (99 mil. visits)
Using 8,100-14,100 Pediatricians		
Training Cost	$810.0 mil.	$1,140.0 mil.
Visit Costs	456.0 mil.	792.0 mil.
Using 8,100-14,100 Pediatric Nurse Practitioners under MD Supervision		
Training Cost	16.2 mil.	28.2 mil.
Visit Costs	456.0 mil.	792.0 mil.

In 1967 the actual consumption of 240 million visits (by children with access to care) was 65% of the difference between the low standard at 184 million and the high standard 261 million. If actual demand in 1980 falls in the same range, (above low and below high standards), then we would expect normal consumption of physician visits by children with access to care to fall 65% of the difference between 162.5 million (low) and 224.9 (high) -- thus around 203 million.

ESTIMATED DEMAND & ADDITIONAL NEED FOR PHYSICIAN VISITS TO CHILDREN (0-16 yr.) in 1980

	Millions of visits	
	Low	High
Normal Consumption by Children with access (demand)	203	203
Unmet Deficits for children with access (mixed demand & need)	57	99
Unmet Deficits for children without access (mixed demand & need)	65	79
Totals	325	381

In the face of need and demand in 1980 in the range of 325-381 million physician visits to children (age 0-16 yrs.), the likely supply of physician (pediatricians and 30% of general practitioners) visits to these people will be approximately 236-240 million. This unmet requirement is one of both absolute amounts and maldistribution of services; both causes would have to be attacked. The use of middle level manpower such as pediatric nurse practitioners to massively increase the productivity of present physicians could help the maldistribution problem if they are wisely distributed.

---

* See footnote on page 49.

Unmet needs can be partially estimated by specific disease categories. However, discussing categories should not be interpreted as necessarily endorsing solutions on a piecemeal categorical basis.

Psychiatric Disease: There are unmet needs for mental health worker care for 10 million persons under 24 years of age, for psychiatric care for 1 million children under 18 years old, for residential psychiatric treatment for 80,000 children.

Somatic Diseases: There are unmet needs controlling our current outbreaks of 9-day measles (rubeola), diphtheria, malaria, serum hepatitis, syphilis and gonorrhea, suicide among young males (white and non-white), and polio. See pages 21-24 of this report.

Diseases of Poverty: There are unmet needs among the 40 million poor and near poor because of the burden of excessive ill health which they bear. The so-called diseases of poverty (see page 25) are inequitably distributed among our population. The average poor person experiences 7-9 times as much tuberculosis, untreated middle-ear infections, impetigo, iron-deficiency anemia, and malnutrition as does the average non-poor person.

Some Health Options for Children and Youth in the Seventies

There are many alternative health options for children and youth; only a few can be discussed here.

Some of the options which might be possible are:

(1) to assure that every child and youth has financial accessibility to adequate personal health services.

(2) to assure that there is an adequate supply of personal health services available for children and youth.

(3) to make major non-medical investments in the health of children and youth such as nutrition, housing, education, jobs.

(4) to assure primary prevention of all the diseases of children and youth for which primary prevention is known.

(5) to assure early control of the specific diseases which have broken out in our children and youth (chronic bronchitis, suicide, accidents, diphtheria, syphilis, gonorrhea, nine-day measles, serum hepatitis, teen and preteen pregnancy, polio, malaria, malnutrition, and the diseases of poverty).

(6) to seek comprehensive family-centered care which integrates acute, chronic, preventive, and maintenance health care.

Let us develop these options in some additional detail.

(1) FINANCIAL ACCESSIBILITY - Many poor people and near-poor can not afford to purchase adequate medical care for their children and youth (even when it is available). The proposed Family Health Insurance Plan (FHIP) would provide health insurance for families with children on a national basis with a sliding scale of contributions which phase down gradually as income level rises among the working poor and near-poor without sharp notches at which eligibility for benefits abruptly stops and without the state by state residency requirements of Medicaid.

(2) SUPPLY - Insuring that people can afford to buy care when it is available is very important; this supplements demand, given that there is available supply. If the supply of services is rigidly restricted (e.g., in poor neighborhoods, in migrant camps, rural areas, Indian reservations), then the supply of services must be increased along with the demand in order to avoid excessive price inflation. However, supply must be increased primarily to reduce inequities in the treatment of poor children and not just to control inflation of medical prices.

One analysis[*] has shown that, in order to provide physician-
type care to the 21.8 million children (under 16) in 1975 who will
not see a physician even once in the year, we can either:

    a. Spend $19 million over 5 years to train 9,500
       pediatric nurse practitioners to work under the
       supervision of 2,360 physicians, or

    b. Spend $950 million to train the number of
       pediatricians who would be necessary to provide
       the equivalent amount of service.

Option b. is 50 times more costly than option a. and would
require a lag time of 10 years to implement as opposed to a 1-3
year lag time for a. Beyond this, pediatric nurse practitioners
could also be used to improve the use of physician visits by the
21-22 million children (under 16) in 1975 and 1980 (see table
on page 60) who saw a physician some but not enough.

If we want to increase the supply of health services for children
who are without access, facilities as well as manpower are
necessary. Facilities such as Neighborhood Health Centers,
Comprehensive M&I and C&Y clinics, Central City Hospital
Outpatient departments would be necessary and might be expanded
into comprehensive family care centers serving (among others)
FHIP beneficiaries. Another facility proposal is that of
creating pediatric group practices based in the schools using
pediatric nurse practitioners and pediatricians providing comprehensive health maintenance care, case-finding, acute sick
and chronic care. The poor, school age child could thus be
reached, but not the poor, pre-schooler or certain categories of
school children.

(3) NON-MEDICAL INVESTMENTS - Many undeveloped countries have learned
that, when faced with extremely bad levels of health status (such
as exist among the poor, the near-poor, migrants, and Indians in
the United States), the maximum return in health status comes
from money spent on non-medical health investments. Proper housing
reduces tuberculosis, other infections and psychological diseases.
Good nutrition prevents infections, certain anemias, and some mental
retardation. Soap and safe water (sanitation) prevent dysentery
and impetigo. Health education can teach people to care wisely
for some of their own illnesses. Income and jobs improve health
status and psychological well-being. Lastly, expensive personal
health services become important to health status much later in
the course of improving the health of very deprived people.

---

* See page 48.

In a study by Galenson and Pyatt* relationships were
sought between investments in food calories per capita,
physicians per population, and hospital beds per population
and their impact on economic development. Investments in
food calories were found to be more important than the
other health inputs. Furthermore, they concluded that
"the direction of causality runs _from_ calories and higher
education _to_ economic growth, although it cannot be denied
that there must be something of the opposite effect as well."**

(4) PRIMARY PREVENTION - Primary prevention can be more cost-
beneficial than treatment. We know that the prevention of
one case of lead encephalopathy (lead poisoning) in a child
saves over $200,000 in later costs related to remedial care.
In dental health an expenditure of 15¢ per person per year
on fluoridation of public water supplies (i.e. $7.50 over
50 years) prevents over $300 worth of dental care; this is
a benefit-cost ratio of 40 to 1 for prevention over
restorative treatment. Of course, some illnesses have no
primary prevention available, and treatment is then the
only available approach.

(5) CONTROL PRESENT OUTBREAKS - Several specific outbreaks of
diseases and health problems among children and youth have
been reported in this paper. An issue has arisen as to
whether these should be approached on a categorical disease
basis. Is the urgency for prompt control of these too
great to allow us to wait for good comprehensive care to
catch up and solve these problems?

(6) COMPREHENSIVE FAMILY-CENTERED CARE - In the long term view
our problems with access to medical care, infant mortality,
morbidity and mortality in children and youth, care of
pregnancy, military disqualification rates, immunization
status, and life expectancy are related to the basic need
for continuous, coordinated, comprehensive medical care of
whole families (the children, the youths, and the parents).
The issue, then, comes back full circle to the options on
financial accessibility and supply of health services.

* "The Quality of Labour and Economic Development in Certain Countries"
(Geneva: International Labor Office, 1964) p. 64

** Ibid., p. 77

SUMMARY by Michael S. March

The aggregate deficits in health and dental services identified above for children and youth are proportionately large in relation to the present volume of services being rendered. When considered in the context of the unmet needs for the total population, it is clear that the country cannot, in the near future, meet its entire health needs, and that priorities will have to be chosen carefully for apportioning available health services and insuring their productivity and yield.

The claim of children and youth for a high priority on the limited available health resources is strong, for in the early developmental years of a human being the entire pattern of life-time health may be set -- for sickness or for good health. In short, preventive health care is generally regarded as the preferable form of health care, and children and youth are a primary focus of effective preventive health care.

Given the evident inability of the nation to meet <u>all</u> its desirable health goals <u>simultaneously</u>, a number of alternative strategies for allocating limited available health resources for children and youth might offer good yields in reduced morbidity and mortality among children and youth and improved life-time health as they grow to maturity.

    a. <u>The very early years</u> - Evidence is accumulating that lack of proper maternal health care, including nutrition, during pregnancy and nursing periods and lack of proper health care and nutrition for infants and little children greatly increase the incidence of prematurity, low birth weight, physical and mental defects, and the rates of infant and child morbidity and mortality. Increased emphasis could be placed on more adequate maternal and infant health care.

    b. <u>Children of the poor and the minorities</u> - HEW studies highlight the disproportionately large gap in health care for the children of the poor and of special groups such as the blacks, Spanish-surname Americans, American Indians, and migrants who are often poor as well as socially deprived. These groups make a high contribution to the excess mortality of the country and to the rate of failures on health tests, such as under the military entrance examinations. Steps to increase health care for the children of the poor and the minority groups could yield marked improvements in their health status, as has been demonstrated under various Federal programs.

    c. <u>Geographic equalization of health resources</u> - Glaring disparities in the distribution of physicians and dentists leave many rural and ghetto areas with heavy concentration of children without the barest essentials of medical and dental care. Measures to induce physicians, dentists, and paramedical personnel to serve in these areas would represent another alternative, high-yield strategy, especially if coupled with improvements in the effectiveness of the health service delivery system.

APPENDIX A

Source No. 33

Health Expenditure Tables (Nos. 1-7)

TABLE 1.--Estimated personal health care expenditures, by type of expenditure, source of funds, and age, fiscal years 1967-69

[In millions]

1967

Type of expenditure	All ages Total	Private	Public	0-18 years Total	Private	Public	19-64 years Total	Private	Public	65 years and over Total	Private	Public
Total	$41,594	$29,163	$12,451	$6,887	$5,276	$1,611	$25,218	$20,024	$5,193	$9,489	$3,843	$5,647
Hospital care	16,814	8,713	8,101	1,560	960	600	11,084	7,404	3,680	4,170	349	3,821
Physicians' services	9,738	8,363	1,375	2,298	2,133	165	5,823	5,347	476	1,617	883	734
Dentists' services	3,158	3,077	81	811	745	66	2,088	2,086	2	259	246	13
Other professional services	1,174	1,094	80	271	243	28	703	688	15	195	158	37
Drugs and drug sundries	5,491	5,282	209	997	962	35	3,223	3,163	60	1,271	1,157	114
Eyeglasses and appliances	1,508	1,472	36	228	222	6	954	926	28	326	324	2
Nursing-home care	1,692	782	910	13	...	7	156	66	90	1,523	710	813
Other health services	2,019	360	1,659	704	...	704	1,187	344	843	128	16	112

1968

Type of expenditure	All ages Total	Private	Public	0-18 years Total	Private	Public	19-64 years Total	Private	Public	65 years and over Total	Private	Public
Total	$46,917	$30,756	$16,161	$7,658	$5,751	$1,907	$27,019	$21,515	$6,104	$11,640	$3,490	$8,150
Hospital care	19,248	9,440	9,808	1,725	996	729	12,134	8,055	4,079	5,389	389	5,000
Physicians' services	10,913	8,626	2,291	2,572	2,350	222	6,469	5,793	574	1,878	483	1,395
Dentists' services	3,490	3,287	203	885	799	86	2,322	2,225	97	283	263	20
Other professional services	1,280	1,148	132	302	265	37	758	729	29	220	154	66
Drugs and drug sundries	5,912	5,642	270	1,083	1,038	45	3,394	3,306	88	1,435	1,298	137
Eyeglasses and appliances	1,658	1,615	43	306	297	9	994	963	31	358	355	3
Nursing-home care	2,070	618	1,452	16	...	10	191	79	112	1,863	533	1,330
Other health services	2,340	380	1,960	769	...	769	1,357	365	992	214	15	199

1969

Type of expenditure	All ages Total	Private	Public	0-18 years Total	Private	Public	19-64 years Total	Private	Public	65 years and over Total	Private	Public
Total	$52,564	$33,835	$18,729	$8,415	$6,189	$2,227	$30,659	$23,884	$6,776	$13,490	$3,762	$9,726
Hospital care	22,531	11,268	11,263	2,069	1,196	873	13,928	9,431	4,497	6,534	641	5,893
Physicians' services	11,916	9,214	2,702	2,809	2,530	279	7,022	6,270	752	2,085	414	1,671
Dentists' services	3,719	3,457	262	946	839	107	2,465	2,341	124	308	277	31
Other professional services	1,396	1,230	166	330	282	48	836	799	37	230	149	81
Drugs and drug sundries	6,278	5,952	326	1,095	1,039	56	3,634	3,544	90	1,549	1,369	180
Eyeglasses and appliances	1,751	1,700	51	308	297	11	1,066	1,049	17	377	374	3
Nursing-home care	2,412	614	1,798	18	...	12	223	86	137	2,171	522	1,649
Other health services	2,562	400	2,162	840	...	840	1,486	384	1,102	236	16	220

Source No. 33

TABLE 2.--Estimated per capita personal health care expenditures, by type of expenditure, source of funds, and age, fiscal years 1967-69

1967

Type of expenditure	All ages Total	All ages Private	All ages Public	0-19 years Total	0-19 years Private	0-19 years Public	19-64 years Total	19-64 years Private	19-64 years Public	65 years and over Total	65 years and over Private	65 years and over Public
Total.................	$206.85	$144.93	$61.92	$91.72	$70.27	$21.46	$235.32	$186.86	$48.46	$503.98	$204.11	$299.93
Hospital care.............	83.62	43.33	40.29	20.78	12.79	7.99	103.43	69.09	34.34	221.48	18.54	202.94
Physicians' services......	48.43	41.59	6.84	30.60	28.41	2.20	54.34	49.90	4.44	85.88	46.90	38.98
Dentists' services........	15.71	15.30	.40	10.80	9.92	.88	19.48	19.47	.02	13.76	13.07	.69
Other professional services	5.84	5.44	.40	3.68	3.30	.37	6.56	6.42	.14	10.36	8.39	1.97
Drugs and drug sundries...	27.31	26.27	1.04	13.28	12.81	.47	30.08	29.52	.56	67.51	61.45	6.05
Eyeglasses and appliances.	7.50	7.32	.18	3.04	2.96	.08	8.90	8.64	.26	17.31	17.21	.11
Nursing-home care.........	8.41	3.89	4.53	.17	.08	.09	1.46	.62	.84	80.89	37.71	43.18
Other health services.....	10.04	1.79	8.25	9.38		9.38	11.08	3.21	7.87	6.80	.85	5.95

1968

Type of expenditure	All ages Total	All ages Private	All ages Public	0-19 years Total	0-19 years Private	0-19 years Public	19-64 years Total	19-64 years Private	19-64 years Public	65 years and over Total	65 years and over Private	65 years and over Public
Total.................	$230.84	$151.32	$79.51	$101.96	$76.57	$25.39	$253.42	$197.41	$56.01	$607.71	$182.21	$425.50
Hospital care.............	94.70	46.45	48.26	22.97	13.26	9.71	111.34	73.91	37.43	281.35	20.31	261.04
Physicians' services......	53.72	42.44	11.28	34.24	31.29	2.96	59.36	53.15	6.20	98.05	25.22	72.83
Dentists' services........	17.17	16.17	1.00	11.78	10.64	1.14	21.31	20.42	.89	14.77	13.73	1.04
Other professional services	6.30	5.65	.65	4.02	3.53	.49	6.96	6.69	.27	11.49	8.04	3.45
Drugs and drug sundries...	29.09	27.76	1.33	14.42	13.82	.60	31.14	30.33	.81	74.92	67.77	7.15
Eyeglasses and appliances.	8.16	7.95	.21	4.07	3.95	.12	9.12	8.84	.28	18.69	18.53	.16
Nursing-home care.........	10.18	3.04	7.14	.21	.08	.13	1.75	.72	1.03	97.26	27.83	69.44
Other health services.....	11.51	1.87	9.64	10.24		10.24	12.45	3.35	9.10	11.17	.78	10.39

1969

Type of expenditure	All ages Total	All ages Private	All ages Public	0-19 years Total	0-19 years Private	0-19 years Public	19-64 years Total	19-64 years Private	19-64 years Public	65 years and over Total	65 years and over Private	65 years and over Public
Total.................	$256.04	$164.81	$91.23	$111.82	$82.24	$29.59	$277.31	$216.03	$61.29	$692.22	$193.04	$499.08
Hospital care.............	109.75	54.89	54.86	27.49	15.89	11.60	125.98	85.30	40.68	335.28	32.89	302.39
Physicians' services......	58.04	44.88	13.16	37.33	33.62	3.71	63.51	56.71	6.80	106.99	21.24	85.75
Dentists' services........	18.12	16.84	1.28	12.57	11.15	1.42	22.30	21.17	1.12	15.80	14.21	1.59
Other professional services	6.80	5.99	.81	4.39	3.71	.64	7.56	7.23	.33	11.80	7.65	4.16
Drugs and drug sundries...	30.58	28.99	1.59	14.35	13.81	.74	32.87	32.06	.81	79.48	70.25	9.24
Eyeglasses and appliances.	8.53	8.28	.25	4.09	3.95	.15	9.64	9.31	.33	19.35	19.19	.15
Nursing-home care.........	11.75	2.99	8.76	.24	.08	.16	2.02	.78	1.24	111.40	26.79	84.62
Other health services.....	12.48	1.95	10.53	11.16		11.16	13.44	3.47	9.97	12.11	.82	11.29

Source No. 33

Table 1.--Estimated public personal health care expenditures, by type of expenditure, source of funds, and age, fiscal years 1967-1969

[In millions]

1967

Type of expenditure	All ages			0-18 years			19-64 years			65 years and over		
	Total	Federal	State and local	Total	Federal	State and local	Total	Federal	State and local	Total	Federal	State and local
Total	$12,451	$7,466	$4,985	$1,611	$959	$652	$5,193	$2,348	$2,845	$5,647	$4,130	$1,517
Hospital care	8,101	4,639	3,463	600	366	231	3,680	1,429	2,253	3,821	2,813	1,008
Physicians' services	1,375	828	547	165	92	73	476	64	412	734	672	62
Dentists' services	81	41	40	66	32	33	3	2	1	13	7	7
Other professional services	80	44	35	28	16	12	15	1	15	37	29	8
Drugs and drug sundries	209	98	111	35	18	17	60	24	35	114	56	59
Eyeglasses and appliances	36	17	19	6	4	2	28	11	16	2	1	1
Nursing-home care	910	507	403	7	3	4	90	46	42	813	457	357
Other health services	1,659	1,291	368	704	424	280	843	771	72	112	96	16

1968

Type of expenditure	All ages			0-18 years			19-64 years			65 years and over		
	Total	Federal	State and local	Total	Federal	State and local	Total	Federal	State and local	Total	Federal	State and local
Total	$16,161	$10,436	$5,725	$1,907	$1,149	$758	$6,104	$2,902	$3,202	$8,150	$6,385	$1,765
Hospital care	9,808	6,043	3,765	729	449	280	4,079	1,676	2,404	5,000	3,918	1,081
Physicians' services	2,293	1,620	673	222	128	94	676	156	520	1,395	1,336	59
Dentists' services	203	103	101	86	44	43	96	49	48	21	10	10
Other professional services	132	88	44	37	23	14	29	6	23	66	59	7
Drugs and drug sundries	270	129	141	45	24	22	88	38	50	137	67	69
Eyeglasses and appliances	43	22	21	9	6	3	31	14	17	3	1	1
Nursing-home care	1,452	898	554	10	5	5	112	59	53	1,330	834	496
Other health services	1,960	1,533	427	769	471	296	992	904	87	199	158	42

1969

Type of expenditure	All ages			0-18 years			19-64 years			65 years and over		
	Total	Federal	State and local	Total	Federal	State and local	Total	Federal	State and local	Total	Federal	State and local
Total	$18,729	$12,351	$6,378	$2,227	$1,346	$882	$6,776	$3,287	$3,488	$9,726	$7,718	$2,008
Hospital care	11,263	7,222	4,042	873	538	336	4,497	1,922	2,576	5,893	4,762	1,130
Physicians' services	2,702	1,920	782	279	164	116	752	182	569	1,671	1,574	97
Dentists' services	262	134	128	107	53	53	124	63	60	21	16	15
Other professional services	166	115	51	48	31	26	37	8	29	81	76	5
Drugs and drug sundries	326	157	169	55	30	26	90	38	52	180	89	91
Eyeglasses and appliances	51	27	24	11	8	3	37	17	19	3	2	1
Nursing-home care	1,798	1,112	686	12	6	6	137	73	64	1,649	1,033	616
Other health services	2,162	1,665	497	840	516	325	1,102	982	119	220	167	53

Source No. 33

TABLE 4.--Estimated personal health care expenditures under public programs, by program and age, fiscal years 1967-69

[In millions]

Program	Total			Federal			State and local		
	1967	1968	1969	1967	1968	1969	1967	1968	1969
All ages									
Total	$12,451	$16,161	$18,729	$7,437	$10,436	$12,351	$5,014	$5,725	$6,378
Health insurance for the aged	3,172	5,126	6,299	3,172	5,126	6,299	---	---	---
Temporary disability insurance	54	55	58	---	---	---	54	55	58
Workmen's compensation (medical benefits)	695	765	850	14	15	17	682	750	833
Public assistance (vendor medical payments)	2,383	3,581	4,421	1,157	1,760	2,186	1,226	1,821	2,235
General hospital and medical care	2,822	2,895	3,027	135	187	200	2,687	2,708	2,827
Defense Department hospital and medical care (including military dependents)	1,432	1,648	1,766	1,432	1,648	1,766	---	---	---
Maternal and child health services	308	335	380	137	159	190	171	176	190
School health	178	190	204	---	---	---	178	190	204
Veterans' hospital and medical care	1,237	1,361	1,465	1,237	1,361	1,465	---	---	---
Medical vocational rehabilitation	67	102	124	51	76	93	17	26	31
Office of Economic Opportunity	103	104	134	103	104	134	---	---	---
Under 19 years									
Total	$1,611	$1,907	$2,227	$959	$1,149	$1,346	$652	$758	$882
Health insurance for the aged	---	---	---	---	---	---	---	---	---
Temporary disability insurance	---	---	---	---	---	---	---	---	---
Workmen's compensation (medical benefits)	---	---	---	---	---	---	---	---	---
Public assistance (vendor medical payments)	524	684	844	254	336	418	270	348	427
General hospital and medical care	112	125	146	40	46	58	72	78	88
Defense Department hospital and medical care (including military dependents)	501	577	618	501	577	618	---	---	---
Maternal and child health services	233	260	313	104	123	156	129	137	157
School health	178	190	204	---	---	---	178	190	204
Veterans' hospital and medical care	---	---	---	---	---	---	---	---	---
Medical vocational rehabilitation	14	20	25	10	15	19	3	5	6
Office of Economic Opportunity	49	51	77	49	51	77	---	---	---
19-64 years									
Total	$5,194	$6,105	$6,778	$2,348	$2,902	$3,287	$2,845	$3,202	$3,488
Health insurance for the aged	---	---	---	---	---	---	---	---	---
Temporary disability insurance	54	55	58	---	---	---	54	55	58
Workmen's compensation (medical benefits)	664	735	817	14	15	17	651	720	800
Public assistance (vendor medical payments)	589	1,132	1,451	286	556	716	303	575	733
General hospital and medical care	1,858	1,911	1,955	75	118	115	1,783	1,793	1,840
Defense Department hospital and medical care (including military dependents)	888	1,022	1,095	888	1,022	1,095	---	---	---
Maternal and child health services	75	75	67	33	36	34	42	39	33
School health	---	---	---	---	---	---	---	---	---
Veterans' hospital and medical care	965	1,048	1,187	965	1,048	1,187	---	---	---
Medical vocational rehabilitation	52	80	97	40	59	72	14	20	24
Office of Economic Opportunity	49	48	50	49	48	50	---	---	---
65 years and over									
Total	$5,647	$8,150	$9,726	$4,130	$6,385	$7,718	$1,517	$1,765	$2,008
Health insurance for the aged	3,172	5,126	6,299	3,172	5,126	6,299	---	---	---
Temporary disability insurance	---	---	---	---	---	---	---	---	---
Workmen's compensation (medical benefits)	31	30	33	---	---	---	31	30	33
Public assistance (vendor medical payments)	1,270	1,765	2,126	617	868	1,052	653	898	1,075
General hospital and medical care	852	859	926	20	23	27	832	837	899
Defense Department hospital and medical care (including military dependents)	43	49	53	43	49	53	---	---	---
Maternal and child health services	---	---	---	---	---	---	---	---	---
School health	---	---	---	---	---	---	---	---	---
Veterans' hospital and medical care	272	313	278	272	313	278	---	---	---
Medical vocational rehabilitation	1	2	2	1	2	2	(1/)	1	1
Office of Economic Opportunity	5	5	7	5	5	7	---	---	---

1/ Less than 0.05.

Table 5. - Annual health care outlays under Federal programs, by program, age and income groups, fiscal year 1969

PRELIMINARY - Subject to change

[In thousands of dollars]

Agency and program	All ages			0-5			6-18			19 and over		
	Total	Indigent 1/	Nonindigent	Total	Indigent 1/	Nonindigent	Total	Indigent 1/	Nonindigent	Total	Indigent 1/	Nonindigent
Total	$12,293,207	$5,125,139	$7,671,579	$446,830	$265,056	$181,774	$847,640	$352,237	$495,103	$11,498,717	$4,507,256	$7,009,702
Department of Health, Education and Welfare	9,355,931	4,467,190	4,898,254	264,704	223,505	41,199	395,423	321,666	73,757	8,695,806	3,922,019	4,783,298
Health Services and Mental Health Administration	355,903	276,696	79,408	88,795	82,787	6,008	112,713	99,024	13,684	154,395	94,678	59,716
Comprehensive Health Planning and services	4,558	3,313	1,245	638	464	174	1,276	927	349	2,644	1,922	722
Health Services Research and Development	2,364	7,364	---	1,105	1,105	---	1,841	1,841	---	4,418	4,418	---
Mental Health	13,020	13,020	---	---	---	---	575	575	---	12,445	12,445	---
Maternal and Child Health	174,595	162,636	12,141	82,386	78,137	4,249	61,686	54,401	7,285	30,523	29,916	607
Indian Health Facilities	14,606	14,606	---	3,081	3,081	---	4,761	4,761	---	6,762	6,762	---
Social Security Administration	6,597,702	2,285,207	4,321,495	---	---	---	---	---	---	6,597,702	2,285,207	4,321,495
Federal Hospital Insurance Trust Fund	4,758,172	1,641,569	3,116,603	---	---	---	---	---	---	4,758,172	1,641,567	3,116,603
Federal Supplementary Medical Insurance Trust Fund	1,839,530	643,638	1,204,892	---	---	---	---	---	---	1,839,530	643,638	1,204,892
Social and Rehabilitation Service	2,383,226	1,890,156	493,401	174,920	139,936	34,984	281,061	221,497	59,564	1,927,245	1,529,723	398,853
Rehabilitation Services and Facilities	98,561	62,093	36,468	---	---	---	19,712	12,418	7,294	78,849	49,675	29,174
Grants to States for Public Assistance	2,284,665	1,827,732	456,933	174,920	139,936	34,984	261,349	209,079	52,270	1,848,396	1,478,717	369,679
Other: Howard University	7,952	4,183	3,769	414	207	207	1,074	565	509	6,464	3,411	3,053
Department of Defense: Military Personnel	1,598,424	---	1,598,424	139,862	---	139,862	419,586	---	419,586	1,038,976	---	1,038,976
Veterans Administration	1,374,056	522,141	851,915	---	---	---	---	---	---	1,374,056	522,141	851,915
Office of Economic Opportunity	126,006	125,356	650	41,463	41,463	---	30,420	30,420	---	54,123	54,123	---
Civil Service Commission	40,748	---	40,748	---	---	---	---	---	---	40,748	---	40,748
Department of Labor: Bureau of Employee's Compensation	16,320	---	16,320	---	---	---	---	---	---	16,320	---	16,320
Other Agencies: Appalachian Regional Development Programs	973	494	479	121	69	52	299	135	164	553	290	263
Peace Corps	6,643	---	6,643	---	---	---	---	---	---	6,643	---	6,643
Soldiers' Home	10,295	---	10,295	621	19	602	1,348	19	1,329	10,295	---	10,295
The Panama Canal	7,160	1,072	6,088	---	---	---	---	---	---	5,191	1,054	4,137
Department of Justice, Federal Prison System	8,886	8,886	---	31	---	31	297	297	---	8,589	8,589	---
Department of Transportation, Coast Guard	771	---	771	28	---	28	183	---	183	557	---	557
United States Information Agency	415	---	415	---	---	---	84	---	84	303	---	303

1/ Based on the Social Security Administration poverty index

Source: Unpublished detailed data from the Office of Management and Budget, as summarized in the "Special Analysis," Budget of the United States, 1971.

Source No. 33

TABLE 6.--Estimated health care outlays under Federal programs, by program, age and income groups, fiscal year 1972

PRELIMINARY - Subject to change

[In thousands of dollars]

Agency and Program	All ages			0-5			6-18			19 and over		
	Total	Indigent 1/	Nonindigent	Total	Indigent 1/	Nonindigent	Total	Indigent 1/	Nonindigent	Total	Indigent 1/	Nonindigent
Total	10,717,244	5,672,014	5,013,271	494,840	294,022	200,812	938,233	399,141	539,114	13,051,633	4,978,851	8,072,318
Department of Health, Education and Welfare												
Public Health and Mental Health Administration	428,509	337,748	90,841	91,217	86,401	4,877	124,427	118,964	5,461	192,685	126,381	
Health Services and...	21,942	16,800	5,137	3,072	2,156	719	5,165	4,766	1,419	12,728	9,748	
Maternal and Child Health...	1,967	1,967		592	192		987	987		2,368	2,368	
Mental Health...	14,570	14,570					812	812		13,758	13,758	
Maternal and Child Health...	187,883	135,243	12,622	80,886	76,446	4,418	42,964	55,331	7,573	46,017	13,186	
Indian Health Facilities...	13,344			4,488	4,488		7,708	7,708		10,947	10,947	
Public Health Administration...	7,537,757	2,412,083	5,125,674							7,537,757	2,412,083	5,125,674
Federal Hospital Insurance Trust Fund...	5,372,333	1,718,147	3,653,186							5,372,333	1,718,147	3,653,186
Federal Supplementary Medical Insurance Trust Fund...	2,165,424	692,936	1,472,488							2,165,424	692,936	1,472,488
Administration...	2,342,126	1,175,844	1,172,733	208,994	167,194	41,800	314,553	247,003	67,523	2,226,702	1,761,650	483,608
Rehabilitation Services and Facilities...	135,801	85,555	50,246	208,994	187,194	41,800	27,161	11,111	10,050	108,640	68,444	40,196
Grants to States for Public Assistance...	7,022,423	2,045,928	122,495				287,306	229,896	57,473	2,116,067	1,692,850	423,211
Other												
Howard University...	7,744	4,324	3,672	602	201	201	1,044	553	496	6,298	3,323	3,170
Department of Defense												
Military Personnel...	1,728,370		1,728,370	151,057		151,057	453,172		453,173	1,122,140		1,146,407
Veterans Administration...	1,539,958	585,184	954,774							1,539,958	585,184	954,774
Office of Economic Opportunity...	148,925	148,125	800	41,200	41,300		40,995	40,995		66,730	65,930	800
Civil Service Commission...	41,185		41,185							41,185		41,185
Department of Labor												
Office of Employee's Compensation...	19,975		19,975							19,975		19,975
Other Agencies												
Appalachian Regional Development Program...	3,200	1,635	1,565	460	230	170	450	450	550	1,800	955	845
...Corp...	3,363		3,363							3,363		3,363
The Panama Canal...	10,543		10,543							10,543		10,543
Department of Justice, Federal Prison system...	7,803	1,216	6,587	673	21	652	379	21	1,429	5,480	1,176	4,304
Department of Transportation, Coast Guard...	11,350	11,350	837	54	18	36				10,971	10,971	904
United States Information Agency...	411		411	28		28				300		300

1/ Based on the Social Security Administration poverty index.

Source: Unpublished detailed data from the Office of Management and Budget, as summarized in the "Special Analyses," Budget of the United States, 1971.

Source No. 33

TABLE 7 —Estimated health care outlays under Federal programs, age and income groups, fiscal year 1971   PRELIMINARY – Subject to change

[In thousands of dollars]

Agency and program	All ages Total	All ages Indigent [1]	All ages Nonindigent	0–5 Total	0–5 Indigent [1]	0–5 Nonindigent	6–18 Total	6–18 Indigent [1]	6–18 Nonindigent	19 and over Total	19 and over Indigent [1]	19 and over Nonindigent
Total..................................	$16,090,473	$6,191,925	$9,899,295	$533,580	$328,546	$205,034	$1,030,414	$479,442	$550,972	$14,526,479	$5,383,937	$9,143,289
Department of Health, Education, and Welfare	12,283,892	5,404,126	6,880,393	338,581	233,825	104,856	525,732	424,876	100,856	11,419,479	4,695,425	6,724,681
Health Services and Mental Health Adm.	452,593	353,904	98,694	101,988	94,616	7,572	137,506	120,310	17,196	213,104	139,178	73,926
Comprehensive Health Planning and Services	41,272	32,482	8,790	5,770	4,547	1,231	11,556	9,095	2,461	23,938	18,844	5,094
Health Services Research and Development	1,315	1,315	---	197	197	---	329	329	---	789	789	---
Mental Health	16,463	15,463	1,040				1,040	1,040	---	15,423	15,423	---
Maternal and Child Health	203,435	190,563	12,873	89,452	64,944	4,506	67,278	59,555	7,723	46,706	46,062	644
Indian Health Facilities	22,399	22,399	---	4,726	4,726	---	7,302	7,302	---	10,371	10,371	---
Social Security Administration	8,774,613	2,632,326	6,142,089							8,774,413	2,632,324	6,142,089
Federal Hospital Insurance Trust Fund	6,460,484	1,938,145	4,522,339							6,460,484	1,938,145	4,522,339
Federal Supplementary Medical Ins. T F	2,313,929	694,179	1,619,750							2,313,929	694,179	1,619,750
Social and Rehabilitation Service, Total	3,028,144	2,393,587	634,979	235,207	188,166	47,041	305,965	302,903	33,062	2,406,972	1,902,518	504,876
Rehabilitation Services and Facilities	172,648	108,768	63,880				34,529	21,754	12,775	138,119	87,014	51,105
Grants to States for Public Assistance	2,855,496	2,284,397	571,099	235,207	108,166	47,041	351,436	281,149	70,287	2,268,553	1,815,082	453,771
Other												
Howard University	9,337	4,911	4,631	486	243	243	1,261	643	598	7,590	4,005	3,790
Department of Defense Military Personnel	1,703,783	---	1,703,783	149,082	---	149,082	447,243	---	447,243	1,107,458	---	1,107,458
Veterans Administration	1,559,662	592,672	966,990							1,559,662	592,672	966,990
Office of Economic Opportunity	177,880	177,180	800	44,200	44,200	---	53,110	53,110	---	80,570	79,870	800
Civil Service Commission	46,523	---	46,523							46,523	46,523	46,523
Department of Labor Bureau of Employee's Compensation	22,660	---	22,660							22,660	22,660	22,660
Other Agencies Appalachian Regional Development Program	7,130	3,630	3,520	900	500	400	2,200	1,000	1,200	4,050	2,130	1,920
Peace Corps	10,059		10,059							10,059		10,059
Soldiers' Home	7,684	1,287	6,397							7,684	1,245	5,636
The Panama Canal	13,030	13,050		654	21	633	21	21		12,595	12,595	
Department of Justice, Federal Prison System	876		876				435	435				
Department of Transportation, Coast Guard	633		633							208		208
United States Information Agency	408		408	35	35					298		298

1/ Based on the Social Security poverty index.

SOURCE: Unpublished detailed data from the Office of Management and Budget, as summarized in the "Special Analysis," Budget of the United States, 1971.

APPENDIX B

Cases Served by MCH Programs of State and Local Health Departments

Table 1.--Number of mothers 1/ provided maternity medical clinic services, by new or carried over status and by residence, fiscal year 1969

	Total number of mothers	New or carried over			Residence		
		New		Carried over from previous year	Metropolitan county		Non-metropolitan county
		Number	Percent		Number	Percent	
Total 2/.........	337,000	218,000	70.1	89,900	163,000	52.3	149,000

Table 2.--Number of mothers 1/ provided maternity nursing services, dental treatment, and hospital inpatient care, fiscal year 1969

	Number of mothers 1/ provided--			Number of days of hospital inpatient care
	Maternity nursing service	Dental treatment	Hospital inpatient care	
Total 2/.........	515,000	42,200	50,400	157,000

Table 3.--Number of children provided well child conference service, by residence and age, fiscal year 1969

	Total			Age			
		Residing in--		Under 1 year		1-4 years	5-17 years
	Number	Metropolitan county	Non-metropolitan county	Total	New this year		
Total 1/..........	1,301,000	---	---	494,000	318,000	590,000	190,000

Table 4.--Number of children provided nursing service by age, fiscal year 1969

	Total	Under 1 year	1-4 years	5-17 years	18-20 years
Total............	1/ 2,326,000	580,000	704,000	894,000	42,400

Table 5.--Number of children provided hospital inpatient care, general pediatric clinic service, dental treatment, and topical fluoride applications, fiscal year 1969

	Hospital inpatient care				General pediatric clinic service	Dental treatment	Topical fluoride applications
	Premature infants		Excluding premature infants--				
	Number of infants	Number of days of care	Number of children	Number of days of care			
Total............	13,500	147,000	15,400	146,000	199,000	1,390,000	466,000

Table 6.--Number of children provided school health examination by physician and screening by other personnel, fiscal year 1969

	Children examined by physician	Children screened by other personnel		
		Visual	Audiometer testing	Dental
Total.............	1,732,000	8,141,000	4,693,000	2,164,000

Table 7.--Number of children 1/ provided immunization, including boosters and revaccinations, by type, fiscal year 1969

	Smallpox	Diphtheria	Pertussis	Tetanus	Polio	Measles
Total.............	2,010,000	3 949,000	2,582,000	4,058,000	3,038,000	1,358,000

Table 8.--Number of children provided the basic series of immunization, by age, and number receiving boosters or revaccinations, fiscal year 1969

	Total 1/	Basic series by age				Boosters or revaccinations
		Total	Under 1 year	1-4 years	5-20 years	
Smallpox	2,010,000	2/1,171,000	116,000	418,000	613,000	839,000
Tetanus immunization,	4,058,000	2/ 1,695,000	723,000	483,000	450,000	2,361,000
Pertussis immunization	2,582,000	2/ 1,372,000	656,000	455,000	226,000	1,210,000
Diphtheria immunization	3,949,000	2/1,675,000	713,000	485,000	438,000	2,273,000
Measles immunization	1,358,000	2/1,358,000	103,000	557,000	570,000	9,500
Polio immunization..	3,038,000	2/1,865,000	618,000	506,000	678,000	1,174,000

Table 14.--Number of midwives and services provided, fiscal year 1969

	Practicing midwives	Deliveries by midwives supervised by a member of the health department	Midwives enrolled in classes or institutes
Total..............	4,300	7,700	2,000

APPENDIX C

Sources of Tables and Graphs

Source No.	Page	Source
1	5	Thomas McKeown, <u>Medicine in Modern Society</u> (New York: Hafner, 1966) p. 35.
2	6	<u>Acute Conditions</u> 1961-62, Vital & Health Statistics, NCHS, Series 10, No. 1, Table 13, p. 19.
3	6	<u>Current Estimates 1968</u>, Vital & Health Statistics, NCHS, Series 10, No. 60, Table 2, p. 6.
4	8	Unpublished data, NCHS, supplied by Mr. Ronald Wilson.
5	9	<u>Current Estimates 1968</u>, op. cit., all tables.
6	10	<u>The Nation's Youth</u>, Children's Bureau publication no. 460, 1968, chart 44.
7	11	<u>Ibid.</u>, chart 43.
8	13	<u>Maternal Nutrition and the Course of Pregnancy</u>, (Washington, D. C.: National Academy of Sciences, 1970) pp. 165, 167.
9	14	<u>The Nation's Youth</u>, op. cit., chart 36.
10	14	<u>Ibid.</u>, chart 37.
11	15	<u>Indian Health Trends and Services</u>, (Washington, D. C.: DHEW-PHS, Indian Health Service, March 1969), p. 9.
12	15	<u>Ibid.</u>, p. 8.
13	16	<u>Maternal Nutrition and the Course of Pregnancy</u>, op. cit., p. 144.
14	17	<u>Supplement to Health of the Army</u>, June 1969, p. 40.
15	18	<u>Ibid.</u>

16   20   U. !. Immunization Survey 1969, NCDC,
                                  Atlanta, Ga., Feb. 1970.

17   21   Vital Statistics of the U. S. and The World
                                  Almanac, 1970.

18   21   Morbidity and Mortality, NCDC, July 4, 1970.

19   23   The Nation's Youth, op. cit., chart 40.

20   24   Ibid., chart 41.

21   25   Annual Supplement (1968) to Morbidity and
                                Mortality, NCDC, Dec. 1969, p. 13.

22   26   Joaquin Cravioto et. al., "Nutrition, Growth,
                                and Neurointegrative Development,"
                                Pediatrics, 38: No. 2, Part II, Aug. 1966,
                                p. 343.

23   27   Ibid., p. 347.

24   28   Suicide Among Youth,   by Richard H.
                                Seiden, P.H.D., M.P.H. for the National
                                Clearinghouse for Mental Health Information,
                                December 1969, p. 14.

25   29   Ibid., p. 17.

26   31   The Nation's Youth, op. cit., chart 39.

27   32   "Pregnancy Patterns Study," The Washington Post,
                                April 8, 1970, based on data from
                                Mrs. Grace Kovar, NCHS.

28   37   The Budget of the United States Government - 1971,
                                Appendix, p. 381.

29   37   1962 Budget of the United States, p. 677.

30   39   Justifications to the Senate for Fiscal 1971.

31   41   Ibid.

32   42   Per Dr. Charles W. Gish, Indiana State Board
                                of Health, "Portfolio for a Pilot Dental
                                Health Program for Children," State Secre-
                                taries Management Conference, June 1969, p. 16.

33   57-63   Unpublished tables prepared by Dorothy P. Rice
                                from data by the Office of Management and
                                Budget.

POPULATION CHANGE IN THE UNITED STATES

and

THE DEVELOPMENT OF FAMILY PLANNING SERVICES

A Discussion Paper for

The White House Conference on Children and Youth

prepared by

The Department of Health, Education, and Welfare, Office of
Population Affairs, Office of the Secretary; Carl S. Shultz, M.D.,
Coordinator; Center for Population Research, National Institute
of Child Health and Human Development: Earl E. Huyck, Ph.D.
and Arthur A. Campbell, principal authors.

PAST POPULATION GROWTH IN THE WORLD
AND IN THE UNITED STATES

Total Population

The earth's population reached its first billion by
1830, its second billion by 1930, its third billion
by 1960, is now at the 3½ billion mark, and, if the
present rate of population growth continues, may
climb to more than 7 billion by the year 2000.
Pictorially, this change can be represented as two
related cable cars--the natural increase car ascending
as the mortality car descends.

The current rate of population growth in the United
States (1.0 percent per year) is the same as that
for the U.S.S.R. and is somewhat higher than that
for Europe (0.8 percent), but is significantly lower
than that for Latin America (2.9 percent), and for
India and Africa, about 2.6 percent (WHCC Chart 2*).

After three full centuries of steady growth, the
population of the United States passed the first
100 million in 1917 and reached the second hundred
million 50 years later in 1967. Thirty years from
now we may be rubbing shoulders with an additional
100 million Americans. The total population of the
United States (including armed forces overseas) was
about 205.4 million in mid-1970--some 25.4 million
or 14.1 percent above the 1960 census figures[1]--and
may increase by 20-24 millions in the 1970's. The
Census Bureau is currently projecting the population
in a range of 266 to 321 millions by the year 2000,
but points out that the population may in fact fall
outside this range[2] (Figure 1).

---

*WHCC Chart refers to the 1970 White House Conference
on Children Chart Book, "Profiles of Children."

Past and Prospective Trends in Numbers of Children
and Youth

The proportion of the U.S. population under 25 years
of age has fluctuated between 42 and 54 percent
since 1900--declining from 54 percent in that year
to 47.5 percent in 1930 and to 41.7 percent in 1950
but rising thereafter to 44.5 percent in 1960 and to
46.5 percent in 1970. However, it is anticipated
that this proportion will decline to 43.5 percent by
1980. The proportion under age 15 has decreased
from 37.0 percent in 1950 to 31 percent in 1960, to
29 percent in 1970 and will likely continue downward
to just over one-fourth of the population in 1980.[3]
(WHCC Chart 5.) The 55 million children now under
14 years of age in the United States plus 4 million
new births each year in the 1970's means that a
total of nearly 100 million children in this decade
will pass through part or all of these stages of
development--prenatal, conception to birth, infancy,
birth to age 1, preschool age 1-5, and school age
6 to 13 (WHCC Chart 6).

As for "youth," as of mid-1969 there were 39.1 million
persons in the United States 14-24 years of age, or
an increase of 44 percent over the 27.2 million of
this age in 1960. Their proportion to the total
population increased from 15 to 19 percent. The
number of young persons of high school age 14-17
increased from 11.2 million in 1960 to 15.5 million
in 1969, and the number of persons of college age
18-21 increased from 9.4 million to 14.2 million in
the interim. The percentage of Whites 14-24 years
(19.0 percent) in 1969 was somewhat less than that
for Negroes and other races (20.7 percent).[4]

Thus, in spite of apparent improvements in the control of fertility in this country and in spite of
the declines in fertility taking place in the 1960's,
the United States has probably entered a period of

renewed population growth given impetus by a rise
in the number of young couples of childbearing age
resulting from the high fertility rates of the
period following World War II.

In the 20 years between 1965 and 1985, the number
of women at ages when births commonly occur will
rise by 58 percent. This will be the most rapid
rise in the population of childbearing age that
has occurred or will occur in the United States
during any period of comparable length in the
present century. As these large numbers of women
have their own children, the size of the child
population will rise again. An inflection point
was reached in 1969 when the number of births rose
3 percent above the number for 1968 (provisional
data).

The U.S. Census Bureau's Revised Interim Projections
(1970)[5] show a range between the highest "B" series
and the lowest "E" series (Figure 2 and Table 1).
The 0-5 Infant and pre-school population (in millions)
under the "B" series would grow from 21.7 in 1970 to
30.8 in 1980 and 44.2 in 2000, but under the "E" series
would increase from 21.3 to 22.8 and to 23.6. The
6-13 school children population would fluctuate under
"B" from 33.3 to 31.2 and to 48.7 and under "E" from
33.3 to 27.9 and 32.4.

The 14-24 youth population under "B" would increase
from 40.3 to 45.4 and to 62.0, but under "E" would
increase from 40.3 to 45.4 and then decrease to
44.6. By the end of the century the numbers may be
closer to the "E" than to the "B" series.[6] (See
also the later section on "'ZPG' and All That: The
Possibilites and Implications of a Stationary
Population".)

Of the components of population change--fertility,
mortality, and migration--mortality, which was the
primary factor from the beginning of time until it
was brought under control relatively recently, and
migration are now of secondary importance in the
United States to fluctuations in fertility.
Accordingly, mortality and migration will be considered first, but major attention will be given
to the past and prospective course of fertility.

MORTALITY

Mortality is decreasing and can go somewhat lower.
The partial control in the late 19th century of
intestinal diseases was followed by the successful
attack on the respiratory infections early in the
20th century.[7] But as control has been gained over
mortality at the perilous threshold of life and
people are living longer, death rates have risen
from the degenerative diseases, especially heart,
cancer, and stroke.

Life Expectancy

Three score and ten will be the average life expectancy for children born during the 1970's in the
United States. From 1900 to 1968 (WHCC Chart 79),
life expectancy for Whites increased from 47.6 years
to 71.1 years; that for all other races from 33.0
years to 63.9 years. There has been a major increase
in life expectancy for all races, yet the life expectancy for non-Whites lags some 30 years behind that
for Whites. For example, 63.9 years for "all other
races" in 1968 was about the level for Whites in the
late 1930's. Life expectancy is highest for White
females and lowest for males, all other races.

Infant Mortality

The risk of death in the first year is higher than
that in any other year under age 65 (WHCC Chart 86).

Accordingly, infant mortality is considered to be
a sensitive indicator of health status.

The steady fall in the level of infant mortality
in the U.S. from 140 prevailing in 1900 to the
present 20 infant deaths per 1,000 live births is
principally attributable to the reduction in just
one disease complex--the pneumonia-diarrhea complex
relating to environmental health and sanitation.
The decline in infant mortality before the advent
of antibiotics is largely attributable to public
health measures. Tuberculosis, diphtheria, and
streptococcal diseases comprise only a small part
of total infant deaths.[8]

About two-thirds of deaths under one year of age
occur in the first week of life (WHCC Chart 85).
The fact that the neonatal death rate has been
far more resistant to change than has the death
rate for infants from the first week of life to
the first birthday suggests that environmental
problems have been able to be brought under greater
control than have those problems related to genetic
background and to delivery. Nonetheless, as we
shall see, there are still significant ethnic
differences among postneonatal rates.

Internationally as of 1967, the United States
ranked 13th in infant mortality. Countries with
lower infant mortality rates tended to be clustered
in Western Europe (Netherlands, United Kingdom,
France, and Switzerland), East Germany, Scandinavia,
Japan, Australia, and New Zealand, with the lowest
rate being 12.9 for Sweden, as compared with 21.7
for the United States (WHCC Chart 81). However,
many of these countries with lower infant mortality
rates had homogeneous populations and relatively
high levels of economic and social status. Infant
mortality for "all other races" has been paralleling
the downward course of infant mortality for Whites

in the United States (WHCC Chart 80). Yet, as of
1968 when the infant mortality rate was 21.8 for
the U.S. population as a whole, that for Whites
(19.2) was only slightly more than half of that
for all other races (34.5). Thus the level of
infant mortality for all other races lags approximately 30 years behind that for the White population.

Infant mortality differentials can be indicated
geographically by regions and by socioeconomic con-
tour maps. Geographically, the South generally has
the highest infant mortality rates (WHCC Chart 82).

In large U.S. cities, high infant mortality is often
linked with low-income groups. (WHCC Chart 83).[9]
Moreover, 1966 Public Health Service data (WHCC
Chart 84) indicates that male infant mortality rates
are highest for Blacks (44.0), somewhat less for
American Indians (39.0), substantially less for
Whites (23.5), and least for Chinese and Japanese
(10-12)--or on a level with that for Sweden.

As one measure of the cost of teenage childbearing,
infants born of teenage mothers have above-average
mortality rates--130 percent higher for mothers
under age 15 and 30 percent higher for mothers 15-19
years of age as of 1960.

Maternal Mortality

As of 1941, maternal mortality rates per 100,000
live births were 266 for Whites and 678 for other
women (WHCC Chart 70). In 1961 the rates were,
respectively, 24.9 and 101.3, and in 1967, 19.5 and
69.5. Expressed in another way, maternal mortality
for non-White women in 1967 was about on a level
of that for White women in the 1940's, or lagging
a generation behind. The mother's health has much
to do with the weight at birth of the infant and
in turn is a determinant of the infant mortality
rate.

<u>Stillbirths, Neonatal Deaths, and Neurological Abnor-</u>
<u>malities</u> at age 1 year were very substantially higher
for infants with birth weights under 5½ pounds than
they were for infants weighing more. Stillbirths and
neonatal death rates for small babies were higher for
Whites than for Blacks (WHCC Chart 71).

<u>Mortality Among Preschoolers</u>

Among preschoolers (here defined as children aged 1-4
years), accidents are the leading cause of death
(WHCC Chart 110). Deaths from accidents per 100,000
preschoolers in 1967 were 28.6 for Whites and 52.0 for
other races; American Indians had particularly high
accidental death rates. Death rates from influenza
and pneumonia for other races (21.8) were three times
that for Whites (6.7)--another indicator of the impact
of environmental factors.

In sum, the U.S. lag behind a number of other nations
with respect to life expectancy and infant mortality
and the differential impact within the United States
with respect to mortality rates for the various racial
and ethnic groupings represent unfinished business on
the social and economic dockets.

MIGRATION

With the decrease in natural increase in the past few
years, immigration has assumed increasing importance (Figure 3).
Net civilian immigration accounted for 9 percent of
the average annual population increase in the 1940's,
but this percentage rose to 11 percent in the 1950's,
to 16 percent in the 1960's, and to 21 percent in
1967.[10]

Effective July 1, 1968, a limit of 170,000 was set
for immigrants of natives of countries outside the
Western Hemisphere, and the ceiling of 120,000 on

Western Hemisphere natives was placed on a first-
come, first-served basis with no limitation on the
number from any one country. Effective November 2,
1966, Cubans admitted or paroled into the United
States up to January 1, 1959, and present in the
U.S. for at least two years, may obtain permanent
residence status.[11]

From 1961 through 1968, more than 309,000 Cuban
refugees registered with the Cuban Refugee Center
in Miami, Florida and 206,000 of these had been
resettled to other areas.[12] Except for a small
group of older women, the Cuban refugees were
skilled, energetic, rapidly learned English and
necessary retraining and became absorbed into metropolitan areas throughout the United States. They
posed transitional social welfare problems but have
become significant contributors to the American
scene.*

FERTILITY

Fertility Trends in the United States

Declining fertility in the United States, rather
than being unique, was the rule for over a century.
During the 19th century the birth rate fell from a
level of about 55 births per 1,000 population in
1800 to 30 per 1,000 by 1910.

During the next three decades of the present century,
the birth rate continued to decline at an uneven
pace to levels below 20 in the 1930's. The lowest
rate recorded (in 1933 and 1936) was 18.4. Then the
birth rate began a long-term rise for the first time
in the history of the United States. The first cul-
mination of this upward trend was a peak birth rate

---

*Internal migration in considered in the section on
"Population Distribution, Mobility, and Internal
Migration" rather than here because it is not a com-
ponent of total growth of the U.S. population.

of 26.6 in 1947; the second peak of 25.3 was reached
in 1957. Since then, the birth rate has come down,
again reaching in 1966 the prewar low level of 18.4
and in 1968 reaching a new low of 17.4. In 1969
the birth rate inched upward by 3 percent to 17.7.

Changes in the birth rate are determined by changes
in the number of women of childbearing age and by
the birth rates they experienced at each age within
the reproductive span. The levels of age-specific
birth rates, in turn, are determined by two factors:
the average number of children that an age group of
women will ultimately bear by the end of the reproductive period of life (referred to as the completed
fertility rate), and the ages at which they have
these children. Analyses of age-specific birth
rates observed over the past 50 years have shown
that both of these factors, completed fertility and
age at childbirth, are important determinants of the
trend in the birth rate.

The virtually uninterrupted transition from large-
to-small families in the United States can also be
demonstrated by the decline in the total fertility
rates by 20-year intervals from 1800 to 1940--7.04;
6.73; 6.14; 5.21; 4.24; 3.56; 3.17 to 2.19. The
fertility rate thereafter rose to 3.52 in 1960.[13]

Concentration on women reaching age 20-24 at different
periods of time provides clues to the future as well
as to the past course of completed fertility (Figure 4). In
these terms, completed fertility declined from an
average of 3.6 children per woman for those women
reaching age 20-24 at the beginning of the 20th century to a low of 2.3 for those reaching this age in
1930, but subsequently increased to a probable 3.3
or 3.4 children for those reaching this age in 1955.
At the present time, it seems likely that the completed fertility rates will decline, but just how
far is uncertain (Figure 5).

Data on the timing of births show that during the 1930's women in the younger years of the reproductive span tended to delay marriage and childbearing. In the 1940's and the early 1950's they more than made up for these delays with relatively high birth rates at the older childbearing ages. At the same time, women who reached the younger childbearing ages soon after the end of World War II tended to marry and have their children earlier than had been true for women of the same ages in the 1930's. As a result of these two overlapping shifts in the timing patterns of fertility, age-specific birth rates were unusually high at both the younger and the older childbearing ages throughout the 1950's. However, this situation could not last indefinitely. The older women began to move out of the reproductive years of life in the late 1950's and early 1960's. Moreover, most of the women who were reaching the later reproductive ages (30 and over) had already borne many children in the 1950's and did not want any more during the 1960's. Consequently, age-specific birth rates at the older ages fell during the 1960's.

Between 1955 and 1965 there was an increase in the median age at first marriage for women and consequently a decline in the percent married among women under 25 years of age.[14] Females tend to marry males two years older, but a developing dearth of "older" males, as pointed out by Glick and others, is restricting marriage opportunities.[15]

There was also a trend toward somewhat later childbearing and, probably, somewhat lower completed fertility on the part of younger women during the 1960's. As a result of these trends, birth rates have tended to be low at both the older and younger ages of the reproductive span in the 1960's.

Changes in the Distribution of Children by Size of Family

Studies by universities and private foundations have shown a long-term trend toward families of moderate size (2-4 children)--from 42 percent of children in the early 1900's to 66 percent today-- and away from very large families or very small families (no children or only one). The distinct trend away from large families resulted in a substantial decline in the proportion of children who were raised in families with large numbers of brothers and sisters. Between the early 1900's and the 1930's the proportion of children born to mothers who eventually had six or more children dropped from 31 percent to 11 percent, and the proportion of "only" children rose from 18 percent to 28 percent.

Since the 1930's, however, there has been a definite trend away from the one-child family, and perhaps only one-in-ten mothers bearing children in the late 1950's and early 1960's will restrict their families to one child. Although there has been simultaneously a slight trend toward larger families, the anticipated proportion (14 percent) of recent mothers who will have six or more children will be less than half that for mothers in the early 1900's.

Decline in Higher-Order Births

Still the rapid decline, since 1960, in the probabilities of having fifth and higher-order births, gives some evidence that control of fertility in the United States has begun to improve. For example, between 1960 and 1968, the annual probability that a woman with four or more previous births would have another child declined sharply from 168 per 1,000 to 80 per 1,000. Not only was this an exceptionally

rapid fall, but the 1968 level is well below the
lowest previously recorded. During the 40 years
before 1960, this probability never went below 159
per 1,000--even during the period of relatively
depressed fertility in the 1930's. Additional data
would be needed, however, to confirm this interpretation. Even among women who have borne three
children, the annual probability of having another
child has declined to the lowest levels ever
recorded in this country. It is only among women
with no, one or two previous births that the annual
probability of having a child has remained at
moderate levels.

In summary, the general picture of fertility control in the United States is one of widespread
failure to time conception successfully and of
failure, among a substantial minority of married
couples, to limit family size to the number of
children wanted.

Fertility by Race

Fertility rates have been consistently higher for
other races than for Whites (WHCC Chart 78) but
show a generally parallel decline. In the 40-year
period 1910-1950 the average number of children
ever born to women 45-49 years of age declined
from 4.1 to 2.3 for Whites and from 5.9 to 2.7
for non-Whites.[16]

Fertility rates (births per 1,000 women 15-44 years
of age) for non-Whites as of 1965 were somewhat
lower than that for Whites as of 1957, indicating
that virtually all components of the population
are participating in the decline of fertility.
The birth rate for American Indians is considerably
higher than those for other elements of the population and has declined only slightly since 1960
(WHCC Chart 77).

According to the Current Population Survey, there
was a decrease in fertility differentials by race
between 1960 and 1969. Rates of young children
under five years of age per 1,000 women 15-49 years
of age declined by about one-fourth for Whites but
by as much as one-third for Blacks. The declines
among Blacks in non-metropolitan areas where fertility formerly was highest were larger than the
declines among either Whites or Blacks in metropolitan areas.[17]

FERTILITY CONTROL

Ends and Means

The need for, and practice of, fertility control
is not new. What is new is the expansion of the
number of people practicing family planning and in
the technology available to them.

Ohlin maintains that in most societies population
growth or stability has in an approximate fashion
been brought into conformity with economic opportunities achieved by social institutions which
adjusted fertility to the prevailing levels of
mortality, e.g., through postponement of marriage,
permanent celibacy, and taboos on sexual intercourse
at certain times. Induced abortion, infanticide,
and contraception also have a long history in most
societies. The French attitude toward family forma-
tion was summarized by the French demographer
LeVoisseur who said, "When the pere de famille has
fewer children, it is because he does not want any
more."[18]

As for the means of fertility control, coitus interruptus, abstention and abortion were in all probability the principal means by which couples reduced
the number of births. Coitus interruptus was probably

the most widely used method of preventing conception throughout Europe and remains so, contributing
significantly, for example, to the recent decline
in the birth rate in Greece from a level of around
30 in the early 1930's to 18 in 1960-62.[19]

Similarly, David points out that in Eastern Europe
and especially in Czechoslovakia, Hungary, and Yugo-
slavia, coitus interruptus remains the most widely
practiced method of conception limitation, with
younger couples favoring modern contraceptive
techniques.[20]

As for abortion, in countries where abortion has been
legalized (Japan and Eastern Europe) there have been
very high rates of abortion reported. Still there
is enough internal, indirect evidence to make it certain that in all industrialized countries abortion
has been, and remains, a major social phenomenon
which must have contributed significantly to the
drop in fertility which eventually followed upon the
reduction of mortality.

According to Miltenyi, the main motivation for legal
abortion among married women in Hungary is the number
of living children. While one-sixth of the childless
married women terminated their pregnancies by abortion (in most cases to postpone childbirth), the
ratio of abortions in pregnancies for those having
one child was more than one-half; and for those having
two children, more than three-fourths.[21]

In the United States, too, it is primarily the married woman who resorts to abortion because she "finds
herself unable to bear another child and maintain a
stable family unit," according to Dr. Edwin Gold,
Professor of Maternal and Child Health at the
University of California at Berkeley. He indicated
that in 1964 in New York City, of the 46.1 percent
of the maternal deaths resulting from criminal

abortions, 54.7 percent were of married housewives with a median age of 25.5 years and an average of 3.2 children.[22]

In the United States fertility control has been the result by and large of individual couples deciding to practice family planning in order to tailor the size of their families to the changing economic and social situation confronting them. To attain this end they use modern methods (oral contraceptives, intrauterine devices, diaphragms, foams, condoms, etc.)

The Control of Fertility in the United States

Nonetheless, one of the more severe problems associated with population growth in this country is poor control over fertility, leading to the birth of unwanted children who suffer various kinds of emotional, physical, and cultural deprivation. Some couples have more children than they want, and others report failures in delaying conception for as long a period as desired. Couples experiencing either kind of failure comprised 56 to 58 percent of the married population of reproductive age, according to estimates based on surveys conducted in 1955, 1960, and 1965. The proportion would be still higher were it not for limitation on fertility imposed by various impairments of the reproductive system.

In most cases, the more serious failure is the inability to prevent conception after a couple has had the number of children desired. On the basis of survey data, it is estimated that 15 percent of the American couples of reproductive age had experienced such "excess fertility" by 1955. By 1960 and 1965 the proportion had increased to 20-21 percent (WHCC Chart 73). However, the increases in these proportions give a misleading impression of actual trends in the ability to control fertility. Apparently one of the major reasons for this increase is

the rise in the proportion of couples who complete
their families in the early portion of the reproductive period of life and are thus exposed for
more years to the risk of having more children than
they want.

The proportion of married couples who have failed
to delay one or more conceptions as long as they
would have preferred, but have managed to avoid
having unwanted children, has varied between 37 and
41 percent in the period 1955 to 1965 (WHCC Chart 73).
Although these timing failures are generally regarded
as less serious than failures to prevent unwanted
conceptions, research undertaken by Freedman and
Coombs has shown that early childbearing and close
spacing of births impose serious obstacles on the
effort of young couples to improve their economic
positions. The burden of too many children too soon
can be so heavy that the couple never manages to
provide adequately for themselves or their children.

Abortions in the United States

A large number of unwanted pregnancies in the United
States are terminated by abortions, many of which
are illegal. WHCC Chart 76 illustrates the greater
incidence of illegal abortions, and therefore the
greater health risk, among women of Black and other
minority races. According to 1967 estimates developed
from a special survey reported by the National Institute of Child Health and Human Development and
appearing in Demography, February 1970, some 4.1
percent of women (1.6 percent among Whites and 10.3
percent among other women) indicated that they have
had an abortion within their lifetime. Nearly one-
fifth of the abortions were illegal.

Illegitimacy in the United States

High U.S. illegitimacy rates provide more evidence
of the failure to time births adequately. Over
half of this country's illegitimate births are
first births, and most of the remaining are second
or third births. Given the average American
couple's desire for two to four children, most of
the women who have illegitimate births would have
had children at some time. Therefore, most births
outside marriage cannot be regarded as "excess"
births that would not have occurred if control of
fertility were adequate, but as poorly timed births.
Between 1940 and 1957, the illegitimacy rate (illegitimate births per 1,000 unmarried women 15-44
years of age) increased threefold (from 7.1 to 21.0).
Since 1957, the rate has remained within the range
of 21-24 per 1,000. Although the illegitimacy rate
appears to have stabilized, the proportion of births
that are illegitimate has risen from 4.7 percent in
1957 to 9.7 percent in 1968. This is partly due to
the increase in the proportion of unmarried women
in the 15-49 age group and partly to the decline in
the number of legitimate births.

The number of illegitimate births by age of mother
increased steadily for all broad age groups through
1965 but thereafter showed slight decreases among
women 25 and over (WHCC Chart 91). But for younger
women there were very significant increases between
1960 and 1968--for those under 15 (from 4,600 to
7,700); for the 15-19 groups (87,100 to 158,000),
and for the 20-24 group (68,000 to 107,900). Illegitimacy rates by age would undoubtedly lessen these
increases, and reporting may have improved, but the
fact that over 7,700 females under age 15 had illegitimate live births in 1968 speaks to a cost to the
individual and to society alike.

Factors Affecting the Interval Between Marriage and Childbirth

According to estimates based on decennial censuses and on sample surveys of the U.S. Census Bureau, fertility rates of women who married between 1940 and 1964 showed that women who did not graduate from high school and go on to college, who married before age 22, or were wives of blue-collar husbands were more likely than other women to have borne their first child by the end of their first year of marriage.[23]

"Shotgun" Marriages in the United States

The 1964-66 National Natality Survey (NNS), the first attempt to obtain estimates for the United States based on a sample of all births registered in the United States, found that 22 percent of legitimate first births occurred to women who had been married less than eight months.[24]

The proportion of women who were married for the first time and had their first births less than eight months after marriage decreased steadily with advancing age--from 38 percent (for women under age 18) to 25 percent (18-19 year olds) to 16 percent (20-21 year olds) to 12 percent (22-24 age group) and down to 6 percent for those 25 years old or older.

Women of other races were younger than White women both at the time of the marriage and at the age of childbearing--26 percent of women of other races as compared to 19 percent of White women had married before their 18th birthday, and 43 percent of women of other races as compared to 32 percent of White women were under age 20 at the time of birth.

Among married women having their first child, 20 percent of White women and 42 percent of women of other races were pregnant at the time of their first marriage.

By level of education, the interval between first marriage and first birth was shorter for married women with one to three years of high school education than for married women at any other level of educational attainment. Approximately 58 percent of this group were under age 18 at marriage and some 69 percent were under age 20 at first birth. Since most U.S. children are about 18 when they graduate from high school, it is likely that a majority of the mothers with one to three years in high school dropped out and married because of pregnancy.

Taking into account both illegitimacy and premarital conceptions, an estimated 33 percent of first births were conceived outside marriage, and of these 45 percent were illegitimate and 55 percent were legitimate. Among White women 27 percent of the first births were premarital conceptions and among other women 68 percent.

Fertility Control and Education

Failure to control fertility successfully is found among all socioeconomic groups in the population, but is more prevalent among those with less education and lower income. For example, in a survey conducted in 1960 among White wives in the 18-39 year age range, 32 percent of those with less than a high school education--as compared with only 11 percent of college-educated wives--reported that they had not wanted another child at the time of their last conception.[25]

By and large the lengthening of the period of education delays the age at marriage and the birth of the first child. Moreover, a considerable body of literature points out the inverse relationship between level of education and fertility. The Census Bureau's release on Educational Attainment, March 1969, for example, attests to the increasing

percentage of the population, age group by age group
from the oldest (75 years and over) to the youngest
(20-21 year olds), who have completed four years of
high school and one year of college or more[26]
(Figure 6).

In fact, most of the Nation's youth are enrolled in
school or have at least completed high school. In
October 1968 some 58 percent of 14-24 year olds
were enrolled in school--almost all those of high
school ages, about one-half of the 18-19 years, and
one-fifth of those 20-24 years old. Moreover, there
were 6.8 million students in college in the Fall of
1968--an increase of 46 percent over those enrolled
in 1964. In the interim, Black enrollment increased
by 85 percent to comprise 6 percent of total college
enrollment.[27]

Focusing on the 25-29 year olds, the youngest age
group beyond the children and youth age group as
defined for this conference, the median number of
school years completed increased from 10.3 in 1940
to 12.1 in 1950, to 12.3 in 1960, and 12.6 in 1969.[28]

In recent years the period of education has been
lengthened for increasing proportions of females as
well as males, Negroes as well as Whites. For
example, between 1966 and 1969 the percentage of
Black males 25-29 years of age who had completed
high school rose from 49 to 60 percent, and of
Black females from 47 to 52 percent. During this
same period the comparable percentage of White
males rose from 73 to 78 percent and that of White
females from 74 to 77 percent.[29]

Between 1960 and 1969 in the 25-29 age group, the
percentage of Whites completing college rose from
11.8 to 17.0 percent, and that for Blacks (while
not strictly comparable in that "other races" were
included in 1960) rose from 5.4 to 6.7 percent.[30]

If the Growth of American Family studies in 1955,
1960, and 1965 are any guide, the lengthening of
education and the availability of educational opportunities for Blacks and "other races" will be a
powerful stimulus to decreasing their fertility and
lessening the differential with White fertility.

As for sanctioned exposure to childbearing during
the educational process, as of 1968 only 6.1 percent
of persons of high school or college age (16-24)
were enrolled in high school or college, married
and living with spouse.[31]

The Low-Education, High-Fertility, Poverty Cycle Evident in Case Studies

Preschool and school-age children are disproportionately represented in poverty areas. Whereas
about 36 percent of the general population is under
age 18, one-fifth of poor persons residing in poverty
areas in 1968 were of preschool age and another
third were children of school age 6-17 years.[32]

The Director of the Illinois Public Aid Association
told the Gruening Committee in 1965 of children
dropping out of school at age 13, 14, or 15: "Caseworkers tell time and again that what happens is
that this boy or girl will come from a family of
five or six and reach the point where they feel they
no longer are getting any individual attention from
their mother...this 14 or 15 or 16 year old feels
no one is interested in him and as a result a frame
of mind occurs in which this individual leaves home
ill-equipped to go into the world. Eventually
another family is started and you have a repetition
of the cycle."[33]

Nor does attempted retraining of welfare mothers
necessarily work out. According to the same Director,
"We will enroll a mother in a course for practical

nursing /but/...one of the major reasons for termi-
nating these courses has been pregnancies...they
have informed the caseworkers of their very strong
desire not to have more children but it happens
nonetheless...an unwanted pregnancy playing a major
role and upsetting plans."[34]

Another study, based on 1966 data, showed that the
fertility rate (births per 1,000 women 15-44 years
of age) for women included in the poor and near-
poor populations (according to criteria developed
by the Social Security Administration) was 55 percent
above that for women not living in poverty. In
poverty areas in 1968 the average number of children
was consistently higher for poor families than for
families above the poverty level, regardless of
race and regardless of whether a male or a female
headed the family unit. The average number of
persons per poor family was 3.9 among Whites and
4.8 for Black and other races. Moreover, female-
headed families had more children per family than
did male-headed families.[35]

The Director of the Illinois Public Aid Commission
has cited cases indicative of the pattern in public
aid families in Illinois--"First of all we find
desertion as a prime cause...a couple is married,
they have a child or two or three, and the income
is sufficient to take care of day-to-day expenses,
but then the fourth or fifth or the sixth child
comes along and it taxes the individual's ability
to pay the bills. There may be a little nagging
and some differences of opinion about where the
money is coming from and how much is needed. The
next thing we know the husband is gone and the wife
and the five or six children have applied for public
aid. In another area we have been particularly
concerned about younger mothers 18-22...who have
not been married, have had a child or two; ...we
have found over and over again the pattern repeating
itself...."[36]

Yet some women in poverty have realized their
plight and sought assistance through family planning clinics. For example, women participated in
the Mechlenberg, North Carolina Clinic because,
as they said, "We knew that we could not support
more than one or two children but we did not know
how to stop producing children." The persons
responsible for that clinic told the Gruening
Committee that "A great many of these women have
seen tensions grow as the number of children grew
beyond the ability of the family to support these
children. Unfortunately many of these unwanted
children were children who were rejected outright.
There is no question about it: unwanted and
rejected children constitute a very serious social
menace in our society today...."[37]

Sex Education: Rational Response to the New-and-
Now Sexuality

In his preface to Lee Rainwater's "And the Poor
Get Children," published in 1960,[38] J. Mayone Stycos
scored the little attention that had been given to
the gathering of data in the sexual sphere. Stycos
pointed out that the Indianapolis study, while
limited to a sample of urban, native, White Protestant
women with at least 8 years of education, nonetheless
indicated that "social class proved to be the most
powerful predictor of family planning behavior."
He emphasized that the Indianapolis questionnaire
included only one small question on attitudes toward
sexual relations and nothing on the actual sexual
relations. Although interviewers could not directly
ask questions on contraceptives, respondents were
willing to talk more freely about sexual matters
than about family income.

The Rainwater sample survey, limited to 46 men and
50 women, pointed to the abysmally low level of
sexual knowledge: "Quite a few women /before marriage/

...did not know that...conception comes about as
a result of sexual intercourse" and further that
the degree of current misinformation concerning
the processes of fertilization is startling indeed."
The woman in the Rainwater sample who remarked,
"The doctor told me all about that stuff but I was
too ashamed to listen," indicates the long way that
has to be traversed to communicate sexual knowledge.
Stycos pointed out, that his own study on "Family
and Fertility in Puerto Rico" produced strikingly
similar findings regarding attitudes toward, and
knowledge of, sex.

But in the 1960's a new sexual awareness developed
to the point where now both back and front views
of the human anatomy are exposed in the Lincoln
Memorial reflecting pool before a large crowd in
the Nation's capital; New York stage and road shows,
and "X" rated movies, etc., run the gamut of exposure of the human body to simulation of sexual acts.
This is not to argue that this is all to the good,
but rather that most social phenomena go to extremes
before they come to strike a balance.

At the same time that there were remarkably swift
changes in attitudes toward sexuality and reporting
on sex attitudes and behavior, there has been a
renascence of interest--pro and con--in sex education. There have been sexual education courses in
some school systems in the United States for decades,
but these have recently encountered strong reaction
from groups who have also fought water flouridation
and other beneficial measures. Yet more sex education is needed, graded according to educational
level and tastefully presented from the ethical as
well as biological point of view. In this connection
the United States may learn from the experience of
some other countries in Western and Eastern Europe[39]
and in Central and South America who are developing
courses in sex education in various sociological and

ideological ambientes. In recent years requests
from foreign governments for family planning assistance from the United States stimulated the development of U.S. policies toward population and family
planning in this country as well as abroad--so a
precedent exists.

If fertility, mortality, and migration are the
determinants of how many people reside in the United
States, social mobility and internal migration indicate where they reside. Indeed "freneticism"--
seemingly endless movement--is one outward characteristic of the American way of life.

POPULATION DISTRIBUTION,
MOBILITY AND INTERNAL MIGRATION

Concentration of U.S. Population

The U.S. population is highly concentrated, with
nine States containing 20 percent of the land area
(California, New York, Pennsylvania, Texas, Illinois,
Ohio, Michigan, New Jersey, and Florida) having over
half the total population, half the children under
5 years of age, and half of those age 5-17 years
(WHCC Chart 8).

Figure 7 shows the percentage changes in the population of States, 1960-1968, a period in which the
population generally continued moving from the center
of country to the borders and coasts. California,
Nevada, Arizona, and Florida, along with Alaska and
Hawaii, grew by 20 percent or more.[40] Washington,
Utah, Colorado, Texas, Georgia, the mid-Atlantic
States, Connecticut, and New Hampshire grew from
15-20 percent. Oregon, Oklahoma, Arkansas, Tennessee,
the Carolinas, some of the deep South and Great Lakes
States, New York and Vermont increased by 7.5-15
percent. Minnesota, Wisconsin, New Mexico, and

Idaho plus a central swath of States (Kansas,
Missouri, Kentucky, Pennsylvania, Massachusetts,
and Rhode Island) grew less rapidly (3.5-7.5 percent). The remaining States (Main, West Virginia,
the Dakotas, Nebraska, Iowa, Montana, and Wyoming)
increased at less than 3.4 percent or suffered
actual population losses.

Between the 1960 Census and mid-1968, California,
now the most populous State, increased its population by nearly 3.5 million while Texas, New York,
New Jersey, and Florida had increases exceeding
one million each. The overall population growth
in these five States amounted to 8.5 million, or
more than 40 percent of the total growth in the
period.

Growth was not uniform throughout the period 1960-
1968, and 1965 marked a transitional point in migration patterns. The Nation's birth rate, which had
been gradually declining since 1957, dropped sharply
between 1964 and 1965 and more gradually thereafter.
Moreover, the sharply increased military commitment
in Viet Nam since 1965 resulted in large shifts of
civilians into the military and of Armed Forces
overseas.

These shifts may have effected some change in the
pattern of net interstate migration. The rate of
natural increase declined at least 3 per 1,000
between 1960-1965 and 1965-1968 in every State, but
even more in the less industrialized States which
historically have had the highest birth rates, e.g.,
from 18 to 12 per 1,000 in the eight States comprising the mountain division. Florida's civilian
in-migration remained high throughout the decade,
but California's slowed, and many of the other fast
growing States (Nevada, Arizona, Connecticut, New
Jersey and Maryland) experienced decided reductions
in immigration. At the same time net out-migration

slackened from Pennsylvania, Iowa, and West Virginia,
which heretofore had consistently heavy net out-
migration.

The changing concentrations and fluctuations of a
few large-scale industries had an impact on the
migration balances of a few States such as Washington
and Vermont.

Mobility and Internal Migration

One-fifth of the population one year of age and
over--some 36 million persons--moved during the
twelve-month period ending March 1969.[41] The annual
variation in the percentage of movers has been small,
ranging between 18.3 and 21.0 percent since 1948
(Figure 8). The Bureau of the Census includes among
"movers" all those moving to another house and considers "migrants" as those moving to a different
county or to another State.

Here we are focusing on migration between States
because of the greater likelihood that institutional
changes, legal and other patterns relating to children
and youth will be affected by long-distance moves
than by short moves. For at least two decades,
3.1-3.6 percent of the population has moved across
State lines each year. Whites have been more prone
to migrate (3.1-3.8 percent) than have "Negroes and
others" (1.7-3.0 percent). Sharper decreases for
"Negroes and others" than for Whites in the recession
years 1954-1956 and 1958-1960 and sharper rebounds
in successive years suggest that migration for
"Negroes and others" is more responsive to fluctuations in the business cycle--which fits with other
information that "Negroes and others" are the last
to be hired in an economic upswing and the first to
be released in an economic downswing. It is also
consistent with Kuznets' earlier determination of
the relationship between the ebb and flow of immigration

into the United States and business cycles here.
Moreover, the proportion of the population migrating
between non-contiguous States has been greater over
the period 1958-1969 (1.9-2.4 percent) than has that
for contiguous States (1.0-1.3 percent). Relatively
more White than "Negroes and others" have migrated
both between contiguous States (2.0-2.6 percent vs.
1.2-1.9 percent).

Finally, data for 1968-69 splitting out the "Negro
and other" group indicate that the "other" ethnic
group has greater migration propensity than has the
Negro group both between contiguous States (1.3 vs.
0.8 percent) and non-contiguous States (2.9 vs. 1.8
percent).

The moving van is not only a fact of American life;
it is also a symbol of the flexibility and adapta-
bility required of individuals (children and youth
as well as adults) and of economic and social institutions involved in the areas of out-migration and
of in-migration.

Urbanization and Suburbanization

The migration flows in the United States have moved
toward the urbs, sub-urbs, and ex-urbs. The metropolitan areas have been about as efficient as
blotting paper in absorbing these flows--the socioeconomic tissue has been weakened when the flow has
been too great.

Over 70 percent of the U.S. population now live in
urban areas; over 60 percent of children under 14
years of age live in these areas, and less than
5 percent of all children live on farms (WHCC Chart 9).

Metropolitan population growth was almost 3½ times
as fast growth in non-metropolitan areas in the 1950's
and somewhat more than 1½ times as fast in the 1960's.

Three-quarters of the 22 million increase in the
population of the U.S. between 1960 and 1969, or
about 16 million persons, was added to metropolitan
areas. Virtually this entire increase occurred in
the suburban areas whereas the population in central
cities changed very little. Both in the 1950's and
the 1960's suburban growth greatly exceeded that of
central cities. Growth rates for the cities, which
were very low in the 1950's (1.0 percent per year)
were even lower in the 1960's (0.1 percent annually).[42]

The Report of the National Goals Research Staff
states:

> Assuming that the trend continues unabated,
> most of the U.S. population growth over the
> next few decades will be concentrated in the
> 12 largest urban regions (Figure 9). These
> twelve metropolitan areas, occupying one-
> tenth the land area, will contain over 70
> percent of the population. Moreover, at
> least 50 percent of the total population will
> be found in three great metropolitan belts:
> Boston-Washington, Chicago-Pittsburgh, San
> Francisco-San Diego. These three centers
> will include an overwhelming proportion of
> the most technologically advanced and the
> most prosperous and creative elements of this
> society.
>
> The continued mechanization of farms will
> lead to a further decline in the use of
> agricultural labor, hence some further
> migration from farms to cities is expected.
> On this basis, the current farm population
> of 10 million, about 5 percent of the total
> population, may drop to 6 million, or only
> 2 percent of the total, by the year 2000.[43]

The Report continues:

> In recent years practically all the growth
> in the metropolitan areas has occurred in
> the suburban rings. Since 1960 the central
> cities as a whole grew about only one per-
> cent--the suburban rings, by 28 percent;...
> the balance has shifted and today more than
> half the people in our metropolitan areas
> live outside the central cities. At the
> same time, rural America--our small cities,
> towns, and farms--has not only exported
> many of its poor to the Central cities,
> but has lost many of its young and able
> bodied...(with the result that there has
> been stagnation and a lack of economic oppor-
> tunity. Rural America now holds only about
> one-third of the total population but contains
> about half the Nation's poor.[44]

Moreover, there have been institution-shaking changes
in the ethnic compostion of the urban areas (Figure
10). The proportion of Whites living in urban areas
increased from 64 percent in 1950 to 70 percent in
1960 and 73 percent in 1970. But the proportion of
Negroes living in these areas has become even more
concentrated during these past two decades, rising
from 62 percent in 1950 to 73 percent in 1960 and to
79 percent in 1970 (WHCC Chart 9). (Even the traditionally rural American Indian is becoming more
urbanized. Whereas prior to 1940 less than one-in-
ten were living in urban areas, by 1960, 28 percent
and by 1970, 35 percent were living there.)[45]

Between 1960 and 1969 the White population in central
cities declined by about 2 million persons[46]--only
adolescents, young adults and the elderly increased
in number. But the White population living in metropolitan areas outside central cities grew by 14 million
in the interim. In the same period 75 percent of the

$3\frac{1}{2}$ million total increase in the number of Negroes occurred in central cities--and three-quarters of this central city increase took place in the population under 25 years of age.

Thus by 1969 only 26 percent of the White population lived in central cities while 38 percent lived in metropolitan rings and 36 percent lived in non-metropolitan areas. By contrast, 55 percent of the Negro population was concentrated in central cities and only 15 percent lived in metropolitan rings; 30 percent lived elsewhere[47] (Figure 11).

As a consequence of these compositional population shifts, the Report of the National Goals Research Staff asserts:

> There may be serious problems of over population and under population in various areas of the United States.... Population shifts of the last two decades have had very detrimental effects on many rural areas while simultaneously greatly aggravating urban problems; much of urban poverty is rural poverty recently transplanted. The great migration of the middle class and of jobs in the central city to the suburbs during the last decade has further aggravated the problems of the city, the poor, and of the Blacks....[48]

The Report goes on to say:

> A most serious aspect of these problems will be the growing inability of the central cities to provide jobs for their residents. Continued migration of the Negro population to central cities will add fuel to already incendiary conditions in central cities ghettos.... Both the National Governors'

conference and the National League of
Cities in their 1969 meetings called
for a more even distribution of population and the provision of social and
economic opportunity for all persons.

As to what can be done, the Report suggests that:

The trends toward megalopolis in some
areas and under population in others
are reversible,...but realization of a
better future will probably require a
coordinated national strategy for
balanced population distribution. The
Federal Government can provide leadership in developing any such strategy,
but public and private institutions
across the country will need to participate in both planning and implementation.[49]

TOWARD TOMORROW AND THE 21ST CENTURY

"ZPG" and All That: The Possibilities and Implications of a Stationary Population

Projections of the population in the United States
by age and sex (interim revisions) 1970-2020 for
regular series B, C, D and E use identical assumptions of mortality and immigration and differ only
according to the fertility assumptions involved.[50]

Whereas today's childbearing families may ultimately
have completed families of perhaps 3.3 children,
the Census Bureau projections assume that women now
starting their childbearing will on the average bear
3.10, 2.78, 2.45, and 2.11 children under the series
B, C, D and E, respectively, during their lifetime.
A completed fertility rate of 2.11 children per woman
is the value needed for the population to exactly

replace itself after the age structure has stabilized. By the year 2000 the total population
projected might range from 321 million for series
B down to 266 million for series E--but of course
the actual population may fall outside this range.

Making the further assumption of "no immigration,"
the Census Bureau has developed a series "X" projection (Figure 12 and Table 2) showing the effect
of the gradual movement toward a stationary--or
levelling off of--population of about 276 million
by 2037. Even so there would be a growth of population in the interim of some 71 million people
or by about one-third the present size of the
population. At that point the crude birth and
death rates would be on the order of 13 per thousand
per year as against today's 18 and 10 respectively.[51]
The median age would be 37.3 years as compared with
27.7 for the present population, and only 20 percent
of the population would be under 15 years of age as
compared with 29 percent today.

Family Size: Problem for the Middle-Income as well as the Low-Income Family

Enke has pointed out:

> What each family wants may not be best for
> all families collectively...each family in
> deciding how many children it will have
> quite reasonably supposes that its decision
> will not affect similar decisions of other
> couples. Each couple therefore assumes
> many things as data that would not be 'given'
> if all other couples were equally fertile...
> family size has long been considered a
> private matter and insofar as each imple-
> ments its own calculations it properly
> assumes that its decisions do not alter
> other couples' decisions, but the aggregate

outcome of such independent decision making
is often such as to affect everyone....[52]

The Report of the National Goals Research Staff
points out that:

> Much more than half the population increase
> is contributed by families that are not poor
> and who regularly practice contraception.
> Although unwanted births pose a significant
> problem, middle class families desire more
> children per family than the average 2.2
> /per ever-married woman/ needed for replace-
> ment, thus, the wanted child is seen as a
> major problem as well as the unwanted child.[53]

In the Gruening Hearings, William Vogt, then Secretary of the Conservation Foundation, stated:

> It is time to substitute biophysical criteria
> for the economic. After all, the millionaire's
> family of 8 children--which he can well 'afford'--
> occupies more space, consumes more raw materials--
> thus helping to exacerbate our balance of pay-
> ments problem--and pollutes both air and water
> more than four times the rate of the school-
> teacher with two children who has a lower
> material living standard.[54]

Vogt went on to say that:

> Much of the social pathology of our cities,
> such as broken homes, riots, dope addiction,
> environmental destruction, and irresponsible
> reproduction seems to grow largely out of
> human densities...to bring in food, carry
> waste away, house, educate, clothe, employ,
> and provide health, exercise and recreation
> for such a vast concentration of human beings
> requires an enormous expenditure per capita.

New York spends hundreds of millions of
dollars--but not nearly enough to provide
anything like a decent living for these
piled-up masses. I doubt if Calcutta
equals this crowding.[55]

Economic Implications of Population Change Moving Toward a Stationary Population

The addage that the past has shaped the present
and the present is shaping the future is pertinent
in considering the interplay between population
change and economic change. Significant patterns
relate to fluctuations in number of labor force
entrants and to the economic implications of a stationary population.

For an earlier America, Kuznets found that major
fluctuations in immigration typically accounted
for the greatest part of total population change.
He then linked these fluctuations to corresponding
swings in the rate of development of the U.S.
economy and suggested that immigration movements
responded to swings in the demand for labor in
the United States.[56]

For the post-World War II period Easterlin found
that there was again an interplay between demographic
and economic forces--but this time fertility rather
than immigration was the yeasty ingredient. He
determined that the unprecedented concurrence of
three circumstances--a Kuznets type expansion
economy, restricted immigration, and a low rate
of labor force entry from the native population
resulting from depressed fertility in the 1930's--
created an exceptional job market for those in
family-forming ages and thereby drastically accelerated their childbearing. A concurrent boom in
agricultural conditions evoked a similar fertility
response on the part of the rural white population.[57]

The converse of the Easterlin hypothesis is that
when the children born during the baby boom became
old enough to enter the labor force, the supply-
demand picture would be relatively less favorable
for them, and fertility would decline. A 1966

research paper presented evidence supporting this
hypothesis. Fertility did decline during the 1960's,
and the economic donditions of young people did
not improve so rapidly as those for older members
of the labor force.[58]

Children and youth coming of age in 1970 face a
buyer's market--a very different labor force demand
situation from what their older brothers and sisters experienced.

Governmental Population Policies Are Not New But Are Evolving

The National Goals' Report points out that "Consciously
or not, the United States has had a population policy
from a relatively early date."[59] Governmental policies
included the provision of free or cheap land, the
advocacy and later restriction of immigration, and
very recently the evolution of a gradual public
policy regarding birth control.

With respect to migration policies, the Report maintains that during "the first hundred years of the
nation, "the Government dispersed population west-
ward," and once the continent was spanned, continued
to encourage regional economic development, e.g.,
through the TVA and other area projects, through
Regional Development Act and the "depressed areas"
legislation of the 1960's. More numbrous are the
implicit policies that have influenced economic
development and population settlement, including
such factors as FHS and VA mortage insurance, the
interstate highway system, tax policies, the
awarding of defense contracts, agricultural research
and support programs--all of which collectively
make an impact "which may not be desirable from
the standpoint of distribution of population and
economic opportunity."[60]

Individuals and individual enterprises have stimulated or helped to implement these Governmental
policies. The last White House Conference of Children
and Youth met shortly after President Eisenhower
contended that birth control is "not our business."

But in the past decade there has been substantial
change, if not a 180-degree change, from that
position. Subsequent platforms and Presidents
of both political parties have come out more strongly
in favor of family planning, citing the staggering
magnitude of the population problem throughout
the world, the need to provide family planning
services to hundreds of thousands of disadvantaged
women and to be concerned over our natural resources
and the quality of our environment in the attempt
to cope with the provision of health and social
services to the next hundred million Americans.

The year 1968 may have marked a low point in the
U.S. birth rate and 1969, an inflection point with
a slightly higher birth rate, but the large numbers
of postwar babies now coming of marketplace - and
marriage-age will generate more births and raise
the crude birth rate even though the age-specific
fertility rate may not increase and in fact may
decrease. Thus there are long term (15-20 year)
wave patterns of reproductive-age women, and the
amplitude of the wave will diminish and become
diffused over time but will have continuing
repercussions on the economy.

As we have seen earlier, the Census Bureau has
demonstrated that we may not reach a stationary
population until 2037--or some 70 years hence.
What then would be the economic implications of
a stationary population?

The Rrench in particular in the 1930's were appre-
hensive over the economic impact of a declining
population--but the United States was also concerned,
and reputable U.S. demographers were signalling
the possibility of a population of 151-185 million
by 1975 with a moderate fertility-control mortality
projection of 175 million by the year 2000 and a
declining population thereafter. The other
fertility-high mortality projection found a population of 151 million by 1970 and subsequent decline.[61]
The best-laid projections may be off the mark by
a million.

So we find Enke debating with those who argue that
a stationary population is "defeatist, even un-
American." He stresses that "in terms of a demographic, economic model, the more slowly population
grows the more capital can be accumulated per member
of the labor force." He points out that there would
be a change in the composition of GNP. With a smaller
proportion of the population being children and youth,
there would be less need for goods and services for
them, but there would be an increase in semi-luxury
goods and in items for the aging and the aged. The
economic consequences of a zero growth population are
desirable on balance even though certain special
minority interests would not benefit."[62]

Population as a Factor in the "Quality of the Environment

Numerous "ZPG" (Zero Population Growth) chapters in the
United States underscore The National Goals' Research
Staff's contention in A Report Toward Balanced Growth:
Quantity With Quality, (July 4, 1970), that "There is a
widespread concern that our own population has been
growing and will probably continue to grow at a rate
that threatens to produce acute social, educational,
economic, and environmental problems."[63]

The Report emphasizes that there are no objective criteria for arriving at an "optimum population" for a given
area at a given time. Rather the question of whether
this country has a population problem is related to
"the quality and safety of our physical and social surroundings. ...The criteria for judging the population
problem in the United States, then, is in terms of its
effect on the quality of life--the kind of life one can
lead in terms of health, education, housing, work, play,
and personal freedom on the one hand and resource utilization on the other. ...The very fact that we have the
world's highest material level of living obscures the
dangers inherent in rapid growth and at the same time
exacerbates many of the difficulties such growth entails."[64]

With the increasing shoulder-rubbing, tension-inducing
density of population in our cities, government is being
increasingly called upon to share in the management of
the near-unmanageable.

President Nixon, in the first Presidential Message to
Congress on "Problems of Population Growth," July 18,
1969, stressed that:

> This population growth will produce serious chal-
> lenges for our society...We have...had to accomplish
> in a very few decades an adjustment to population
> growth which once spread over centuries...The great
> majority of the next hundred million Americans will
> be born to families which looked forward to their
> birth and are prepared to love them and care for
> them as they grow up. The critical issue is whether
> social institutions will also plan for their arrival
> and be able to accommodate them in a humane and
> intelligent way. We can be sure that society will
> not be ready for this growth unless it begins its
> planning immediately....[65]

President Nixon proceeded to raise several questions
regarding living space, natural resources and quality of
the environment, education, health care, transportation,
etc. when "many of our institutions are already under
tremendous strain as they try to respond to the demands
of 1969." He emphasized that:

> All of these questions must now be asked and answered
> with a new sense of urgency. The answers cannot be
> given by government alone, nor can government alone
> turn the answers into programs and policies. I
> believe, however, that the Federal Government does
> have a special responsibility for defining these
> problems and for stimulating thoughtful responses....[66]

Toward this end, President Nixon proposed the creation
of a Commission on Population Growth and the American
Future, which was subsequently established by Congress
in March 1970.

THE DEVELOPMENT OF FAMILY PLANNING SERVICES

The Federal Government has supported the provision of family planning
services for over three decades, but it has only been within the
last five years that the support has been a significant factor in
extending the availability of services to the medically indigent.
Before the mid-"sixties" Federal involvement was largely clandestine.
It was only following statements of President Johnson and Secretary
Gardner of Health, Education and Welfare that family planning became an
established segment of Federally supported health services. Since
that time there has been a rapid expansion of Federal effort in
support of family planning services and research into improved methods
of contraception.

Until the middle of the last decade the stimulation and the leadership in the development of family planning education and services
was through the efforts of private individuals and organizations.
Even professional societies were slow to recognize the importance
of the problem and to become involved in the dissemination of information and the provision of services.

In 1916, Mrs. Margaret Sanger opened in Brooklyn, New York, the
first family planning clinic in the United States. With this as
a beginning, birth control leagues were shortly started in several
other U.S. cities, consolidating themselves under the name of the
National Birth Control League. This organization soon changed its
name to the American Birth Control League (ABCL). In 1923, the
Clinical Research Bureau of the ABCL was opened in New York City.
By 1929, almost 10,000 persons annually were seeking contraceptive
services from the Bureau. In 1931, a resolution supporting the
provision of family planning services was passed by the Public Health
Committee of the New York Academy of Medicine. Radio censorship
of the topic of family planning ended in 1935 and this led to the
beginning of the discussion of family planning in mass communication
media. In 1941, the ABCL changed its name to the Planned Parenthood
Federation of America, and following a subsequent merger is now
known as Planned Parenthood-World Population. This organization
through its affiliates has developed a nationwide network of family
planning service clinics. [67]

State and local health agencies, particularly in the South, from
the mid-thirties onward began to include birth control services
among the other public health preventive services which they offered.

Federal Support

The first Federal support for local family planning services was
made available under the maternal and child health formula grants

to States established under the Social Security Act of 1935. Funds
became available to the States in 1936. Authorizations for this
program have been increased by the Congress from time to time, most
recently in 1967.

The Social Security Act Amendments of 1963 set up a 5-year program
of project grants to pay up to 75 per cent of the cost of comprehensive health care to mothers and infants in low-income areas
where health hazards are higher. Family planning services are
regarded as an essential ingredient of the comprehensive maternity
and infant care projects. The authorization for the maternity and
infant care project grants was extended by the 1967 amendments.
Family planning services were provided to 53,439 women in 1966,
the first year such services were reported, and to 86,500 women
in 1969, the most recent year for which figures are available.
In 1963, the year in which the program was established, the infant
mortality rate was 25.2 per thousand live births. In the most recent
year, 1969, for which figures are available, the infant mortality
rate (provisional) was 20.7 per thousand live births, a reduction
of almost 18 per cent. Through Maternity and Infant Care project
grants and maternal and child health formula grants over 480,000
women received family planning services during fiscal year 1969.

The Social Security Act Amendments of 1967 established for the
first time categorical grants for family planning services. These
grants could be made to any State health agency, with the consent
of such agency, to the health agency of any political subdivision
of the State, and to any other public or nonprofit private agency,
institution, or organization to pay not to exceed 75 per cent of
the cost of the project. Not less than 6 per cent of the amount
appropriated under Title V of the Social Security Act shall be
available for family planning services. Funds became available
for this program during fiscal year 1969, and during that fiscal
year 79 projects in 41 States had been approved with an obligation
of almost $12 million. These projects were continued through fiscal
year 1970 (one of the projects was split for administrative reasons)
and 51 new projects were funded, for a total of 131 projects in
43 States and three jurisdictions supported through an obligation
of $22.8 million, $15.5 million for continuations and $7.2 million
for new projects. Information is not yet available as to how many
women received services through these projects. For fiscal year
1971, $33.5 million has been requested for this family planning
services project grant program. An additional $17.8 million has
been requested for family planning services for fiscal year 1971
under the other Title V programs.

Under the Economic Opportunity Act of 1964 the first family planning project was funded in fiscal year 1965. The 1967 amendments to the Economic Opportunity Act established family planning as a special emphasis program. During FY 1969 OEO expended $13.8 million; has available in FY 1970 $22.0 million; and has requested $24.0 million for fiscal year 1971 for family planning services projects. In 1969 there were 244 funded projects in 42 States and Puerto Rico designed to serve 350,000 women. In fiscal year 1970 over 250 projects were supported.

Unmet Need

A recent study financed by OEO indicated that 1,800 out of approximately 3,000 counties in the U.S. offered no family planning services whatsoever, and that 90% of approximately 4,000 non-profit general care hospitals in the U.S. in which most low-income mothers deliver babies, offer no family planning programs at all.[68]

These statistics indicate a substantial lack of subsidized family planning services. Other studies have shown the severe medical, social and economic consequences which uncontrolled fertility in an already problem-ridden living environment engenders. These consequences include high infant and maternal mortality rates which contribute to the U.S. ranking 13th in the world in rates of infant mortality. (A recent study in the city of New Orleans showed that although only 26% of the female population of reproductive age there were poor, they accounted for 72% of the still-births, 80% of the maternal deaths and 68% of the infant deaths.)

Other consequences to low-income people deprived of family planning services center around the entrapment in the cycle of poverty which occurs when families are unable to improve their economic position due to their large size and to the inability of the mother to either finish her education or to work where work is available.

Grantees, sponsored by State and local health departments and private non-profit organizations, must now match Federal funds with a rigid share of the total cost. This has proved to be a sizeable demand upon limited resources of State, city and county governments as well as upon private groups and has significantly reduced the size of programs in those areas where the need for the programs is greatest.

National Goal

In his Message to the Congress of July 18, 1969 on Population Growth and the American Future, President Nixon stated that it is clear that the domestic family planning services supported by the Federal Government should be expanded and better integrated. It is his

view that no American woman should be denied access to family planning
assistance because of her economic condition. He then established
as a national goal the provision of adequate family planning services
within the next five years to all those who want them but cannot
afford them, and said that this we have the capacity to do. "In
order to achieve this national goal, we will have to increase the
amount we are spending on population and family planning."[69] The
President also spoke of the need for legislation to help the Department of Health, Education, and Welfare implement this important
program by providing broader and more precise legislative authority
and a clearer source of financial support.

Through various estimates about 5 million women have been identified
as being in need of subsidized family planning services. With the
resources available through HEW and OEO programs in fiscal year
1969 about one million women were served. It is estimated that
about one million and a half were served during fiscal year 1970;
and about two million will probably be served with funds available
from these two agencies during fiscal year 1971. This underlines
the President's statement that a marked increase in funds available
will be necessary if we are to achieve the national goal.

The following table represents an estimate of the funds required
to support family planning services to achieve the President's goal:

Selected Family Planning Activities - Cost Estimates*
(In millions)

Organization	Authorizing legislation	Fiscal year				
		1971 budget	1972 estimate	1973 estimate	1974 estimate	1975 estimate
Maternal & Child Health Services, HSMHA:						
(1) Maternal & child health formula grant to the States.	Title V, Social Security Act.	$13.1	$15	$15	$15	$15
(2) Maternity & infant care project grants.	do	4.7	5	5	5	5
National Center for Family Planning Services, HSMHA: Project grants for services, operational research & training.	do	33.5	34------------------------------			
	Asministra-tion proposal (H.R. 15159).	12.0	51	130	175	220
Total services		63.3	105	150	195	240

*These figures represent only staff estimates of costs under these programs. They
should not be construed as committing the Department or the Administration to
requesting or spending such funds for fiscal years after 1971.

POPULATION RESEARCH

In his Message to the Congress on Population Growth, President Nixon said, "...... increased research is essential. It is clear, for example that we need additional research on birth control methods of all types and the sociology of population growth."[70]

Expanded population research is an essential component of our efforts to help couples achieve voluntary control of the number and spacing of their children to improve our understanding of problems associated with population change, and to help policy makers and program administrators deal effectively with these problems while preserving or increasing freedom of choice for individuals. Specifically, increased research is needed in four major areas: (1) the development of new contraceptives; (2) the safety of various methods of fertility control; (3) the social, psychological, and economic determinants and consequences of changes in population; and (4) the methods of making available safe and effective contraceptive services to all couples who wish to use them.

If couples are to exercise satisfactory control over their fertility they must have access to contraceptives that are effective, safe, inexpensive, reversible, and acceptable to various population groups. No presently available method fulfills all of these criteria. The oral steroids and the intrauterine devices represent remarkable improvements in contraceptive technology, but it is well recognized that they are not satisfactory in all respects. Probably no single method will be universally satisfactory, and the appropriate goal is the development of an array of methods that will be suitable for a variety of applications.

The need for new methods of fertility control is emphasized by the facts presented earlier that approximately one-fifth of the married women of reproductive age report that they have exceeded the number of children that they or their husbands wanted. In addition, approximately 40 per cent of wives report in national surveys that they have had one or more pregnancies sooner than desired. Altogether these figures indicate that a majority (approximately 60 per cent) of American couples have failed to control their fertility in accordance with their own desires. Although it is clear that specific methods of contraception were not to blame in all reports of poor control over fertility, it is equally clear that better methods and better access to them would go far toward reaching the goal of completely voluntary control of couples over their own fertility.

Contraceptive Development Program

Although individual research projects on reproductive biology have
been supported by the National Institute of Health for many years,
these efforts were not specifically directed toward the development
of new contraceptive methods and the total volume of support was
relatively small. In 1963, for example, only $3.4 million were
spent by all NIH on research projects in reproductive biology.
It is only within the past two years that a major effort has been
launched for the stated purpose of developing new methods of fertility
control. In its initial phase, this program has been directed
toward the expansion of knowledge about the reproductive system
in order to find new ways of intervening in the reproductive process.
As new methods of intervention are found, they will have to be
tested for effectiveness and safety before they can be released
for use by large numbers of people. Both the search for these
methods and their development and testing will require many years
and large expenditures of money.

Parallel with the program of contraceptive development, there must
be expanded research on the safety of various methods of fertility
control that have been developed in the past and will be developed
in the future. As the experience with the oral steroids has shown,
it is not always possible to identify with certainty medical effects
that occur among small proportions of users early in the testing
of a compound. Yet it is highly important that these effects be
determined so that physicians and the general public are aware of
the side effects and possible hazards of various methods of fertility
control.

In 1967, at the request of Congress, NIH began its program to study
the medical effects of contraceptives in use, particularly the oral
steroids. This program has expanded slowly since that time, but,
as the hearings before the Monopoly Subcommittee of the Select
Committee on Small Business indicated, a greatly increased research
effort is required to enable physicians to become fully aware of
all the potential hazards of various drugs that are being taken
now and may be taken in the future to control fertility. Such research may also make it possible to identify certain types of
individuals for whom various methods are especially hazardous, so
that these patients may be referred to other methods of fertility
regulation.

Social Science Research

In the social and behavioral sciences, a great deal of research
is needed on both the consequences and the determinants of changes in
population growth, distribution, and structure. With respect to
the consequences of population change, we do not now have the kind
of information that permits us to state with confidence the effects

that various patterns of population growth and distribution would have on the social and economic life of our country and on our physicial environment. We know, in general, that population size acts as a multiplier of existing problems originating from a variety of other sources, but we require much more detailed information about the consequences of population change in order to provide adequate information to the public as well as to government officials responsible for formulating policies that affect population change.

Research must also help us learn a great deal more than we now know about the social, economic, and psychological factors determining population change in order to provide a better basis for the formulation of effective policies and programs to deal with population problems.

Although a number of government agencies, such as the Census Bureau and the National Center for Health Statistics, provide information that is essential to the conduct of population research in the social sciences, the major sources of support for university-based investigators in the social sciences have been the private foundations. In view of their limited resources it is clear that the Federal government will have to provide the funds needed for the rapid expansion of population research in the social and behavioral sciences.

An important component of efforts to moderate rates of population growth and to enable couples to exercise voluntary control over their fertility consists of family planning service programs. The coverage of these programs must be increased and they must become more responsive to the needs of the various sectors of the public that they serve. Both of these goals require increased research on the operational aspects of family planning programs. One major objective of such research is the development and improvement of methods for establishing program goals and priorities in various locations and among various groups of individuals to be served. Another goal is to find ways of bringing information about available services to individuals who need them but have not yet been reached, and to insure continuity of service once it is begun. Program operators also need a better understanding of efficient staffing patterns and ways of using personnel in service programs. In addition to improving the efficiency of services, operational research is needed to evaluate the effectiveness of various programs, and, wherever possible, to quantify measures of success in meeting overall goals.

RECENT LEGISLATION

The Act establishing the Commission on Population
Growth and the American Future was signed by
President Nixon on March 16, 1970. One of the tasks
of the Commission is "to conduct an inquiry into...
the various means appropriate to the ethical values
and principles of this society by which our Nation
can achieve a population level properly suited for
its environmental, natural resources, and other
needs." The Commission is now functioning and its
interim report will be due in the Spring of 1971,
and its final report will be submitted in the Spring
of 1972.

Within the month, the Administration will have the
task of implementing the "Family Planning Services
and Population Research Act of 1970." This Act
establishes an Office of Population Affairs directed
by a Deputy Assistant Secretary within DHEW, delineates
the functions of the Deputy Assistant Secretary for
Population Affairs, and requires that a five-year
plan for the development of family planning services,
population research, and training of the necessary
manpower to carry out these programs be submitted
within six months to the Congress. Annual progress
reports during the five-year period are required.
The Act authorizes project grants and contracts for
family planning services. For this purpose, the
following sums are authorized:

FY 1971	$30,000,000
FY 1972	$60,000,000
FY 1973	$90,000,000

The Act authorizes formula grants to States for
Family Planning Services. The following sums are
authorized:

FY 1971	$10,000,000
FY 1972	$15,000,000
FY 1973	$20,000,000

The Act authorizes training grants and contracts
for this purpose. The following sums are authorized:

FY 1971	$ 2,000,000
FY 1972	$ 3,000,000
FY 1973	$ 4,000,000

The Act authorizes grants and contracts for bio-
medical, contraceptive development, behavioral, and
program implementation research. For these purposes,
the following sums are authorized:

FY 1971	$35,000,000
FY 1972	$50,000,000
FY 1973	$65,000,000

The Act authorizes grants and contracts for developing
and making available family planning and population
growth information and educational materials. For
this purpose, the following sums are authorized:

FY 1971	$ 750,000
FY 1972	$ 1,000,000
FY 1973	$ 1,250,000

The Act grants the Secretary the right to make and
promulgate appropriate regulations. The Act pre-
scribes voluntary participation by the individual in
any part of the program, and prohibits the use of
funds appropriated in programs where abortion is a
method of family planning.

The Act establishing the Commission on Population
Growth and the American Future and the Family Planning
Services and Population Research Act constitute and
complete the legislative package requested by the

President in his Population Message. The establishment of the National Center for Family Planning
Services implemented the organizational change mandated by the President. The Center for Population
Research had been established the previous year.

The growth of the HEW Population Research Programs
now administered by the National Institutes of
Health Center for Population Research during the
last five years is shown in the following table:

FY 1967	FY 1968	FY 1969	FY 1970	FY 1971
$7,743,000	$7,668,000	$10,806,000	$15,541,000	$28,341,000

The Center for Population Research will have the
major responsibility for the administration of the
population research funds appropriated under the
new Act.

The growth of the major controllable HEW Family
Planning Services programs during the last five
years is shown in the two following tables:

Funds available for family planning services through
programs now administered by the Health Services and
Mental Health Administration, Maternal and Child
Health Service:

FY 1967	FY 1968	FY 1969	FY 1970	FY 1971
$5,500,000	$6,500,000	$8,800,000	$8,800,000	$17,800,000

Funds available for family planning services through
programs now administered by the HSMHA National Center
for Family Planning Services:

FY 1967	FY 1968	FY 1969	FY 1970	FY 1971
---	---	$11,909,000	$22,800,000	$33,515,000

The National Center for Family Planning Services will
have the major responsibility for family planning
services funds appropriated under the new Act.

There are two large HEW programs which support the
provision of family planning services over which the
Department has no direct control - the public assistance programs for social services and medical services
authorized under Titles IV and XIX of the Social
Security Act.

The Office of Economic Opportunity has been a major
source of support for family planning services.
During the last five years OEO support has increased
as follows:

FY 1967	FY 1968	FY 1969	FY 1970	FY 1971
$4,800,000	$9,000,000	$15,000,000	$22,000,000	$24,000,000

The growth of State programs in recent years has been
directly related to the availability of Federal funds.
With the increase in official agency programs, the
private sources of support for both services and
research have tended to level off or decline.

398

FOOTNOTES

1. U.S. Department of Commerce, Bureau of the Census, Current Population Reports: Population Estimates and Projections, Series P-25, No. 449, August 18, 1970.

2. Ibid., Projections of the Population of the United States by Age and Sex (Interim Revisions): 1970-2020, Series P-25, No. 448, August 6, 1970.

3. Ibid., Population Estimates, Series P-25, No. 321, November 30, 1965.

4. Ibid.; Technical Studies, "Characteristics of American Youth,". Series P-23, No. 30. February 6, 1970.

5. Op. cit.,"Projections...1970-2020", Series P-25, No. 448, August 6, 1970.

6. Ibid.

7. Thomlinson, Ralph, Population Dynamics, Random House, 1965, pp. 109-110.

8. Population Crisis: A Condensation of United States Senate Hearings on the Population Crisis with an introduction by Former Senator Ernest Gruening, Chairman of the Subcommittee on Foreign Aid Expenditures during the 1965-1968 Hearings; Socio-Dynamics Industries, Inc., Washington, D.C., 1970, p. 321. Testimony of Dr. Walsh McDermott, Professor of Public Health at the Cornell University Medical College, during the 1967-68 Hearings.

9. Ekhardt, Abramson, Pakter, and Nelson, "An Epidemiological Approach to Infant Mortality, Archives of Enviornmental Health, Vol. 20, No. 6, June 1970.

10. U.S. Department of Commerce, Bureau of the Census, Statistical Abstract of the United States, 1969, p. 6.

11. Ibid., p. 86.

12. Ibid., p. 92.

13. Thomlinson, op. cit., p. 166 citing Ansley J. Coale and Melvin Zelnik, New Estimates of Fertility and Population in the United States, Princeton University Press, Princeton, 1963, Table 2.

14. U.S. Department of Commerce, Bureau of the Census, Series P-20, No. 186, August 6, 1969, citing Nos. 62 and 144.

15. Parke, Robert, Jr. and Glick, Paul C., "Prospective Changes in Marriage and the Family," _Journal of Marriage and the Family_, Vol. 29, No. 2, May 1967, pp. 249-256.

16. Thomlinson, _op cit._, citing Grabill, Kiser, and Whelpton, _The Fertility of American Women_, 1958, p. 3.

17. U.S. Department of Commerce, Bureau of the Census, Series P-20, No. 189, August 18, 1969.

18. Ohlin, Goran, _Population Control in Economic Development_, Development Centre Studies, OECD, Paris, 1967, Ch. 5.

19. _Ibid_.

20. David, Henry P., _Family Planning and Abortion in the Socialist Countries of Central and Eastern Europe: A Compendium of Observations and Readings_; New York: The Population Council, 1970, p.30.

21. Miltenyi, K., "Social and Psychological Factors Affecting Fertility in a Legalized Abortion System," W.P.C. Belgrade, 1965, paper no. 334, cited by K.H. Mehlan, M.D. in _Family Planning and Population Programs: A review of World Developments_, edited by Bernard Berelson and others, University of Chicago, 1966.

22. _Population Crisis_, _op. cit._ pp. 229-230. Testimony of Dr. Kermit Krantz, Kansas City, Kansas.

23. U.S. Department of Commerce, Bureau of the Census, Series P-20, No. 186, August 6, 1969.

24. Kovar, Mary Grace, the "Interval from First Marriage to First Birth," paper given at the annual meeting of the Population Association of America, Inc., Atlanta, Ga., April 17, 1970, provides the basis for this sub-section.

25. U.S. Department of Commerce, Bureau of the Census, _Current Population Reports: Consumer Income_, Series P-60, No. 67, "Socio-Economic Trends in Poverty Areas, 1960-1968," December 30, 1969.

26. _Ibid._, _Current Population Reports: Population Characteristics_, Series P-20, No. 194, February 19, 1970.

27. _Ibid._, _Technical Studies_, _op.cit._

28. _Ibid._, _Current Population Reports: Population Characteristics_, Series P-20, No. 194, February 19, 1970.

29. _Ibid._, Series P-20, No. 189, August 18, 1969.

30. Ibid., No. 194, February 19, 1970.

31. Ibid., Technical Studies..., Series P-23, No. 30, February 6, 1970.

32. Ibid., Current Population Reports: Consumer Income, op cit.

33. Population Crisis, op. cit., pp. 124-25. Testimony of Harold O. Swank, Director, Illinois Public Aid Commission, Springfield, Illinois, speaking in 1965 on behalf of the American Public Welfare Association.

34. Ibid.

35. Current Population Reports: Consumer Income, op. cit.

36. Population Crisis, op. cit., Swank Testimony.

37. Ibid., pp. 126-8, Testimony of Wallace H. Kuralt, Director of the Department of Public Welfare, Mechlenberg, N.C.

38. Rainwater, Lee, And the Poor Get Children: Sex, Contraception, and Family Planning in the Working Class. Chicago: Quadrangle Books, 1960.

39. David, op cit.

40. U.S. Department of Commerce, Bureau of the Census, Current Population Reports: Population Projections, Series P-25, No. 436, "Estimates of the Population of States, July 1, 1968 and 1969," January 7, 1970.

41. Ibid., Current Population Reports: Population Characteristics, Series P-20, No. 193, "Mobility of the Population in the United States, March 1968 to March 1969," December 26, 1969, and No. 189, August 18, 1969, provided the basis for this sub-section.

42. Ibid., Series P-20, No. 197, "Population of the United States by Metropolitan, Non-Metropolitan Residence, 1969 and 1960," March 6, 1970.

43. National Goals Research Staff, A Report Toward Balanced Growth: Quantity With Quality, Ch. 2, "Population Growth and Distribution," July 4, 1970, pp. 39-61.

44. Ibid.

45. U.S. Department of Commerce, Bureau of the Census, Series P-20, No. 197, op. cit.

46. Ibid.

47. Ibid.

48. National Goals, op. cit.

49. Ibid.

50. U.S. Department of Commerce, Bureau of the Census, Projections...
    (Interim Revisions), op. cit., provides the basis for this
    sub-section.

51. Enke, Stephen, "Zero United Stated Population Growth: When, How,
    and Why," TEMPO, General Electric Company, Center for Advanced
    Studies, Santa Barbara, Calif., January 1970, 70 TMP-35, p. 25.

52. Ibid., "The Economics of Having Children," reprinted from
    Policy Sciences, Vol. I, No. I, Spring 1970.

53. National Goals, op. cit.

54. Population Crisis, op. cit., pp. 242-3.

55. Ibid.

56. Easterlin, Richard A., The American Baby Boom in Historical
    Perspective, National Bureau of Economic Research, Occasional
    Paper No. 79, 1962, 32p.

57. Ibid., p. 30.

58. Kiser, Clyde V., Grabill, Wilson H., and Campbell, Arthur A.,
    Trends and Variations in Fertility in the United States. Harvard
    University Press, 1968, pp. 252-3.

59. National Goals, op. cit., p. 47.

60. Ibid., p. 51.

61. Whelpton, Pascal K., Forecasts of the Population of the United
    States: 1945-1975, U.S. Bureau of the Census, Washington, 1947.

62. Enke, "Zero United States Population Growth...," op. cit.

63. National Goals, op. cit.

64. Ibid., p. 42

65. "Problems of Population Growth: The President's Message to the
    Congress...July 18, 1969", Weekly Compilation of Presidential
    Documents, July 21, 1969, pp. 1000-1008.

66. _Ibid._

67. U.S. Department of Health, Education, and Welfare, National Center for Health Statistics, _Health Resources Statistics: Health Manpower and Health Facilities, 1970._ PHS Publication No. 1509.

68. U.S. Office of Economic Opportunity, Family Planning Program, Office of Health Affairs, _Need for Subsidized Family Planning Services: United States, each State and County, 1968,_ Washington, D.C.

69. "Problems of Population Growth: The President's Message to the Congress...July 18, 1969," _Weekly Compilation of Presidential Documents_, July 21, 1969, pp. 1000-1008.

70. _Ibid._

Figure 1. Total Population of the United States[1], Actual 1930-1960 and Projected[2], 1970-2037

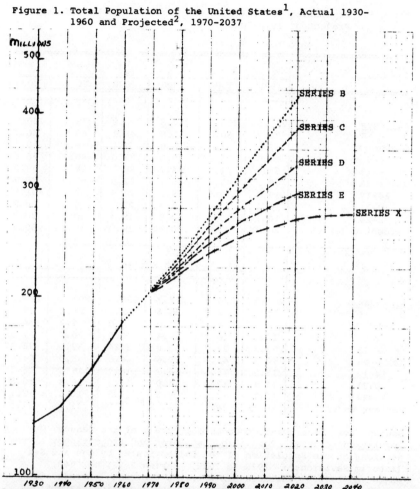

Source: Current Population Reports: Population Estimates and Projections, "Projections of the Population of the United States by Age and Sex (Interim Revisions): 1970 to 2020," Series P-25, No. 448, August 6, 1970, U.S. Dept of Commerce, Bureau of the Census.[1] [1]Includes armed forces overseas. [2]Projection series B,C,D, and E use the same mortality and migration assumptions but different fertility assumptions. Series "X" uses the same fertility assumption as Series "E" but makes no allowance for migration and leads to a stationary population in the year 2037.

Table 1. Population[1] of Children and Youth in the United States, Projected[2] 1970-2020

Age group	B Series					
	1970	1980	1990	2000	2010	2020
	---in millions---					
All ages	205.5	236.8	277.3	320.8	376.2	440.2
0 - 5	21.7	30.8	35.8	40.1	49.5	56.3
Under 1	3.7	5.5	6.0	7.1	8.6	9.7
1-5	18.0	25.2	29.8	33.0	40.9	46.6
6 - 13	33.3	31.2	44.7	48.7	57.5	69.0
14 - 24	40.3	45.4	45.1	62.0	67.9	80.3
14-17	15.8	15.9	18.6	23.9	25.4	31.5
18-21	14.4	17.0	15.6	22.7	24.4	28.9
22-24	10.1	12.5	10.9	15.4	18.2	20.0
Percent under 15	28.2%	27.8%	30.8%	29.5%	30.2%	30.3%

Age group	E Series					
	---in millions---					
All ages	205.1	225.5	247.7	266.3	283.7	299.2
0 - 5	21.3	22.8	24.4	23.6	24.8	25.3
Under 1	3.3	4.0	4.0	4.0	4.2	4.2
1-5	18.0	18.8	20.4	19.6	20.7	21.0
6 - 13	33.3	27.9	32.0	32.4	32.1	33.8
14 - 24	40.3	45.4	39.6	44.6	45.0	44.9
14-17	15.8	15.9	14.7	16.7	16.0	16.6
18-21	14.4	17.0	14.0	16.3	16.4	16.3
22-24	10.1	12.5	10.9	11.6	12.6	12.1
Percent under 15	28.6%	24.1%	24.3%	22.6%	21.5%	21.1%

Source: U.S. Department of Commerce, Bureau of the Census, Current Population Reports: Population Estimates and Projections, "Projections of the Population of the United States by Age and Sex (Interim Revisions): 1970 to 2020," Series P-25, No. 448, August 6, 1970. [1]Includes armed forces overseas. [2]Projection series B and E use the same mortality and migration assumptions but suggest the impact on age groups of a range of possible fertility assumptions.

405

Figure 2. Population[1] of Children and Youth in the United States,
Actual, 1930-1960 and Projected[2], 1970-2020

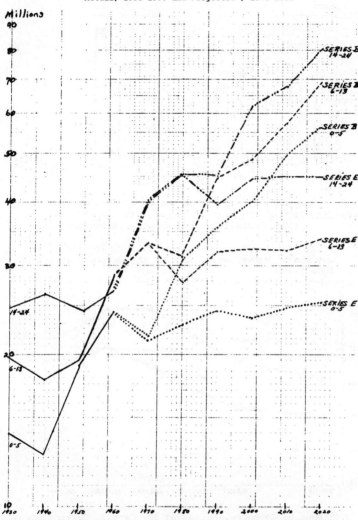

Source: Current Population Reports: Population Estimates and
Projections, "Projections of the Population of the United States
by Age and Sex (Interim Revisions): 1970 to 2020," Series P-25,
No. 448, August 6, 1970. [1]Includes armed forces overseas.
[2]Projection series B and E use the same mortality and migration
assumptions but suggest the impact on age groups of a range of
possible fertility assumptions.

Figure 3.   Immigrants Admitted to the United States, 1950-1968

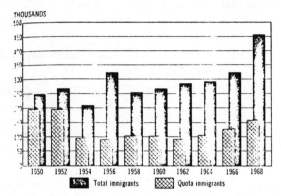

Source: U.S. Department of Commerce, Bureau of the Census,
Statistical Abstract of the United States, 1969, p. 87.   Data
from Dept. of Justice, Immigration and Naturalization Service.

Figure 4.   Births Per 1,000 Women by Age 23, for Selected Birth
Cohorts of Women, by Color, for the United States:
June 1965

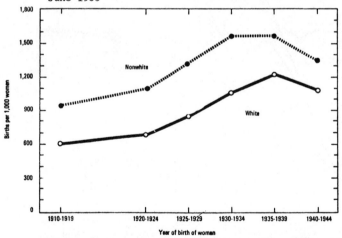

Source: U.S. Dept of Commerce, Bureau of the Census, Current Population
Reports: Population Characteristics, "Marriage, Fertility, and Child-
spacing, June 1965," Series P-20, No. 186, August 6, 1969.

Figure 5. **TOTAL FERTILITY RATES FOR THE TOTAL POPULATION, BY CALENDAR YEARS, 1925 TO 1990**

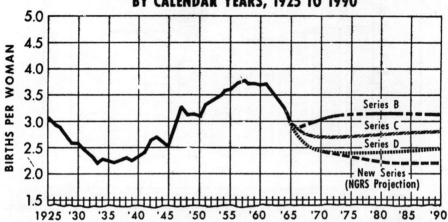

Notes: Total fertility rates represent sums of age-specific birth rates for a given calendar year.

Source: National Goals' Research Staff, A Report Toward Balanced Growth: Quantity with Quality, Ch. 2, "Population Growth and Distribution," July 4, 1970, p. 41.

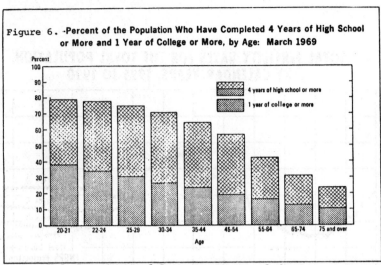

Figure 6. -Percent of the Population Who Have Completed 4 Years of High School or More and 1 Year of College or More, by Age: March 1969

Source: U.S. Department of Commerce, Bureau of the Census, <u>Current Population Reports: Population Characteristics</u>, "Educational Attainment, March 1969," Series P-20, No. 194, February 19, 1970.

Figure 10. Metropolitan Areas: Average Annual Percent Change in Population, by Race, 1950-1960 and 1960-1968

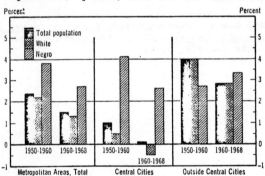

Source: U.S. Department of Commerce, Bureau of the Census, <u>Statistical Abstract of the United States</u>, 1969, p. 4.

Figure 7. Percentage Change in the Population of States,
         1960-1968

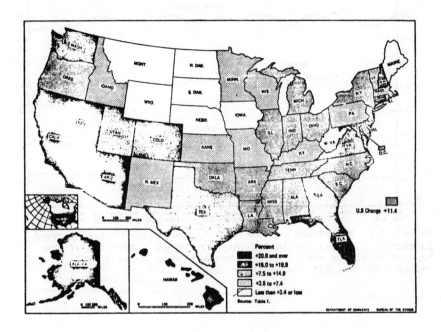

Source: U.S. Department of Commerce, Bureau of the Census,
Current Population Reports: Population Estimates and Projections,
"Estimates of the Population of States, July 1, 1968 and 1969,
Series P-25, No. 436, January 7, 1970.

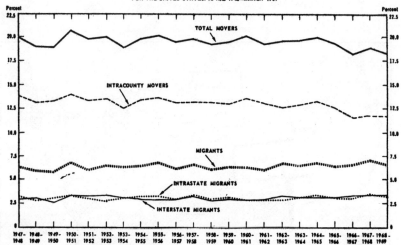

Figure 8. MOVERS BY TYPE OF MOBILITY AS PERCENT OF THE POPULATION 1 YEAR OLD AND OVER, FOR THE UNITED STATES: APRIL 1948—MARCH 1969

Source: U.S. Department of Commerce, Bureau of the Census, Current Population Reports: Population Characteristics, "Mobility of the Population of the United States, March 1968 to March 1969," Series P-20, No. 193, December 26, 1969.

411

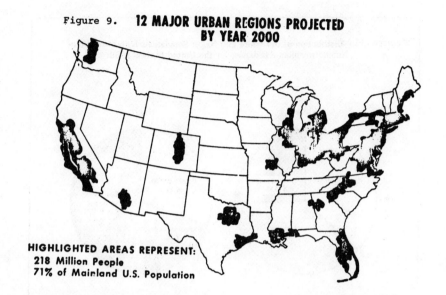

Figure 9. **12 MAJOR URBAN REGIONS PROJECTED BY YEAR 2000**

HIGHLIGHTED AREAS REPRESENT:
218 Million People
71% of Mainland U.S. Population

Source: National Goals' Research Staff, <u>A Report Toward Balanced Growth: Quantity with Quality</u>, Ch. 2, "Population Growth and Distribution," July 4, 1970, p. 45.

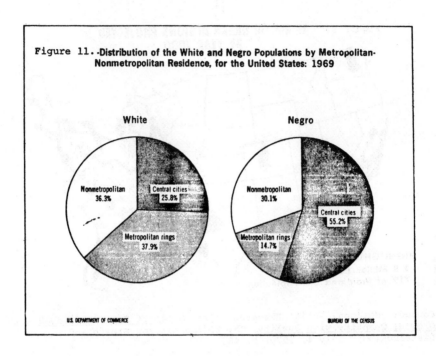

Figure 11.--Distribution of the White and Negro Populations by Metropolitan-Nonmetropolitan Residence, for the United States: 1969

Source: U.S. Department of Commerce, Bureau of the Census, Current Population Reports: Population Characteristics, "Population of the United States by Metropolitan-Nonmetropolitan Residence: 1969 and 1960," Series P-20, No. 197, March 6, 1970.

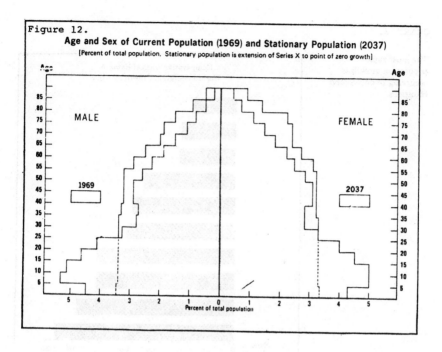

Figure 12.

Age and Sex of Current Population (1969) and Stationary Population (2037)

[Percent of total population. Stationary population is extension of Series X to point of zero growth]

Table 2. Total Population and Population Under Age 25 Extended
to Point of Zero Growth, 1970-2037

Year	Total	Age		
		0 – 4	5 – 14	15 – 24
		in millions		
1970	204.7	17.4	41.2	36.2
1980	220.5	18.6	34.4	40.9
1990	237.5	19.3	38.0	34.1
2000	250.3	18.2	37.7	37.8
2020	270.4	18.7	37.6	36.4
2037	275.6	18.7	37.0	37.1

Source: U.S. Department of Commerce, Bureau of the Census,
<u>Current Population Reports: Population Estimates and Projections</u>,
Projections of the Population of the United States by Age and
Sex (Interim Revisions): 1970 to 2020," Series P-25, No. 448,
August 6, 1970. [1]Includes armed forces overseas. [2]Series "X"
uses the same fertility assumption as the "E" series but makes
no allowance for migration and leads to a stationary population
in 2037.

CHART 2.

The most rapid
population growth is
occurring in developing
countries.

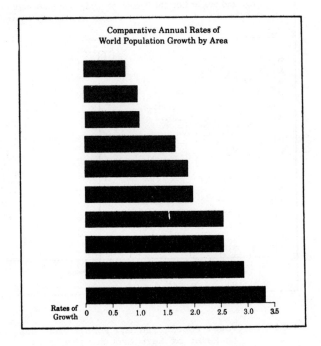

Comparative Annual Rates of
World Population Growth by Area

CHART 5.

Since 1900, the
percentage of persons
under age 25 has
varied widely.
It is now 47 percent;
in 1980 it is expected
to be 44 percent.

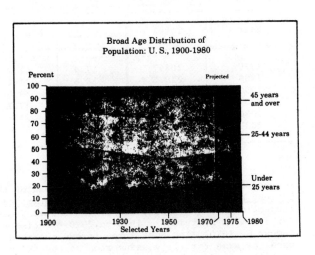

Broad Age Distribution of
Population: U. S., 1900-1980

CHART 6.

As in prior decades,
at least one-fourth of
the population will be
under age 15.

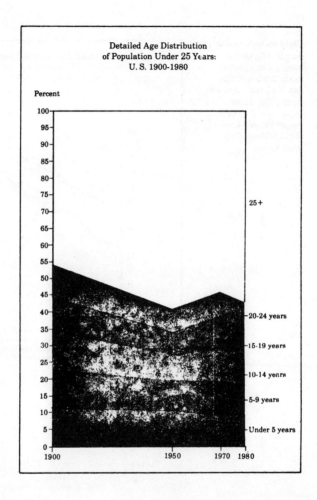

Detailed Age Distribution
of Population Under 25 Years:
U. S. 1900-1980

Percent

CHART 79.

Children born during this decade will, on the average, live seventy years. Although the gap has been narrowing since 1900, white children still have a longer life expectancy than children of all other races.

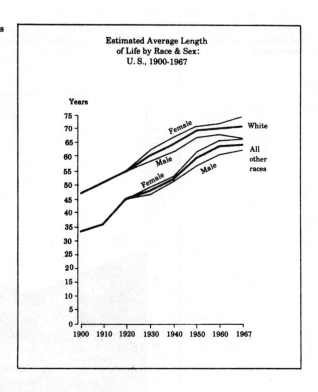

Estimated Average Length
of Life by Race & Sex:
U. S., 1900-1967

The risk of death in the first year is higher than that for any other year under sixty-five.

Premature births, congenital malformations, and postnatal asphyxia account for more than fifty percent of all infant deaths.

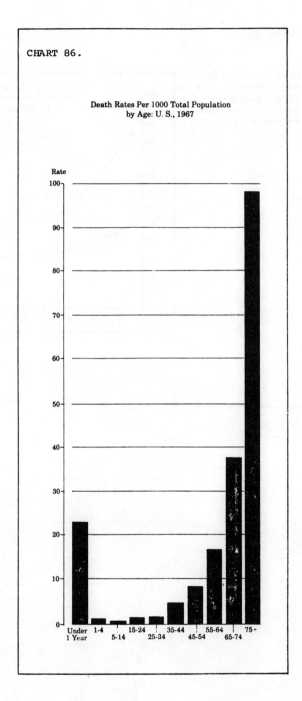

CHART 86.

Death Rates Per 1000 Total Population
by Age: U.S., 1967

CHART 85.

Death rates in the first
week of life have
declined much more
slowly than those in the
first year of life.

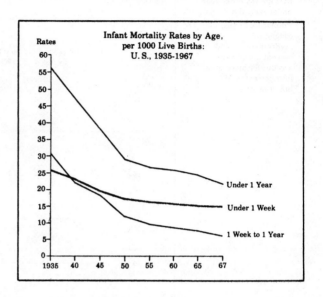

Rates

Infant Mortality Rates by Age,
per 1000 Live Births:
U. S., 1935-1967

Under 1 Year

Under 1 Week

1 Week to 1 Year

CHART 81.

But they are still higher
than the rates in twelve
other major developed
nations.

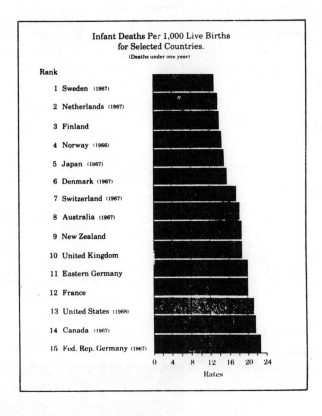

Infant Deaths Per 1,000 Live Births
for Selected Countries.
(Deaths under one year)

Rank

1 Sweden (1967)

2 Netherlands (1967)

3 Finland

4 Norway (1966)

5 Japan (1967)

6 Denmark (1967)

7 Switzerland (1967)

8 Australia (1967)

9 New Zealand

10 United Kingdom

11 Eastern Germany

12 France

13 United States (1968)

14 Canada (1967)

15 Fed. Rep. Germany (1967)

0   4   8   12   16   20   24
Rates

CHART 80.

Infant mortality rates
in the United States are
continuing to decline.

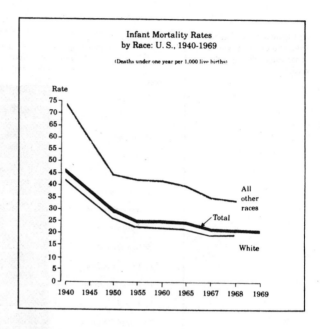

Infant Mortality Rates
by Race: U. S., 1940-1969

(Deaths under one year per 1,000 live births)

CHART 82.

The South generally has
the highest infant
mortality rates.

CHART 83.

In large cities, infant
mortality is often linked
with low income groups.

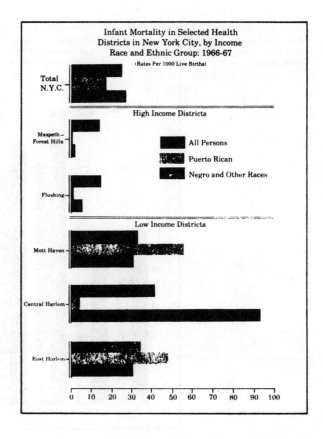

Infant Mortality in Selected Health
Districts in New York City, by Income
Race and Ethnic Group: 1966-67
(Rates Per 1000 Live Births)

CHART 84.

Overall, Negroes and
American Indians suffer
the highest rates of
infant death.

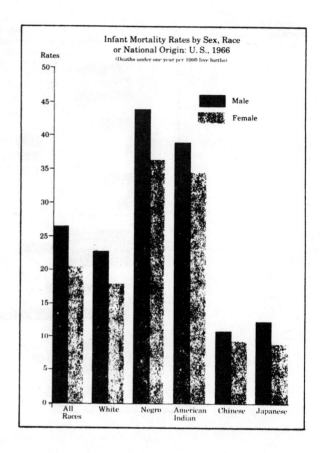

Infant Mortality Rates by Sex, Race
or National Origin: U.S., 1966
(Deaths under one year per 1000 live births)

Improved health services
have contributed to sharp
declines in maternal
death rates, but a large
difference remains
between the rate
for whites and the
rate for other races.

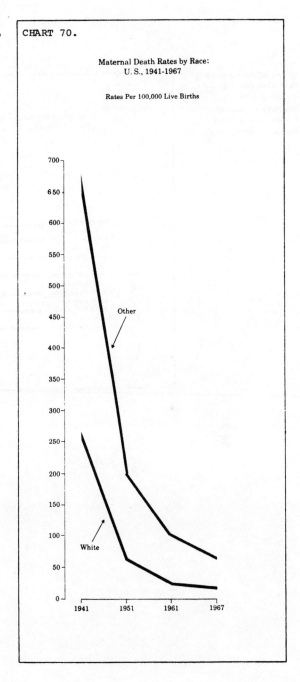

CHART 70.

Maternal Death Rates by Race:
U. S., 1941-1967

Rates Per 100,000 Live Births

424

CHART 71.

Infant mortality rates
vary with the child's
weight at birth. And
the mother's health
has much to do with
the child's birth weight.

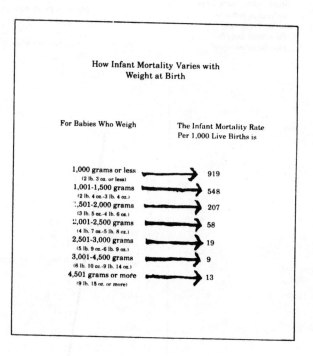

How Infant Mortality Varies with
Weight at Birth

For Babies Who Weigh

The Infant Mortality Rate
Per 1,000 Live Births is

1,000 grams or less
(2 lb. 3 oz. or less)
919

1,001-1,500 grams
(2 lb. 4 oz.-3 lb. 4 oz.)
548

1,501-2,000 grams
(3 lb. 5 oz.-4 lb. 6 oz.)
207

2,001-2,500 grams
(4 lb. 7 oz.-5 lb. 8 oz.)
58

2,501-3,000 grams
(5 lb. 9 oz.-6 lb. 9 oz.)
19

3,001-4,500 grams
(6 lb. 10 oz.-9 lb. 14 oz.)
9

4,501 grams or more
(9 lb. 15 oz. or more)
13

CHART 110.

Accidents are the major
health hazard to
preschool children after
age one.

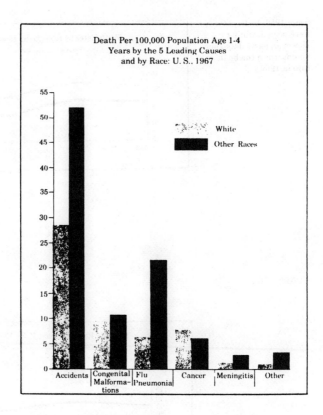

Death Per 100,000 Population Age 1-4
Years by the 5 Leading Causes
and by Race: U.S., 1967

CHART 77.

Since 1957, birth rates
have been declining.
However, early data show
an upturn in the birth
rate in 1969.

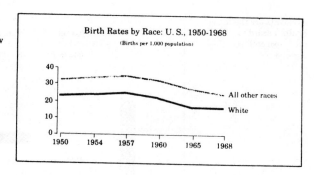

CHART 78.

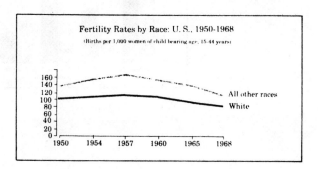

CHART 73.

Nearly sixty percent of
married women report
more pregnancies than
wanted or pregnancies
earlier than wanted.

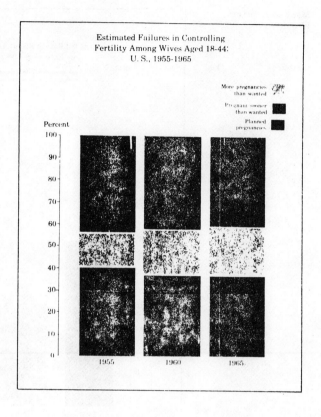

Estimated Failures in Controlling
Fertility Among Wives Aged 18-44:
U. S., 1955-1965

More pregnancies
than wanted

Pregnant sooner
than wanted

Planned
pregnancies

Percent

CHART 76.

Many abortions are
illegal.

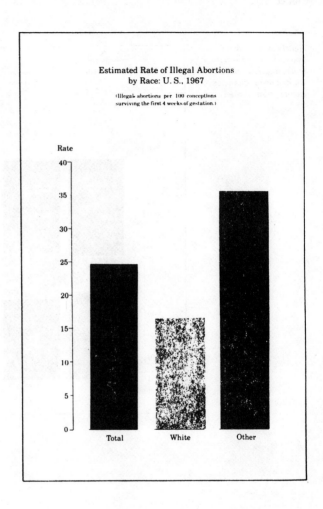

Estimated Rate of Illegal Abortions
by Race: U. S., 1967

(Illegal abortions per 100 conceptions
surviving the first 4 weeks of gestation.)

The number of
illegitimate live births
has been steadily
increasing.

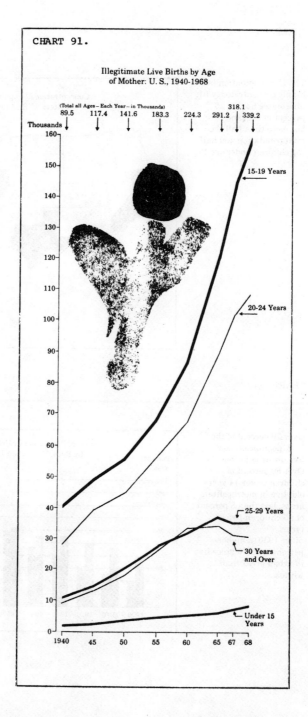

CHART 91.

Illegitimate Live Births by Age
of Mother: U. S., 1940-1968

CHART 8.

The U. S. population is
highly concentrated, with
nine states having 20
percent of the land area,
but more than half the
total population and half
the children under age 17.

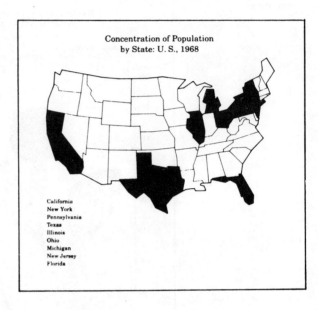

Concentration of Population
by State: U. S., 1968

California
New York
Pennsylvania
Texas
Illinois
Ohio
Michigan
New Jersey
Florida

CHART 9.

Over 70 percent of the
U. S. population now
live in urban areas.
Over 60 percent of
children under 14 years
old, live in metropolitan
areas; less than 5 percent
of all children live on
farms.
Since 1950, a higher
percentage of Negroes live
in urban areas than
whites.

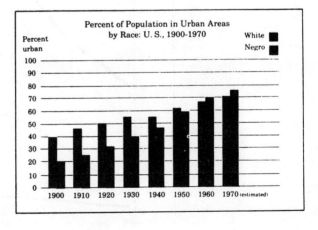

Percent of Population in Urban Areas
by Race: U. S., 1900-1970

THE BACKGROUND PAPER
ON
FOOD AND NUTRITION
FOR THE
1970-71 WHITE HOUSE CONFERENCE
ON CHILDREN AND YOUTH

THE UNITED STATES DEPARTMENT OF AGRICULTURE

DECEMBER 1970

OVERVIEW

In the last decade the importance of proper nutrition for mothers and children has been reemphasized by several related developments:

* Findings by researchers on nutrition, health, and learning have increasingly indicated that hunger and malnutrition can stunt the physical growth and impair the mental development of children. The most crucial influence of nutrition on potential mental development is from 3 months before birth to about 3 years of age, the period during which a child's brain grows most rapidly.

* Data from surveys of national food consumption show that iron in the diets of some groups of infants and children under 3 years was about 50 percent below recommended amounts. Several age groups of girls and young women were found to have calcium and iron intakes that were 30 percent or more below the recommended amounts.

* As an outgrowth of the national effort to overcome poverty in the last half of the 1960's, there has been a painful discovery that some 10 million children lived in poverty--and that many of these children, plus many others from nonpoor families, were inadequately nourished. For instance, selected data from a nutritional survey of families in the lowest fourth of incomes show (a) heights of children under 7 years of age showing poor growth achievement, (b) poor tooth development and numerous caries, and (c) some presence of rickets associated with vitamin D deficiency.

* Until the last few years, food assistance and welfare programs were found to be not reaching many millions of the poor, who were the most likely to be ill-fed.

* The 1969 White House Conference on Food, Nutrition, and Health stressed that "every American should have access to knowledge of nutrition and its relation to health as well as a means to assure food to meet his nutritional needs."

The nutritional status of people in the United States depends to a marked degree upon the food purchases by families and the quality of their nutritional knowledge and practice. However, the Federal Government, with the cooperation of local and State governments, has substantially improved and expanded its food and nutrition assistance programs in recent years to meet the foregoing problems. New nutritional assistance programs have been created and older programs have been redirected, all with increased emphasis on assisting the poor and the children. Total Federal funds for food and nutrition were increased from $.4 billion in fiscal year 1960, to $.8 billion in 1965, and $1.6 billion in 1970. Within these totals, the portion for children and youth under age 21 is estimated to have grown from $.3 billion in 1960 to $1.1 billion in 1970.

Legislation was recommended by the President to provide for further expansion of the Food Stamp Program and he has supported proposals to expand child nutrition programs. The Budget for 1971 reflected the increases by providing a total of $2.5 billion for food and nutrition. The legislative proposals for reform of the public assistance system by adoption of the Family Assistance Plan represented a closely related major step toward increasing the purchasing power of poor families with children so they would have greater means to buy food and other necessities.

Food assistance programs to counteract malnutrition are reaching children in various ways. Nearly 21 million children are being served through the school lunch program, including 5.3 million needy children who receive free or reduced-price meals. The goal is to reach 6.6 million of these needy children with school lunches. In 1970 about 500,000 youngsters through high school age got one good meal a day through summer recreation programs in poor areas of several cities. Breakfast at school is reaching about 500,000 children in 1970. The availability of school food services has been inhibited by lack of space, equipment, and funds, although rapid improvements have been made recently. Continuing attention should be given to the nutritional quality and acceptability of the meals once the service is available. Participation in the Food Stamp Program rose to 8.8 million people in October 1970 as compared with 2.7 million in October 1968. Participation in the Commodity Distribution Program was 3.6 million in 1970 and 3.5 million in 1968 which reflects the emphasis of expanding food assistance in the form of Food Stamps rather than by distribution of commodities.

Many large and complex nutrition education programs are conducted by the U.S. Department of Agriculture, the U.S. Department of Health, Education, and Welfare, and several national organizations. An example is the Expanded Food and Nutrition Education Program, focused on low-income families. In May 1970 this program included more than 7,000 aides in 1,030 counties in the 50 States, Puerto Rico, the Virgin Islands, and the District of Columbia. The Extension Nutrition Education Program in FY 1970 supported an accelerated youth activity to reach disadvantaged young people who live in cities. It is anticipated that 225,000 youths will be reached in 1970.

Among the most urgent unmet needs in reaching optimum nutritional health are economic resources to enable families to buy adequate food; consumption of more milk, fruits, and vegetables to supply calcium, iron, vitamins A and C in adequate amounts; and nutrition education for all consumers, with special attention to teaching children and youth the relation of food to health.

Coordination of national, State, and local nutrition education programs with concern for continuity is needed. Nutrition education must be a long-term effort which must expand and reach people more effectively as new knowledge becomes available about what determines their food choices. Children are a key group in the process of educating the Nation to adopt better nutritional practices. However, there are still children and youth of every age hungry and malnourished, often because their families are too poor to buy the right food or lack knowledge of sound nutrition practices.

THE BACKGROUND PAPER ON FOOD AND NUTRITION

FOR THE 1970-71

WHITE HOUSE CONFERENCE ON CHILDREN AND YOUTH

INTRODUCTION

In this country of great wealth in food supplies and technological knowledge of nutrition, there are children and youth of every age who are malnourished and hungry. On every front, the public is being made aware that despite our affluence, all is not well with the food intake and the nutritional status of many of its children and youth. There is a "nutrition gap" and everything possible must be done to close it.

For some, the nutrition gap is between food supply and dietary needs; for others, it is between knowledge and application. The cause may be singular or plural--insufficient resources to secure food, poor selection and poor food habits even though resources are sufficient, ignorance or disregard on the part of parents and their children for the importance of food to health, and lack of motivation for change. In food assistance programs, the gap is often between what is being done and what needs to be done.

Participants in this conference can contribute much in developing ways to eliminate these causes and thus close the nutrition gap.

Malnutrition in children and youth, endangers the individual and the society in which he lives. It can be found at every socioeconomic level of affluence or poverty but is much more common among the poor.

The physical results of malnutrition can be readily recognized and measured. These include a child's slow growth and his failure to reach his growth potential, structural weakness (sometimes overt physical defects) in bone and muscle, and impairment of normal functioning of body processes. The extent of damage depends on when the energy or nutrient deprivation occurs, the specificity of the deprivation, how long it lasts, and how severe it is. The degree to which such effects can be reversed depends on the same factors plus the intensity and duration of the rehabilitation regimen.

Since the 1960 White House Conference on Children and Youth, a great deal of research has been reported which points to a relationship between nutrition and the growth, development, and functioning of the brain. Brain and nerve tissue are built and nourished by the same bloodstream as bone and muscle. For the central nervous system, there is the same relation between the supply of the needed building materials, final structure, and ability to function as there is for other structures of the human body. Any growing organism is more vulnerable to deprivation--a reduced supply of needed building materials--then one that has attained its growth.

The most crucial time for the influence of nutrition on the structure of the brain and other parts of the central nervous system is during its period of most rapid growth, from 3 months before birth until 6 months after birth and continuing, but at a much reduced rate, until the child is about 3 years old.

Even though many children in the United States may be malnourished, only a very few have been subjected to the severe protein-calorie deprivation that has been shown to be a causal factor in experimental animals in the development of abnormal behavior and learning ability.

When malnutrition in children in the United States is described, the dietary deficiencies are usually in vitamins and minerals. On the basis of present knowledge, there is no basis for believing that children with low levels of blood hemoglobin or of vitamins or of minerals are consequently susceptible to the development of long-lasting mental retardation. Mildly inadequate or borderline intakes of specific nutrients can interfere with learning and performance. Thiamin deprivation causes anxiety, irritability, depression, and increased sensitivity to noise and pain. Inadequate amounts of nicotinic acid result in lassitude, apprehension, and depression. A deficiency of vitamin B_{12} causes mental confusion. Inadequate iodine causes a low basal metabolic rate and physical and mental languor. Insufficient iron results in lowered hemoglobin and reduced capacity of the blood to carry oxygen needed by the tissues for normal functioning. In their early stages, mild forms of undernutrition are accompanied by an increase in motor restlessness. In later stages, depression of motor activity sets in. All these manifestations disappear when the deficiency is corrected.

Beyond the changes that occur in specific deficiency diseases, the effect of nutrition on the functioning of the central nervous system cannot be separated from the effect of a whole complex of environmental factors. Malnutrition in man never occurs in isolation, free of other environmental factors. Nor does mental ability develop or function in the abstract without relation to culture. There is a synergistic action between the nutritional status of children and the education, economic status, motivation, and responsiveness of their parents. All of these are known to influence total performance. In this area we have few specific quantitative measurements. We know, however, that the lessened energy, the inability to concentrate, and the easy fatigue that accompany undernutrition are likely to cause inferior ability to cope with one's environment and to achieve one's objectives.

The right food and the physical and mental vigor that can result from such food are among the greatest potentials for achieving a high level of health and well-being in our Nation's children and youth.

To combat hunger and the recognized nutrition gap, food delivery systems to low-income families have been expanded. At this writing, over 10 million people are being served and pending legislation will probably expand these systems and the complementary ones aimed at infants and children. As of September 1970, over 98 percent of our people were living in counties with family food programs. Because people must know how to buy and prepare food to be properly fed, food education programs were expanded or activated in the schools, in homes, sponsored by governments and by the private sector.

The 1969 White House Conference on Food, Nutrition, and Health stressed that "every American should have access to knowledge of nutrition and its relation to health as well as a means to assure food to meet his nutritional needs." Professionals and nonprofessionals, public and private sectors have all concurred with this statement.

Vital nutrition information is available from both government and private groups. They share this information and reinforce each other's efforts. Within the Federal Government, nutrition knowledge is exchanged through the Interagency Committee on Nutrition Education.

All this represents much effort with at least one major net result. Assuming continuation of the present momentum and the social and political commitment for expanding food delivery systems and increased welfare payments, we are making some headway against hunger. We must, however, find ways to progress farther and faster.

The sections that follow in this report present background information on the areas of food and nutrition as related to children and youth about which we have the most specific information, and which offer the greatest potential as springboards for future actions to achieve improved nutrition for the Nation. These areas are nutritional status and food consumption, food assistance, and nutrition education.

NUTRITIONAL STATUS AND FOOD CONSUMPTION

Nutrition and health workers frequently study the nutritional status and food intakes of population groups as a means of making a general assessment of where a group stands in relation to the nutrition and food "standards" associated with optimum health. Such information is used to identify needs and plan the direction of food assistance and education programs designed to meet these needs and thus improve nutritional well-being.

Data for the past decade come chiefly from two sources. One source includes many studies of special population groups rather specifically characterized by age, location, socioeconomic status, and other factors. The studies have included some physical or biochemical measures for assessment of the nutritional status on over 13,000 children and youth in the United States, Puerto Rico, and the Virgin Islands. Similarly, dietary studies have included a total of almost 25,000 children and youth. Most of these studies have been focused on low-income groups, including Caucasians, Indians, Negroes, Orientals, and Puerto Ricans. Infants and preschool children, teenagers, pregnant women, and people over 50 years of age have received particular attention.

The other source of data on nutritional status and food intake is provided by three nationwide studies--two of nutritional status and food intake and one of food intake only.

The most widely used measurements taken to assess nutritional status include height and weight, and the concentration of hemoglobin and selected vitamins, particularly A and C, in the blood. Other measurements on blood, such as protein and iron-binding capacity, and the urinary excretion of thiamin and riboflavin, may be made also but are used less frequently than the other measurements. The dietary studies involve taking records of the kind and amount of foods eaten, calculating the nutritive value, and comparing the intakes of different nutrients with the Recommended Dietary Allowances (RDA's) established by the Food and Nutrition Board of the National Academy of Sciences-National Research Council.

STUDIES OF SPECIAL POPULATION GROUPS

Results of studies of special population groups can be summarized as follows:

Height and weight in relation to age are useful measures of general nutritional status. They have long been used to judge the general adequacy of the quantity and quality of the food intake--both past and present. Results of the studies that have been made of various groups of children indicate a generally consistent relation between height

and weight for age and socioeconomic status. Heights and weights of
children from low-income families are clustered below the averages on
the height-weight charts of Caucasian children of predominently middle-
class origin. The deficit in height and weight has been particularly
true for children of Negro migrant workers, impoverished black families,
and culturally deprived homes, and children on Indian reservations and
from rural areas in Puerto Rico.

Obesity, overweight for height, was found in 10 to 20 percent of
the adolescents studied and most of them were from middle- or upper
middle-income families. Among low- and poverty-income families,
obesity is found more frequently among the women than the children.

Anemia is one of the most prevalent manifestations of malnutrition
among children and young women beginning with the teen years. In the
absence of overt disease or excessive blood loss, anemia is caused by
inadequate intakes of nutrients needed for blood building, particularly
iron. Hemoglobin levels below 10 grams per 100 milliliters of blood are
usually considered as evidence of anemia and such levels are referred
to as "unacceptable."

The incidence of anemia varies with the ages of the children,
being highest in those under 2 years of age. For example, in a study
of children and youth in Comprehensive Health Services Projects, 28
percent of the children from 1 to 2 years had unacceptable values but
the occurrence dropped to 2 percent for the children 5 to 13 years. A
peak in the incidence probably occurs for the teen years for girls.
Anemia is almost twice as prevalent among children of low-income families as among those of higher income families.

Blood levels of selected nutrients, particularly vitamins A and
C and protein, are used to assess nutritional status. Blood levels of
a nutrient are related rather directly to the level of nutrient intake.
The relation between different blood levels and clinical symptoms of
varying degrees of severity, however, is not clearcut except in extreme
deficiency, and extreme cases are rare in the United States.

In an effort to identify blood levels that may be only marginal in
protecting against nutritional deficiency, certain low levels are
designated as "unacceptable." These low levels may be forerunners of
overt clinical symptoms of deficiency and the person with such blood
values is referred to as "at risk" of developing deficiency symptoms.
To illustrate: It is exceedingly rare to have a report of clinical
signs of advanced vitamin A deficiency in a child in the United States.
The incidence of unacceptable blood levels of vitamin A, however, runs
from 20 to 50 percent in children of impoverished families.

Dietary studies constitute an important part of any assessment of
nutritional status. Information gained from such studies cannot be used
to diagnose the presence or absence of malnutrition, but it does indicate the levels of intake of energy and essential nutrients.

Comparison of these levels with the Recommended Dietary Allowances shows the relative adequacy of the intake which then becomes an important adjunct to the evaluation of the total health picture. In addition, dietary studies can provide valuable information on eating patterns, food habits and attitudes, and sources of nutrients. Such information is basic when there is a need for upgrading food and nutrient intakes by nutrition education, for planning programs of food assistance and of food fortification.

In the studies reported, the nutritive quality of the diets was generally related to economic status and level of education. The poorest diets were those of people in rural communities in Puerto Rico, Indians on reservations in the West, Eskimos, Aleuts and Indians in Alaska, Negro migrant agricultural workers, and teenagers from low-income families in urban areas in the Northeast. The nutrients most frequently in short supply were calcium and vitamins C and A. This indicated that the foods most needed to improve diets were milk, citrus fruits, and green and yellow vegetables. Low intakes of iron seemed to be the major problem in diets of preschool children.

A survey in the north central region has identified some factors that influence the diets and nutrient intakes of preschool children. Mothers' nutrition knowledge, mothers' attitudes toward meal planning and food preparation, and parental permissiveness were factors influencing the nutritive quality of diets of the preschool children. Permissiveness was a strong negative factor. The amount of money spent for food and the number of members in the family were related to levels of intakes of calories, protein, fat, and carbohydrates. The amount of money spent and the education of the mother were the more important factors affecting calcium, thiamin, riboflavin, and ascorbic acid intakes. Ascorbic acid intake was influenced more by socioeconomic characteristics of the family than by any other nutrients in the diet. The children's intake of iron was related statistically only to the mothers' education.

NATIONWIDE STUDIES

Beginning in 1965, results of three nationwide studies have been contributing recent and broad assessment of food intakes and nutritional status of children and youth. They are:

The Nationwide Survey of Food Consumption was conducted in the spring of 1965 by the U.S. Department of Agriculture and provides data on a one-day's food intake of a representative sample of 14,519 men, women, and children. Findings have been reported on quantities of food and the nutritive quality of diets for total United States, four income classes, two urbanizations, and two regions.

The National Nutrition Survey was initiated in 1968 to determine the prevalence of malnutrition and related health problems in the United States. The survey was sponsored by the Public Health Service, U.S. Department of Health, Education, and Welfare, and carried out under contract by agencies in the 10 States selected for the study-- Texas, Louisiana, New York, Kentucky, Michigan, California, Washington, South Carolina, West Virginia, and Massachusetts. The sample was randomly selected from the lowest income quartile and included approximately 24,000 households and 96,000 individuals. Data from clinical examinations and biochemical analyses and information on diets and socioeconomic factors related to health have been released for two States--Texas and Louisiana. Data from the other States are being analyzed.

The Survey of Nutritional Status of Preschool Children was initiated in November 1968 to evaluate the nutritional status of approximately 5,000 preschool children in the United States. The survey is being conducted by the Department of Pediatrics, Ohio State University, and the Children's Hospital Research Foundation in Columbus, Ohio, and is supported in part by a grant from the Maternal and Child Health Service, U.S. Department of Health, Education, and Welfare. The children were selected at random in a national probability sample of the United States. Some 25,000 households from 74 primary sampling units in 40 States are included in the 2-year survey. For each child in the survey, there is an evaluation of dietary intake, a physical examination, and a battery of biochemical determinations. Some data from clinical examinations have been published.

THE NATIONWIDE SURVEY OF FOOD INTAKE OF INDIVIDUALS

This study is the first to obtain information on a nationwide basis of the food eaten in a 24-hour period by individuals of all ages. The sample for children and youth included approximately 8,000 persons from birth to age 19. Results of the survey are summarized below:

For most of the sex-age groups from infants to young adults, average diets approached (90 to 100 percent) or were above the Recommended Dietary Allowances (RDA's) set by the Food and Nutrition Board of the National Academy of Sciences-National Research Council in 1968 for energy, vitamin A value, thiamin, riboflavin, and ascorbic acid. For all income groups, calcium and iron were the nutrients most often below allowances. In the low-income families the nutrients most often below recommended allowances, in addition to calcium and iron, were ascorbic acid and vitamin A value.

Charts 1 and 2 show the sex-age groups between infancy and 34 years of age with nutrient intakes below the allowances and the magnitude of deficiency for all individuals studied and for those from families with incomes under $3,000.

NUTRIENT INTAKE BELOW RECOMMENDED ALLOWANCE
In all Households

SEX—AGE (YEARS)	PROTEIN	CALCIUM	IRON	VITAMIN A VALUE	THIAMINE	RIBO-FLAVIN	ASCORBIC ACID
MALE AND FEMALE:							
UNDER 1			****				
1—2			****				
3—5			**				
6—8							
MALE:							
9—11		*					
12—14		**	***		*		
15—17		*	*				
18—19							
20—34							
35—54		*					
55—64		**					
65—74		**					
75 & OVER		***		*		**	*
FEMALE:							
9—11		***	****		*		
12—14		****	****	*	*		
15—17		****	****		**		
18—19		***	****	*	*		
20—34		***	****		*	*	
35—54		****	***		*	**	
55—64		****			*	*	
65—74		****	*	*	**	**	
75 & OVER		***		*	**	***	

BELOW BY: * 1—10%   ** 11—20%   * 21—29%   **** 30% OR MORE**

AVERAGE INTAKE OF GROUP BELOW RECOMMENDED DIETARY ALLOWANCE, NAS—NRC, 1968
U.S. DIETS OF MEN, WOMEN, AND CHILDREN, 1 DAY IN SPRING, 1965

U.S. DEPARTMENT OF AGRICULTURE   NEG. ARS. 5947-69 (4)   AGRICULTURAL RESEARCH SERVICE

Chart 1

NUTRIENT INTAKE BELOW RECOMMENDED ALLOWANCE
In Households With Incomes Under $3,000

SEX—AGE (YEARS)	PROTEIN	CALCIUM	IRON	VITAMIN A VALUE	THIAMINE	RIBO-FLAVIN	ASCORBIC ACID
MALE AND FEMALE:							
UNDER 1			****				***
1—2			****				**
3—5		*	**				***
6—8		**	*	*	*		*
MALE:							
9—11		***		**	*		
12—14		****	***	**	**		
15—17		***	**	*	*		**
18—19		***					
20—34				*			
35—54				*			*
55—64		**					***
65—74		**		*			*
75 & OVER		****		***		***	****
FEMALE:							
9—11		****	****		*		
12—14		****	****	***	**		
15—17		****	****		**		**
18—19		****	****		**	**	***
20—34		****	****			**	**
35—54		****	****	**	*	**	**
55—64		****		**	**	**	**
65—74		****	*		**	**	**
75 & OVER		***	**	**	***	***	**

BELOW BY: * 1—10%   ** 11—20%   * 21—29%   **** 30% OR MORE**

AVERAGE INTAKE OF GROUP BELOW RECOMMENDED DIETARY ALLOWANCE, NAS—NRC, 1968
U.S. DIETS OF MEN, WOMEN, AND CHILDREN, 1 DAY IN SPRING, 1965

U.S. DEPARTMENT OF AGRICULTURE   NEG. ARS. 5948-69 (4)   AGRICULTURAL RESEARCH SERVICE

Chart 2

When averages for several nutrients are below the recommended allowances for a sex-age group, it is safe to conclude that some persons within that group had diets in need of improvement. When averages are more than 30 percent below recommendations, as in calcium and iron, the proportion of persons in these groups with diets in need of improvement is almost certain to be high.

Infants and preschool children.--Average diets of infants and young children met the recommended allowances for all nutrients studied except iron. For children under 3 years, diets averaged about half of the allowance for iron. Infants up to 2 months consumed relatively more iron than older infants (3 to 11 months), probably because some were given formulas fortified with iron.

Intake of ascorbic acid averaged below the allowance for infants aged 0 to 2 months. These infants had an average of 67 grams of vegetables and fruits, but only a small proportion of it was tomatoes and citrus or dark green and deep yellow vegetables. Also low in ascorbic acid were diets of 1- and 2-year-old children in rural low-income families (under $3,000) in the North and of infants and young children in both urban and rural families with incomes under $5,000 in the South.

A major problem in diets of children aged 1 to 5 years was the low intake of iron. Other studies have shown that calcium, vitamin A, and ascorbic acid also are short in the diets of many children.

Children 6 to 11 years.--For the United States as a whole, nutrients supplied by the diets of boys and girls aged 6 to 8 and boys 9 to 11 years old averaged 90 percent or more of the RDA's for all major nutrients. Diets of girls aged 9 to 11 were low in calcium and iron for the U.S. average. In the South the average iron and calcium intakes of girls 9 to 11 years were about two-thirds of the RDA's, and iron was a similar problem for northern girls in this age group.

The relationship of unfavorable diets to low income is indicated by average nutrient supplies among children in families with incomes below $3,000. Low-income children in the 9 to 11 year group living in the rural North had relatively low intakes of calcium, iron, and vitamin A value. In the rural South, only calcium intake was low for low-income children in this age group. Low intakes of calcium, iron, and vitamin A are related to low levels of consumption for milk products and dark green and yellow vegetables.

Grain products and meats contribute the greatest amounts of iron to the diet. The boys met the allowances for iron; the girls 9 to 11 years did not, even though substantial amounts of these foods were eaten.

Average consumption of milk for children 9 to 11 years was a little over two cups, compared with the 3 or more cups suggested by USDA. Girls drank less milk than boys on the average, but obtained more of it away from home. Milk consumption was higher at successively higher levels of income.

Teenagers, 12 to 17 years.--As children progress into the teen years, the difference between the food patterns of boys and girls increase. Teenage boys (12 to 17 years of age) generally had satisfactory diets but many teenage girls did not eat foods that provided the recommended amounts of nutrients. The younger teenage girls (12 to 14 years) tended to drink more milk and eat more citrus fruit and tomatoes, cereal products, and potatoes than the older teenage girls (15 to 17 years). Boys continued to eat larger amounts of these foods as they moved into the later teens. Soft drinks were consumed in greater quantities by the older teenagers. However, the boys did not decrease their milk drinking with the increased consumption of soft drinks to the extent that the older girls did. This substantial displacement of fluid milk intake by soft drinks by the older girls was reflected in their low calcium intakes.

Teenagers in the lowest income groups had the least favorable average intakes of calories, calcium, iron, and ascorbic acid in most parts of the country. The largest amounts of soft drinks and grain products were consumed by teenagers in the low-income groups, whereas larger quantities of milk and citrus fruit tended to be consumed by teenagers in the higher income groups. Urban boys, 15 to 17 years, from low-income families in the South appeared to drink less fluid milk than those 12 to 14 years of age, whereas their northern counterparts drank more than the younger boys.

Calories, calcium, iron, and vitamin A were the nutrients in shortest supply in the diets of teenage girls. The low calcium and caloric intakes of the older teenage girls reflected a decreased consumption of milk, grain products, and other protein-containing foods. In most instances low vitamin A values could be traced to the low intakes of dark green and yellow vegetables. Dietary iron intake tends to be proportional to the caloric content of the diet. Thus, the lower iron intakes of girls compared with boys was related in part to their lower total caloric intakes.

Young adults.--Average diets of young men in the age groups 18 to 19 and 20 to 34 supplied adequate amounts of the major nutrients, but the diets of young women in this age range were inadequate in calcium and iron. The milk consumption of these young women was lower than amounts recommended by most nutritionists.

In low-income families in the South, 18- to 19-year old men obtained less than two-thirds of the allowance for calcium and ascorbic acid. Several groups of young women in the South had average diets below two-thirds of the allowances for ascorbic acid and vitamin A value. In low-income families of the North, average intakes of ascorbic acid and vitamin A value were less than two-thirds of the allowances for young women 18 to 19 years in urban areas.

Low consumption of tomatoes and citrus fruits by these groups accounted for the low intakes of ascorbic acid. Consumption of dark green and deep yellow vegetables accounted for some of the variations in intakes of vitamin A.

Good nutrition is especially important to young women because many of them are bearing children. An adequate state of nutrition for the pregnant women is an important factor in the normal course of pregnancy and having a healthy infant.

There were 147 pregnant women in the nationwide sample. By age, 8 percent were 15 to 19 years, 76 percent were 20 to 34, and 15 percent, 35 to 54. A comparison of the average diets with a recommended food pattern indicated the need for increased consumption of milk and milk products and fruits and vegetables. This is shown in table 1.

Table 1.--Diets of pregnant women, recommended and 1965 food consumption survey

Food	Suggested dietary pattern per day during the latter half of pregnancy [1]	Average dietary intake [2] of pregnant women-- 1965 survey	
		15 to 19 years	20 to 34 years
Milk (any kind)[3] -----cup--	4	1-2/3	1-1/3
Lean meat, fish, poultry or meat alternate (use liver or heart frequently) -----ounce--	5	6-1/2	6
Egg----------------each--	1	1	3/4
Fruits and vegetables (1 serving = 1/2 cup) ----servings---	5	3-3/4	3-3/4
Whole grain or enriched cereal			
Cooked-------------cup--	1/2 to 3/4	1/4	1/8
Ready-to-eat (Dry)--do--	3/4	1/16	1/6
Whole grain or enriched bread-----------slices--	2 to 3	4	3

1/ U.S. Dept. HEW, Children's Bur. Pub. No. 4, Prenatal Care. 1965
2/ Approximate
3/ Calcium equivalent

The nutritive value of the diets of the pregnant women in the survey bears out this conclusion. Diets were 30 to 50 percent below the recommendations for calcium and 20 to 35 percent below for iron and vitamin A value. Only in protein were the diets of pregnant women comfortably above the recommended allowance of the Food and Nutrition Board.

THE NATIONAL NUTRITION SURVEY

The completed data will furnish important information for interpretation within the population sampled; that is, the lowest income quartile.

Selected results from Texas and Louisiana, of the 10 States surveyed, are available at this time. Within these two States, over 13,000 individuals were studied. Black Americans constituted one-half of the sample, Spanish-speaking Americans from Texas constituted more than one-fourth, and white Americans less than one-fourth of the sample. Over half of the surveyed population was under 20 years of age. Two-thirds of the households in the Texas sample and 53 percent of the Louisiana sample were below the poverty level.

In one sample of children, the heights of those under 7 years of age reflected the poor growth achievement of white, black, and Mexican-American children. Poor tooth development and a high rate of dental caries were found. Caries were seldom treated in the children of these relatively low-income groups. The percentage of carious, unfilled teeth was often above 50.

The most striking clinical finding in the children examined, other than the poor condition of their teeth, was the physical evidence associated with rickets due to vitamin D deficiency. This was observed in some children in each State.

Many determinations of the food intake and biochemical measurements of the sample showed serious deficiencies as indicated by unacceptable blood values for key nutrients (table 2).

Although clinical signs of vitamin A deficiency were found infrequently, low plasma concentrations of vitamin A and low dietary intakes gave evidence of a problem with this vitamin in both States. Children had greater percentages of blood values considered unacceptable than adults.

Table 2.--Percentage of children with unacceptable blood values by
type of deficiency and age, special survey, Texas and
Louisiana

| Deficiency and age group | Percent unacceptable blood values | | | |
| | Texas | | Louisiana | |
	Boys	Girls	Boys	Girls
Hemoglobin:				
Less than 6 years ------------:	13	9	40	35
6 to 9 years ------------------:	12	9	50	40
10 to 16 years ----------------:	16	13	46	34
Vitamin A:				
Less than 6 years ------------:	79	80	40	45
6 to 9 years ------------------:	82	78	33	33
10 to 16 years ----------------:	68	66	19	16
Vitamin C:				
Less than 6 years ------------:	9	11	10	12
6 to 9 years ------------------:	11	10	8	10
10 to 16 years ----------------:	13	13	12	10

THE SURVEY OF NUTRITIONAL STATUS OF PRESCHOOL CHILDREN

In general, the data being accumulated in this study of nutritional
status indicate that iron deficiency is a fairly common occurrence among
preschool children in the United States, regardless of socioeconomic
status. The incidence is greatest, however, among the poor. Although
not all anemia is due to iron deficiency, it appears that a preschool
child with anemia frequently has iron deficiency. Relatively few children in the study were found to be receiving inadequate protein in
their diets. No children have been detected with scurvy, but a significant number of the preschool children in low-income families had
intakes of vitamin C that were well below recommended levels. Plasma
levels of ascorbic acid correlated well with recent dietary intakes of
vitamin C. Calculation of nutrient intakes has yet to be published.

Selected findings are now available on 725 children, 1 to 6 years
of age, from 518 families in 15 States. Seven percent of these children
had hemoglobin values judged as anemic, but about 45 percent had an iron
deficiency based on the iron-binding capacity of the blood plasma.
Among the children in the poverty area, the incidence of anemia rose to
20 percent, and presumably the deficiency in iron-binding capacity would
have been correspondingly high.

UNMET NEEDS

The greatest unmet needs in attaining optimum nutritional health for all the Nation's children and youth include:

(1) Economic resources to enable families to purchase adequate kinds and amounts of food for their children. The relation between a low-income and a poverty status and the incidence of manifestations of poor nutrition are unmistakeable. School feeding as discussed in the next section has been the most concerted public effort to bridge the gap between the need and supply of food for children. This program holds the key to the most immediate, massive attack on the problem of underfed, hungry children of school age.

The other vulnerable groups of children and youth, preschool children and pregnant and lactating teenage mothers in economically deprived homes, are target groups in line to receive increasing attention through special feeding programs in childcare centers or extra allowances in food assistance programs either in kind or purchasing power.

(2) Consumption of more milk and fruits and vegetables to provide the nutrients most often found in short supply--calcium, iron, vitamins A and C. In addition, these foods supply other important nutrients and energy. Some food suppliers and educators advocate increased fortification of staple foods to supply needed amounts of minerals and vitamins.

Calcium and iron could be added to all bread, bakery products, flour, mixes, and pastas for a cost of not more than $15 million annually. The value of such a practice, however, is limited because the age and sex groups that need the largest amount of these nutrients consume the smallest amounts of such foods. The same is true of iron fortification of milk. Boys consume the largest amounts of these foods and their intakes of calcium and iron are more adequate than the intakes of the girls.

(3) Nutrition education for all consumers, with special attention to teaching children and youth the relation of food to health. Important as are economic resources to procure food, they do not guarantee wise food selection to meet nutritional needs. Children and their families are entitled to be informed of simple principles of good food choices and motivated to practice them.

FOOD ASSISTANCE PROGRAMS

Federal food assistance programs reach children in two ways. First, a series of child nutrition programs provide food services in elementary and secondary schools, day-care centers, organized summer activity programs, and institutions. Second, family food assistance programs for those in economic need reach children in their homes.

CURRENT STATUS

The increased awareness of hunger and malnutrition during the 1960's resulted in a national commitment expressed by the President on May 6, 1969, in his "Hunger Message" to Congress: "The moment is at hand to put an end to hunger in America itself for all time."

Public awareness also brought forth new legislation, increased funds and resources, and general recognition of the plight of millions of people who lacked money to buy adequate diets, During 1969 and 1970, the number of children and families getting food help through U.S. Department of Agriculture programs gained dramatically:

• The hope of reaching 6.6 million needy children with free or reduced price school lunches became a practical goal during the fall of 1970. In total, nearly 21 million children are being served through the school lunch activity, including those who can pay the regular price along with the needy youngsters. Earlier, through the 1960's, free and reduced price meals annually benefited about 10 percent of total participation. In 1960, about 12 million children participated.

• Some 500,000 youngsters through high school age in poor areas got at least one good meal a day during the summer months of 1970. They were served through recreation programs in several cities including Chicago, Atlanta, and Washington, D.C.

• Breakfast at school, inaugurated in 1968, for needy youngsters who arrive hungry is gaining. Some 500,000 children benefited from the added nourishment of milk, cereal, and fruit juice each school morning in 1970.

• Participation in the Food Stamp Program rose to 8.8 million people in October 1970, compared with 3.3 million a year earlier, largely as a result of improvements in the program. Participants now receive enough stamps to buy at least the food necessary to attain USDA's "economy diet."

•The Commodity Distribution Program for families was improved during 1969 and 1970, now providing fortified and enriched foods and a wider variety than ever before. Some 24 foods are currently available for donation. Participation which reached a peak of over 7 million people in 1962, stood at 3.5 million in October 1970, as the Food Stamp Program was steadily expanding.

•A total of 12.3 million people were being helped by a family food assistance program in October 1970. No figures are available on ages of participants in either the stamp or commodity program.

•The supplemental food program, operating on a test basis in 262 areas at the end of fiscal year 1970, provided extra allotments of nutritious foods to some 170,000 pregnant women, infants, and young children in October 1970.

•The goal of nationwide availability of a family food assistance program is virtually met. As of October 31, 1970, only 10 of the 3,129 counties and independent cities of the Nation are without a family food program commitment, and less than 1 percent of the U.S. population·resides in those 10 areas.

Charts 3 through 8 show participation and funding of Child Nutrition Programs.

CHILD NUTRITION PROGRAMS
Federal Reimbursement (Cash Assistance Only)

Million Dollars

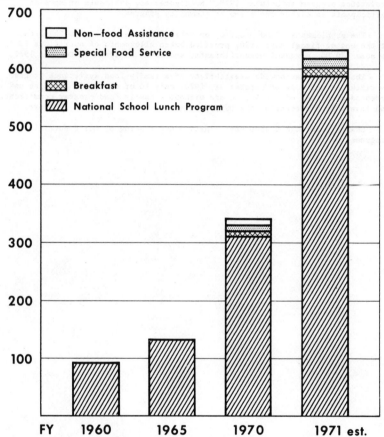

FY   1960   1965   1970   1971 est.

FOOD AND NUTRITION SERVICE Program Reporting Staff

Chart 3

PARTICIPATION[1] IN SCHOOL LUNCH AND SCHOOL BREAKFAST PROGRAMS

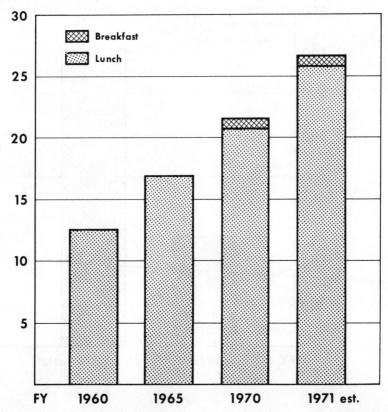

Millions of students

FY 1960 1965 1970 1971 est.

Breakfast
Lunch

[1] Peak month average daily participation

FOOD AND NUTRITION SERVICE Program Reporting Staff

Chart 4

PARTICIPATION IN SPECIAL
FOOD SERVICE PROGRAMS

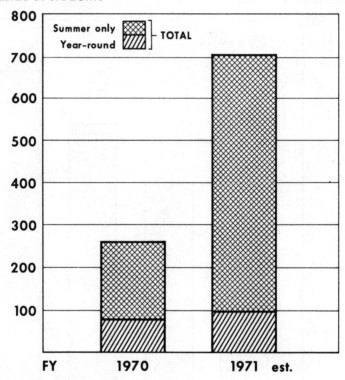

Thousands of students

FOOD AND NUTRITION SERVICE Program Reporting Staff

Chart 5

CHILDREN RECEIVING FREE AND REDUCED PRICE MEALS IN SCHOOL LUNCH AND SCHOOL BREAKFAST PROGRAMS [1]

Millions of students

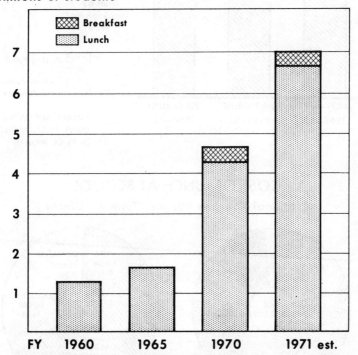

[1] Peak average daily participation multiplied by percentage of free and reduced price meals to total.

FOOD AND NUTRITION SERVICE Program Reporting Staff

Chart 6

CHILDREN GETTING LUNCH AT SCHOOL
(National School Lunch Program)

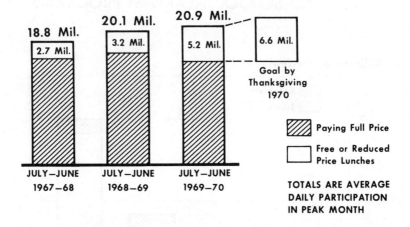

18.8 Mil.
2.7 Mil.

20.1 Mil.
3.2 Mil.

20.9 Mil.
5.2 Mil.

6.6 Mil.

Goal by
Thanksgiving
1970

JULY—JUNE
1967—68

JULY—JUNE
1968—69

JULY—JUNE
1969—70

Paying Full Price

Free or Reduced
Price Lunches

TOTALS ARE AVERAGE
DAILY PARTICIPATION
IN PEAK MONTH

COST OF LUNCH AT SCHOOL
(National Average 60¢ for "Type A" Lunch)

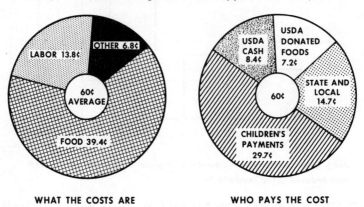

LABOR 13.8¢   OTHER 6.8¢

60¢
AVERAGE

FOOD 39.4¢

WHAT THE COSTS ARE

USDA
CASH
8.4¢

USDA
DONATED
FOODS
7.2¢

STATE AND
LOCAL
14.7¢

60¢

CHILDREN'S
PAYMENTS
29.7¢

WHO PAYS THE COST

EXPENDITURES FOR FOOD ASSISTANCE

The Federal budget request for all Child Nutrition Programs -- school lunch, breakfast, milk, special nonschool food service, equipment, State administrative expenses, and value of donated foods -- for the fiscal year ending June 30, 1971, totals approximately $1 billion. That's an increase of more than $300 million from fiscal year 1970, and compares with a total of $306 million spent in 1960 for school lunch and milk, the only programs then available.

In addition, for the lunch program, value of contributions by State and local sources (excluding payments by children) is expected to reach $730 million in the 1970-71 school year, compared with about $230 million in 1960-61.

Budgets for other food assistance programs in fiscal year 1971 are food stamps, $1.2 billion, double the amount for 1970; commodity distribution to families, $272 million, about $10 million above 1970 and compares with $140 million in 1960-61; supplemental foods for mothers, infants, and children, $40 million--about $7 million more than the 1970 fiscal year. Neither food stamps nor supplemental foods were available in 1960.

PRESENT PROGRAMS

Child Nutrition

National School Lunch Program

This is the oldest and most extensive of the child nutrition programs. Federal assistance to school lunch programs began in the 1930's. The National School Lunch Act, which provided substantive legislation for a program of cash assistance, was passed in 1946.

The National School Lunch Program is a grant-in-aid program operated through State educational agencies. Any public or nonprofit private school of high school grade or under is eligible to receive Federal assistance for its lunch program, if it agrees to operate its lunch program on a nonprofit basis, serves a lunch meeting specified nutritional standards, and serves lunch free or at a reduced price to children unable to pay the full price of the lunch. In those States where State educational agencies cannot disburse funds to nonprofit private schools, such schools may participate in the program under a direct agreement with the U.S. Department of Agriculture.

From the passage of the Act through 1961, Federal assistance was available in the form of: (1) Cash assistance to reimburse schools for a portion of the food costs of the lunch service; (2) foods especially purchased for school lunch programs; (3) other foods acquired by the Department of Agriculture under farm market stabilization programs; and (4) technical assistance in menu planning, buying guides, and other aspects of school food service management.

From 1962 through the 1969-70 school year, those schools with concentrations of children from low-income families (the children needing free or reduced price lunches) were eligible for additional assistance to finance the food costs of their lunch programs.

As the 1970-71 school year opened, significant changes were put into effect in the National School Lunch Program as a result of the passage of P.L. 91-248 in May 1970. These program changes, among other things, are designed to make effective the program's requirement that needy children receive a free or reduced price lunch; to foster more rapid expansion of the program to all elementary and secondary schools; and to strengthen the nutrition education potential of school food services.

Under the new provisions of law, school officials must:

(1) Develop and publicly announce eligibility standards for free and reduced price lunches, which take into account family income, family size, and the number of children in school and preschool programs;

(2) Not later than January 1, 1971, serve free and reduced price lunch to children from families with incomes at or below "annual income poverty guidelines" established by the Secretary of Agriculture ($3,720 for a family of four for the 1970-71 school year);

(3) Strengthen procedures to protect the anonymity of the children who receive free and reduced price lunches; and

(4) Develop a simple system for families to apply for free and reduced price lunches, and provide for a fair hearing procedure.

P.L. 91-248 also significantly changed the type of Federal financial assistance that is available in the service of free and reduced price school lunches. Beginning this school year, any school is eligible for such special cash assistance if special assistance is required to meet the need for free and reduced price lunches. Also, such special assistance is no longer limited to only the food costs of a lunch program.

To encourage better long-range school lunch planning, State educational agencies are required to develop annual plans of operation to provide free and reduced price lunches to needy children and to extend the program to all schools within the State. The Act also provides for increased financial support for school lunch programs from State appropriated funds.

P.L. 91-248, for the first time, authorizes the use of a portion of the
Federal appropriation in child nutrition programs to undertake nutrition
education and training for participating children, for workers, and for other
program cooperators; and for special developmental projects. The new Act
also authorizes use of some Federal funds to finance child food service
surveys and evaluation and for a National Advisory Council.

Special Milk Program

In 1954, the Special Milk Program was authorized. Under it, schools and
nonprofit institutions for children receive Federal assistance for the service
of fluid milk to children.

School Breakfast Program

In 1966, the Child Nutrition Act authorized Federal cash assistance for
school breakfast programs. The previous program of commodity assistance to
school breakfast programs was continued. First consideration was given to
those schools which draw their attendance from areas in which poor economic
conditions exist and to those schools in which a substantial proportion of
the children must travel long distances daily to school.

Cash assistance is used to help finance the food costs of the breakfast
program, but broader assistance is available to those schools with a "severe
need" to carry on an effective breakfast program. Patterned after the lunch
program, the breakfast served must meet specified nutritional standards;
and needy children are to be served free and reduced price breakfasts under
conditions that protect their anonymity.

Nonfood Assistance Program

In 1966, the Child Nutrition Act authorized Federal assistance to schools
in low-income areas to purchase needed equipment to begin, maintain, and
improve their school feeding programs.

State Administrative Expenses

In 1966, the Child Nutrition Act authorized Federal funds to assist
State educational agencies to carry out broadened responsibilities for
school feeding programs.

Special Food Service Program for Children

In 1968, Federal cash assistance (in addition to the previous program of commodity assistance) was made available to assist nonresidential, nonprofit institutions including day care centers and summer day camps in the operation of their food service programs for preschool and school-age children. (Residential nonprofit institutions and summer camps for children are eligible for commodity assistance and for the Special Milk Program.)

Cash assistance is used to help finance the food costs of these special food service programs but broader assistance is available in those situations where there is a "severe" need to carry on an effective program. Assistance may also be provided to help finance the cost of needed food service equipment.

Family Food Assistance

Since the mid-1930's, the Commodity Distribution Program has been available to provide food assistance to low-income families, although its size and scope have varied. Needs during the 1960's brought about the revival of the food stamp approach, first utilized between 1939-43. Beginning in 1961, a food stamp program was operated on a small-scale pilot basis. In 1964, the Food Stamp Act was passed.

Counties or other political units can elect which of these two programs they will utilize to provide food assistance to low-income families. Under the Commodity Distribution Program, the participating family is assisted through direct food donations. Under the stamp program, the food purchasing power of participating families is increased by changing the money they normally spend for food into food stamps of a higher monetary value.

Significant actions have been taken to improve the quality of family feeding programs, and other improvements are underway.

The Food Stamp Program was liberalized in December 1969 to reduce purchase requirements and to increase the level of the Federal food subsidy.

Other proposed changes in the Food Stamp Program are before the Congress. As examples, these proposals call for uniform national standards of eligibility; free stamp allotments for the poorest families; a more flexible program under which eligible families could elect the level of investment and assistance (the variable purchase plan); and strengthened programs of outreach.

It is expected that, ultimately, most areas of the country will transfer from the commodity program to the Food Stamp Program. (In September of 1970, about two-thirds of the counties in the country were operating or approved to operate a stamp program.)

In the interim, under the Commodity Distribution Program, the kinds and qualities of available foods have received increased attention. For example: Donated supplies of cornmeal, corn grits, and rice provide the regular B-vitamin enrichment but have higher levels of iron; a higher protein-content macaroni has been utilized; vitamins A and C are added to instant potatoes and vitamins A and D to nonfat dry milk; a special bread flour has been developed for the Navajo Reservation. Other enrichment and fortification programs are underway and policies for the use of engineered foods have been developed.

Federal funds have been made available, beginning in 1970, to assist States to begin commodity programs in counties without a family food program and to improve the quality of operating programs. (The Food Stamp Act authorizes some Federal matching of within-State food stamp operating costs.)

Within both family assistance programs, actions are underway to support pilot programs of supplemental food assistance designed to further improve nutrition among low-income new mothers and expectant mothers, infants, and young children. These pilot programs take two forms--the direct donation of selected foods or the use of special food certificates good for the purchase of selected foods in retail stores.

A Nutrition and Technical Services Staff is being organized within the Food and Nutrition Service. The Staff will develop a nutrition education program for food assistance participants and assist in carrying it out.

Participation and Funding

Included in this section are statistical summaries of participation and funding of food assistance programs, prepared by the Food and Nutrition Service, U.S. Department of Agriculture. Tables 3 through 6 indicate outputs and obligations by selected years (1960, 1965, 1970) for Child Nutrition Programs, Food Stamp Programs, Commodity Distribution Program, and Special Milk Program.

Table 7 indicates funds for Child Food Services apportioned to States for FY 1970. Table 8 indicates participation in the School Lunch Program for FY 1970, and Table 9 indicates participation in Family Food Assistance Programs as of June 1970.

Table 3.--Child nutrition programs: Outputs and obligations, by selected years

Category	1960	1965	1970
Outputs:			
School lunch			
Number of lunches served (mil.).:	2,153	2,892	3,594
Average number of children			
served (mil.) 1/.............:	12	16	20
Free and reduced price lunches			
Number of lunches served (mil.).:	217	286	736
School breakfast			
Number of breakfasts			
served (mil.).................:	...	...	68
Average number of children			
served (thou.)...............:	...	...	2/ 377
Nonfood assistance			
Number of schools equipped	...	...	6,371
Nonschool food program			
Number of meals served (thou.)..:	...	...	49,475
Peak number of children			
served (thou.)...............:	...	...	246
Obligations (thou.):			
Federal 3/......................:	$225,672	$402,821	$595,908
State and local.................:	775,837	1,089,954	1,663,700
Total.........................:	1.001.509	1.492.775	2.259.608

1/ Children enrolled in schools of high school grade and under. Age
distribution not available.
2/ Peak served 497,760 children.
3/ Includes commodity distribution under Section 32, Section 416 and
Section 6.

Table 4.--Food Stamp Program: Outputs and obligations, by selected years

Category	1960	1965	1970
Outputs:			
Average participation (thou.).....:	(1/)	425	4,343
Average number of children			
participating (thou.) 2/........:	(1/)	204	2,085
Number of areas...................:	(1/)	110	1,747
Obligations:			
Federal (thou.)...................:	(1/)	$32,494	$549,649

1/ The first project opened May 29, 1961.
2/ Children enrolled in schools of high school grade and under. Age
distribution not available. Estimate of under 18 years of age based on 18th
Decennial Census data.

Table 5.--Commodity Distribution Program: Outputs and obligations, by selected
        years

Category	1960	1965	1970
Outputs:			
Schools			
Peak number of children served (mil.) 1/............:	16	20	23
Peak number of children in non-ala-carte school lunch program served (mil.) 1/......:	13	17	21
Institutions			
Peak number of persons served (mil.)................:	2	3	3
Peak number of children served (mil.) 2/............:	1	2	2
Needy families			
Peak number of persons served (mil.)................:	4	6	4
Peak number of children served (mil.) 1/ 2/..........:	2	3	2
Obligations (thou.):			
Federal			
Schools......................:	$132,025	$272,408	$259,044
Institutions...................:	15,748	29,818	20,698
Needy families.................:	59,410	226,883	291,157
Total......................:	207,183	529,109	570,899

1/ Children enrolled in schools of high school grade and under. Age
distribution not available.
2/ Age distribution of institutional recipients not available. Estimate
of under 18 years based on 18th Decennial Census data.

Table 6.--Special Milk Program: Outputs and obligations, by selected years

Category	1960	1965	1970
Outputs:			
Number of half-pints of milk reimbursed (mil.)..............:	2,384	2,967	2,868
Average number of children served (mil.) 1/.............:	13	16	16
Obligations (thou.):			
Federal 2/.......................:	$80,277	$97,195	$102,124

1/ Children enrolled in schools of high school grade and under. Age distribution not available.
2/ Excludes administrative expenses.

Table 7 indicates a total of $417,126,810 in Federal funds for Child Food Services, apportioned to the 50 States, the District of Columbia, and five territories, for FY 1970 (column 8). This was an increase of $6,000,000 over the previous year.

$44,800,000 was for cash aid in schools that are located in needy areas, under Section 11 of the National School Lunch Act (column 2). These funds provide additional assistance to selected needy schools where State and local sources as well as children's payments are inadequate to meet program requirements for free and reduced price lunches to needy children. This was nearly 4 1/2 times the $10,000,000 in needy-area aid provided the previous year.

$10,000,000 was for food assistance in the School Breakfast Program, largely in schools in needy areas (column 3). These funds are for the local purchase of foods, and funds from local sources meet the cost of preparing and serving the breakfasts. This was a gain of $6,500,000 over the previous year.

$10,000,000 was for reimbursement up to 75 percent of the cost of obtaining equipment for needy schools for the initiation, expansion, or improvement of lunch or breakfast programs (column 4). This was an increase of $9,250,000 over the previous year.

$67,000,000 is primarily to expand free or reduced price lunches and breakfasts to children from low-income families (column 5). This was $24,000,000 more than for 1969.

$15,000,000 is for Special Food Service for Children in Day-Care and Recreation Centers and other nonschool situations (column 6). This was $5,825 more than for 1969.

$102,285,810 was to help pay the cost of milk served to children by schools and child care organizations (column 7). This was the same as for the previous year's amount.

In addition to these cash allocations, the U.S. Department of Agriculture donated food amounting to $213,000,000 to the States for their use in food service programs to children. This was an increase of about $6,000,000 over the amount of food aid to schools last year.

Table 7.--Initial apportionment of funds for child food services, by States, Fiscal Year 1970

State	NSLP lunch (1)	Needy areas (2)	Breakfast (3)	Equipment (4)	Additional needy (5)	Nonschool food serv. (6)	Special Milk (7)	Total funds (8)
Alabama	$ 5,594,572	$ 2,060,866	$ 294,870	$ 332,929	$ 2,571,095	$ 572,582	$ 1,878,670	$ 13,305,584
Alaska	189,886	143,083	58,311	11,300	64,971	62,638	28,892	559,081
Arizona	1,535,038	553,125	117,187	91,349	488,608	149,310	416,822	3,351,439
Arkansas	3,152,936	1,661,006	188,001	187,629	1,586,211	372,403	1,117,695	8,262,881
California	6,308,394	1,252,434	126,112	375,408	3,793,102	604,943	8,948,698	21,588,791
Colorado	1,785,284	203,452	128,140	106,241	480,575	140,695	947,678	3,852,065
Connecticut	1,482,306	129,612	114,880	88,211	390,038	106,595	1,775,091	4,086,733
Delaware	449,274	45,325	69,664	26,736	99,123	69,252	382,934	1,142,808
District of Columbia	260,564	281,173	61,405	15,506	239,423	92,470	618,710	1,569,251
Florida	6,667,867	2,551,184	341,846	396,800	1,911,910	439,008	1,978,478	14,289,093
Georgia	7,583,774	2,345,735	381,935	451,305	2,804,306	619,983	1,685,552	15,872,610
Guam	162,849	4,238	22,128	9,691	47,328	6,832	---	253,066
Hawaii	1,035,166	139,824	95,308	61,602	148,964	75,880	157,502	1,714,246
Idaho	746,186	56,441	82,660	44,405	191,870	86,276	187,844	1,395,682
Illinois	4,818,475	531,641	260,900	286,744	2,339,257	443,703	6,637,287	15,318,007
Indiana	3,963,886	242,993	223,496	235,888	1,024,736	252,887	2,972,080	8,915,966
Iowa	2,990,407	259,802	180,887	177,957	964,731	232,947	1,806,283	6,613,014
Kansas	1,953,057	199,858	135,483	116,225	601,073	161,295	1,103,140	4,270,131
Kentucky	4,860,838	1,619,214	262,754	289,265	2,071,335	469,864	2,012,642	11,585,912
Louisiana	6,814,355	1,712,845	348,258	405,518	2,304,838	518,361	708,274	12,862,459
Maine	936,392	121,248	90,985	51,724	281,959	107,310	507,190	2,190,778
Maryland	2,213,957	252,631	146,903	115,251	819,355	199,413	2,446,903	6,210,913
Massachusetts	3,972,926	689,681	223,891	236,426	887,179	185,429	3,535,303	9,730,835
Michigan	4,171,349	386,950	232,576	248,234	1,904,077	377,557	5,028,335	12,349,078
Minnesota	3,907,793	328,249	221,041	232,550	1,091,340	257,223	2,661,225	8,692,621
Mississippi	4,596,439	1,803,176	251,183	273,532	2,501,348	558,427	1,386,354	11,370,459
Missouri	4,164,863	624,993	232,292	247,848	1,543,363	360,436	2,397,322	9,571,117
Montana	506,896	107,953	72,186	30,165	193,501	88,076	203,874	1,202,651
Nebraska	1,330,582	234,089	108,238	79,182	489,342	145,839	637,916	3,025,188
Nevada	149,825	25,005	56,558	8,916	44,663	58,585	150,271	494,023
New Hampshire	539,092	48,705	73,596	32,081	99,467	68,875	531,971	1,393,787
New Jersey	2,306,363	453,142	150,947	137,250	1,074,922	211,584	3,806,956	8,141,464
New Mexico	1,258,409	630,712	105,080	74,887	471,294	145,793	731,992	3,418,167
New York	10,864,792	6,270,297	525,542	646,556	4,383,296	621,624	9,728,443	33,040,550
North Carolina	8,045,458	2,961,222	402,273	478,958	3,579,038	777,291	3,646,881	19,894,121
North Dakota	632,358	111,660	86,432	49,533	311,315	110,247	354,775	1,856,320
Ohio	6,723,925	954,383	344,300	400,136	2,100,418	445,565	6,571,318	17,560,045
Oklahoma	2,302,851	550,036	150,394	137,041	1,066,434	259,879	1,128,116	5,595,151
Oregon	1,488,037	117,670	117,130	88,452	350,186	113,986	616,752	2,890,313
Pennsylvania	6,554,204	731,682	335,872	390,036	2,694,173	339,717	5,041,290	16,287,974
Puerto Rico	4,449,843	1,262,241	244,766	264,807	1,922,281	277,473	---	8,421,411
Rhode Island	312,338	93,018	63,671	18,587	197,927	83,829	510,874	1,280,244
South Carolina	5,069,579	2,913,221	271,891	301,687	2,185,393	494,187	642,176	11,878,234
South Dakota	664,417	131,089	79,081	39,539	367,239	121,937	363,942	1,767,244
Tennessee	5,198,197	1,659,572	277,520	309,341	2,465,558	551,132	1,938,642	12,399,962
Texas	8,567,923	2,000,927	425,010	509,871	4,842,457	1,034,245	4,131,466	21,511,899
Utah	1,500,858	295,318	115,691	89,315	177,546	83,128	343,019	2,604,875
Vermont	334,738	65,679	64,651	19,920	123,397	73,251	265,202	946,838
Virginia	4,959,310	1,426,945	267,064	295,125	2,013,091	458,607	1,986,936	11,407,128
Virgin Islands	175,334	50,243	22,674	10,434	21,921	3,164	---	283,770
Washington	2,108,663	231,486	142,294	125,485	560,277	145,484	1,451,393	4,765,082
West Virginia	2,981,640	741,590	136,735	117,926	1,110,939	275,779	644,903	5,009,512
Wisconsin	3,122,504	269,475	186,669	185,818	908,170	216,203	3,419,572	8,308,411
Wyoming	275,806	34,443	62,167	16,413	72,770	64,790	110,226	636,920
Samoa, American	95,195	27,278	19,167	5,665	18,470	2,666	---	168,441
Trust Territory	---	---	---	---	---	9,865	---	9,865
TOTAL	$168,041,000	$44,800,000	$10,000,000	$10,000,000	$67,000,000	$15,000,000	$102,285,810	$417,126,810

Table 8.—National School Lunch Program: Number of children and schools participating (elementary and secondary schools), fiscal year 1970 [1]

STATE	Total U.S. enrollment [2] No. of Children	Average daily participation No. of Children	Enrollment participation Percent	Total Schools [3] Number	Schools in program Number	NSLP schools: of total Percent	Average daily attendance No. of Children	Attendance participation Percent
NORTHEAST								
Connecticut	753,800	202,470	26.9	1,523	820	53.8	475,875	42.5
Delaware	144,700	64,261	44.4	275	176	64.0	115,989	55.3
District of Columbia	172,300	44,492	25.8	282	176	62.4	75,000	59.3
Maine	262,900	111,151	42.3	1,039	663	63.8	175,714	63.3
Maryland	998,300	324,182	32.5	1,676	1,076	64.2	785,144	41.3
Massachusetts	1,364,300	563,255	41.3	3,132	1,646	52.6	877,058	64.2
New Hampshire	179,600	72,507	40.4	603	374	62.0	139,706	51.9
New Jersey	1,735,400	331,281	19.1	3,170	1,287	40.6	773,363	42.8
New York	4,283,600	1,455,466	34.0	6,750	4,493	66.6	3,081,413	47.2
Pennsylvania	2,893,300	918,494	31.7	6,208	3,874	62.4	2,115,184	43.4
Rhode Island	221,900	43,516	19.6	526	226	43.0	130,500	33.3
Vermont	117,700	64,701	55.0	549	447	81.4	108,171	59.8
West Virginia	429,400	194,486	45.3	1,540	1,311	85.1	324,563	59.9
Total	13,557,200	4,390,262	32.4	27,273	16,569	60.8	9,177,680	47.8
SOUTHEAST								
Alabama	873,500	545,623	62.5	2,336	1,387	59.4	739,493	73.8
Florida	1,463,800	831,991	56.8	2,437	1,795	73.7	1,204,089	69.1
Georgia	1,144,800	815,414	71.2	2,299	1,847	80.3	1,011,711	80.6
Kentucky	792,700	518,561	65.4	2,023	1,664	82.3	818,407	63.4
Mississippi	610,600	404,610	66.3	1,428	987	69.1	543,938	74.4
North Carolina	1,229,400	811,720	66.0	2,529	1,895	74.9	1,014,660	80.0
Puerto Rico	727,500	330,542	44.8	2,513	2,420	96.3	660,000	50.1
South Carolina	672,900	478,395	71.1	1,524	1,171	76.8	610,791	78.4
Tennessee	928,500	562,056	60.5	2,109	1,685	79.9	748,826	75.1
Virginia	1,128,500	633,967	56.2	2,224	1,785	80.3	1,051,209	60.3
Virgin Islands	15,500	14,524	93.7	48	35	72.9	16,703	87.0
Total	9,587,700	5,947,403	62.0	21,470	16,671	77.6	8,419,827	70.6
MIDWEST								
Illinois	2,803,500	891,636	31.8	5,851	3,581	61.2	2,004,645	44.5
Indiana	1,353,500	575,739	42.5	2,823	2,164	76.7	1,012,736	56.8
Iowa	755,800	414,298	54.8	2,350	1,877	79.9	591,589	70.0
Michigan	2,478,800	601,225	24.3	4,340	2,545	58.6	1,996,686	37.7
Minnesota	1,056,800	575,238	54.4	2,907	1,833	63.1	940,387	61.2
Missouri	1,225,100	585,314	47.8	2,951	2,582	87.5	1,026,000	57.0
Nebraska	387,700	206,068	53.2	2,699	810	30.0	358,707	57.4
North Dakota	168,600	93,172	55.3	974	513	52.7	134,128	69.5
Ohio	2,755,000	904,795	32.8	5,126	3,340	65.2	1,571,028	57.6
South Dakota	186,800	85,412	45.7	1,639	293	17.9	117,420	72.7
Wisconsin	1,212,900	436,281	36.0	3,296	2,260	68.6	855,195	51.0
Total	14,384,500	5,369,178	37.3	34,956	21,798	62.4	10,208,521	52.6
SOUTHWEST								
Arkansas	473,100	311,400	65.8	1,445	982	68.0	442,957	70.3
Colorado	573,000	233,244	40.7	1,433	1,138	79.4	483,344	48.3
Kansas	574,400	260,438	45.3	2,133	1,514	71.0	400,368	65.0
Louisiana	1,007,000	730,271	72.5	2,399	1,672	70.9	933,299	78.2
New Mexico	299,200	138,587	46.3	810	582	71.9	255,852	54.2
Oklahoma	630,700	272,904	43.3	1,873	1,259	67.2	401,254	68.0
Texas	2,893,600	1,064,005	36.8	5,837	4,008	68.7	2,279,474	46.7
Total	6,451,000	3,010,849	46.7	15,890	11,155	70.2	5,196,548	57.9
WESTERN								
Alaska	74,200	30,201	40.7	391	177	45.3	58,687	51.5
Arizona	446,200	189,086	42.4	861	560	65.0	302,210	62.6
California	5,052,800	883,690	17.5	8,665	4,300	49.7	2,263,659	39.0
Guam	25,800	13,720	53.2	46	35	76.1	22,988	59.7
Hawaii	202,600	137,755	68.0	335	218	65.1	172,340	79.9
Idaho	191,300	80,730	42.2	629	518	82.4	136,869	59.0
Montana	193,300	62,955	32.6	1,058	469	44.3	114,560	55.0
Nevada	124,300	21,266	17.1	273	113	41.4	44,196	48.1
Oregon	526,900	211,032	40.1	1,490	1,100	73.8	346,589	60.9
Samoa, American	9,300	7,604	81.8	38	32	84.2	8,267	92.0
Utah	311,700	168,635	54.1	599	520	86.8	283,780	59.4
Washington	871,700	302,091	34.7	1,890	1,465	77.5	754,018	40.1
Wyoming	91,600	38,567	42.1	453	218	48.1	72,388	53.3
Total	8,121,700	2,147,332	26.4	16,718	9,725	58.2	4,580,551	46.9
GRAND TOTAL	52,102,100	20,865,024	40.0	116,307	75,918	65.3	37,583,127	55.5

[1] Data represent the average number of children in the program during December 1969 and number of schools in April 1970. The number of schools and children may have been higher in some States during other months, but these were the peak months nationally.

[2] From: Digest of Educational Statistics, 1969 Edition. Private School enrollment estimated by Office of Education.

[3] From: Preliminary data supplied by Office of Education based on 1968-69 school year.

Table 9.--Families (or persons) participating in Food Assistance Programs,
  by State, June 1970

State	:	Participation	
	:	Food Stamp	:Commodity distribution
		Number	Number
Alabama....................		154,587	235,335
Alaska.....................		23,037	---
Arizona....................		---	107,272
Arkansas...................		149,642	6,244
California.................		805,869	232,866
Colorado...................		112,249	---
Connecticut................		111,782	---
Delaware...................		---	27,013
District of Columbia......		75,745*	---
Florida....................		16,832	265,487
Georgia....................		141,342*	166,275
Hawaii.....................		18,703	---
Idaho......................		9,003	16,331
Illinois...................		433,443	---
Indiana....................		103,082	51,864
Iowa.......................		82,326*	4,227
Kansas.....................		9,179	35,323
Kentucky...................		208,770	59,157
Louisiana..................		353,599	38,124
Maine......................		8,453	66,461
Maryland...................		112,319	1,433
Massachusetts..............		3,465*	141,564
Michigan...................		288,970*	31,934
Minnesota..................		105,845*	15,558
Mississippi................		280,844	101,166
Missouri...................		88,737	192,994
Montana....................		20,975	16,277
Nebraska...................		42,216*	1,428
Nevada.....................		---	8,596
New Hampshire..............		---	16,377
New Jersey.................		202,920	---
New Mexico.................		110,990	20,280
New York...................		106,419*	607,775
North Carolina.............		147,834	127,237
North Dakota...............		16,101	17,024
Ohio.......................		406,057*	17,622
Oklahoma...................		---	230,550
Oregon.....................		37,296	93,249
Pennsylvania...............		356,658	17,483
Rhode Island...............		40,438*	---

Table 9.--Families (or persons) participating in Food Assistance Programs, by State, June 1970 -- continued

State	Participation	
	Food Stamp	: Commodity distribution
	Number	Number
South Carolina..............	213,357	--
South Dakota.................	18,858	21,104
Tennessee....................	263,594	29,115
Texas.......................	146,653	317,048
Utah........................	27,053	--
Vermont.....................	20,754	--
Virginia....................	94,986	46,738
Washington..................	221,710	--
West Virginia...............	195,919	--
Wisconsin...................	71,934	46,091
Wyoming.....................	9,401	1,851
U.S. total...............	6,469,946*	3,432,473
Outlying areas		
Guam.......................	--	2,313
Puerto Rico................	--	537,498
Virgin Islands............	--	4,143
Trust Territories.........	--	915
Total......................	--	544,869
GRAND TOTAL................	6,469,946*	3,977,342

*Estimated.

SOME UNMET NEEDS

The Federal food program tools, together with imaginative planning and innovative actions, are the foundation for child nutrition programs in the 1970's. The availability of school food services, especially in many urban situations, is still inhibited by lack of space and equipment. To help alleviate technical problems, the services of food management concerns are now authorized in Federally aided child feeding programs; existing food service facilities in some schools are being used to prepare meals for delivery to satellite schools; others are developing central sites, with prepared meals delivered to all the attendance units in the school system. Research is underway to develop nutritious, palatable engineered or precooked meal components that would not require elaborate inschool preparation and service facilities.

Continuing attention needs to be given to the nutritional quality and acceptability of the meals offered to children, once the food service is available. Only by achieving excellence in this area will children elect to participate in such food service programs and, thus, will the programs be laboratories for the development of sound food habits which will carry over into adult life.

Sound financing of quality food services for children will call on the skills and resources of local, State, and Federal Governments and private agencies. To achieve their intended benefits to children, quality food services must be accompanied by reasonable prices, with special provision for those children who are unable to pay those prices.

NUTRITION EDUCATION PROGRAMS

There is important evidence in all available data that income is a strong determinant in setting nutritional status, but income or years of schooling alone, or amount of money spent for food, do not in themselves guarantee adequate diets.

If adequate income and years of schooling do not influence enough of us to choose wisely, what can or should be done? We can and should:

. Encourage use of certain food supplements.

. Fortify foods that are consumed by large proportions.

. Require all salt be iodized.

. Develop unique and highly nutritious foods for those considered particularly vulnerable--infants, children, pregnant and lactating women, and the aged. However, in a county where freedom of choice is the model for much of our living, making such products available does not guarantee that people will choose to use them in the proper amounts.

The 1965 Food Consumption Survey of individuals pointed to the failure of the diets of children and youth to meet the Recommended Dietary Allowances for several nutrients, especially calcium, iron, vitamin A, and ascorbic acid. Decreased use of milk and milk products, fruits, and vegetables was the primary contributor to the inadequacy of these nutrients in diets of children.

To achieve desirable levels of nutritional health through wise selection, a need exists to help people understand the importance of nutritionally sound diets. This need calls for better nutrition education.

Nutrition education, as described here, is confined to those programs conducted by the USDA and USHEW and a number of national organizations. There are many programs and they are large and complex. Because a full description would require a volume in itself, extremely brief summaries are included in this inventory.

INVENTORY OF PRESENT PROGRAMS

U.S. Department of Agriculture

Agricultural Research Service

The Consumer and Food Economics Research Division of ARS prepares research-based guidance materials used in nutrition education programs. These programs may be geared to children and youth but the materials are not used exclusively with this group. The materials include food plans at different levels of cost to help families with preschool and school age children select nutritious and satisfying meals that they can afford.

The Division cooperates with the Department's Food and Nutrition Service in developing special materials for child feeding programs such as the menu planning guide and recipes for the national school lunch program.

ARS supplies the secretariat for the Interagency Committee on Nutrition Education. It also issues "Nutrition Program News" to provide an exchange of information on nutrition education for all population groups, including children and youth.

Cooperative Extension Service

In a new program which focuses on low-income families, aides work with low-income families in their own homes, or with small groups. The aides are selected from areas in which they are to work, and are trained and supervised by Extension home economists.

In May 1970, the Expanded Food and Nutrition Education Program involved more than 7,000 aides in 1,030 counties in the 50 States, Puerto Rico, the Virgin Islands, and the District of Columbia. These aides have helped almost three million individuals in over 600,000 families to have better diets.

These totals include about two million infants and children under 19. Families reached during the first year were 33.1 percent Caucasian, 48 percent Negro, 16.5 percent Spanish-American, 1.9 percent Indian, 0.1 percent Oriental, and 0.4 percent classified as other.

The Extension Nutrition Education Program in FY 1970 provided for an accelerated youth activity to reach disadvantaged young people who live in our cities. Work is done through volunteer leaders in 4-H type groups. It is anticipated that 225,000 youths will be reached in 1970, about 350,000 in 1971, and 500,000 by 1972.

Extension's other 4-H programs reached 718,085 girls and 37,548 boys with 4-H food-nutrition information during 1969. Another 146,000 youths were reached in special teenage nutrition programs. About 36 percent of these 4-H members live on farms, 36 percent are from rural nonfarm areas and cities of up to 10,000, and 23 percent are from cities above 10,000 and suburbs of larger cities. Over a third come from families with incomes under $3,000. Extension is now reaching over a million youth with 4-H or 4-H type food-nutrition education.

To improve knowledge of the importance of nutrition among 4-H members, a set of nationally developed project manuals has been developed, each geared for a particular age group. Three in the series of five, have been introduced within the past 18 months, and sales have run over 850,000 copies in 37 States. The fourth manual was made available in September, and the final one is projected for early 1971.

A series of twelve 15-minute nutrition films is being produced for television use. It tells 9- to 11-year-olds about food and what makes it important to people. The TV viewing is supplemented with a manual suggesting projects these young people can try in their own homes.

During the summer of 1970, at least 25 States expanded their 4-H camping programs to include nutrition day camps. Making learning fun through creative involvement has led to the development and use of nutrition games, songs, puppet shows, and drama.

Teenagers working with younger 4-H'ers as "junior leaders" tend to learn more about nutrition themselves. Some 35,000 youths are now serving as junior or teen leaders in nutrition, and this total is expected to be greatly increased.

Extension's nutrition programs for adults also include many innovative approaches, which result in benefits to the entire family. Series of nutrition lessons for young homemakers--usually 18- to 24-year-olds--have been used in almost all States. Over half the young families reached have incomes of $3,000 or less. Correspondence and TV courses have been developed for homemakers who are housebound by very small children. Because some homemakers do not have time to attend meetings, specially designed brief information leaflets are made available at such places as laundromats, grocery stores, beauty parlors, lunchrooms, and in places where women work.

In addition to demonstrations by aides in the Expanded Nutrition Program, Extension home economists in 1969 gave demonstrations to 800,000 families on planning balanced meals and preparing donated or low-cost foods.

Farmers Home Administration

In the Farmers Home Administration, 43 assistant county supervisors (home economists) located in 21 States and Puerto Rico work with individual caseloads of approximately 100 families in a "Family Service Program" to help low-income farm and nonfarm families raise their standards of living.

The Family Service Program of FHA home supervisor is to assist families in raising their nutritional levels. A variety of educational methods is used to achieve for each family: (1) A sufficient amount and variety of food to meet dietary needs; and (2) the production, selection, preservation, preparation and serving of food in a manner acceptable to family members.

A Special Garden Project launched in 1968 is an example of the unique FHA approach that provides credit as well as information to help solve a problem. Purpose of this project was to improve diets and to release funds to provide other essential family needs that otherwise would be used to purchase food. The 3,703 families comprising 21,338 persons enrolled in the project produced at home 3,844,410 pounds of fruits and vegetables with a value of $538,217.40 at retail cost.

In this family-focused program large numbers of children and youth are being reached.

Food and Nutrition Service

Family Food Assistance Programs (donated foods, food stamps). -- The Food and Nutrition Service seeks the cooperation of the Extension Service, OEO Emergency Food and Medical Services, CAP, VISTA, Public Health Service, Welfare Administration and Office of Education of U. S. Department of Health, Education and Welfare, State educational institutions, and the food industry, in carrying out nutrition education activities for low-income families. Donated foods are made available for food demonstrations for recipients and for the instruction and training of professional and volunteer teachers of nutrition.

In May 1970, the Extension Service's Expanded Nutrition Education Program reached more than 200,000 persons under 19 who were participating in a USDA-food assistance program. Additional persons were reached by other cooperating agencies. The potential audience in this age group is an estimated 50 percent of the more than 10 million persons participating in the Food Stamp and Family Food Donation Programs.

A guide developed by Extension Service is included in "A Teaching Kit--Food for Thrifty Families," supplied free to any agency providing nutrition educa-tion for food assistance families. The kit also includes 23 recipe leaflets, developed by FNS and the Agricultural Research Service, for distribution to the families being reached. The Daily Food Guide and recipe leaflets are also being printed in Spanish.

A "Food Makes the Difference" series of materials includes: "Ideas for Leaders Working With Economy Minded Families" and related leaflets for fami-lies using donated foods and food stamps (provided free and in quantity); a

"Smart Shoppers" series of illustrated recipes and related reproducibles; and a slide series with narrative guides (prepared cooperatively with industry) such as "The Basic Four Ways to Good Meals," "Milk the Magnificent," and "Milk Basic to Good Nutrition."

Child Nutrition Programs (School Lunch, Breakfast, and Special Food Service Programs). -- Present Act: Serving an adequate lunch each day to school-age children, is a practical demonstration of good nutrition education. All program material prepared and released by the Department emphasizes the nutritional values of participating in the program. Local school officials are, in turn, encouraged to emphasize this factor in their activity with children and their parents in promoting a sound school feeding program.

The school lunch program is available in schools that are attended by about 42 million of the estimated 51 million children in the Nation's schools. On an average day, approximately 21 million children participate in this practical demonstration of adequate nutritional intake. In addition, over 500,000 children are exposed to such nutritional educational experiences in the school breakfast program and an additional 100,000 are exposed daily in the Special Food Service Program which operates primarily in child-care centers serving preschool children.

Among the educational methods used to promote nutrition education are national, State, and local workshops and training programs for school lunch personnel; national workshops for State School Lunch Directors and supervisory personnel; person-to-person nutrition education sessions with local lunchroom managers during administrative reviews of the programs; and annual analyses of State agency operations.

The Future: The enactment of Public Law 91-248 provides authority to earmark one percent of the funds appropriated for nutritional training and education of workers, cooperators and participants in these programs and for necessary surveys and special studies of requirements for food service programs. This enabling legislation, contingent upon the availability of funds, will greatly accelerate the Department's activity in nutrition training and education in the future.

While posters, slides, and fact sheets are provided for use by school lunch workers, the basic items are the menu planning guides which translate nutrition facts into simple instructions for planning nutritionally adequate meals.

Office of Information

USDA's Office of Information employs all of its information facilities to support the food programs of the Department and to distribute information on food and nutrition for the public. Much of this information is aimed at the family unit including children and youth.

A major portion of this food and nutrition information and education effort is coordinated by the Office of Information in its "Food Makes the Difference" campaign. More than 15,000 packets of these information materials have been distributed.

Other outlets for food and nutrition subjects are: Consumer Time, a weekly radio tape feature service to 350 stations; Across the Fence, a 30-minute weekly television program seen on 87 major stations; Down to Earth, weekly television featuretts going to about 400 stations; TV Home Features, consumer-oriented slide features furnished monthly to about 200 stations; Service, a monthly newsletter distributed to about 6,800 people who report to individual consumers; Food and Home Notes, a weekly newsletter going to about 5,600 food page editors of daily and weekly newspapers and other news media; Copy Lines, a bimonthly feature service to about 480 magazines and weekly newspaper editors; Agriculture Yearbook for 1969, Food for Us All, includes six chapters dealing with nutrition and food for children and youth.

More than 3,000 slide sets and filmstrips dealing with food and nutrition were sold during fiscal 1970. Leaders in this record year include Improving Teenage Nutrition (235); Basic Four Ways to Good Meals (305); and How Food Affects You (557).

Department of Health, Education, and Welfare

Office of Child Development -- Head Start

Head Start nutrition education programs are designed for children 3 to 6 in poverty and low-income groups throughout the country, except for the Parent-Child Centers where children under 3 years and their parents are included. These programs are carried on during mealtime.

A Project Head Start film on nutrition, "Jenny Is a Good Thing," in English and Spanish is distributed through 32 Modern Talking Picture Service Film Libraries. It is currently being shown in movie theaters and has reached 550,000 patrons since June 1970. A nutrition kit of printed materials is available and being used.

Office of Education -- Focus on the Schools

The principal goal of nutrition education in the elementary school is to offer wide experiences with a variety of foods. The children study about foods, where they come from, how they are prepared, and actually prepare and taste them. They identify foods that are important to good health.

The Head Start and Follow Through Programs have offered many experiences with different foods for young children who come from backgrounds of limited family meal patterns.

School administrators and teachers recognize the school lunch as a very important factor in the growth and development of children, and the development of improved study habits and learning.

In the junior and senior high schools, opportunities are provided to students for a more concentrated study of food and nutrition. Units of study included are science, biology, health, and physical education. More time is spent on food and nutrition in home economics classes in the high schools; some have semester or year courses. Most of the estimated 3 million students in these courses are girls, but boys are electing to enroll in larger numbers.

Future Homemakers of America, the national organization of 600,000 students in home economics in the schools, sponsors projects such as improving teenage eating habits, assisting with elementary children at lunch time, and operating fruit and juice bars at athletic games. These experiences expand their understanding of food and nutrition.

Young adults enrolled in some of the community colleges and vocational technical schools have the opportunity to acquire food and nutrition knowledge in elective courses in "Consumer and Family Life Skills" or in "Personal Nutrition" offered by the home economics departments.

Under Title I of the Elementary and Secondary Education Act of 1965, (P.L. 89-10), this Bureau allocates funds to local educational agencies to strengthen programs for disadvantaged children. In FY 1968, almost $26 million were allotted and provided food for about 1.2 million school children. Another $18.7 million went for health, dental, and medical services for 1.2 million children.

Title III of Public Law 89-10 provides funds for planning and development of innovative or exemplary education programs. One such project undertook a comprehensive approach to a "pilot breakfast program." Several projects related to improving health education and health services, and two dealt with homemaking education. Nutrition education was an important element in each.

Public Health Service -- Community Health Service

The Health Services Development Grant Program under Section 314 (e) of the Public Health Service Act has as a major goal the elimination of inequities in access to and receipt of care for certain especially disadvantaged population groups.

The grant program had funded 41 neighborhood health center projects as of April 1970. Twelve have arranged for donated food, supplemental food, or food stamp programs as a part of the other services offered. Provision of direct nutrition education services to patients is or will be an integral part of 24 of the centers when all become operational.

Migrant Health Program. -- Under the Migrant Health Program, nutrition education is generally directed to women and girls, including teenaged mothers.

The effort is chiefly through migrant health grant-assisted projects which now operate in local areas of 35 States. About 5 percent of the potential are being reached.

The PHS prepared a film, "Safe Food" with an accompanying discussion guide. It also has prepared lists of materials in Spanish and English.

Indian Health Service

Malnutrition in the Indian and Alaska Native population is a medical as well as a socioeconomic problem. It is related to a lack of basic food and economic resources, plus a lack of needed knowledge regarding the best use of those limited resources. A family-centered approach is used in nutrition education programs for this population.

There is no single dietary pattern characteristic of the more than 250 Indian and Alaska Native tribal and village groups. Eating practices of each reflect a great variety of cultural factors, the impact of transitions in Indian and Alaska Native society, and a lack of conformity in eating patterns of all residents of any given geographical area.

Concerted educational efforts on food and nutrition are directed toward the infant and preschool child where nutrition related illness and under-achievement in growth and development are prevalent. Special emphasis is given to teenagers and young adults. Females in the childbearing years (14 to 44) merit particular concern regarding food practices.

Major attention is given to involving the Indian himself in food and nutrition education programs. Nutrition aides and technicians are being trained and used in their home communities where they can make a unique con-tribution to the nutritional health of the indigenous population.

Maternal and Child Health Service

Expansion of comprehensive health and medical care projects for expectant mothers and their infants as well as for children and youth has afforded excel-lent opportunities to extend nutrition services, including nutrition education, to more mothers and children, particularly those in low-income families. About 300 nutritionists and dietitians are working through these projects as members of health teams in such activities as prenatal and family planning clinics, well-child conferences, pediatric clinics, school health programs, adolescent clinics, and day-care centers.

Parents, families, and the public are given information and guidance about nutritional needs and feeding of infants and children through group meetings and use of mass media. Efforts are made to reach children and youth as early as possible with nutrition education by working with staff, children, and parents in developing school health programs, comprehensive programs for school-aged pregnant girls, and preschool programs.

Maternal and Child Health Services employ home economists as members of health teams to focus more attention on the problems of home management and family economics. These home economists work with small groups of mothers in the waiting room of the clinic, make home visits, conduct teaching trips to the grocery store, and use a variety of approaches to reach and teach mothers, children, and families.

Increasing numbers of trained aides and volunteers from the low-income neighborhoods are working in Maternal and Child Health Services. With guidance from the health teams, they teach mothers and children how to overcome problems in such areas as food selection, preparation and storage, home management, budgeting, and care of clothing.

National Organizations

American Medical Association

Nutrition education programs of the American Medical Association (AMA) are geared to the medical and allied health professions as well as to educators. Through these professions AMA is able to reach the desired audiences.

"Today's Health," a monthly AMA publication written for the layman, frequently contains articles on child health which include nutrition. In addition, the column, "Let's Talk About Food," edited by Dr. Philip White, contains information pertaining to nutritional needs of infants and children. A book published under this title is in its third printing.

Pamphlets on nutrition geared directly to children or teenagers are distributed through physicians' offices.

The AMA is helping to develop a service delivery model in Chicago utilizing two mobile units to serve the south side of Chicago. The Council on Foods and Nutrition is exploring the possibility of holding a resource conference which would define the gaps or needs of nutrition services in communities. With this information, it might be possible to establish a nutrition service center in conjunction with the service delivery model. The nutrition problems of vulnerable groups, such as children and adolescents, would be an important segment of this program.

The Council on Foods and Nutrition has sponsored symposia on infant nutrition, adolescent nutrition, and nutrition in human development. The most recent one held in February 1970 pertained to "The Role of Malnutrition in the Pathogenesis of Slums." Lectures given at this symposium related to the effect of malnutrition on infants and children.

American National Red Cross

When the needs for foods and education have become most apparent, the American National Red Cross has played an outstanding role in teaching family economics as well as establishing food distribution centers. Nutrition education was also taught by paid and volunteer professional nutritionists.

In 1952 the Nutrition Program was phased out on a national level because of insufficient funds. The program became the responsibility of each area office and some 3,300 chapters.

Nutrition is a part of Red Cross Programmed Nursing courses and has helped to keep the program alive in chapters. Today's awareness of the needs for food and nutrition education has stimulated Red Cross chapters to increase their activities in these fields.

In Red Cross programs, proper nutrition is being taught as a part of courses on care of the sick and injured, mother-baby care, fitness for the future, and home nursing. The classes are taught by nurses and nutritionists.

Red Cross Youth programs develop health and safety materials for use in U.S. elementary and secondary schools and train college students to use these materials in teaching nursing and safety in foreign countries.

Chapters participate in USDA's supplementary food programs by helping with certification and transportation of food to people and people to food.

Industry Groups

Many widely used nutrition education tools are made available through sponsorship of the food industry and are utilized by educators in schools, government agencies, and private groups. These organizations frequently use highly skilled communication experts to produce high-quality aids.

The food industry is promoting a Nutrition Awareness Campaign to be repeated annually.

Youth-Serving Organizations

Nutrition education is an important element in many youth-serving programs, especially those with physical fitness or homemaking components. In addition to those already mentioned, Girl Scouts of U.S.A., Boy Scouts of America, Girls Clubs of America, Boys Clubs of America, Y.M.C.A., and Y.W.C.A. all reach large numbers of both rural and urban youth. Church-sponsored groups and numerous other clubs are also active in making nutrition information available to youth and their families.

SUMMARY

Many channels are available to reach large numbers of people who have inadequate diets. On-going programs are employing techniques to improve diets.

Young children - Some programs are aimed at the homemakers who have young children. The Head Start Program is geared to the preschool child--and his or her mother--with a Follow-Through program adapted for the 6- to 11-year-olds.

School Age - Children in the elementary grades are exposed to nutrition training in their classes and through the nationwide school lunch, breakfast, and milk programs. Home economics classes in high school are channels for nutrition education adapted to the needs of teenagers.

Informal Education - Starting at the elementary school age and extending into high school levels, youth have opportunities to participate in many national organizations which sponsor informal nutrition education.

Young Adult (18 to 24) - Fewer educational programs and less research has been aimed at this age group, partly because of their mobility.

Families with Most Need - Welfare and family assistance programs offer opportunities for educational services to improve nutrition of families in need. Nutrition programs of the State Cooperative Extension Services, supported by the Department of Agriculture and land-grant universities, are reaching large numbers of hard-to-reach homemakers with assistance in planning and preparing food for their families. In addition, food is being made available to poor families through the many food assistance programs.

UNMET NEEDS

To improve the food choice of adults and children, those of us who plan nutrition education need to know more about what influences choice of food: what homemakers and their children know about the relationship between food and health and their knowledge of the nutritive value of foods; whether they have any idea of the need for different foods for various family members; and their ideas on handling food to preserve its nutritive value, appearance, and flavor. We need to know, with some precision, what adults and children know, in order to know what we need to teach.

At the same time, we must involve curriculum planners in the development of nutrition education programs and improve the nutrition training of teachers, teachers of teachers, and other professionals who are concerned with nutritional health of people.

We need greater overall coordination of national, State, and local programs, with concern for continuity of services for those who migrate. We need aides who can work with and understand different cultures, and we must provide materials written in simple terms and several languages.

Last, but not least, is the need for sustained monitoring of the impact of our education programs.

Nutrition education is not a short-run program. It must be viewed as a long-term effort which must expand, develop new ideas, and reach people more effectively as more knowledge becomes available about nutrients in foods and dietary needs and food practices of individuals. Each generation must be taught to make wise use of the food choices that will be available to it.

MAJOR AREAS OF CONCERN

The exact nutritional status of the Nation and what to do to improve it is a complicated issue. Not the least of the problems involved is where to start an accurate evaluation. Those taking part in the White House Conference are faced with the entire issue.

A systems analysis could produce a design for a massive coordinated food system to include all the areas that affect goal achievement -- the complexity of inputs that influence the actual nutritional state of people, and particularly of children and youth. That would include, among other factors, economic limitations; environmental conditions; agricultural technology, production, and productivity; food processing and marketing; wholesomeness, quality, and fortification of food.

In tandem with each of these aspects would be the curbing or stimulus effect of the available technical knowledge about human nutrition. Family life, food habits, health conditions, housing and home facilities, health and welfare programs, could be justifiably included. Education should be added -- not only nutrition education -- but how we should educate, and what influence nutritional status has on educability.

Running through all areas would be the consideration of placing responsibility for achievement -- Federal, State and local, private sector, or the individual himself -- and a set of options for each. Of course, a continuing check must be run on the progress made in each area.

Such an effort would be tremendously costly, involving all of the disciplines implied in the different areas. Time alone has prohibited much consideration along this line in advance of the Conference.

In any event, we must not simply await more definitive studies before attempting to cope with many of the problems of improving the nutritional status of children and youth.

Certainly the availability of food is basic to good nutritional status, and this is first priority. But we know that availability alone, whether assured by adequate income or food delivery systems, does not guarantee proper diets -- neither does general education or specialized nutrition education, in the form we have had it. We know that, in addition, we must be aware of general health and psychological factors.

One-shot treatments will not work. Complex and intergenerational problems require complex and sustained attack.

Expressions of goodwill and a national commitment are not enough. Massive investment of money and personal effort are needed to start us on the way toward truly good nutritional status in the United States. We

must have strong and coordinated leadership at the Federal level, so that
we may help the States and local areas develop programs to reach children
and young adults, and their parents and their teachers.

> The chart that follows plots the major areas
> of concern involved in achieving nutrition goals.
> All of this assumes on-going research on nutritional
> needs, food consumption, and human behavior for the
> creation and assessment of possible options.

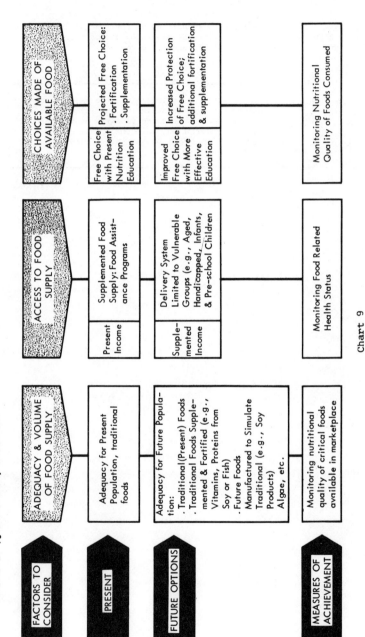

NUTRITIONAL GOALS

or GOAL 1   Recommended Daily Allowance — Nat'l. Academy of Science
   GOAL 2   ²/₃ Rec'd Daily Allowance

FACTORS TO CONSIDER	ADEQUACY & VOLUME OF FOOD SUPPLY	ACCESS TO FOOD SUPPLY	CHOICES MADE OF AVAILABLE FOOD
PRESENT	Adequacy for Present Population, traditional foods	Present Income	Supplemented Food Supply: Food Assistance Programs	Free Choice with Present Nutrition Education	Projected Free Choice: . Fortification . Supplementation
FUTURE OPTIONS	Adequacy for Future Population: . Traditional (Present) Foods . Traditional Foods Supplemented & Fortified (e.g., Vitamins, Proteins from Soy or Fish) . Future Foods Manufactured to Simulate Traditional (e.g., Soy Products) Algae, etc.	Supplemented Income	Delivery System Limited to Vulnerable Groups (e.g., Aged, Handicapped, Infants, & Pre-school Children	Improved Free Choice with More Effective Education	Increased Protection of Free Choice; additional fortification & supplementation
MEASURES OF ACHIEVEMENT	Monitoring nutritional quality of critical foods available in marketplace	Monitoring Food Related Health Status	Monitoring Nutritional Quality of Foods Consumed

Chart 9